MW01180708

literaturen im kontext *literatures in context*

arabisch – persisch – türkisch *arabic – persian – turkish*

Series Editors
Verena Klemm, Sonja Mejcher-Atassi, Friederike Pannewick,
Barbara Winckler

Advisory Board
Beatrice Gründler (Yale), Angelika Neuwirth (Berlin),
Sunil Sharma (Boston)

Vol. 38: The Andalusian Music of Morocco
Al-Āla: History, Society and Text

Reichert Verlag Wiesbaden 2013

The Andalusian Music of Morocco

Al-Āla: History, Society and Text

Carl Davila

Reichert Verlag Wiesbaden 2013

Bibliografische Information der Deutschen Nationalbibliothek
Die Deutsche Nationalbibliothek verzeichnet diese Publikation
in der Deutschen Nationalbibliografie; detaillierte bibliografische Daten
sind im Internet über http://dnb.d-nb.de abrufbar.

© 2013 Dr. Ludwig Reichert Verlag Wiesbaden
ISBN: 978-3-89500-913-6
www.reichert-verlag.de

Das Werk einschließlich aller seiner Teile ist urheberrechtlich geschützt.
Jede Verwertung außerhalb der engen Grenzen des Urhebergesetzes ist ohne
Zustimmung des Verlages unzulässig und strafbar.
Das gilt insbesondere für Vervielfältigungen, Übersetzungen,
Mikroverfilmungen und die Speicherung
und Verarbeitung in elektronischen Systemen.
Printed in Germany

Table of Contents

List of Illustrations

Track List for the Accompanying CD

Track	Title & Source
1	*Tawāšī Mīzān Quddām Ramal al-Māya* Jawq ʿAbd al-Krīm ar-Rāyis (directed by Mohamed Briouel) Recorded live at the 8th *Mahrajān* in Fez, 2001 (provenance unknown)
2	*Šaḏarāt min al-Qāʾim wa-niṣf al-Māya* L'Ensemble Artistique Al Baàth de la Musique Andalouse de Fes directed by ʿAbd al-Fattāḥ Benmūsā (proprietary recording, 2012)*

* Used with permission of the artist. All rights remain with the performers. I wish to thank Si Benmusa for his cooperation in producing this CD.

Preface

The past two decades have seen a dramatic growth of interest in the cultural legacy of Islamic Spain, al-Andalus. Two areas in particular, poetry and music, have received special attention from the academy. On the literary side, discussion has dealt (at times acrimoniously) with the origins and historical significance of the two Andalusi[1] strophic poetry forms, the *muwaššaḥ* (pl. *muwaššaḥāt*) and the *zajal* (pl. *azjāl*). Building on the work of Martin Hartmann (1897), Emilio García Gómez (1943) and Samuel Miklos Stern (1974), scholars like Federico Corriente (1980, 1988 et al.), Alan Jones (1980, 1988, 1991), James T. Monroe (1986, 1987, 1989) and others have advanced the field to the point that we now have a fairly rich and nuanced understanding of these distinctive poetic forms and their linguistic characteristics. Even if some aspects of this poetic legacy remain on the table for discussion, scholarship has created a much clearer picture of its significance than when Hartmann first pointed out the interesting linguistic promiscuity of some of these poems. If the scholarly community might be said to have come up short in any way, it would be in the production of readable English translations that could make the delights of Andalusi strophic poetry available to a wider audience. A notable exception is James T. Monroe's useful student anthology, *Andalusian Strophic Poetry*. Beyond the world of scholarship, though, Andalusi strophic poetry has not yet received its due as one of the world's great poetic traditions.

The same cannot be said of the musical aspect of the Andalusi cultural legacy. One calls to mind first the recordings by Eduardo Paniagua and his family who, along with Luis Delgado, took the "early music" approach in attempting to reconstruct (perhaps *represent* is a better word) the Arabic, Christian and Jewish musical styles of al-Andalus, drawing upon a handful of written documents from the era but also taking hints from the music of contemporary descendant traditions, such as *al-Āla* in Morocco, *al-Ġarnāṭī* in Algeria, and the Syrian/Lebanese *muwaššaḥāt*. But beyond these more scholarly efforts, "Andalusian Music" is also becoming a bona fide sub-genre of World Music, with CDs by North African groups and singers like Amina Alaoui and Francoise Atlan finding their way into many of the better music shops in Europe and the United States alongside those of Delgado and the Paniaguas. Through these recordings the musical-poetic legacy of al-Andalus is beginning to acquire a wider audience, which shows at least the power of music as an "international language" capable of contributing to the survival of a poetic tradition.

[1] I will be using *Andalusi* here and throughout to mean "Arab-Andalusian" from the Middle Ages, as distinct from both *Andalucí* (referring to things from the modern Spanish province of Andalucía) and *Andalusian* (referring mainly to the modern North African musical-poetic traditions).

It seems to me, though, that a further link can be made here, one that underscores the role of music in the production and presentation of Andalusi *muwaššaḥāt* and *azjāl* in the Middle Ages. Although the scholarly community is not in complete agreement as to whether these strophic poems were *originally conceived* as such, literary and other evidence leaves no doubt that they did at least come to serve as song lyrics in al-Andalus. Thus, after a long period of interest in the linguistic, structural and metrical aspects of these poems, scholarly attention to the role of music in the Andalusi poetic legacy is on the upswing, as shown by the wealth of papers on music-related topics presented at the third and fourth conferences on the *muwaššaḥ*, which were held at the School of Oriental and African Studies in London in 2004 and 2007. (The proceedings of the earlier conference have recently been published in a volume entitled *Muwashshah: Proceedings of the Conference on Arabic and Hebrew Strophic Poetry and Its Romance Parallels*). In short, if the parallel musical legacy of al-Andalus is left out, the tale of the Andalusi strophic poetry is far from complete. The present work is meant in part as a contribution to the discussion surrounding this dual heritage.

However, this book looks beyond the narrow confines of Andalusi literary or musical studies, embracing both aspects of this double cultural legacy as manifested today in this Moroccan musical-poetic tradition to explore the complex relationship between written poem and oral-musical rendition as they function historically and culturally within the boundaries of *al-Āla*. The argument first assesses what I refer to in Part One as the "standard narrative" of its history. It then revises and complicates that narrative by emphasizing the shifting social and economic contexts surrounding and supporting *al-Āla* as part of the musical heritage of al-Andalus, from its semi-legendary birth in ninth-century Cordoba, through a middle period when it became established within rather different social conditions in North Africa, and into the modern era in which the social and economic bases of the tradition have been radically transformed by processes associated with modernization. Through examining *al-Āla* in these terms, I seek to place its history on a more substantial footing, and also to underscore the significance of changes in society and economy in the evolution of cultural traditions generally.

Part Two of this book reorients the discussion along more theoretical lines, proposing a "value theory of tradition" and using it to analyze the social-economic history of *al-Āla* presented in Part One. In essence, I am arguing that the social and economic relations surrounding the Andalusi musical heritage can together be described in terms of *value*, that is, the importance attaching to meaningful action within social context. Doing so enriches our understanding of how continuity, preservation and change have produced the contemporary *Āla* tradition. Moreover, the analysis that emerges from this discussion helps to explain how and why cultural traditions like *al-Āla* change and decline, and therefore helps to account for the somewhat precarious status of *al-Āla* in Moroccan society today.

Parts One and Two, taken together, thus use *al-Āla* as an in-depth test case for talking about writing and performance as social-cultural forms through Graeber's three domains of value, the social, the economic and the linguistic. (Chapter 5 in Part One takes up this third domain by exploring the role of oral processes in forming the textual corpus that defines the contemporary tradition, and what that reveals of the tradition's history.)[2] In this way, the voice and the pen are shown to engage complementary values, which allow them to coexist within the boundaries of the contemporary *Āla* tradition.

Acknowledgments

I was guided to this project. From the curious way that the Andalusian music entered my life, to the many fortuitous twists and turns the research led me through, the Creative Intelligence touched my life in many ways. So I want to give thanks to those individuals and institutions who were my guides, exemplars and benefactors in this project. Whether they realize it or not, they have changed my life.

The research presented here is partly the result of several months of fieldwork in Fez, and other cities in Morocco, carried out in the summers of the years 2001 and 2002, and during some 30 months' residence in Fez between October of 2002 and March, 2006. It was aided by a number of individuals in Morocco, Spain and the United States, who deserve specific thanks for their contributions. My research began with the help of Omar Ghiati and the master of the Andalusian orchestra he performs in, ʿAbd al-Fattāḥ Benmūsā. To these two men I own a debt of gratitude for their hospitality and gracious assistance in my work, pointing me toward valuable resources and introducing me to a number of my most important contacts within the community of Andalusian musicians, music lovers and scholars in Morocco. Sī Benmūsā especially has always given generously of his time, allowed me to observe his orchestra in rehearsal and performance whenever possible, and provided much-needed insider information, both in scholarship and in terms of performance practice within the branch of the tradition as it is performed in Fez.

[2] For those readers interested in the third of Graeber's analytical domains of value, the linguistic, my other work on this subject, *Pen, Voice and Context* (forthcoming) offers a thorough discussion of this topic as part of a critical translation of one of the large musical suites of *al-Āla*, *Nawbat Ramal al-Māya*.

I also owe a great deal to the faculty at the Andalusian music conservatory in the Fez Medina, Dār ʿAdīl: Sīdī Aḥmad Turašī, Sīdī ʿAbd al-Raḥīm al-ʿUṯmānī and Sīdī Aḥmad Šīkī, who were very gracious in allowing me to observe classes at that institution.

I further extend my warmest thanks to my sponsor in Fez, Dr. ʿAbd al-Malik aš-Šāmī, of the Faculty of Arts and Sciences in Fez, who provided me with invaluable insight into the history of the tradition, more than once steering me toward otherwise unsuspected opportunities and resources. Moreover, he gave me access to several major events held by the musical community of Fez which otherwise were open only to invitation. This work could not have come to fruition without his generosity and hospitality. Likewise to his brother, Professor ʿAbd as-Salām aš-Šāmī and his son, Omar, my thanks for invaluable assistance with materials at the Museum of Andalusian Music in Fez.

Thanks go also to the library staff at the Arabic Language Institute in Fez, a welcome refuge on cold, rainy winter days, as well as to my professor of Arabic at ALIF, Mohamed Ezzahraouy.

To Mehdi Chaachou, *raʾīs* of Jawq al-Ḥāyik at-Tetuani, I offer my sincere thanks for many delightful moments in his company, as well as for his hospitality and insight into the tradition as it exists in Tetuan. Also in Tetuan, Professor M'hamed Benaboud and Sīda Ḥasna Dāwūd were extremely helpful in opening doors for me to the Andalusian music community there. Thanks to them both, and to Sīda Ḥasna especially for allowing me to view a number of her father's manuscripts and documents related to the Moroccan Andalusian music tradition at the Dāwūdiyya library she oversees.

To Dr. Malik Bennūna, I offer my very special thanks for his years of devotion to studying the texts of the tradition. His unmatched knowledge of the poetry of *al-Āla* provided insights crucial to my understanding of the literary dimension of the tradition. His door was always open, and he always shared his research with me in the most generous and unselfish manner.

My thanks also to Professor Awatif Bouamar of al-Maʿhad al-Waṭanī lil-Mūsīqā wa al-Raqṣ in Tangier for allowing me to observe her classes, and to her and the other members of Jawq Abnāʾ Ziryāb, for their hospitality. And to Professor Driss Srairi of the Centre National de Coordination et de Planification de la Recherche Scientifique et Technique in Rabat, who gave enthusiastically of his time and provided access to the Andalusian music materials in his possession.

I would like to thank fondly here Dr. Dwight Reynolds, of the University of California at Santa Barbara. Dwight's enthusiasm for the Andalusian music traditions across North Africa and the Middle East is truly contagious, and our conversations on the subject have always been stimulating and enlightening. I was fortunate indeed to have him close at hand in Granada for three years during my research, always ready to provide a sounding board and valuable perspectives on my work. In the same breath I should also mention Professor Jonathan Shannon of Hunter College, CUNY, for hours of insightful conversation and camaraderie. To have two such scholars to "talk shop" with - in English - was very welcome, indeed.

And last - when she should be first - I want to thank my dissertation advisor, Dr. Beatrice Gruendler. Her kindness and keen intellect, in due measure, saw me through the highs and lows of this project. Words cannot capture my gratitude for her support and efforts on my behalf over the years. When traveling the seas, the help of a master sailor can be the difference between sailing and drowning.

The research embodied in this work was funded in part by grants from the American Institute for Maghrib Studies, the J. William Fulbright Fellowship fund, the Fulbright-Hays Dissertation Research fund; and by grants and fellowships from the Yale University Graduate School of Arts and Sciences.

On transliteration

Consonants:

ʾ	=	ء *	*ḍ*	=	ض
b	=	ب	*ṭ*	=	ط
t	=	ت	*ẓ*	=	ظ
ṯ	=	ث	ʿ	=	ع
j	=	ج	*ġ*	=	غ
ḥ	=	ح	*f*	=	ف
ḫ	=	خ	*q*	=	ق
d	=	د	*k*	=	ك
ḏ	=	ذ	*l*	=	ل
r	=	ر	*m*	=	م
z	=	ز	*n*	=	ن
s	=	س	*h*	=	ه
š	=	ش	*w*	=	و
ṣ	=	ص	*y*	=	ي

(final) -*a*, or -*at* in construct = ة

āh = اة (in plurals of nouns with weak third radical, as: *wāšin*, pl. *wušāh*)

* Initial *hamza* and *waṣla* are not transliterated.

Vowels:

Short vowels are rendered by their nearest English equivalents: *a*, *i* and *u*.
Long vowels are rendered: ا = *ā*, ي = *ī* and و = *ū*
Dipthongs: *aw* and *ay*

Grammatical inflection is not rendered, except where needed for clarity or where called for in weak-third-radical constructs, as with *Ibn Abī Ṭālib*. *Tašdīd* in the definite article is indicated by doubling of the appropriate consonant, with hyphenation. Prepositional prefixes and the definite article are connected to nouns with / - /, but *hamzat al-waṣl* is not transcribed when elided. Thus, the opening *āya* of the Qurʾān would be rendered:

bi-smi llāhi r-raḥmāni r-raḥīm

Proper names:

For Arab authors, historical figures and other individuals bearing formal titles, I have preferred in general to render their names in their classical or colloquial Arabic form, except where conventions already exist in English (for example, *Ibn Khaldun* but then *ʿAbd al-Karīm ar-Rāyis*). I have avoided Latinized renderings of notable figures from the Middle Ages (*Ibn Bājja*, not *Avempace*) and abbreviated *ibn* in construct when rendering full Arabic names, except where the person is commonly known by a *nasab*, thus: *Abū Bakr b. Yaḥyā aṣ-Ṣāyiġ Ibn Bājja*. In a number of cases, Moroccan names have contracted the *nasab*, which now appears in print in contracted form with altered vowels (sometimes thus even in Arabic script). I have retained most of these: *Benmūsā*, *Bennūna*, etc. *Hamza* is conserved in formal Arabic renderings, except in cases where it is lost in a particular usage (usually Moroccan, but sometimes francophone, thus: *Ibn ʿAbd Allāh Muḥammad b. al-Ḥusayn al-Ḥāʾik at-Tiṭwānī*, but *Jawq al-Ḥāyik al-Tetuani*). Note also that francophone renderings of vowels in some proper names have been retained in cases where clarity seemed to me to call for it, as for example *Jawq al-Ḥāyik al-Tetuani*. In some cases, the francophone version of a name is common in Morocco, in which case I have adopted it (e.g.: *Mohamed Briouel*). For other Moroccan individuals, I have used either the francophone or the formal Arabic spelling, depending upon how I was introduced to him or her (thus: *Omar* and *Mehdi Chaachou*, but *Sīda Ḥasna Dāwūd*). In cases where I cite works by an Arab author in both Arabic and a European language, I have used the Arabic version of the name but included the foreign version in brackets: Bennūna (Bennouna), Malik.

For Rosa,
who stood by me and made it possible,
for Beatrice,
who gave me room to discover it,
and for my mother.

Al-Āla: History, Society and Text

Introduction

1. *Opening doors*

The musical-poetic tradition known as the Andalusian Music entered my life through a strange combination events in the summer of 2001. Certainly, I had heard the music before, resounding from the music shops and cyber cafes of Fez, where I was studying Arabic. But the tradition really entered my life by other means. One day in June of that year, I was wandering the streets of the Ville Nouvelle in desperation. I had come to Fez that summer on a grant from my graduate school to study Arabic and to develop contacts relating to my supposed dissertation topic, the cultural aspects of national sentiment in Morocco. Yet, for at least a month prior to my arrival, I had been haunted by the feeling that something was wrong. The thought was lurking in the back of my mind that somehow I had started down a long path that I had only a superficial interest in. So there I was, spending my grant money in this foreign country chasing a topic that I knew somehow I could never finish. I just did not have a passion for it; that much had become clear. I was, as I thought of it then, in the wrong place and the wrong time, and so what could I possibly do about it? As I stood by the park in front of the Tajmuʿatī Mosque, a sense of despair began to take hold of me. I looked up at the clear blue Moroccan sky and said one word aloud: "Help!"

I took a few steps, and then I was struck with an inspiration. Of course, I thought, I am indeed in the wrong place: what am I doing stumbling around the Ville Nouvelle, when I should go to the old city, the Medina! I did not know exactly what I was looking for, but somehow I knew I would find it in the spiritual and cultural heart of Fez. Immediately, I hailed a taxi and asked to be taken to Bab Bou Jaloud, the main gate at the upper end of the Medina.

The Medina of Fez sprawls across a hillside northeast of the Ville Nouvelle, reaching down to and beyond the river Wad Fas. Its bewildering maze of stucco-brown streets and alleys seems to be woven like a great, many-veined leaf around two large avenues, al-Talaa al-Saghira and al-Talaa al-Kabira, which descend from Bab Bou Jeloud down to the river, now almost completely obscured by streets and buildings. These two brick avenues serve as the main lifelines reaching from the upper end of the Medina into its vast, web-like interior.

Jumping out of the taxi, I plunged into the teeming atmosphere of the old city, oblivious to the heat, the press of the crowd, the lumbering pack animals, the pungent smells of fried fish and lamb tagine coming from the restaurants, the cloud of would-be guides and young boys hovering around me near the gate. Not knowing where to go exactly, I simply let my feet carry me to the left and down the crowded artery of al-Talaa al-Kabira. After a few moments of expectation, eyes drinking in the rush of details, I noticed a young man, a foreigner, approaching from the opposite direction. He was rather unkempt and was wearing a Moroccan-style hooded sweater in spite of the summer heat. But what caught my eye was the fact that he was carrying a guitar on his back: music! I wanted to stop him, but before I could react, he had disappeared behind me into the crowd, so I turned and pushed my way back up the street after him. I caught up with him finally just outside the gate and, not knowing what else to say, asked him if he knew anyone who could teach me some Arabic songs. It seemed like a logical way to begin.

Together we set off in search of two American music students, two women whom he had never met, but whom a Moroccan man in a cafe had mentioned to him the night before. My new acquaintance did not have their names, nor even their address, only a "map" consisting of two lines scribbled on a scrap of paper along with the name of a street. After several false starts and about an hour of wandering, we found what appeared to be the right street. We could not find the name, but the corner looked a bit like the "map." But which was the right house? I stopped a woman passing by with her three young children and asked about the two American women. She had never heard of them, but said we should ask "Mishmisha" ["Little Apricot"], and she told one of her sons to take us to "Mishmisha's" door just around the corner.

I knocked, and heard a woman with a distinctly American accent shout, "Go away!" Surprised, I knocked again and explained in English that we were two American students looking for "Mishmisha." The door opened, and the woman invited us in, apologizing, saying the neighborhood children had been pounding on her door all day and then dashing off when she opened it.

"Mishmisha's" real name was Michelle. She was an American graduate student who had been living in the Medina for some years. Everyone knew her, it seemed, and she knew everyone. She said she had not heard of any female music students, but when I explained my mission, she suggested I visit Abdelfettah Seffar at his cultural center, Fes Hadara. He would certainly be able to help me, she said.

A day or two later, I visited Fes Hadara, an old palace that had been converted into a show place for decorative arts, especially Abdelfettah's trade, plasterwork. It is a huge and lovely place, full of trees swaying in peaceful breezes, water fountains and shady patios. Theatrical and musical events are held there, especially around the time of the Fez Festival of Sacred Music in June. Abdelfettah told me that he hosts music lessons for children from time to time, and he offered to put me in touch with the music teacher, Omar Ghiati. I left Fes Hadara full of hope that at last I was on track.

The day I met Omar was a turning point in my academic life. Through him I was introduced to a musical and literary phenomenon that has thrived in Morocco for more than half a millennium but which has been marked by the rapid cultural and economic transformations which have overtaken nearly every corner of the globe. A new phase in the development of the tradition has begun, and this fact is not lost on the more reflective members of the Andalusian music community in Morocco. I soon realized that I had arrived on the scene at a fascinating moment in the tradition's development, a point at which a fresh insight might help clarify the processes forcing change upon the tradition and its participants.

What is more, I discovered that there is a sizable gap in the literature on this tradition. I regret to say that academic interest in the Moroccan Andalusian music tradition has been confined almost entirely to Arabic, French and Spanish scholarship. Fewer than half a dozen articles and not a single book-length work hitherto had appeared in English dealing with this or any of the North African Andalusian music traditions. This is a pity, it seems to me, because these art forms are full of surprises and rewards for the scholar, whether one looks at the music itself, or the poetic corpus which the musical tradition has helped to preserve within Moroccan popular culture.[1] Given the distinctive intellectual perspectives which they bring to bear, British and North American scholars have something valuable to contribute to the study of the Andalusian music traditions, including *al-Āla* in Morocco.

I was aware of none of this when I met Omar. In fact, the day of our first lesson at Fes Hadara, I still had no clear idea of my purpose. I simply knew somehow that a suitable topic for my research might emerge if I started learning the music familiar to the people of Morocco. Music and singing had been dear to me since childhood, so I believed that my love of music would provide the spark of passion to carry me through the years of research and writing that lay ahead. Abdelfettah gave us a room on the ground floor of his own house, adjacent to the gardens of Fes Hadara. Omar asked me what I wanted to learn, and I told him I was interested in common songs in Arabic, songs of everyday life, rather than the Westernized music from CDs that was taking over the neighborhood music shops.

Omar proved to be an amiable and patient teacher. He has a sweet singing voice and accompanies himself on the *ʿūd* (the Arabic lute) and sometimes on the

[1] In addition to two survey articles on the Moroccan tradition by Philip Schuyler (1978, 1979), only three other articles have appeared in English. Dwight Reynolds has published two articles, one on the larger Arab-Andalusian music tradition in *Charting Memory: Recalling Medieval Spain* (1999), and a survey of Andalusian music in the *Cambridge History of Arabic Literature* volume on al-Andalus (2000); and Owen Wright offers a similar survey in *Arab-Islamic Culture in Andalusia* (1996). At the time of this writing, the first book in English on Arab-Andalusian music, Ruth Davis' book on the Tunisian tradition, *Maʾlūf*, has just been published; and two other books are in production that deal with the various Arab-Andalusian music traditions of the Mediterranean world, one by Dwight Reynolds and one by Jonathan Shannon.

darbūka (the vase-shaped Middle Eastern drum), as well. After a singing a couple of songs which I was not particularly struck by, he sang a song with an absolutely enchanting melody, whose words spoke sweetly the longing of lost love:

أنا قد عَيَى صَبْري   وَجِسْمي فَنَى ... جِسْمي فَنَى
أَنْتَ يا مُنَى قَلْبي   عايشْ في الهَنَى ... في الهَنَى
لِقاضي الهَوى أَشْكِي   يَحْكُمْ بَيْنَنا ... بَيْنَنا
يَشْهَدُ العِبادْ جُمْلا   عَلَى مَن ظَلَمْ ظَلَمْ
عَلَى مَن ظَلَمْ فينا   وَارْضَ بِالبِعادْ ... بِالبِعادْ

My patience has worn thin
    and my body has withered away...withered away
You, the desire of my heart
    live well in good health...in good health
To the Judge of Love I appeal
    to judge between us...between us
All the people bear witness together
    against one who did wrong...did wrong
Against one who did wrong to us
    so be content with the distance (between us)...
        with the distance (between us)[2]

When he finished singing, I exclaimed, "What was that?" I knew immediately that whatever kind of music it was, I wanted to learn it. Omar called it *al-mūsīqā al-andalusiyya* ("Andalusian music") and said he knew many of the Andalusian songs. He said it would be a pleasure to teach me some of them.

Over the following four weeks, Omar and I met about ten times. He taught me perhaps half a dozen songs, which I recorded on a portable cassette recorder, writing down the words as he dictated them. I wish I could convey the magic that seemed to embrace us in those sessions. Each new song was like a voyage of discovery, opening me to new melodic and textual dimensions of the tradition. Songs of praise of the Prophet Muḥammad, songs of golden sunsets, bright sunrises and morning breezes in meadows, and of love and the beauty of the beloved, such was the range of themes I

---

[2] As I learned later, this song is a *zajal*, which means it is a polyrhyming poem in Andalusi colloquial Arabic, that comes from a portion of the tradition called Quddām ar-Raṣd, which means that the melodic mode is *ar-raṣd* and the rhythmic meter is *al-quddām*. See the discussion of song types later in this chapter.

encountered in my first meeting with the Moroccan Andalusian music. Above all I was struck by the beauty of many of the melodies, as they came floating and dancing from Omar's voice and *ʿūd*. There was something strangely "medieval" in them, and yet their purity and clarity gave them a timeless quality as well.

Moreover, I found the richness of much of the poetic material very pleasing. As I worked through translations of the songs I was learning, questions arose in my mind: Where exactly did these poems come from? How did they come to be set to music? How did they manage to survive into the 21st century? As a parting present near the end of my time in Fez that summer, Omar gave me a copy of an anthology entitled *Min waḥy ar-rabāb*, ("From the Inspiration of the Rabab") which he said contained most of the Andalusian songs, arranged by musical mode.

Thus, after my desperate appeal for help and a series of chance encounters, Omar had opened the door to my research for me, in both its performed and textual dimensions.

2. *An overview of the tradition*

The chapters that follow explore some of the historical, cultural and textual aspects of the Moroccan Andalusian music tradition, framing it within its historical and cultural contexts in order to show how its oral-performed dimension has combined with the use of printed anthologies of the texts to preserve it into the 21st century. However, let us begin with a brief outline of the tradition as it exists today, in order to introduce some of its key concepts and terminology.

2.1 *al-Mūsīqā al-andalusiyya and al-Āla*

The musical tradition known in Morocco today as the Andalusian music (*al-Mūsīqā al-andalusiyya*) is also known as *al-Āla* ("instrument"). The name *Andalusian music* is a relatively recent appellation, which probably came into broad use in the early 20th century, as a product of French colonial interest in the music. It carries some historical and rhetorical weight, given the cultural associations attaching to al-Andalus as a high point of Arab-Islamic culture. On the other hand, many Moroccan scholars prefer the label *al-Āla*, which appears to have been the most common name for the tradition before the arrival of the French in 1912. It does not carry the same ideological significance, but it also is not tainted by colonial associations. Its main significance lies in the fact that it distinguishes this particular tradition, whose songs are organized into suites (*nūba*, pl. *nawbāt*) characterized by certain musical modes and performed on musical instruments, from *as-samāʿ*, a similar tradition in Morocco which draws upon much the same musical and poetic resources and is organized in much the same way, but is commonly performed a cappella. For the purposes of the present work, "Andalusian music" and *al-Āla* are treated as synonymous. *Al-Āla* is used most often here, because it is preferred by the tradition's Moroccan afficionados.

2.2 *The structure of* al-Āla

This combined instrumental and vocal genre normally is performed by an ensemble ranging from perhaps half a dozen (a group sometimes called a *farqa* > formal Arabic *firqa*, pl. *firaq*) to twenty or more (a *jawq*, pl. *ajwāq*). Traditionally, the instrumentalists also sing the songs, so that the idea of a separate chorus did not exist within the tradition until very recently and still remains an unusual practice.

Al-Āla, like its sister traditions in Algeria and Tunisia,[3] is organized into large suites of songs and instrumental compositions grouped according to their musical modes. In Morocco today there are eleven of these suites (*nawba*, or colloquially, *nūba*; the plural being *nawbāt*[4]), each named after its primary melodic mode (*ṭabᶜ*, pl. *ṭubūᶜ*, literally: "nature" or "characteristic"). In keeping with common usage in Morocco, in this work I will use the colloquial *nūba* when referring to these suites generically. However, when referring to the name of a specific suite, I will use the more formal *Nawbat* in construct, as for example, *Nawbat Ġarībat al-Ḥusayn*. This seems appropriate, since these grand suites comprise highly formalized collections of instrumental and vocal material, which represent the collective effort of composers, poets and musicians over the course of several centuries.

A *nūba* comprises a series of songs and instrumental pieces, all composed in either the primary *ṭabᶜ* for which the *nūba* is named or a specific secondary *ṭabᶜ* that may also be included in the *nūba*. There are eleven *nawbāt* in the Moroccan tradition today, which are commonly listed in the following order:

Ramal al-Māya
al-Iṣbahān
al-Māya
Raṣd aḏ-Ḏīl
al-Istihlāl
ar-Raṣd
Ġarībat al-Ḥusayn
al-Ḥijāz al-Kabīr

[3] A similar musical tradition also exists in Libya, though it has been more heavily influenced by Turkish and Egyptian music than is the case with the other North African Andalusian traditions.
[4] This term *nūba* (literally, a "turn") has been the subject of considerable discussion among scholars of the tradition. See §4 below.

al-Ḥijāz al-Mašriqī
ʿIrāq al-ʿAjam
al-ʿUššāq

A *nūba* comprises five movements (*mīzān*, pl. *mayāzīn* colloquially, or rarely, *mawāzīn* in formal Arabic, "measure" or "poetic meter"), each based upon and named after a single musical rhythm (*īqāʿ*, pl. *īqāʿāt*, "rhythm"). The tempo can change dramatically within the performance of one *mīzān*. For example, some sections of *mīzān al-basīṭ* may shift from being counted as six pulses to three. However a triple meter like *al-basīṭ* will never change to a duple one or vice versa, and the basic pattern of accented pulses within the system remains essentially the same, so that musicians do not consider that the musical meter has changed. The five *mayāzīn* are presented in the following order:

al-Basīṭ [5]
al-Qāʾim wa-Niṣf
al-Bṭāyḥī
ad-Darj
al-Quddām

Thus the Moroccan Andalusian music today theoretically comprises 11 x 5 or 55 musical movements, each with a distinctive combination of *ṭabʿ* and *īqāʿ*. Two *nawbāt*, *ar-Raṣd* and *al-Ḥijāz al-Mašriqī*, are exceptions in that they have only four *mayāzīn*: al-Qāʾim wa-Niṣf has been lost from each. In addition, there are two *mayāzīn* which do not belong to any *nūba*, having been assembled in relatively recent times. One, al-Quddām al-Jadīd (literally, "the New Quddām"), is composed of songs that are thought to have belonged to *nawbāt* that are now lost (termed *yatāmā*, s. *yatīm*, "orphans", though specialists in the tradition could not tell me when the loss and recomposition actually took place). The other, Quddām Bawākir al-Māya, is said to have been assembled in the time of the Alawite sultan Mūlāy Slīmān (r. 1792-1822). The sultan, it is said, was very fond of *ṭabʿ al-Māya* and insisted that the *nūba* of that mode be performed upon demand. His court composer reminded him that this mode is traditionally held to be best performed at sunset; doing so at any other time of day was considered to be less than propitious. However the sultan insisted, so to satisfy his patron, the musician composed a separate *mīzān* that could be performed at any time of day, calling it Quddām Bawākir al-Māya – the word *bawākir* (plural of *bākira*), meaning "harbingers", since this *mīzān* could be performed before the time expected for its *ṭabʿ*.

---

[5] There is no obvious relationship between the musical meter *al-basīṭ* and the poetic meter of the same name.

Figure I-1 represents the overall organization of the Moroccan Andalusian music tradition.

	al-Basīṭ	*al-Qāʾim wa-Niṣf*	*al-Bṭāyḥī*	*ad-Darj*	*al-Quddām*
Ramal al-Māya	x	x	x	x	x
al-Iṣbahān	x	x	x	x	x
al-Māya	x	x	x	x	x
Raṣd aḏ-Ḏīl	x	x	x	x	x
al-Istihlāl	x	x	x	x	x
ar-Raṣd	x	—	x	x	x
Ġarībat al-Ḥusayn	x	x	x	x	x
al-Ḥijāz al-Kabīr	x	x	x	x	x
al-Ḥijāz al-Mašriqī	x	—	x	x	x
ʿIrāq al-ʿAjam	x	x	x	x	x
al-ʿUššāq	x	x	x	x	x
					Quddām Bawākir al-Māya
					al-Quddām al-Jadīd

Figure I-1: *The basic organization of the Moroccan Andalusian music tradition*

A number of these *nawbāt* include songs and instrumental passages composed in subsidiary or secondary *ṭubūʿ*, some of which are said to be related to the primary *ṭabʿ*.[6] For example, in addition to the primary mode *ramal al-māya, Nawbat Ramal al-Māya* includes three secondary *ṭubūʿ*: *inqilāb al-ramal, ḥamdān* and *al-ḥusayn*. Of these four, *ramal al-māya* and *inqilāb al-ramal* are both said to be derived from the *ṭabʿ al-māya*.

[6] See Appendix 2 for a table of the nawbāt and their associated *ṭubūʿ*. Some of these modes are said to be "derived" from others, and these relationships are commonly expressed in two ways. Some works relating to the tradition present a diagram of a tree, the *šajarat aṭ-ṭubūʿ*, which shows some modes as branches from others that are more fundamental. In other cases one finds a poem attributed to one ʿAbd al-Wāḥid b. Aḥmad al-Wanšarīsī (d. 955/1549?), *Ṭabāʾiʿu mā fī ʿālami l-kawni arbaʿun* ("The temperaments of things in the world of existence are four").

Altogether, then, there are 25 *ṭubūʿ* dispersed among the eleven *nawbāt*, with one, *as-sīka,*[7] being employed in both *Raṣd aḏ-Ḏīl* and *Ġarībat al-Ḥusayn.*[8] In this work, names of *nawbāt* and *mayāzīn* will be capitalized, *nawbāt* appearing in italics, but lower case italics will be used for the *ṭubūʿ* and *īqāʿāt* as such.

Not being a specialist in the music of the Arab world, I will not be dealing with the *ṭubūʿ* or *īqāʿāt*, nor indeed with any of the musical material as such, except insofar as is necessary to clarify the performed context of the tradition's texts. There are two reasons for this choice. The *ṭubūʿ*, though interesting, are fraught with many complications and ambiguities, requiring lengthy discussion that will not contribute much to the argument in this particular work. They deserve attention in their own right.

More important, I find that historical questions which center on the musical aspects of the tradition are problematic, at best. The Arabic-speaking world, including its Andalusi branch, lacked precise musical notation until after the importation of Western music theory and script in the modern era. The first efforts to write down parts of the Moroccan Andalusian music tradition date only to the 1930s, and of course the earliest audio recordings are not much older than that. Consequently we have little clear documentary evidence of how these songs and instrumental pieces actually sounded before the 20th century. We find numerous references to names of notes and their corresponding strings and fingerings on the *ʿūd*, but for everything else we are dependent upon oral tradition alone. As the present work mainly concerns placing the performed texts within their cultural frame, I prefer not to become involved in these musicological questions.

A *nūba* is composed of both songs and instrumental passages, and the latter are of two basic types. Every performance begins with an instrumental passage called *buġya* (pl. *buġayāt*, "object of desire" or "wish"; some also refer to this passage as *mšāliya*, roughly, "uplifting"). A slow and stately melody performed *rubato*, the *buġya* serves to introduce the *ṭabʿ* to the listener. Each primary *ṭabʿ* has its proper *buġya*, and one will always hear the *buġya* for the principal *ṭabʿ* of the *nūba* as the concert begins. Sometimes, a performance will include material from more than one *nūba*, in which case the *buġya* for each successive primary *ṭabʿ* will be performed before continuing on with material from the corresponding *nūba*. (I know of no *buġayāt* for secondary *ṭubūʿ* like *al-ḥusayn* or *ḥamdān*.) The *buġya* melody is fixed, but each instrument renders it in a

---

[7] Or *aṣ-ṣīka*, sources differ on the spelling.

[8] Contemporary authors differ on number of *ṭubūʿ*: ar-Rāyis (1982), names 25, Guettat (2000, p. 379) lists 26. Ar-Rāyis gives brief summaries of these *ṭubūʿ* in his own introductions to each *nūba*. The main source for the information in these summaries is the introduction to *Kunnāš al-Ḥāʾik*, the earliest complete anthology of the tradition. In general, I have followed ar-Rāyis, who was one of the most highly regarded performers and *jawq* leaders of the 20th century.

distinctive fashion. Moreover, outstanding instrumentalists, especially the leader of the orchestra, usually take the opportunity to explore the *ṭab*ʿ by improvising around each note of the *buġya*. The length of the *buġya* depends largely upon the direction of the orchestra leader and the performance context. For shorter, or less formal performances, the *buġya* may last only half a minute or so. In longer or more formal concerts, the orchestra may devote a couple of minutes to the *buġya*, giving the audience more time to experience the full color of the *ṭab*ʿ, and the star performers a chance to illuminate its nuances.

Following the *buġya* one or more *tawāšī* (s. *tūšiya*, "embroidery") typically are performed. These are fixed instrumental passages performed at tempo that introduce the *mīzān*. Some *mayāzīn* also have *tawāšī* which fall at specific points in the *mīzān*, that is, immediately before, after or in the midst of specific songs. Some *tawāšī* are strikingly beautiful compositions in their own right, and a number of them are quite famous. Nowadays, one sometimes finds CDs that feature these instrumental interludes, and it is not unheard-of for an orchestra at a large *mahrajān*, or festival, to perform a series of *tawāšī*, rather than the usual mixture of vocal and instrumental pieces.

The first track on the accompanying CD presents a selection performed by Jawq ʿAbd al-Karīm ar-Rāyis under the direction of Mohamed Briouel, which was recorded in 2001 at the Eighth Mahrajān of Andalusian music in Fez. It begins with the *buġya* to *Nawbat Ramal al-Māya*, followed by the *tūšiya* from Quddām Ramal al-Māya. This is a very famous *tūšiya*, in part because of its exceptional beauty, but also because it belongs to *Nawbat Ramal al-Māya*, which is devoted thematically to praise of the Prophet Muḥammad, and so this *tūšiya* is frequently performed during Ramaḍān and on other religious occasions. Note that the *buġya* flows directly into the *tūšiya*, without a clear break in the music. This is typical of *al-Āla*: songs and instrumental passages proceed in an uninterrupted succession.

The heart of *al-Āla* is its vocal material. Here again one finds several types. Often, a *tūšiya* will be followed by a short, improvised vocal solo called *inšād*. The *munšid*, or singer, extemporizes on one poetic verse, usually without tempo, sometimes inserting nonsense syllables (*tarāṭīn*). It is a chance for the singer to explore the melodic possibilities of the *ṭab*ʿ while displaying his or her skill, much as the instrumentalists do in the *buġya*. The *inšād* is marked by a highly stylized performance which reflects both the singer's talents and the distinctive characteristics of the tradition itself. Another type of solo improvisation takes place in the *baytayn*. This may fall almost anywhere in the performance, and involves the *munšid* singing two lines of verse (hence, *baytayn*, lit. "two verses"). Unlike *inšād* (but like the *buġya*), the melody for *baytayn* is fixed. The *munšid* elaborates this melody by adding decorations, playing with the lengths of notes and so on, just as the instrumentalists do in the *buġya*.

These two types of improvisation represent the pinnacle of the singer's art, and thus are reserved for the most accomplished singers in the ensemble. An especially fine performance of either may be interrupted with applause and exclamations of admiration and encouragement from the audience. The singer often responds to the encouragement by enhancing his performance: repeating a well-received passage, inserting *tarāṭīn* into the text, or lifting the melody to a higher register.

The second selection on the CD presents the beginning of al-Qāʾim wa-niṣf al-Māya as performed by L'Ensemble Artistique Al Baàth de la Musique Andalouse de Fes (under the direction of Abdelfattah Benmūsā). It commences with *buġya* and *tūšiya* which lead to the first few *ṣanāʾiʿ* of the *mīzān* and a performance of *inšād* by Anwar Barrada.

Most of the vocal material in the tradition falls under the heading of *ṣanʿa* (pl. *ṣanāʾiʿ*), which means a "song" or "composition" (literally, "a work" or "a piece of craft"). The number of *ṣanāʾiʿ* in the tradition has been estimated at well over 700 individual pieces, ranging from two-line poems (invariably composed in Classical Arabic), through a large number of songs of three to perhaps a dozen lines (in Classical or Andalusi colloquial Arabic, or a mixture of both), to a few songs of up to 20 lines (most of them composed in Moroccan colloquial Arabic). These songs are generally sung by the instrumentalists themselves, although nowadays there are a few well-known singers who are recognized as such in their own right and are not expected to play instruments. The second track on the CD proceeds to a series of *ṣanāʾiʿ* from Quddām al-Māya, performed by Jawq Benmusa, which illustrates both the singing technique within the *ṣanʿa*, but also the continuous nature of the performance, as one *ṣanʿa* flows into the next with no break.

The structure of a *mīzān* performance, or indeed any performance of the tradition, is based upon song tempo. Much like the *tūšiya* on the CD, the music begins at a relatively slow and stately tempo and gradually accelerates toward a climax at the end of the *mīzān*. Formally speaking, the *mīzān* proper (that is, after the *buġya*) is divided into three sections, which ʿAbd al-Fattāḥ Benmūsa (2003) terms *marāḥil al-mīzān* (s. *marḥala*, "the stages of the *mīzān*"). The first *tūšiya* is generally performed in a slow to moderate tempo. It is followed by *taṣdirat al-mīzān* ("commencing" the *mīzān*), the first *ṣanʿa* that establishes a slow tempo for the following five or six songs. Together these first slow-tempo songs are referred to as *muwassaʿ al-mīzān* ("the extension" of the *mīzān*), the first *marḥala*. This is followed by a series of slightly faster songs, called *al-qanṭara* ("the bridge"). The third *marḥala*, *al-inṣirāf* ("the departure"), is the fastest. *Inšād* or *baytayn* may occur at any point in the progression, at the orchestra leader's discretion. Often, one of these solo vocal passages is inserted after a particularly intense or well-known series of songs, in order to raise the aesthetic tension by stopping the rhythm for the vocal solo. Also, some *mayāzīn* have more than one *tūšiya*. These other *tawāšī* are generally separated from each other, and some are associated with particular *ṣanāʾiʿ*. In many cases, these extra *tawāšī* are designed to fall within or introduce a specific *marḥala*. The orchestra leader may plan the performance so that a *tūšiya* falls between *al-muwassaʿ* and *al-qanṭara*, or between *al-qanṭara* and *al-inṣirāf*, to serve much the same musical purpose as the vocal solos just described.

A typical *mīzān* performance may be diagrammed as in Figure I-2.

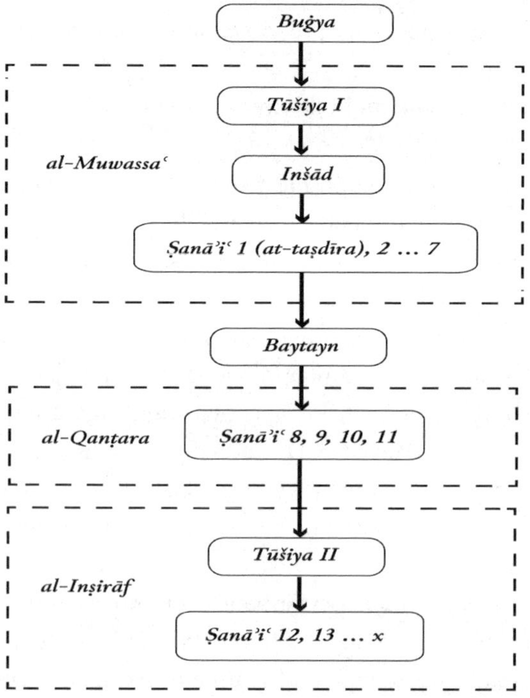

Figure I-2: *Diagram of a typical mīzān performance*

The vocal material in the Andalusian music tradition lies at the heart of this work, so it is important to understand terms used for the various types and structures of these songs. Moroccans traditionally categorize *ṣanāʾiʿ* according to two sets of criteria, structural and linguistic, which are held to describe all the vocal contents of the tradition. However, on examination it becomes clear that these criteria are not completely adequate. The linguistic labels (Classical Arabic, Andalusi Arabic, Moroccan *dārija*) are in fact more complicated and less distinct in practice than the terms seem to allow. Moreover, the *tawšīḥ* and *zajal* also shade into one another structurally to some extent. So the categories that emerge from this system are not always used consistently, which can create some confusion and misunderstanding. The traditional terminology, however, serves well enough for most purposes.

Structurally, *ṣanāʾiʿ* are divided into non-strophic (*mawzūn*, "properly-formed poetry") and strophic varieties. *Mawzūn* songs are formed according to the classical rules of prosody for Arabic verse (*ʿilm al-ʿarūḍ*): they adhere to a specific poetic meter and to a single end rhyme. As with Classical Arabic verse, they are represented on the page as lines divided into two hemistiches:

________________ x ________________ a
________________ y ________________ a

The first hemistiches of each line frequently rhyme, as well (a technique known in classical Arabic poetics as *tarṣīʿ*, lit. "inlay" or "ornamentation") :

________________ x ________________ a
________________ x ________________ a

The majority of these poems are two or three lines in length, with only a very few examples of four or more lines. Many of these *ṣanāʾiʿ*, especially in *Nawbat Ramal al-Māya*, are selected from longer poems in Classical Arabic. In classical poetic terms, they could be termed *qarīḍ* or *qalīḍ*. Within the contemporary Andalusian music tradition, they are typically referred to simply as *ṣanʿa* (that is, a song text that is unmarked as to structure or language) and then by poetic meter. In a few cases, non-strophic poems that appear to be *mawzūn* answer to no poetic meter and are indicated by the word *ṣanʿa* only. Several *qarīḍ* poems have been identified as deriving from poems by well-known figures such as al-Mutanabbī (two verses in Bṭāyḥī al-Iṣbahān), Abū Tammām (two verses in Quddām al-Māya) and even the 9th-century legal scholar, aš-Šāfiʿī (two verses found in both Quddām al-Ḥijāz al-Mašriqī and Quddām ʿIrāq al-ʿAjam).

Strophic *ṣanāʾiʿ* are of three basic types: *tawšīḥ*, *zajal* and *barwala*. These categories are in theory both linguistic and structural. As their names suggest, the first two resemble the well-known varieties of Andalusi poetry, the *muwaššaḥ* and the *zajal*. Although the most careful discussions of these genres of poetry note an ideal structural distinction between them,[9] it is more practical for the study of *al-Āla* to regard linguistic register as the decisive difference.[10] Broadly speaking, *tawšīḥ* (pl. *tawāšīḥ*) refers to a

[9] See for example: Stern (1974), Chapter 4, Monroe (1986), Liu and Monroe (1989) and Zwartjes (1995).
[10] A full discussion of the significance of linguistic register in the tradition appears in my forthcoming book, *Pen, Voice, Context: Nūbat Ramal al-Māya in Cultural Context*.

ṣanʿa with a varying rhyme scheme composed in formal Arabic that may (but frequently does not) also adhere to a single poetic meter. *Zajal* (pl. *azjāl*) in contrast refers to a similarly-formed *ṣanʿa* composed in Andalusi colloquial Arabic.

Clearly *tawāšīḥ* and *azjāl* are modeled on strophic poetry from al-Andalus. They are, however, only short selections of one or sometimes two strophes (termed *dawr*, pl. *adwār*, “a turn”), whereas the typical Andalusi *muwaššaḥ* or *zajal* was four or five *adwār* in length. A *dawr* from one of these Andalusi-style strophic poems usually has five lines, with the first three rhyming together (formed like the independent-rhyme section of a *muwaššaḥ*, or *ġuṣn*), and the last two rhyming differently (like the common-rhyme part of a *muwaššaḥ*, or *qufl*):

________________	v	________________	b
________________	w	________________	b
________________	x	________________	b
________________	y	________________	a
________________	z	________________	a

As with *mawzūn* songs, it is not unusual to find *tarsīʿ*:

________________	x	________________	b
________________	x	________________	b
________________	x	________________	b
________________	y	________________	a
________________	y	________________	a

This type of five-line *ṣanʿa* is known as a *ḫumāsiyya* (“pentain”). Some strophic *ṣanāʾiʿ* have an introduction (termed a *maṭlaʿ*, lit. “starting point”) of two lines that rhyme with the *qufl*, producing a *subāʿiyya* (“septain”):

________________	t	________________	a
________________	u	________________	a
________________	v	________________	b
________________	w	________________	b
________________	x	________________	b
________________	y	________________	a
________________	z	________________	a

Other variations on these basic patterns are possible, including a *rubāʿiyya* ("quatrain"), for example:

________________ w	________________ b
________________ x	________________ b
________________ y	________________ b
________________ z	________________ a

and a *sudāsiyya* ("sextain") :

________________ u	________________ b
________________ v	________________ b
________________ w	________________ b
________________ x	________________ b
________________ y	________________ a
________________ z	________________ a

and occasionally we find a variation on the *ḫumāsiyya* format with a single-line *maṭlaʿ* and *qufl*:

________________ v	________________ a
________________ w	________________ b
________________ x	________________ b
________________ y	________________ b
________________ z	________________ a

In addition, many Andalusi-style strophic poems in the tradition carry more elaborate *tarsīʿ* emphasized by the melodies in which they are set. Such cases usually are represented on the page using lines of three (or more) segments. For example:

________ x	________ y	______________ b
________ x	________ y	______________ b
________ x	________ y	______________ b
________________ z	________________ a	
________________ z	________________ a	

As with some of the *mawzūn* poems, both *tawāšīḥ* and *azjāl* are found in the tradition that derive from strophic poems by specific authors, both Andalusi and North African.

Examples from *Nawbat Ramal al-Māya* include poems by Ibn al-Fāriḍ (d. 632/1235), Aḥmad ar-Rifāʿī (d. 578/1182) and Abū l-Ḥasan aš-Šuštarī (d. 667/1269), among others .

The last structural-linguistic category is the *barwala* (pl. *barāwil*), which is probably a relatively late addition to the tradition, as it does not appear in any of the manuscripts which lie behind the modern printed anthologies which contain *barāwil*. These poems are composed in Moroccan (some scholars say North African) colloquial Arabic. They vary considerably in length, structure and rhyme pattern (poetic meters in the traditional sense are unknown in them), but despite their colloquial language and variable structure, they are nevertheless laid out on the page following the conventions of Arabic poetry described above. Very little background scholarship has been done on these *ṣanāʾiʿ* and the poetry that lies behind them, and written sources are almost nonexistent. An aspect of some interest in these poems is their complex relationship with Moroccan colloquial Arabic, a subject dealt with in some detail in my forthcoming study of *Ramal al-Māya*. Here it can be said that, because these texts belong to a poetic register of language, they stand at some distance from truly day-to-day colloquial Moroccan Arabic.

Al-Āla is not simply a written, poetic tradition, but a performed one, as well. For reasons which will be explored in the chapters that follow, it cannot be categorized as either oral or written. Rather, it bears characteristics of both. One way this becomes important lies in the complicated relationship between the printed and the performed text of *al-Āla*, a distinctive feature of this relationship being the presence of nonsense syllables, *tarāṭīn* (a term derived from the formal Arabic verb رَطَنَ , "to jabber, talk gibberish"). These are integral elements of many of the *ṣanāʾiʿ* in the tradition, referred to as *šuġl* (from the verb for "to be busy, occupied"), though they never appear in print. Nevertheless, they must be memorized along with the poetic text and music. Here are two examples of *tarāṭīn*. The first is a single verse from a *ṣanʿa ḫumāsiyya* in Mīzān Bṭāyḥī of *Nawbat Ġarībat al-Ḥusayn*:

أَنْتَ أَحْلَى مِن المُنَى يا لا لا لا لا   وَمِن الماءِ أَعْذَبُ يا لا لا لا لا

You are sweeter than desire *ya la la la la*
and sweeter than sweet water *ya la la la la*

In addition to يا لا لا لا لا being inserted after each hemistich of this *ṣanʿa*, the second hemistich of each line (including the *tarāṭīn*) is repeated (the *tarāṭīn* having a different melody). Another, somewhat more complex example can be found in a *zajal* from *mīzān*

Quddām al-Istihlāl, in which the *tarāṭīn* given below are inserted after each line, but only after the line has been repeated with a variation in melody. Here are two lines from this *zajal*, with the appropriate repetitions added:

مَسَكَتْ عِناني   وَهَيَّجَتْ حُرَقى
مَسَكَتْ عِناني   وَهَيَّجَتْ حُرَقى   ها نا نا نا طايْ طِيرِراي
كَأَنَّها البَدْرُ   في دُجَى الغَسَقي
كَأَنَّها البَدْرُ   في دُجَى الغَسَقي   ها نا نا نا طايْ طِيرِراي

She seizes my bridle
  and provokes my agitation
She seizes my bridle
  and provokes my agitation *ha na na na ṭāy ṭīrī rāy*
It's as if she's the full moon
  in the darkness of the night
It's as if she's the full moon
  in the darkness of the night *ha na na na ṭāy ṭīrī rāy*

In not a few cases, *tarāṭīn* comprise prolonged passages interpolated between or even within phrases of the text.

The printed text thus stands in a complex relationship to the text as performed. As this touches on historical, textual and cultural aspects of the tradition, a discussion of this relationship represents an important theme throughout the pages to come.

2.3 *Performers and performances*

The social-cultural aspects of the music's performance is a key subject of Part 1. Here, I think it useful to introduce the essential terminology and describe very briefly the various formats in which the music is presented today. A more detailed picture emerges in the discussion of the history of the tradition, that follows, especially in Chapter 4, which deals with the handing down of the tradition across generations.

In Morocco today, *al-Āla* is performed by two kinds of ensembles. A smaller ensemble, consisting of perhaps half a dozen musicians, is usually called a *farqa* ("group" or "band"). One sometimes finds this sort of group performing in public in support of a large vocal group (as for example during religious festivals), where the Andalusian music is only one part of the repertoire of the chorus. However, this type of ensemble has a long history within the tradition, and is ideally suited for informal, private gatherings or for smaller private parties. Figure I-3 is a photograph of Farqa Šīkī performing at Fes Hadara in the spring of 2004. Anas Attar, *ra ʾīs* of Jawq al-Brīhī, is second from left, playing *rabāb*; to his left is Professor Aḥmad Šīkī of the National Conservatory in Fez; and on the far right is ʿAzīz ʿAlamī, also an instructor at the Conservatory, who performs in Jawq Briouel.

Instruments in the *farqa* typically include *ʿūd* (Arabic lute), *kamān* ("violin," from the Turkish *kamānja*), *ṭār* (a small frame drum with cymbals mounted in the frame) and *darbūka* (vase-shaped, Middle Eastern-style hand drum). Occasionally one finds *qānūn* (an Egyptian- or Turkish-style lap zither), *rabāb* (a two-stringed rebec) or viola as well. The leader of the *farqa* nearly always plays either *ʿūd* or *kamān*. (Farqa Šīkī opts for an unusual, more ancient instrumentation featuring *suwīsan* – a three-stringed cognate of the *ʿūd* with at round neck and leather-covered sound box – instead of *kamān*.)

Figure I-3: *Farqa Šīkī*

Figure I-4: *Rabāb*

Figure I-5: *Ṭār*

Figure I-6: *Suwīsan*

A larger ensemble is called a *jawq* (pl. *ajwāq*, "orchestra"). Its leader is called the *ra'īs* (sometimes colloquially *rāyis*, pl. *ru'asā'*, "chief"), and the best-known *ajwāq* are lead by highly-skilled musicians who possess an extensive knowledge of the tradition. Because the tradition is regarded as a very refined and sophisticated art form, the *ra'īs* of a distinguished *jawq* commands a great deal of respect from performers and audiences alike. The role of the *ra'īs* is analogous to that of a big band jazz orchestra leader. As is usually true for the big band leader, the *ra'īs* performs with the group, and like the jazz band leader, he is called upon to make many aesthetic decisions for each performance. (However unlike jazz, the Andalusian music employs very little improvisation, and so a *ra'īs* has considerably less creative freedom than a jazz band leader.) In addition, an experienced and well-educated *ra'īs* is constantly educating the musicians of his *jawq* in the nuances and subtleties of the tradition. For this reason, such a *ra'īs* is also known as *mu'allim* ("teacher"), which is a sign of very high respect within the Andalusian music tradition.

Figure I-7: *Jawq Temsemānī performing at the National Festival in Fez, in May 2003.*

The *jawq*, as it is known today, may comprise from eight to twenty musicians, always including the following instruments: a *rabāb* (never more than one), an *ʿūd* (sometimes more than one), several *kamān*, a *ṭār* (sometimes two), and *darbūka* (sometimes two). A number of *ajwāq* have adopted the *qānūn*, and often include one or two violas, as well. Some *ajwāq* have incorporated other stringed instruments, such as the cello and contrabass. Some of the more famous *ajwāq* have added piano, while an even more controversial development has been the introduction of wind instruments such as the *nāy* (reed flute), transverse flute, saxophone and clarinet.[11] Occasionally, a larger *jawq* may include a chorus of from one to four singers. Further discussion of the *jawq*, and of the role of the *raʾīs* in the perpetuation of the tradition is presented in Chapter 4.

The *jawq* is generally considered the premier format for performing *al-Āla*. Each of the main cities in the north of Morocco in which the Andalusian music has taken root is home to at least one *jawq*, while the most important centers (Fez, Tetuan, Tangier, Rabat and Casablanca) have several (the actual number is difficult to determine since musicians may participate in more than one *jawq*, and sometimes a sub-group of musicians belonging to one *jawq* may appear together under a different name).[12] The *jawq* is invariably the form in which the tradition is presented at the large

[11] I have never seen nor heard of a *jawq* that included brass instruments.

[12] Until recently, there was a *jawq* based in Marrakech in the south of the country. My informants tell me that the tradition is no longer practiced there. When I showed some of them a recent CD, allegedly by

festivals of Andalusian Music, which are held in Tangier, Fez, Casablanca and Chefchaouen each year, and which feature notable *ajwāq* from around the country. The size of the *jawq* gives the music a grand and majestic quality, while the variety of instruments brings a richness to the sound. It is no wonder that Andalusian music scholars and musicians sometimes compare the Andalusian music tradition with Western orchestral music.

Members of the *jawq* in a formal concert wear a particular costume. In Fez, men usually wear a white or off-white *jallāba* (a long-sleeved, hooded caftan; the hood is never worn in performance) over tight-fitting white trousers and white stockings, a red felt "Fez" hat with a black tassel (*tarbūš*) and yellow pointed slippers (*darbūš*). Musicians from other cities may wear white or other-colored slippers, and sometimes a striped *jallāba*. For women, the costume is very colorful, featuring a brightly-colored satin or silk *jallāba* with matching slippers. They may also wear a headdress with an embroidered veil tied up in the hair and draped down the back and shoulders.

Andalusian music performances take a number of formats. A collection of *ṣanāʾiʿ* may be performed along with other styles of music. This might happen, for example, at a wedding or other private celebration where *al-Āla* is welcomed but not necessarily the primary focus. (In the past, *al-Āla* was often the music of choice for a wedding party, especially among middle-class Fassis, but my informants indicate that this far less common today than it once was.) In such a case, the musicians will be versed in a wide variety of musical styles. Thus, their knowledge of the Andalusian tradition may not be very extensive. Songs from the tradition often will be performed at religious celebrations, such as the birthday of the Prophet Muḥammad or during one of the ʿĪd holidays. On such an occasion, other styles of music may also be heard, including those of the closely-related *madīḥ* (praise of the Prophet) tradition. The ensemble in this case might be a smaller version of a well-known *jawq*, or perhaps a *farqa* of musicians versed in several styles of music. The quality of the performance in this case is likely to be very high, as the musicians for these festivities are usually carefully chosen. In either of these two examples, the number and variety of songs from the Andalusian tradition will typically be very limited.

During the month of Ramadan, Moroccan television presents short videotaped programs of Andalusian music in the afternoons, as the time for breaking the fast approaches. Rarely more than 30 minutes or so in length, these performances nearly always are drawn from *Nawbat Ramal al-Māya*, which is devoted to praise of the

---

"Jawq Marrakech," I was told that the leader of the group had stopped performing, and that all the other musicians in the jawq were from elsewhere. My own inquiries in Marrakech revealed that indeed no one is teaching the tradition there: instruction is not available at the local branch of the National Conservatory of Music and Dance, and a private conservatory that once offered instruction is now closed.

Prophet Muḥammad. (I have also heard *Nawbat al-Māya* in this context, as it is devoted to sunset imagery – the time for breaking the fast.) During the rest of the year, Moroccan television presents feature concerts of *al-Āla* from time to time, which may last up to an hour or more. These videotaped concerts always involve full *ajwāq*, in keeping with the formality of the occasion.

During the ʿĪd celebrations at the end of Ramadan, influential individuals – such as an important local official or his wife – might sponsor a party featuring a *farqa* or small *jawq* playing selections from *Ramal al-Māya*. This would be, of course, a highly formal affair open only to invitees from the local elites and influential families. The associations of Andalusian music lovers also sponsor other private performances and performance series.[13] These special *ḥafalāt* (s. *ḥafla*, "party, gathering") may happen at any time of the year, but typically occur in the spring, or during one of the religious festivals, or sometimes during festivities marking the crowning of the king – as was done during the reigns of the past two monarchs, Muḥammad V and Hasan II.

Among formal concerts of purely Andalusian music, there are two basic types. The longest and most formal is the performance of a *nūba*. A true *nūba* performance requires that songs from all five *mayāzīn* be played, which also implies the appropriate *buġya* and *tawāšī*, as well. According to my informants, this was once considered the standard performance format. However, because its length and modal uniformity are very demanding for modern listeners accustomed to performances that are fast-paced and varied, a whole *nūba* is never performed these days – indeed, there is little hard evidence that it ever really was: the oldest concert programs available (from the 1950s) do not show performances of entire *nawbāt*. In any case, it is now typical for a *jawq* to perform a series of songs from a single *mīzān* (or *marḥala*), and then perhaps follow that with songs from another (often unrelated) *mīzān*. Usually these *mīzān* performances include all three *marāḥil*, though sometimes a more lively version beginning with *buġya* followed only by the *inṣirāf* will be performed. This sort of performance allows the *raʾīs* more flexibility, and the listener more variety. Such is the case at the national festivals, and at many of the private concerts sponsored by the music lovers' associations.

13 The role of the private music lovers' associations is discussed in Chapter 3 §4.2.

Figure I-8: *Jawq Briouel performing during ʿĪd at Musée Batha, December 6, 2002. The* ra'is, *Mohamed Briouel, is seated just left of center, playing* kamān. *Notice Aḥmad Šīkī and ʿAzīz ʿAlamī on the right, as well.*

Perhaps the most ancient performance format, and one which has received little attention from scholars, is the informal private gathering: a group of friends who happen also to be Andalusian music aficionados come together at someone's home to play the music and socialize. I had the privilege to be invited to one such gathering. An account of this event is found in Chapter 3 §4.2.

Judging from these various performance contexts, and from the teaching of the music in the National Conservatory (also discussed in Chapter 4), it is fair to say that the Andalusian music serves as the national classical music for Morocco. Because of its elite associations and the sophistication of much of its poetry, its immediate audience is limited to the better-educated (and wealthier) strata of society who can afford to join one of the associations of music lovers that play an important role in sponsoring concerts and festivals featuring the music. For this reason, some regard the music as having a certain bourgeois image, and so it is often dismissed by younger people as being irrelevant to their lives in modern Morocco. There is no doubt that this musical tradition has little direct appeal to generations raised in a world whose soundtrack is electronic and percussive, and whose musical models come as much from the West as from the Arab world itself. Moreover, the Andalusian music is and always has been essentially an urban and Arab phenomenon that scarcely touches the lives of Morocco's rural, largely Berber population.

Despite these limitations, many young Moroccans participate in what I would call the music's secondary audience. Although they may never own an Andalusian cassette or CD, and may never attend a live concert of the music, young people in a city like Fez cannot avoid growing up with this literary-musical tradition in their environment. It can be heard echoing from music shops in the streets of the Medina, on weekly broadcasts on the radio, in cyber cafes and coffee shops, and of course on the television, as already described. In this way, its erudite and historical associations (summed up in the adjective *aṣīl*, meaning "authentic" or "pure") reach them on an abstract emotional level that connects less with their active tastes in music than with their sense of themselves as a people with a common history and cultural background, that is, a *nation*. In short, *al-Āla* appears to reach even non-aficionado Moroccans as part of a cluster of cultural elements that help them define themselves in a world increasingly characterized by the blurring of boundaries and the bending of identities through economic and cultural influences from abroad.

3. *Texts and innovations*

As a literary phenomenon, *al-Āla* exists as a collection of *ṣanāʾiʿ* that have been collected into a number of printed anthologies. Three books in particular, *Majmūʿ azjāl wa tawšīḥ wa ašʿār al-mūsīqā l-andalusiyya al-maġribiyya al-maʿrūf bil-Ḥāʾik* (1977) by ʿAbd al-Laṭīf Ibn Manṣūr, *Al-turāṯ al-ʿarabī al-maġribī fī l-mūsīqā : mustaʿmalāt nawbāt al-ṭarab al-andalusī al-maġribī : šiʿr, tawšīḥ, azjāl, barāwil – dirāsa wa-tansīq wa-taṣḥīḥ Kunnāš al-Ḥāʾik* (1979) by Idrīs Ibn Jallūn, and *Min waḥy ar-rabāb* (1982) by ʿAbd al-Karīm ar-Rāyis, effectively define the boundaries of the tradition. As the titles of the first two suggest, the *Kunnāš al-Ḥāʾik* (compiled around the year 1788) functions for aficionados as a kind of urtext that both put the tradition on a literary footing, and has come to symbolize the *aṣīl* character of the tradition itself. Only the intervention of the last great anthologist, al-Jāmiʿī near the end of the 19th century even remotely compares to the importance of the *Kunnāš*. Yet al-Jāmiʿī's work was much shorter and was only collected very recently into a comprehensive version (embodied in *Min waḥy ar-rabāb*), and so musicians and aficionados treat it more as an additional resource than as a foundational text.

In theory at least, no new *ṣanāʾiʿ* have been composed since the time of al-Jāmiʿī. In practice, several performers in recent years have introduced *ṣanāʾiʿ* that they claim to have "discovered" in works by their masters before them. Given that musical transmission across generations in this tradition is entirely oral, without the benefit of an accurate, practical method of musical notation (a situation discussed in more detail in Chapters 4 and 8 below), these claims of discovery stretch credibility. The more likely scenario is that these performers found texts in existing manuscript versions of the *Kunnāš* – probably already associated with particular *mayāzīn* – and composed appropriate melodies for them.

These phenomena highlight three important characteristics of *al-Āla* as a performed tradition: its conservative nature, the important role played by manuscript anthologies, and the significance of the oral-literary interplay that characterizes the tradition as a whole. That contemporary performers feel the need to justify their own compositions by attributing them to an earlier generation (and basing them upon manuscript versions of the *Kunnāš*) shows that composition and innovation are not highly valued.[14] Rather, the *aṣīl* character of a particular *ṣanʿa* depends upon a link to an existing corpus of texts that is understood as inherently bounded and complete. The processes by which this corpus was formed can only be understood in light of the manuscript traditions that lie behind it, a topic taken up in Chapter 5. The fact that the corpus itself is represented as a literary phenomenon, deploying all the conventions of representing poetry on the page, illustrates well the significance of this literary aspect in the face of the oral processes that lie behind it. The implications of this curious dual oral/textual character of *al-Āla* are discussed in Part 2 of this book.

4. *The* nūba *in history and theory*

Because of this conservatism, *al-Āla* is widely regarded in Morocco and elsewhere as the North African genre nearest to the music of al-Andalus, while among Moroccans the style performed in Fez is thought to be the most conservative and thus the most authentically "Andalusian." This point touches upon to the question of the "Andalusian-ness" of the tradition. As was mentioned earlier, the expression *al-Mūsīqā l-andalusiyya* was made current by French scholars studying the tradition, and it appeared in writing only in the early 20th century. Moroccan scholars attribute it to Alexis Chottin, the Protectorate official most intimately involved with scholarly study of *al-Āla*. Recent research by Jonathan Glasser suggests it emerged in the late 19th century in Algeria, in connection with French colonial discourses of national/ethnic identity. How much influence Algerian views of the Andalusian musical heritage actually had in Morocco is debatable. However al-Ḥāʾik, writing in his *muqaddima* near the end of the 18th century, distinguishes the 25 *ṭubūʿ* in the *nūba* tradition as being of Andalusi origin. Thus the idea that the *nūba* tradition has roots in the music of al-Andalus certainly was in the air in Morocco well before the French took control of

[14] In *Pen, Voice, Text,* however I present data and an argument demonstrating that this situation is in fact significantly more complicated than it first appears to be.

Algeria in 1830. Insofar as the lion's share of the poetry in the tradition either comes from Andalusi authors or has been composed on Andalusi models, the music's Andalusi pedigree is at least plausible.

Yet, these beliefs should not mislead us into thinking that the Moroccan Andalusian music is in fact "closer" in some demonstrable way to the original music of al-Andalus than, for example, the Algerian *mālūf*. We simply do not know how the medieval music sounded, nor do we know much about its performace practice after the 13th century, and so any such comparisons must remain in the realm of conjecture. Moreover, there is no doubt that the tradition has undergone significant development in Morocco over the five centuries since the fall of Granada.

The structure of the tradition – the *nūba* form – certainly has evolved since its arrival in Morocco. One of the ongoing discussions among scholars concerns its origins and development. It is widely recognized (Sawa, 1989; Wright, 1993; Cortés, 1997; Guettat, 2000; aš-Šāmī, 2001) that the word first appears in a musical context in the *Kitāb al-Aġānī*, referring to a poet's or singer's *turn* to perform for the caliph. This *turn* could happen either in the context of a series of musicians or poets performing on one occasion, or else a performance on a regularly scheduled day of the week. (Sawa 1989, 115-117, 120) The *Aġānī* was written in Iraq in the 10th century, however, and its use of the term *nūba* had nothing at all to do with a suite of songs, as Sawa points out.

An account that may refer to a suite form used in al-Andalus is found in Ibn Ḥayyān's 11th-century *al-Muqtabis*. The anthologist included a passage in his biography of Ziryāb that says the famous composer recommended beginning with a recitative followed by three song types, *al-basīṭ*, *al-muḥarrak*(*a*) and *al-hazaj*, a passage that is widely understood as referring to a primitive *nūba*.[15]

> ورأوه صوابا ايتمروا عليه إلى اليوم ، كما استمر كل مغنٍ افتتح الغناء بطريقة
> نفسه على الابتداء بالنشيد أول شدْوه بأي نقر كان ، ويأتي بالبسيط إثره ، ويختتم
> بالمحركات والأهزاج ، بما رسم زرياب لهم ...

> They thought it proper to continue it up till today, just as every singer continued to do, beginning singing in his own style, commencing with *našīd* as the first of his song in whatever rhythm there was; and then came *al-basīṭ* immediately afterwards; and he concluded with *al-muḥarrakāt* and *al-ahzāj*, according to what Ziryāb set down for them ...

---

[15] 2003, p. 324. Ibn Ḥayyān's source for this passage is *Kitāb Aḫbār Ziryāb*, which is lost. This passage is cited in full in Chapter 2 §1.2b. On Ibn Ḥayyān's sources for Ziryāb, see §1.2 of the same chapter.

The word *nūba* does not appear in reference to a sequence of songs in al-Andalus until *al-Mutʿat al-asmāʿ fī ʿilm al-samāʿ* by the 13th-century Tunisian author Aḥmad at-Tīfāšī.[16] At-Tīfāšī mentions a *nūba* which involves four elements: *našīd*, *ṣawt*, *muwaššaḥ* and *zajal*. Cortés García (1997) presents a complicated argument on linguistic evidence from other sources that the first two are styles of vocal rendition, and that therefore the first is related to the Moroccan *inšād*. Obviously the second two are genres of sung poetry, so this raises the problem of how terms from two different registers of meaning fit together as movements in a suite of songs.

They do not have to, because at-Tīfāšī presents us with enough information to solve this puzzle, if we read at-Tīfāšī's comments in their context. At-Tīfāšī was writing about what he understood was performance practice in al-Andalus in his day, based upon information he gleaned from Andalusian migrants to Tunis.[17] At-Tīfāšī's Chapter 11 is entitled *Fī qawānīna l-ġināʾi l-andalusī mansūba kulli šayʾin minhu li-mulḥinihi wa-ālātihim fīhi* ("On the Modes of Andalusian Song, Everything Being Ascribed to Its Composer and Their Instruments (in Playing) It"). The main portion of the chapter is a catalog of four modes (*al-Ḫusrawānī*, *al-Muṭlaq*, *al-Mazmūm* and *al-Mujtaṯṯ*), each of which contains some songs *fī ṭarīqati n-našīd* ("in the *našīd* manner") and some *fī ṭarīqati ṣ-ṣawt* ("in the *ṣawt* manner"). At the beginning of the list, immediately after introducing the mode *al-ḫusrawānī* and *fī ṭarīqati n-našīd*, the author explains that *našīd*

> وهو المعروف عند أهل الأندلس بالاستهلال والعمل يبدؤونه بنغمات ثقيلة شيء
> بعض شيء ثم يخرجون عنها إلى نغمات خفيقة تحصل بين الحالين فتثير من
> الطرب ما يُرتاح له

> ...is known among the people of al-Andalus as *al-istihlāl* and *al-ʿamal* and they begin (*al-našīd*) with slow [or "heavy"] notes, little by little, then they leave them for light notes (which) fall between the two parts, and so it stimulates the pleasure that is felt for it.[18]

---

[16] Chapters 10 and 11 edited and published by Muḥammad b. Tāwīt aṭ-Ṭanjī under the title "aṭ-Ṭarā'iq wa-l-alḥān al-mūsīqiyya fī Ifrīqiya wa-l-Andalus" (1968); English translation in Liu and Monroe (1989) pp. 35-44.

[17] Including Ibn Saʿīd al-Andalusī, the author of *al-Muġrib fī ḥulā l-Maġrib*. More on at-Tīfāšī in Chapter 2 §1.1 and §2.

[18] aṭ-Ṭanjī, p. 104.

Then, when introducing the songs in *al-ḫusrawānī* that are *fī ṭarīqati ṣ-ṣawt*, at-Tīfāšī indicates that *ṣawt* is "*ʿamal*, all of it without *istihlāl*".[19]

Lois Faruqi's dictionary of Arabic musical terms (1981) indicates that *al-istihlāl* refers to a "vocal prelude" and that *al-ʿamal* signifies vocal or instrumental music coming after the prelude. If this is correct then we should read *wa* in the passage cited above as *wāw al-muṣāḥaba*: *an-našīd* is "*al-istihlāl* followed by *al-ʿamal*." Thus at-Tīfāšī is giving us two similar genres of song, both with sung verses of poetry, but one (*našīd*) with a kind of prelude (*al-istihlāl*), and the other (*ṣawt*) without.

Moreover, at-Tīfāšī is quite explicit in describing the various examples he provides of both *našīd* and *ṣawt* (none of which are strophic poems). In each case, he notes the author of the poetry, and the composer of the music. He even records when a later composer has changed some part of the music. Since *an-našīd* therefore is a composed musical piece that combines a prelude (probably vocal, to judge from the name, though that is not completely clear from at-Tīfāšī's description) with sung verses, the connection Cortés García wants to make between it and the improvised Moroccan *inšād* seems tenuous. (Perhaps the modern *baytayn* is a closer analogy.) In any case, at-Tīfāšī is writing about, not *styles of rendition*, but *genres of song*.

The last piece of the puzzle is at-Tīfāšī's comments regarding the *nūba* itself:

ومن مغنّي الأندلس رجالا ونساء من يغني خمس مائة نوبة ونحوها والنوبة عندهم
مشيد وصوت وموشّح وزجل .

> Among the men and women of al-Andalus are those who (are able to) sing approximately 500 *nūba*s. The *nūba* among them is a *našīd* and a *ṣawt* and a *muwaššaḥ* and a *zajal*.[20]

At-Tīfāšī appears to be saying that the *nūba* of al-Andalus in his day consisted of four songs: the first with a prelude followed by non-strophic verses, the second with only non-strophic verses, then a *muwaššaḥ*, and finally a *zajal*.

Viewing this structure in schematic form reveals its aesthetic logic. Figure I-9 represents at-Tīfāšī's 13th-century *nūba*. *Našīd* provides an introduction that leads to the first song. *Ṣawt* continues in the same vein with another vocal number in non-strophic form. At-Tīfāšī's examples show that these are both based upon classical-style poetry in formal Arabic. The *muwaššaḥ* follows, introducing strophic poetry into the performance. The *muwaššaḥ* is composed in formal Arabic, like the *našīd* and *ṣawt*, but it

---

[19] p. 106.
[20] p. 114.

ends with a passage (the *ḫarja*) that introduces the possibility of a non-formal register of language, usually colloquial Arabic but occasionally with Romance or Hebrew expressions. The strophic *zajal* continues in the same register, being composed in colloquial Arabic with the possibility of some non-Arabic insertions.

Thus the *nūba* described by at-Tīfāšī seems to have been designed to play upon the linguistic registers current in 13th-century al-Andalus by commencing in a traditional, formal one with the *našīd* and *ṣawt*, but then moving by stages into an amusingly non-formal register with the *zajal*. The expressive possibilities of a performance like this would be very interesting.

Element	*Našīd*		*Ṣawt*	*Muwaššaḥ*	*Zajal*
Type	*Prelude*	*Song*	*Song*	*Song*	*Song*
Arabic	*Istihlāl*	*ʿAmal*	*ʿAmal*	*Muwaššaḥ*	*Zajal*
Format	*(Instrumental or vocal)*	*Mawzūn*	*Mawzūn*	*Strophic*	*Strophic*
Register		*Formal Arabic*	*Formal Arabic*	*Formal -> Colloquial*	*Colloquial*

Figure I-9: *Progression in the 13th-century* nūba *of at-Tīfāšī*

At-Tīfāšī's *nūba* does not look much like the *nūba* or *mīzān* we know in Morocco today. The only obvious similarity lies in the use of *muwaššaḥ* and *zajal* as compositional elements in the suite, which otherwise appears quite short when compared to the modern Moroccan version (even given *muwaššaḥāt* and *azjāl* of five or more strophes). We find here little that speaks to the role of tempo in the performance, and no indication of modes or musical meters as structural elements, contrary to the modern Moroccan *nūba*. Nor does this *nūba* appear to have movements as such – unless one considers a song type to be a movement. Indeed, there is little that connects these four types of song to one another in any way, other than their being performed in one "turn" and the inferred play on linguistic registers.

The Moroccan *nūba* brings together three elements not mentioned in at-Tīfāšī's suite model that together bind the *ṣanāʾiʿ* into something more than a collection of (possibly unrelated) songs: modal unity, movements based upon rhythmic unity, and generally increasing tempo within each *mīzān* (but not for the *nūba* as a whole). A *nūba* combining these elements is not mentioned at all in any extant works before

Muḥammad al-Būʿaṣāmī's early anthology, *Īqād aš-šumūʿ li-laddat al-masmūʿ bi-naġamāt aṭ-ṭubūʿ* in the first half of the 18th century, and it does not come into full expression in writing until *Kunnāš al-Ḥāʾik* at the end of that century.

In sum, at-Tīfāšī refers to a performance unit known as a *nūba*, but it has no structural relationship to the modern version. If we take care not to let a desire to find some connection across the five and a half centuries between at-Tīfāšī and al-Ḥāʾik cloud our vision, we can see that no clear relationship can be established based upon at-Tīfāšī alone. As Wright (1993) points out, the absence of clear documentary evidence leaves us groping in the dark.[21]

Given the evidence we have at hand, we may wonder whether the rhythm-based *mayāzīn* we know as structural elements in the *nūba* might have been a North African invention. This is not by any means certain. The fact that most of the North African Andalusian music traditions make use of rhythm-based movements would seem to indicate that they share a common origin in some type of performance practice (perhaps originating in al-Andalus) that emphasized rhythm as a structural element. Indeed, Dwight Reynolds (2013) has uncovered a manuscript, portions of which appear to date to the 15th century, or perhaps earlier. This manuscript, first described in the early 20th century by Philippe El Khazen, although not organized into *nawbāt*, uses the terms *inṣirāf, darj,* and *bṭāyḥī* to refer to rhythms or movements. Reynolds notes that the *Maʾlūf* Andalusian music of Tlemcen also uses these terms in this way. If the dating of this manuscript proves to be correct, it would suggest that North African Andalusian music traditions were using a rhythm-based movement already within a few generations of 1492. This seems very early to be a true innovation, and it could indicate that such a structure did exist in al-Andalus prior to the Christian conquest.

However, in the Moroccan context, the idea of a *mīzān* in the sense of a movement based upon rhythmic unity does not appear in a written source before *Īqād aš-šumūʿ* in the first half of the 18th century. Aš-Šāmī (2001, p. 5) attributes the idea of five *mayāzīn* in the Moroccan context to the book *Aġānī as-sīqā fī ʿlm al-mūsīqā* by Ibrāhīm at-Tādilī (d. 1894). Mīzān ad-Darj certainly seems to be a relatively late arrival in the Moroccan tradition (in its written form, anyway), since no *mīzān* by that name appears in any of the *Kunnāš* manuscripts (Cortés García, 1996, 49-50), nor indeed in the original versions of any of the al-Jāmiʿī manuscripts. Moreover, while it is now accepted as a standard part of the *nūba*, its present location in the *nūba* was not established canonically even in the 1970s.[22]

---

[21] p. 1043.

[22] We should not take the absence of *mīzān ad-darj* from the *Kunnāš* manuscripts at face value. Cortés García (1996) argues that al-Ḥāʾik almost certainly did not include everything that was performed in his time, and there is no reason to assume that the songs comprising this *mīzān* were not present in some

The *barwala* song form featuring Moroccan colloquial Arabic is without question also a North African addition to the *nūba*. Cortés García (1996) maintains that these songs are broadly associated with *mīzān ad-darj*, which leads her to conclude that they entered the tradition at the same time as *ad-darj*, which she places in al-Jāmiʿī's era. This is problematic, because by no means are all *barāwil* found in *ad-darj*. For example, *Nawbat ʿIrāq al-ʿAjam* contains six *barāwil*: three in Mīzān ad-Darj and three in Mīzān al-Quddām. *Nawbat Ramal al-Māya* contains eight *barāwil*, two of them in al-Quddām. While the exact historical relationship of the *barwala* to *mīzān ad-darj* and to the *nūba* as a whole is not entirely clear, there can be no doubt that they represent North African additions to the *nūba*.

Such is the state of research into the historical development of the Moroccan *nūba*. To a large extent it has been stymied by gaps in the historical record. Yet documentary evidence does suggest that its rhythmic structure has evolved over the past two centuries or so with the inclusion of *mīzān ad-darj*, while the repertoire of *ṣanāʾiʿ* has expanded to include at least one new type of song that did not originate in al-Andalus. Where these developments belong in the narrative of the *nūba*'s history remains unclear. According to Ahmed Piro, the rhythm *ad-darj* was a part of the *Samāʿ* repertoire for a very long time before it became integrated into *al-Āla* and was performed as part of *mīzān al-bṭāyḥī* before being set aside as a separate *mīzān*.[23] Thus it is possible that musicological study of the modern *al-bṭāyḥī*, as well as further study of *as-Samāʿ*, would shed light upon this question.

5. *The organization of this book*

This work is divided into two parts. Part 1 deals with the history of the Andalusian music tradition, from its earliest roots in al-Andalus to its modern circumstances. Chapter 1 considers the historiographical tradition that lies behind the modern narrative of the music's history, arguing that it overlooks significant social and economic factors that shaped the tradition throughout its history both in al-Andalus and in North Africa. Chapter 2 explores the earliest phase of the music's history by discussing the principal social and economic institutions that shaped the careers of two founding-father figures, Ziryāb and Ibn Bājja, placing special emphasis on the signficance of oral and written processes. The following chapter brings the history up to the present day in Morocco by tracing the social and economic factors that have shaped the tradition in its North African incarnation. Chapter 4 offers social-cultural data that illustrate the interplay of oral and written processes in the modern context,

---

regional versions of the tradition. The problem of *mīzān ad-darj* and its relationship to the modern *nūba* is discussed in more detail in Chapter 5 §3.2.

[23] For more on this subject, see *Pen, Voice, Text*.

and the ways in which these processes interact with the formal institutions that surround the tradition today. Finally, Chapter 5 turns attention to the literary component of the tradition. Study of the manuscripts that form the basis of the modern anthologies further underscores the significant role played by oral processes in the formation of the contemporary tradition.

In Part 2, Chapters 6 and 7 combine to construct a theory of tradition that explains the significance of oral and literate processes in terms of value. This theory defines orality and literacy, not as mutually-exclusive *technologies* (as is so often the case in the literature), but as culturally-informed *processes* that may coexist within a single tradition because they draw upon distinct sets of values. By interpreting the data in Part 1 through the lens of this theory, Chapter 8 illustrates the *mixed-oral* character of the Moroccan Andalusian music tradition, and how crucially it depends upon the social values which both orality and literacy embody.

Al-Āla: History, Society and Text

Part 1 — A Social History of the Moroccan Andalusian Music

Prologue to Part 1

Modern writers on the history of the Moroccan *Āla* invariably assume that the music descends directly from the elite music of al-Andalus. Such an assumption seems reasonable at first glance, yet despite the attribution of the tradition to al-Andalus by contemporary performers and audiences, it has little basis in what an historian would consider evidence: there is no written music to look to for confirmation, nor do we find a continuous array of materials linking the earliest era of music in Muslim Spain to the modern day. Rather, we have only a handful of accounts from biographical and *adab* literature, and a few references scattered in historical works between Ibn al-Qūṭiyya in the mid-4th/10th century and al-Maqqarī in the 11th/17th. No work detailing the musical culture of al-Andalus comparable to the *Kitāb al-Aġānī* has survived (though Yaḥyā b. al-Aṣbahī al-Ḥuj al-Mursī is said to have written one in the 6th/12th century). The situation for Morocco between the 6th/12th and 12th/18th centuries – the period during which we infer that the musical forms of al-Andalus took root in North Africa – is similar, if even less rich in detail. Music itself seems to have been a suspect activity in this era except among the religious brotherhoods, if we are to judge by the apologetics put forward by some who wrote on the subject.

The chief piece of direct evidence we have linking *al-Āla* to al-Andalus is the presence of Andalusi strophic poetry in the tradition. This by itself does not suffice, of course, but combined with the attribution of the music to al-Andalus by Moroccans themselves (and the evident structural similarities amongst all the North African Andalusian traditions) it provides some indication that the modern literary-musical tradition has inherited something from the music of al-Andalus, in spirit if not entirely in substance.

I do not mean to argue against the Andalusi origin of *al-Āla,* but merely to point out that the standard narrative of the history of the Moroccan Andalusian music begins on an unsure footing. Like all historical narratives, it relies upon inference to some degree, and it embodies a set of beliefs about the meaning of history that have determined the form of the narrative and to some extent its content. Of course, inferences and beliefs of this kind are unavoidable, but examining them can reveal overlooked details in the sources that may allow the construction of a more convincing narrative. The idea that the narrative is problematic encourages us to pull on some of its loose threads and discover where they lead.

Part 1 takes up the history of *al-Āla* in this spirit. Without denying the validity of the standard narrative, insofar as it preserves some useful basic facts and points to the principal sources available today, these four chapters explore the development of the tradition from a rather different point of view than has been presented to date. For a variety of reasons, the standard narrative has operated exclusively within what I call the Great Men-Great Deeds model of historiography. Chapter 1 examines this model to show how the standard narrative mirrors a very long tradition of Arabic historiography that supplied the basic format for it, in effect a more-or-less direct, uncritical transcription of the sources into modern language. Chapter 2 next offers an alternative view of the early history of elite music in al-Andalus, one that accepts the importance of two founding-father figures, Ziryāb and Ibn Bājja, but shifts the focus toward the social milieu surrounding these two men, and especially toward the institutions which helped shape their careers. Chapters 3 and 4 extend this approach, Chapter 3 seeking to uncover the institutional structures that underlay the tradition in North Africa in the early-modern period, and Chapter 4 reviewing the music's contemporary conditions with special attention to the social frame which surrounds it and to the development of the formal institutions which now support it, in particular the National Conservatory of Music and Dance. One of the touchstones of Part 1 is the role of oral processes in the transmission of the tradition between generations. Chapter 5 completes the picture presented in Part 1 by looking to the literary dimension of the tradition for direct evidence of these oral processes, evidence that sheds further light upon the Moroccan history of the tradition.

Part 1 thus serves two purposes.

First, I want to raise the level of discussion on the history of the music of al-Andalus and its descendants. A significant issue confronting the music, one which lies in the background of much of the literature by Moroccan scholars, is its changing status within Moroccan public culture. The ongoing debate over how best to preserve the tradition indicates the concern felt in some quarters over the music's future. The standard narrative has not changed in any important way for more than half a century since the first Western scholar to study *al-Āla*, Alexis Chottin, and as a result, it offers no more insight into the status of the tradition today than it did in Chottin's time. Reframing the discussion allows new kinds of questions to arise that address the present moment of *al-Āla*. By exploring the social and economic foundations of the tradition in the past, we can perhaps arrive at a new perspective on these phenomena in the present.

A larger aim of Part 1 concerns the significance of the oral and written processes that inform the tradition. These five chapters bring to light historical and cultural data which will be analyzed using tools developed in Part 2, and which concern the meaning of orality and literacy and their social underpinnings. Together, Parts 1 and 2 form an argument about the importance attaching to artistic traditions in their social contexts, an argument that carries implications for how we view the effects of economic and cultural globalization at the local level today.

One touchstone in Part 1 is the concept of *institution*. This word can indicate several related social phenomena, so before proceeding with the discussion, the reader needs so understand this word as used here. In its most specific meaning, this word refers to a large organization that 1) is in some way legally constituted or formed according to a set of established (usually written) rules, 2) has a certain amount of prestige or social value associated with it, and 3) can maintain itself across more than one generation because it is not tied to particular individuals. A bank and a university would be examples of *formal institutions* of this kind. Sometimes, though, we use the word to refer to certain important social practices that have some kind of legal standing, such as marriage. An *informal institution* like marriage would seem at first glance to have little in common with a bank or university, and yet it meets all three criteria above. *Formal institution* thus refers to a specific organization, a collection of people, and an *informal institution* represents a more or less formalized way of doing things that plays a role in organizing society. An important feature of either kind of institution is that it is governed or defined by some form of written rules or laws. These laws may be (and often are) created by a government, but they may also be created from within the institution itself. In this, an institution is distinct from a *tradition*, which answers to similar criteria but operates within society in a less formalized (but also more subtle) way.[1]

For example, the fact that non-Muslims may not enter a mosque in Morocco is not a tradition in Moroccan society because it is codified in law and has as its basis legal argumentation from the literature on Islamic law. It is part of the larger institution of the mosque. On the other hand, the fact that few women go to the mosque is a tradition in Moroccan society (and not part of the institution), because it has no formal legal standing. Instead, the practice derives from assumptions that are taken for granted as comprising the fabric of daily life. Both are practices that help organize behavior in society, but only one can be said to have meaning in a legal context.

In the renarration of the music's history that follows, institutions figure prominently because they tend to operate at the intersection of social and economic arrangements. This is obviously true for modern formal institutions like banks and universities, but also for pre-modern institutions both formal and informal. The Islamic *waqf* (or *ḥabūs*, a bequest made according to the prescriptions of Islamic law for the public disposition of private funds or property) is a good example of a formal institution whose roots lie in the pre-modern era and which serves both economic and social ends. Similarly marriage, perhaps the most ancient informal social institution, has

[1] See Part 2, Chapter 6.

undeniable economic aspects since it invariably entails some kind of agreement about the sharing and disposition of property and so on.

The following discussion examines *al-Āla* in light of the social institutions and contexts that have surrounded it at various stages in its long history. This renarration of the music's history owes a great deal to Max Weber, for through it we may observe the progressive rationalization and institutionalization of certain aspects of the tradition, even while others continue to draw upon older forms of organization. In the interplay between the two lie both the past and the future this fascinating literary-musical tradition.

Chapter 1
The Standard Historical Narrative of the Andalusian Music

Attributing the roots of *al-Āla*, the Moroccan Andalusian music as it is known today, to Islamic Spain has proven to be quite popular. This theme serves as the central feature of the mythos that surrounds this North African tradition and is part and parcel of a well-defined standard narrative of the tradition's history that simultaneously establishes its cultural significance in contemporary Morocco and yet downplays in dramatic fashion any North African influences on it. Certainly the poetic dimension of *al-Āla*, at least, owes something to al-Andalus, as can be seen from the many *ṣanāʾiʿ* whose texts are structured like Andalusi strophic poems of the Middle Ages – some of which in fact derive from well-known Andalusi poets. However, the earliest text relating specifically to *al-Āla* dates only to the first half of the 12th/18th century – the scholarly treatise-anthology *Īqād aš-šumūʿ li-laḏḏat al-masmūʿ bi-naġamāt aṭ-ṭubūʿ* ("Lighting Candles for the Enjoyment of Hearing the Notes of the Modes") by Muḥammad al-Būʿṣāmī, who probably died in 1151/1738. Before that, the identifiable traces of *al-Āla* in historical sources thin out dramatically, to the point that it becomes impossible to link it clearly with al-Andalus through the sources alone. So what, then, is in fact *Andalusian* about this tradition?

Even if one accepts the tale of Andalusi origins, the standard narrative that has been mustered by twentieth-century scholarship to give this attribution form and support seems problematic in other ways. The facts put forward in the narrative, while they are not *wrong* per se, do not represent much more than a collection of names associated with a handful of events regarded as significant in one way or another. From the point of view of the contemporary historian, a number of issues go unexplained, even unnoticed as issues, in the centuries-long parade of Great Men and their Great Deeds. Economic and social concerns, for example, are taken for granted in the sources, and for the most part in the standard narrative as well, even as the modern observer comes to wonder not just *who* but *why*. Likewise, certain events in the narrative – the Reconquista migrations from al-Andalus to North Africa, for example – certainly were significant, and yet it is not difficult to see that the emphasis the standard narrative puts on them raises questions beyond those it seeks to answer: Why would these particular migrations prove to be more significant than the many movements of musicians, poets and literati between al-Andalus and North Africa that characterized the entire period prior to the fall of Granada? Why would the apparently large numbers of migrants in these cases, as such, matter when the music in question clearly was created by elites for elites? Through being tied so closely and uncritically in form and content to the sources themselves, the standard narrative of the Andalusian music's history remains silent on precisely those themes and topics that seem most interesting and noteworthy to the modern observer.

This chapter sets the stage for those that follow by turning a critical eye to the standard narrative itself. Through exploring its main features and the authors most commonly associated with it, a clear picture of its limitations emerges. In addition, its characteristics can be seen to flow more or less directly from the tradition of Arabic historiography itself, which provides the model and narrative ethos for the standard narrative of the tradition's history.

1. *The name, al-mūsīqā l-andalusiyya*

A good way to begin this reassessment of the history of *al-Āla* would be with the common name for the tradition, "the Andalusian music," whose background touches upon two themes that run through this and the following chapters: the problems inherent in the tradition's history as it is commonly retold, and the complex relationship between oral and literary processes that have formed the tradition as we know it today.

The expression *Andalusian music* probably was an artifact of oral tradition adopted by twentieth-century Western scholarship and then taken up by North African scholars. Certainly it never appears in scholarly texts associated with *al-Āla* before the era of the French Protectorate (1912-1956). In 1929, in his introduction to the pamphlet *Le conservatoire de musique marocaine de Rabat*, the French Protectorate official Prosper Ricard noted the existence of a music lovers' association in Oujda of the 1920s called "L'Andalousia."[1] Recent work by Jonathan Glasser[2] pushes the origin of this concept in print back to late nineteenth-century Algeria and the work of the anthologist Edmund Nathan Yafil. This is consonant with the fact that the *al-Ġarnāṭī* style of music straddles the Moroccan-Algerian border, including Oujda, for of course the name *al-Ġarnāṭī* points directly to the kingdom of Granada in al-Andalus. On the other hand, modern Moroccan scholars tend to attribute the expression *al-mūsīqā l-andalusiyya* specifically to Alexis Chottin, the first French scholar to study *al-Āla*. Contemporary Moroccan *Āla* aficionados are of course familiar with Yafil's anthology of the Algerian branch of the Andalusi heritage, but given the greater influence of Chottin's scholarship among *Āla* musicians, and the fact that I find no indication in his writings that he was aware of

[1] See also Guettat, 2000, p. 235 n. 49; and Chapter 3 §4.2a.
[2] Unpublished ms., 2005.

Yafil's work, it seems unlikely that the attribution of *al-Āla* to al-Andalus originated with Yafil.

It is likely, however, that the idea was not wholly of European manufacture. Probably it was a general association made with al-Andalus that belonged to oral tradition in circulation before either Chottin or Yafil. Although the traditional name for the music was *al-Āla,* and the expression *al-Mūsīqā l-andalusiyya* does not appear in Moroccan sources before the 20th century, nevertheless the links to al-Andalus are not hard to discover.

The most obvious link to al-Andalus lies in some of the *ṣanāʾiʿ* which are performed today in Morocco whose lyrics can be traced directly to Andalusi poets, and others which are of unknown origin but clearly have been constructed using Andalusi models. In addition we know that a number of Andalusi poets whose works were set to music crossed the Straits of Gibraltar into North Africa, the most famous of these men being Abū Bakr b. Yaḥyā aṣ-Ṣāʾiġ Ibn Bājja (b. Saragossa 461 / 1070 – d. in Fez 532 / 1139) and Abū l-Ḥasan aš-Šuštarī (b. in Guadix 611 / 1212, d. in Egypt 667 / 1269). Moreover, we find today differences between the music of the Middle East and that of the Islamic West, which seem to suggest a separate path of musical development in the western part of the Arabic-speaking world, a path that presumably included influences drawn from al-Andalus. Chottin summarized these differences in his survey of traditional Moroccan music, *Tableau de la musique marocaine* (1939).[3] While he certainly oversimplified the situation, his comments are not completely off the mark. The Moroccan musicians of Chottin's time and before probably were aware of these obvious links and so attributed the music's origins to al-Andalus as a matter of local, informal knowledge. The specific appellation *la musique andalouse* was most likely a product of Chottin's encounter with this informal attribution, which he and other Protectorate scholars then took up and promoted.

Two decades later the Moroccan scholar, Muhammed al-Fāsī, held a lecture-demonstration of *al-Āla* (1962) in which he described the tradition as Moroccan music of Iraqi-Andalusi origins. He based the latter half of this attribution upon the cultural interchange between Baghdad and al-Andalus in the 3rd / 9th century embodied in the figure of Ziryāb, the eminent composer-musician who arrived in Cordoba from Baghdad in 207 / 822. As will be apparent later in this chapter, Ziryāb functions within the accepted narrative of *al-Āla*'s history as the founding father of Andalusi courtly music, and so of the North African traditions, as well.

Bearing in mind al-Fāsī's point about the synthetic nature of *al-Āla,* we might wonder what would be the most appropriate point at which to begin reviewing its history. Modern historical accounts often begin with the earliest phase of music in

[3] pp. 89-90.

Arab-Islamic culture shortly after the death of the Prophet Muḥammad, and follow with the music of the late Umayyad and early Abbasid dynasties, typically described in terms of two important musical influences, one emanating from conquered Persia and the other from Medina in Arabia. However, all of this serves merely as preface to what is considered to be *al-Āla*'s real point of origin: al-Andalus. The music of al-Andalus always comprises the main and most substantial part of the historical discussion.

Two ideas lie behind this emphasis on al-Andalus. One is practical: very little material has been uncovered to date on music and musicians in Morocco prior to the 20th century. By comparison, the historical and literary materials from al-Andalus are richer, so we should not be surprised to see historians focusing on the historical moment for which they have the most information. Perhaps just as important is the image of al-Andalus itself. To judge from the tone of Chottin's works (and to a lesser extent those of his Spanish contemporary, Patrocinio García Barriuso), the idea that the tradition originated in al-Andalus may have served for Western scholars as a way to explain how such a sophisticated musical art form was to be found in Morocco. The perceived brilliance of al-Andalus allowed these scholars to avoid the troublesome fact of North African contributions to the music.

Ironically, the same might be true for North African scholars as well, though for different reasons. By adopting the name *al-Mūsīqā l-andalusiyya*, they have been able to link their classical music heritage to the shining star of al-Andalus, a pinnacle of Arab-Islamic civilization. Thus a North African scholar like Mahmud Guettat emphasizes the more distant (but more seductive) al-Andalus and writes of the centuries between the fall of Granada and the appearance of the earliest anthologies of the tradition in the 19th century as an era of *decadence and loss*, deemphasizing positive developments that he acknowledges did occur in this period.[4]

Whether or not one believes that the Moroccan *Āla* is in some degree Andalusi, the standard narrative of its history as put forward by modern scholarship certainly presents it as such, and this has become part of the music's mythos. So we must take the Andalusi dimension of the history into account if we are to understand the music's place in contemporary Morocco. This chapter considers the standard narrative in its general form, and then explores its relationships to traditional modes of Arabic historiography. Chapter 2 then studies in detail two central figures in the music's Andalusi history, Abū l-Ḥasan ʿAlī b. Nāfiʿ Ziryāb (b. Iraq 172/789? – d. Cordoba

[4] One wonders whether military defeat and economic subjection by Western powers in the 20th century played a role in this, as well. Based upon interviews with musicians in Morocco and elsewhere, Professor Jonathan Shannon of the City University of New York suggests that associating this form of music with al-Andalus draws upon the prestige attaching to things European as part of a social identity within contemporary Moroccan society. (interview, 4/2/2005)

242/857) and Ibn Bājja, who exemplify *al-Āla*'s Andalusi history. Examining their stories allows us to explore the foundations of the standard narrative in the sources which it draws upon as well as in the underlying historiographical tradition.

To repeat the accepted history of the Moroccan Andalusian music in detail would serve little purpose here. Scholars writing in Arabic, French and Spanish have produced a number of works that deal amply with it. The outstanding examples include Chottin's *Tableau de la musique marocaine* (1939), García Barriuso's *La música hispanoárabe en Marruecos* (1940), Christian Poché's *La musique arabo-andalouse* (1995), and Guettat's two main works *La musique classique du Maghreb* (1980) and *La musique arabo-andalouse: L'empreinte du Maghreb* (2000). These works deploy the standard narrative of the early history of music and music theory as it was known in al-Andalus, and to some extent in North Africa during the centuries following the fall of Granada.[5]

To be sure, each of these authors approaches the history from his own perspective, and some offer more detail than others. García Barriuso and Guettat, in particular, highlight certain aspects of the narrative by culling valuable details from the sources. García Barriuso uses materials first brought to light by Julian Ribera (1922) to add color to his account of al-Andalus. Guettat's work is especially rich in names and in the theory of music as it developed throughout the medieval Arabic-speaking world, and he presents an interesting theory that North Africa had its own musical heritage that contributed in some way to the modern "Andalusian" music. Yet, when one looks past the details put forward by these authors and examines the basic structure and assumptions that inform their works, one sees that each presents only a rather fragmentary narrative, one that is not difficult to summarize because ultimately it reduces to a series of familiar episodes. Furthermore, none of these authors offers an analytical approach to the narrative, and so at times it can be difficult to interpret the significance of some of the information they present.

For example, the standard narrative tells us that Ziryāb added a fifth cord to the *ʿūd*, which the sources say was red and related to spirit. Evidently at least in the time of Ibn Ḥayyān al-Qurtubī (d. 469/1076), whose history of the Andalusi Umayyad dynasty, *al-Muqtabis*, is the principal source for this detail, Ziryāb was held to have brought recognizable elements of Greek musical philosophy with him to al-Andalus. Ibn Ḥayyān, writing in the second half of the 5th/11th century, gives a relatively complete account of the relationships between the strings of the *ʿūd*, colors and the body humors[6], material that Abū l-ʿAbbās Aḥmad al-Maqqarī (b. Tlemcen 986/1577, d. Cairo 1041/1632) reproduces in his own principal work, *Nafḥ aṭ-ṭīb min ġuṣn al-Andalus*

---

[5] Ibn ʿAbd al-Jalīl (1988) also provides a widely-read version of the standard narrative.

[6] *as-Sifr aṯ-ṯānī min al-Muqtabis*, 2003, pp. 317-318.

ar-raṭīb.[7] Much later, Muḥammad b. al-Ḥusayn al-Ḥā'ik (d. after 1788?) included comments in his song anthology, *Kunnāš al-Ḥā'ik*, on the relationships between the *ṭubūʿ*, the body humors and the times of day.[8] Yet these sources tell us little about the actual uses of this philosophy, whether in the domain of healing arts or performance practice. For example, there are no descriptions of performances centering on a particular mode because it was evening, or the new moon was rising, or the performer wished to induce a particular emotion or healing state. So, while we may note the persistence of certain philosophical ideas about music within the Andalusian tradition from at least the end of the 4th/10th century through the beginning of the 14th/19th century, their practical application (if any) remains uncertain. However, modern historians overlook the absence of such accounts, and simply present these philosophical concepts as clear descriptions of the therapeutic uses of music in al-Andalus.

In much the same way, a number of personalities appear in various retellings of the history, but apart from Ziryāb and Ibn Bājja, we find only a handful of names associated in one way or another with music in al-Andalus and with the Andalusian tradition in Morocco, and sometimes the modern historian omits or overlooks meaningful elements in the story. For example, al-Maqqarī (followin Ibn Ḥayyān's *al-Muqtabis*) gives the names of some singers who were known during the reign of the Umayyad emir of Cordoba, al-Ḥakam I (r. 180/796-206/822), just prior to Ziryāb's arrival: ʿAjfā', ʿAllūn and Zirqūn.[9] He also writes that al-Ḥakam's successor, ʿAbd ar-Raḥmān II (r. 206/822-237/852), owned three famous female slave singers from Medina, whose singing style was very influential in the music of the day: Faḍl, ʿAlam, and Qalam. Their influence waned after Ziryāb's arrival.[10] However a curious problem with chronology arises here, since al-Maqqarī (still following Ibn Ḥayyān) states clearly that Ziryāb arrived in Cordoba in the very year that ʿAbd ar-Raḥmān came to power. How influential could Faḍl, ʿAlam, and Qalam actually have been if they were eclipsed almost immediately by Ziryāb? Were they already moving in courtly circles before the death of al-Ḥakam? If so, what became of the other three famous singers, ʿAjfā', ʿAllūn and Zirqūn? The standard narrative remains silent on this question, even though Ibn Ḥayyān gives a partial answer (ʿAbd ar-Raḥmān owned his three women slave singers

---

[7] *Nafḥ aṭ-ṭīb* (1968), v.3 p. 126.

[8] Ibn Jallūn at-Tuwaymī (1979, 15-32) summarizes this material in the introduction to his redaction of the *Kunnāš*, and then reproduces al-Ḥā'ik's *muqaddima* in its entirety. Ibn Manṣūr (1977) reproduces al-Ḥā'ik's *muqaddima*, as well. Ar-Rāyis, also summarizes the effects of the *ṭubūʿ* in *Min waḥy al-rabāb* (1982) in short comments introducing each *nūba*.

[9] *Nafḥ* ..., 1968, v.2 p. 85. See also Guettat (2000), p. 106.

[10] *Nafḥ* ..., 1968, v.2 pp. 96, 97, 98.

before he came to power).[11] In any case, the entire question seems to have escaped the notice of modern scholarship. This lack of critical discussion of the historical sources is symptomatic of the treatment the accounts of Ziryāb receive in the standard narrative, as we shall see in Chapter 2.

As a third example, Guettat gives an annotated list of about two dozen names associated with the history of the music, mostly poets and authors of works about music.[12] However several of these individuals are only parenthetically connected with the musical tradition in al-Andalus. He mentions Ibn ʿAbd Rabbih (d. 328/940) and Ibn Rušd (d. 595/1198), for example, though the latter was a philosopher who wrote about music, and the former was a poet and author of an encyclopedia, *al-ʿIqd al-farīd*, one book of which deals with music and the lives of musicians (none of whom hailed from al-Andalus, in fact).

Another interesting detail that appears in Guettat's work is the idea that the Moroccan composer and Sufi ʿAbd ar-Raḥmān al-Fāsī (1040/1631-1096/1685) "replaced the themes of *Nawbat Ramal al-Māya* with exclusively religious themes."[13] Unfortunately, Guettat offers this tantalizing tidbit without any supporting documentation. Al-Fāsī's only surviving work on music, *Kitāb al-Jumūʿ fī ʿilm al-mūsīqī wa-ṭ-ṭubūʿ*, says nothing on the matter.[14] One might ask as well what the theme of *Ramal al-Māya* was *before* al-Fāsī's innovation. No speculation has been offered to date on this question.[15] The translation and commentary on this *nūba* in my book, *Pen, Voice, Text*, reveals that a substantial number of the poems in *Ramal al-Māya* borrow imagery from love poetry, so it is not unreasonable to suppose that this *nūba* was at one time devoted to the theme of love (and it can hardly be described as dealing "exclusively" with relgious themes today). The point is that such questions have never entered the purview of the modern histories of *al-Āla*.

---

[11] *as-Sifr aṯ-ṯānī*, p. 307.

[12] 2000, pp. 111-118.

[13] Guettat (2000), p. 258, see also (1980), p. 190.

[14] Ibn Jallūn (1979, p. 15) reports that according to the modern scholar Muḥammad al-Fāsī the man who changed the theme of *Ramal al-Māya* was Abū l-ʿAbbās Aḥmad b. Muḥammad b. ʿAbd al-Qādir al-Fāsī. Levi-Provençal in *Les historiens…* (1991/1922, p. 242) indicates that he was the nephew of the well-known Sufi ʿAbd ar-Raḥmān, and that he died in 1164/1752. (This confusion does not, however, explain Guettat's, 2000, erroneous date for the elder al-Fāsī of 1650.) I have not been able to find a written source for this story prior to Ibn Jallūn; possibly it derives from oral tradition handed down within the al-Fāsī family and/or among *Āla* musicians.

[15] Bennūna (interview, 3/29/2005) suggests that *Ramal al-Māya* prior to al-Fāsī's intervention was devoted to love poetry (*ġazal*). He bases this on the predominance of this kind of imagery in *Ramal al-Māya* in the earliest *Kunnāš* manuscript, and indeed, much of the material in the contemporary *nūba* relies upon this type of imagery, as well. It is likely that al-Fāsī's innovation applied also to the Sufi-oriented *samāʿ wa-madīḥ* Andalusian tradition. All the poetry in that tradition is devoted to praise of Muḥammad and other religious themes, though the *ṣanāʾiʿ* often also draw images from love poetry.

Information on performance practice is rare also, for some potentially important sources have been lost. We know of at least one encyclopedic work from the 6th/12th century on music in al-Andalus, *Kitāb al-Aġānī al-andalusiyya* by Yaḥyā b. al-Aṣbahī al-Ḥuj al-Mursī, and two treatises on music and composition (*Risāla fī ta'līf al-alḥān* by ʿAlī b. Saʿīd al-Iqlīdsī, possibly from the 4th/10th century, and *Risāla fī l-mūsīqā* by Abū Ṣalt ad-Dānī in the early 6th/12th century). A fragment of Aḥmad b. Yūsuf al-Tīfāšī's (d. 650/1253) encyclopedia has survived, and a portion of it, entitled *Mutʿat al-asmāʿ fī ʿilm as-samāʿ* ["Pleasure for the Ears in the Art of Listening"], deals with music. It does offer some tantalizing clues, albeit from a scholar working in Tunis from secondhand sources.[16] But our knowledge of performance practices for the whole of al-Andalus cannot rival what is known of eighth- and ninth-century Iraq from Abū l-Faraj al-Iṣfahānī's single work, *Kitāb al-Aġānī*.

Modern historians have devoted much laudable effort to uncovering Arabic sources for the music of al-Andalus and its relationship to that of North Africa, and to presenting this material in a coherent fashion. Certainly, this chapter and the next rely heavily upon their groundwork, which has culled the most important accounts about music in al-Andalus from the classical Arabic literary genres of history, biography, *adab* (that is, the literature of social refinement) and poetry. Indeed it is the work of such scholars that even allows us to speak of a history of Andalusian music.

Yet the historical dimension of Andalusian music studies nevertheless remains neglected. This becomes evident in nonspecialist surveys of the subject (such as the entry in the *Garland Encyclopedia of World Music*[17]), which rely upon an historical narrative first presented by Chottin and others in the early 20th century. Still, even scholars specializing in the Andalusian music tend to accept much of the material they find in their sources at face value, without inquiring too deeply into it or devoting much attention to the context surrounding events and people. In particular, information that complicates the story rarely finds its way onto the page. With a very few exceptions, we find a standard narrative in the modern literature populated largely by a handful of brilliant but rather flat characters.

2. *The standard narrative*

Modern works on the North African Andalusian music, whether by Arab scholars like Mahmoud Guettat (1980, 2000) or ʿAbd al-ʿAzīz b. ʿAbd al-Jalīl (1988, 2000), or by Western authors like Manuela Cortés García (1996), generally present a single, standard

---

[16] Published in 1968 in the journal *al-Abḥāṯ* by Muḥammad b. Tāwīt al-Ṭanjī under the title "*aṭ-Ṭarā'iq wa-l-alḥān al-musīqiyya fī Ifrīqiya wa-l-Andalus.*"

[17] Wendt (1998) pp. 532-548.

narrative whose main points seem to be well-established and agreed upon. Figure 1.1 presents them in schematic form.

This table of course represents a simplification, but it highlights two important features. One is that we find three large gaps of about three centuries each where nothing of importance appears to happen: between Ziryāb in the 3rd/9th century and Ibn Bājja in the 6th/12th, between Ibn Bājja and the fall of Granada at the end of the 9th/15th century, and between Granada and al-Ḥāʾik at the end of the 12th/18th century. As presented in modern histories these gaps contain lists of musicians, composers and writers on music theory. Notably absent is information on the circumstances surrounding these individuals, a sense of an historical progression or development that they participated in. Nor do modern histories attempt to place them within a larger, meaningful framework that might shed some light upon, for example, the significance of music in the courtly life of al-Andalus.

Date	Event
711	Muslims conquer Iberia, bringing with them their work and camel-driver songs (*ḥudāʾ*), which coexist with native Iberian musical forms to comprise the "Andalusian music" of the day.
750s	ʿAbd ar-Raḥmān I ad-Dākhil founds the western Umayyad emirate in Cordoba. The Umayyads bring with them the courtly music of Damascus.
822	Ziryāb arrives, bringing with him the courtly music of Abbasid Baghdad and revolutionizing musical practice and teaching in al-Andalus.
ca. 1100	Ibn Bājja combines the "songs of the Christians" with those of the Middle East to produce a new and distinctively Andalusian style of music.
1492	The fall of Granada: a wave of migrants pours into North Africa; Andalusian music is cut off from its country of origin.
1500s - 1700s	Period of stagnation and loss: no significant changes in the tradition occur, apart from sporadic efforts at compositions and commentary.
late 1700s	al-Ḥāʾik collects what remains of the tradition into an anthology.
late 1800s	al-Jāmiʿī compiles the tradition as he finds it in his day and founds the first conservatory dedicated to the Andalusian music of Morocco.

Figure 1.1: *A basic chronology of the history of the Andalusian music tradition*

Second, the narrative ties the arrival of the music of al-Andalus in North Africa directly to the Reconquista. Most modern authors present stages of emigration from al-Andalus to North Africa that roughly parallel the fall of major urban centers to the Christians. Thus Chottin and others speak of waves moving from Cordoba after 1236, from Seville after 1248, and so on. Moreover, these waves become associated with specific destination cities in North Africa, and this in turn becomes a means of explaining regional differences across the modern Andalusian traditions. While these details may be true, they cannot be the whole story, because we know of other migrations to al-Andalus that were not connected with the Reconquista.[18]

Modern scholarship characterizes the earliest phase of Arab-Andalusian music, the first half-century or so after the initial conquests, as consisting of various camel-driver and work songs (*ḥudāʾ*) in use among laborers and common soldiers and their families. Sometimes they also mention the native Iberian music present when the conquerors arrived. Ibn ʿAbd al-Jalīl (1988) adds some complexity to the story by pointing out the presence of a slave class composed of Visigoths, Franks, "Slavs"[19] and other ethnicities captured during the conquests. These people also brought their own distinctive musical forms to al-Andalus, as indeed did the Berbers who comprised the majority of the conquering armies, and who are practically invisible as cultural actors in the standard narrative. In general, the modern authors paint a very simple picture of the early musical culture of al-Andalus. In this, they draw chiefly from at-Tīfāšī and Ibn Khaldun (d. 808/1406), who in turn draw from earlier works by 9th- and 10th-century scholars like Ibn Ḫurradāḏbih (d. ca. 300/913) and Ibn Salama (d. after 307/920).[20] Moreover, because this was the music of the common people, far removed from the aristocratic music held to be the source of the modern *Āla*, its presence in the modern histories serves merely as a backdrop for the proper subject of the history: the courtly music of al-Andalus. Not surprisingly, these categories and emphases reflect exactly those found in the sources themselves, as for example with Ibn Khaldun, who mentions "folk" music only in passing in the *Muqaddima* and devotes his attention to elite music.

[18] Their role in establishing the music of al-Andalus in North Africa will be explored in Chapter 3.

[19] The word used in the sources and taken up by Ibn ʿAbd al-Jalīl is *ṣaqāliba*, a curious word whose root, *ṣaqlab*, Corriente (1997) finds already in the *Lisān al-ʿArab* as meaning *eunuch*, an early borrowing from the Middle Latin *sclavus*, "slave", which (like its English cognate) derives from *slovēne* ("Slav"). Dozy (1981 [1881]) attributes this Arabic signification to the presence of castrated men of that ethnicity in Muslim lands. It probably refers to fair-skinned people from the Balkans, but in this context it probably meant not only natives of the Black Sea region, but elsewhere as well, including Occitania, Cataluña and Galicia. Some of these captives converted and became clients of influential Muslims, but often they retained their state of servitude. They eventually came to represent an important class of palace servants and even military leaders, whom the Caliphs ʿAbd ar-Raḥmān III and al-Ḥakam II especially relied upon as political counterweight to the Arab aristocracy. See also: Levi-Provençal (1932), pp. 29-31.

[20] See at-Tīfāšī, Chapter 11 (aṭ-™anjī, p. 114); also the *Muqaddima* of Ibn Khaldun, Part V, Chapter 32 on al-Ġināʾ (2004 p. 391, passim).

According to the standard narrative, Ziryāb arrived at Algeciras on the Spanish coast, having traveled there from Baghdad at the invitation of the Umayyad prince of Cordoba, al-Ḥakam I. Our principal source for him, Ibn Ḥayyān al-Qurṭubī, tells us he was met by the musician al-Manṣūr the Jew, who informed him that al-Ḥakam had died, but that his son, ʿAbd ar-Raḥmān II, was also a great lover of music. Al-Manṣūr persuaded Ziryāb to seek patronage from ʿAbd ar-Raḥmān. He did so, and was welcomed grandly into the prince's circle.

Ziryāb's arrival in al-Andalus is universally regarded as the point when the elite Arab-Andalusian music tradition begins; everything in the musical culture of al-Andalus after Ziryāb owes its existence to him. As Chottin remarks:

> Mais, sans Ziryāb, l'Ecole Andalouse eût sans doute continué à n'être qu'un écho l'Ecole Persane et n'aurait pas acquis une personnalité originale. (1939, p. 85)

The modern authors appear to be justified in presenting this image of Ziryāb as a founding father of the Andalusian music tradition, because Ibn Ḥayyān describes him as the most important musician of his time. After mentioning ʿAllūn and Zirqūn, he continues:

> هؤلاء كانوا المقدمين في مغنيه الى ان طرأ عليه من المشرق الأعلى زرياب العراقي صاحب الغناء العجيب بالأندلس فختم على اختياره وغلب على قلبه فرقاه فوق جميع من كان عنده من ذكر وأنثى ممن يشاركه في صناعته وأمال عليه من إحسانه وخوّله من اختصاصه ما تجاوز به حال الضيوف المحبوبين المجتهدين إلى منزلة الأهلين المؤثرين المشتاركين والوزراء المختصين القربين فالأحاديث عنه بذلك في الناس فاشية وآثرره بعدُ بينهم شاهدة لائحة

> These were the foremost of [ʿAbd ar-Raḥmān II's] singers until Ziryāb the Iraqi, the master of marvelous song in al-Andalus, came to him from the Middle East. He put an end to his choosing and conquered his heart. He raised him above everyone (else) who was with him, whether male or female, among those participating with him in his art. He enriched him from his beneficence and granted him his exclusive lands, by which (Ziryāb) surpassed the state of the desirable guests vying for the preferred position with (the prince) and the rank

> of the preferred, intimate ministers. And thus the stories about him circulate among the people because of that, and his legacies among them afterwards bear witness clearly.[21]

For Ibn Ḥayyān, Ziryāb serves rhetorically as the first important point of intersection with the music of the Middle East. Even though other singers had come to al-Andalus from the East before him, Ziryāb's eminence as a musician and aesthete put him above all others. *Al-Muqtabis* tells us he brought new fashions in clothing, hairstyles and perfumes, and even influenced culinary tastes (for example, by teaching the cognoscenti of Cordoba the delights of asparagus). Although not all of this is completely credible,[22] there is no reason to doubt Ibn Ḥayyān's claim that Ziryāb's influence in Cordoba extended beyond the domain of music. Because he was trained in Baghdad and exposed to life at the Abbasid court, the figure of Ziryāb provides the standard narrative with one clear link between the two centers of high culture in the Arab world of the time.

For the two centuries following Ziryāb the standard narrative offers few specifics beyond a handful of names. Ziryāb founded a "school" in Cordoba that brought fame to four of his eight sons and one of his two daughters. García Barriuso also names two female slave singers from this school, Metzas and Maṣābīḥ. In addition, Guettat mentions (on the authority of an unnamed source) one Abū l-Qāsim b. al-Firnās (d. 273/888), who "codified" the music of al-Andalus. Ibn ʿAbd Rabbih (d. 328/940) devoted one book of his *al-ʿIqd al-farīd* to music; and ʿAlī b. Saʿīd, a shadowy figure variously identified by modern scholars as "al-Andalusī," "al-Iqlīdsī" (d. early 4th/10th c.?) or "al-Maġribī" (in which case possibly ʿAlī b. Mūsā Ibn Saʿīd, the author of *al-Muġrib fī ḥulā l-Maġrib*, d. 685/1286), wrote the *Risāla fī taʾlīf al-alḥān* (now lost, as well).[23]

The standard narrative turns next to the period from the Ṭāʾifa States through the Almoravids (roughly from the collapse of the Umayyad caliphate in 1031 until the arrival of the Almohads in 1155). Although Guettat describes this as a "new period for western Islam and the two societies, North African and Andalusian, as much on the political and social map as artistically and culturally" (2000, 112), we find only more references to individuals, of whom Guettat names several.[24] Abū Ṣalt Umayya ad-Dānī (d. 528/1134) was born in al-Andalus but made his fame in Ifrīqiya (Tunisia) by writing

---

[21] *as-Sifr aṯ-ṯānī...* p. 308; compare *Nafḥ...* (1968) v. 3 p. 125.

[22] Dwight Reynolds, in his forthcoming book, points out that asparagus was eaten in Iberia in Roman times. Perhaps Ziryāb made it a fashion among 9th-century Muslim aristocracy?

[23] See García Barriuso, p. 40; Guettat (1980), pp. 100-101, and (2000), pp. 111-112.

[24] 1980, p. 102; 2000, pp. 112-113.

an important treatise on music (known only from an anonymous Hebrew translation). Yaḥyā b. al-Aṣbahī, mentioned above, wrote the lost *Kitāb al-Aġānī al-andalusiyya* in this era. Abū l-Ḥakam al-Bāhilī (484/1093-548/1155) "emigrated to the Mašriq [Middle East]," and Aḥmad al-Ḥaddād (d. 558/1165) also wrote a lost treatise on music.

García Barriuso (pp. 42-43) for his part enriches the parade of names somewhat with a handful of short comments on the importance of Seville and Cordoba to the music of al-Andalus, based upon references found in Julian Ribera's *La Música de las Cantigas*, and drawing primarily from al-Maqqarī's *Nafḥ aṭ-ṭīb*. For example, he relates an anecdote from al-Maqqarī (who cites Ibn Saʿīd's *al-Muġrib*), about a comment which the Cordoban philosopher Ibn Rušd made to the Sevillan poet Ibn Zuhr (both of whom died ca. 594/1198):

> ما أدري ما تقول غير أنه إذا مات عالم بإشبيلية فأريد بيع كتبه حملت إلى قرطبة
> حتى تباع فيها وإذا مات مُطرب بقرطبة فأريد بيع تركته حملت إلى إشبيلية

> I do not know about what you say, except that when a scholar dies in Seville, and his books are to be sold, they are taken to Cordoba to be sold there; and when a musician dies in Cordoba, and his belongings are to be sold, they are taken to Seville.[25]

Without doubt, though, the most important individual in the era after Ziryāb is Ibn Bājja. He serves as a second founding father according to the modern authors, being solely responsible for a new and distinctive style of music that distinguished the Andalusian musical tradition from that of the Middle East. A famous passage from the 13th-century Tunisian at-Tīfāšī, always referred to in modern histories of the Andalusian music tradition, suggests as much:

> إلى أن نشأ ابن باجة الإمام الأعظم واعتكف مدة سنين مع جوارٍ محسنات ، فهذب
> الاستهلال والعمل ومزج غناء النصاري بغناء المشرق واخترع طريقة لا توجد إلا
> بالأندلس . مال إليه طبع أهلها فرفضوا ما سواها

> ...until Ibn Bājja, the greatest master, appeared and devoted himself for some years (to working with) expert female slave

---

[25] *Nafḥ* … II p. 11.

> musicians. He improved the *istihlāl* and the *ʿamal;*[26] and he combined the songs of the Christians with those of the Middle East, inventing a style found only in al-Andalus. The temperament of the people (there) inclined to it, and they rejected everything else.[27]

The modern historians conclude from this that Ibn Bājja single-handedly reinvented the music of al-Andalus, setting the tradition on a new aesthetic course and laying the foundations for the music known in North Africa today as Andalusian.

Ibn Bājja died in Fez during Almoravid rule in al-Andalus and North Africa; the standard narrative has little to say about developments in the music of al-Andalus in the three centuries following him, throughout the latter Almoravid and the whole of the Almohad dynasties, until the conquest of Granada by the Christians in 1492. Guettat does add some color to the picture in a passage entitled "L'ambiance musicale." He describes the "the great interest borne by the Andalusians for the musical art" by referring to accounts in Ibn Bassām (*aḏ-Ḏaḫīra fī maḥāsin ahl al-jazīra*), at-Tīfāšī and al-Maqqarī about "academy-conservatories" in Cordoba and Seville training young women in singing and linguistic arts, and about private parties at the homes of aristocrats.[28]

However, the most important events from this period noted in the modern histories are the various migrations of Andalusians to North Africa from regions captured by the Christians. These migrations are summarized in Figure 1.2, which combines data in *Tableau…* and *La musique…* drawn primarily from al-Maqqarī. Muḥammad Razzūq takes a somewhat different approach by presenting the spread of the music to North Africa in terms of two phases: an *Išbīliyya* ("Sevillan") stage extending from the Almoravid period until the end of the Marīnid dynasty in the mid-15th century, and a *Ġarnāṭiyya* ("Granadan") stage extending from the Waṭṭāsid dynasty in Fez (mid-15th century) until the advent of the Protectorate in the early 20th century.[29] As the names suggest, Razzūq focuses first on Seville as the emblem of musical culture in al-Andalus, and then on Granada as epitomizing the end of Muslim rule in Iberia (including the eventual expulsion of the Moriscos from Spain in 1610). These categories are problematic for two reasons. Although they are named after cities in al-Andalus, they are defined in terms of dynastic succession in Morocco. This mixing of cronologies allows Razzūq to reduce a complicated set of migrations down to two

---

[26] See: Introduction, §4.

[27] p. 115 in aṭ-Ṭānjī's edition of *al-Mutʿat al-asmāʿ fī ʿilm as-samāʿ*.

[28] 2000, pp. 108-111.

[29] 1996, pp. 29-30; 1998 pp. 297-298.

stereotypical stages that erase important historical realities: the *Išbiliyya* stage extends two centuries past the fall of Seville, while the *Ġarnāṭiyya* stage outlasts the fall of Granada by some four centuries. Razzūq's periodization does highlight the idea that the migrations of the late 15th century and afterwards represent rather different historical conditions from those that came before. While the migrations of the two earlier centuries may have been stimulated by Christian conquest to one degree or another, they did not carry the sense of a final separation from the music's Andalusi sources that characterized the events of the late 15th century.

Modern scholarship has suggested a connection between these diverse migrations and regional stylistic variations in the music, both within Morocco and between Morocco and the other states of North Africa,[30] though little solid evidence exists to support this inference. It may be no accident that the region around Tlemcen, Algeria, and Oujda, Morocco, which received a large wave of settlers from the Morisco expulsion of 1610, should be home to a style of Andalusian music known on the Moroccan side of the border as *al-Ġarnāṭī*, that is, "Granadan." Yet as with the expression *al-Mūsīqā l-andalusiyya*, the origin of the name *al-Ġarnāṭī* remains obscure and may be relatively recent. A systematic comparison of contemporary regional stylistic variations might help build a bridge to the migrations as described in the sources, but such a project would require precise data on the regional styles that does not exist at the moment. Indeed, the first attempt to describe local variants within Morocco in musical terms with any sort of precision have been published only very recently in Morocco,[31] so analysis of this question from an historical-musicological point of view remains only a promising possibility.

---

[30] For example, Chottin (1939) p. 94, García Barriuso, pp. 84-85

[31] see Benmūsā (2003) pp. 64-120.

Period	Migration
10th & 12th c.	Seville —> Tunis & Tripoli
12th c.	Cordoba —> Tlemcen Valencia —> Fez
1236	Fall of Cordoba to Ferdinand III of Castile 500,000 —> Tlemcen
1248	Seville —> Granada & North Africa; fall of Valencia to Jayme d'Aragon 200,000 —> Granada & Fez
14th c.	Valencia & Granada —> Marinid Fez & Tetuan
late 15th c. & >1492	Granada —> Wattasid Fez, Tetuan & Chefchaouen, Algiers
>1610	Final expulsion of Moriscos —> Fez, Tlemcen & Tunis

Figure 1.2: *Migrations from al-Andalus to North Africa*

Guettat (1980, 2000) argues against a simplistic view of one-directional flow of influence. He sees in the long history of cultural exchange between al-Andalus and North Africa musical influences flowing from North Africa to al-Andalus that helped to shape the musical styles that ultimately returned to North Africa and are embodied in the regional traditions of Morocco, Algeria, Tunisia and Libya. The complexity of the influences suggested by Guettat in this model certainly seem credible, but because he does not support this interesting hypothesis with much direct evidence, it has more the flavor of inference than firmly grounded fact.

The principal theme associated with Andalusian migrations to North Africa in the standard narrative is that they were conditioned by the Christian conquests. While such migrations certainly were important, there were other migrations as well, but these non-Reconquista migrations have no place at all in the standard narrative. Chapter 3 §1.1 addresses this problem by suggesting a more inclusive framework for understanding the role of Andalusian migrations in the music's history.

The third gap in the standard narrative spans approximately three centuries from the fall of Granada to the appearance of al-Ḥāʾik, the author of the first comprehensive anthology of *al-Āla*. This era covers the evolution of the music in

Morocco itself, but the narrative is characterized at this point by a lack of even the simplest gestures at providing context for the parade of names characteristic of it. García Barriuso, after a lengthy discussion in which he denies the existence of either Arabo-Berber or Arabo-Jewish music in al-Andalus, leaps all the way to al-Ḥāʾik and the importance of Tetuan in the music's history.[32] Only in a footnote does he mention "el Haxch Al-lal al Batla" (al-Ḥājj ʿAllal al-Baṭla) as the Moroccan composer of *Nawbat al-Istihlāl* in the first half of the 18th century.[33] For Chottin, this was an era of "exile, anarchie, décadence" in which only al-Baṭla (d. mid-18th c.?) and the theoretician ʿAbd ar-Raḥmān al-Fāsī appear, and in which "the door of composition was closed forever."[34] Guettat presents a longer list of names that suggests the "door of composition" was not so firmly closed as Chottin believed.[35] In both his major works, however, Guettat mainly discusses in rather vague terms the role of religious brotherhoods in the preservation of musical culture in Islam, a narrative which offers little insight into the Moroccan Andalusian music as such.[36]

Finally, two topics generally appear alongside the history in works by modern authors, and though these topics do not belong to history as such, no account of the standard narrative would be complete without them. Performance practice and music theory in al-Andalus appear to represent a break from the Middle East. Since the modern authors all trace the music of al-Andalus back to the Middle East, they generally discuss the changes the music underwent in the course of its development in both the east and the west. Because no clear evidence exists for the sound of the music of that time, such narratives comprise mainly accounts of musical influences that contributed to the development of Arabic music in the early Middle Ages (that is, Persian practice and Greek theory), and the emergence of the predominant "*ʿūd*ist school"[37] of Baghdad. Music theory in these accounts concerns *ʿūd* cord arrangements and fingerings, and rhythmic principles, all based primarily upon the writings of Yaʿqūb al-Kindī (d. 259/874) and the practice of Isḥāq al-Mawṣilī (d. 235/850) as described in the *Kitāb al-Aġānī*.

Later developments in the Middle East, the works of al-Fārābī (d. 337/950), Ibn Sīnā (d. 427/1037) and others, are not thought to have influenced music in al-Andalus to any appreciable extent. Al-Andalus thus inherited directly only the earliest phase of the high musical art in the Middle East – and of course Ziryāb, as the reputed

[32] *La música hispano-musulmana…* pp. 84-92

[33] *La música hispano-musulmana…* p. 91.

[34] *Tableau…* p. 98. Chottin here is borrowing the traditional phraseology used to describe the end of the practice of *ijtihād* in Islamic *fiqh*, apparently wanting to suggest an analogy. But see n. 16, above.

[35] 1980, pp. 182-283; and 2000, pp. 247-248.

[36] 1980, pp. 178-180; 2000, pp. 220-228. But see also Chapter 3 §1.2.

[37] Guettat (2000) Chapter 4.

pupil of Isḥāq al-Mawṣilī, provides the one link that makes this inheritance possible from the point of view of the standard narrative.

The other secondary topic is poetry, specifically the invention of the strophic forms, the *muwaššaḥ* and the *zajal*. Over the past decade or so, scholarly interest in the *muwaššaḥ* has evolved away from focusing on its structural and linguistic features and toward a greater interest in the role of music in the genesis and development of these poetic forms. The standard narrative merely notes the abundance of poetry labeled *tawšīḥ* and *zajal* in the modern Andalusian music traditions, assumes that the primary context for the strophic poetry of al-Andalus was musical, and therefore concludes that the invention of these forms was a milestone in the history of the music. The exact relationship between poetic text and performed song is rarely considered. On occasion, the comments of Ibn Sanā᾽ al-Mulk (d. 608/1211) come into play, but only on the level of description, and the problem of this Egyptian author writing about the poetry of al-Andalus never figures in the discussion.

3. *Historiography and the standard narrative*

The portion of the standard narrative presented thus far covers almost a millennium. Here it is presented in abbreviated form in order to highlight two characteristics: that the entire narrative is built upon a relatively small number of sources, and that it is dominated by accounts of individuals.

For the Andalusi portion of the narrative, which is the primary concern of this chapter and which covers the six and a half centuries between Ziryāb and 1492, the most commonly cited source is *Nafḥ aṭ-ṭīb fī ġuṣn al-Andalus ar-raṭīb* by Abū al-ʿAbbās Aḥmad b. Muḥammad al-Maqqarī, who died in 1040/1632. This is a relatively late work, written more than a century after the fall of Granada, half a millennium after Ibn Bājja, and eight centuries after Ziryāb's arrival in Cordoba. Even so, modern authors often cite al-Maqqarī as a primary source, without acknowledging the problems suggested by al-Maqqarī's distance from many of the events he describes. Given the scarcity of historical sources for the music of al-Andalus, and the richness of detail one sometimes finds in *Nafḥ aṭ-ṭīb*, we can understand why modern historians rely so heavily upon it. Moreover, much of al-Maqqarī's material relating to the earliest period in al-Andalus comes from *al-Muqtabis* of Ibn Ḥayyān. Since he is reasonably faithful to those parts of *al-Muqtabis* that have hitherto been available for comparison, we may assume that he took similar care with other sources that are not available elsewhere. Nevertheless, unqualified dependence upon al-Maqqarī tends to discourage critical assessment of al-Maqqarī's shortcomings (some of which are detailed in Chapter 2).

The next most commonly cited source is at-Tīfāšī's *Mutʿat al-asmāʿ fī ʿilm as-samāʿ*. Written about a century after Ibn Bājja in Ifrīqiya at the far eastern end of the Maġrib, these two chapters of his encyclopedia (most of which has been lost) contain a number of historical details, his comments about Ibn Bājja being most important. They also present material on Ziryāb, and on a number of songs (*aṣwāt*) that circulated in al-Andalus and North Africa at the time. At-Tīfāšī says little about his own sources for the two musicians in question, though Chapter 2 §1.1 will offer some speculation on this point.

Nearly as important as at-Tīfāšī for the music of al-Andalus is the *Muqaddima* of Ibn Khaldun, which contains a section "on the craft of song" in both the Middle East and al-Andalus (*Faṣl fī ṣināʿat al-ġinā'*: Chapter 5, part 32) and a section on *muwaššaḥāt* and *azjāl* (the final *faṣl* of Chapter 6). We find both Ziryāb and Ibn Bājja in the *Muqaddima*, as well.

Modern historians derive the main part of the biography of Ziryāb from Ibn Ḥayyān al-Qurṭubī, whose book *al-Muqtabis* is known only through fragments of the original and citations by other authors, such as al-Maqqarī. Until very recently, the passage on Ziryāb existed only in manuscript form, limiting access to it. However in 2003 Maḥmūd ʿAlī al-Makkī edited and published it. The published manuscript reveals that al-Maqqarī's version abbreviates Ibn Ḥayyān's narrative. In particular his account of Ziryāb omits the bulk of the material Ibn Ḥayyān offers on female slave singers and their role in the courtly musical culture of 3rd/9th-century Cordoba. This is a significant omission indeed, as Chapter 3 will make clear.

Three other sources for the musical history of al-Andalus are sometimes referred to: Ibn ʿAbd Rabbih's *al-ʿIqd al-farīd*, *aḏ-Ḏaḫīra fī maḥāsin ahl al-jazīra* by Abū l-Ḥasan ʿAlī Ibn Bassām (d. 542/1147), and *al-Muġrib fī ḥulā al-maġrib* by ʿAlī b. Musā Ibn Saʿīd al-Andalusī. These authors supply biographical details for a few poets and musicians.

The standard narrative that has been constructed from these sources comprises little more than a series of biographical sketches set within a chronological framework. The music provides the unifying theme, but otherwise these individuals have been abstracted from time and place in order to present a smooth progression without reference to the vagaries and conditions that shape a complex cultural form like a musical tradition. Even the few departures from this format, such as Guettat's passage on the musical environment of al-Andalus noted above, run parallel to the temporal frame and outside the narrative structure. Guettat's passage covers a broad expanse of time (from the Ṭāʾifa States through the Almohad dynasty) and so ignores his own periodization. Furthermore, he presents it as a supplement to, not an integral retelling of, the standard narrative. The same may be said of the Andalusi migrations to North

Africa: they appear as an interlude – a rupture that describes a rupture – and not as integral elements in the narrative.

In short, the standard narrative reflects an overarching emphasis on individuals (Great Men) whose contributions to the music of al-Andalus (Great Deeds) exist only in the context of the unifying theme, the music itself. In this sense, the standard narrative is modular: no qualitative difference distinguishes each of the individual links in the progression, and so individual accounts in the progression are logically and structurally interchangeable with one another. Indeed, we might go so far as to say that the standard narrative does not even represent the history of a *tradition* at all, for a tradition stands not upon simple facts or the Great Deeds of Great Men, but upon a cluster of beliefs and practices that depend in a meaningful way upon the social relationships among the participants in the tradition. In its structure, the standard narrative of the Andalusian music's history is indistinguishable from the history of a dynasty.

The Great Men-Great Deeds approach is concerned only with the *what* of history, that is to say, with the basic facts, the catalog of artifacts and the acts of important people. This kind of material certainly provides a necessary foundation, even if the historical narrative that results obscures other potentially important details. The Great Men-Great Deeds approach to the Arab-Andalusian music tradition also has the virtue of fitting very nicely with history as it was conceived and presented by the Arabic sources themselves. The modern scholar does not have to delve past the surface presented by the sources, for all the material necessary to the narrative is there, in plain sight. The author need only string the pieces together.

From its beginnings in the early Islamic period, Arabic historical literature was constructed from the same raw materials that provided the basis for both religious tradition and law: the *ḫabar* (pl. *aḫbār*), or narrative account of a single event or utterance. Initially the principal variety of *ḫabar* was *ḥadīṯ* (pl. *aḥādīṯ*), something the Prophet Muḥammad (or sometimes one of his Companions) said or did, as reported at first via oral tradition, and later in written collections. For the first century or so after his death, such accounts proliferated in various regions where the Prophet's associates settled, forming the basis for local solutions to novel questions of religious practice and law. At first such accounts were associated with the name of one or more famous individuals who were regarded as the authoritative source(s) of the story or utterance. An account about the Prophet, for example, might be attributed to his wife ʿĀʾiša or one of his close associates such as Abū Hurayra or ʿUmar. A natural extension of this was to relate a succession of transmitters (*isnād*, from the verb أسند , "to lean upon something"), which led back to the Prophet or one of his Companions, and through whom the *ḥadīṯ* was propagated from this original narrator.

In the course of the first century after the Prophet, these accounts became the basis first for justifying religious practice in various regions, and eventually for overtly legal argument. This type of legal reasoning first crystallized around the figure of aš-Šāfiʿī (d. 143/767), whose followers established the school of legal conventions that now bears his name. With the flourishing of *ḥadīṯ* accounts over time, it became desirable to distinguish between "authentic" *aḥādīṯ* and those of later invention. The solution arrived at was to examine the *isnād*, and this gave rise to *ʿilm ar-rijāl* (the study of the character of each link in the chain of transmitters) with the aim of establishing criteria for rejecting inauthentic accounts, based upon personal reputation and the likelihood that each individual had actually met those before and after him or her in the chain. By the middle of the third century of the Hijra, more or less authoritative compilations of *aḥādīṯ* emerged that attempted to encompass and codify, if not the whole of the traditional material associated with the Prophet, at least the main issues and subjects dealt with by these accounts, along with sufficient *isnād* material to establish their authority. This basic format (a traditional account with an *isnād* prefixed to it) has remained the basic structure of *aḥādīṯ* for centuries.

Alongside these developments, in the early 2nd/8th century the project of *ḥadīṯ* preservation and verification, and the collecting of stories about the Prophet's military expeditions (*maġāzī*) provided the raw materials for composing prophetic biography (*sīra*), which often incorporated oral, *ḥadīṯ*-like material and sometimes even Judeo-Christian literature, to form a kind of universal history or history of prophetic mission. The earliest *sīra* that has survived relatively intact is that of Ibn Isḥāq (d. 143/761), which we have today only in a revision by Ibn Hišām (d. 196/813).[38] The basic structural foundation for this type of biographical work was the same as that of *ḥadīṯ*, namely the *ḫabar*: individual narrative accounts of deeds and utterances, supported by reference to an earlier authority or chain of authorities.

In addition, an early preoccupation with religious history led to the compilation of narrative accounts concerning the early conquests (*futūḥ*), the acts of the early caliphs, the conflict between ʿAlī and Muʿāwiya and other important events and themes of early Islam. This material, at first derived from both oral and written accounts, formed the basis of formal history as such. Another important influence on the early development of Arabic historiography was the collection in writing in the 2nd/8th century of ancient accounts of tribal battles and feats of heroism (known in Arabic as *ayyām al-ʿArab*, roughly: "the battle-days of the Arabs") dating from the *Jāhiliyya* era before Islam. Ad-Dūrī (1983) notes that the *ayyām* literature led to "the survival of a

---

[38] A very thorough discussion of the development of Arabic historiography may be found in Franz Rosenthal's *A History of Muslim Historiography* (1968). A more concise but equally valuable Arab perspective is offered by ʿAbd al-ʿAzīz ad-Dūrī's *The Rise of Historical Writing Among the Arabs* (1983).

certain style in relating accounts, i.e., the pseudo-historical storytelling style" (20) that emphasized episodic events rather than long-term development or processes, just as was the case with *aḫbār*-based *sīra* and *ḥadīṯ*.

By the early ninth century historians were borrowing the tools of *isnād* and *isnād* criticism as a way of verifying the accounts they incorporated into their histories. What had served originally as a way of asserting in writing the veracity of essentially oral traditions became a way for literary material to masquerade as oral tradition, thus importing something of the prestige that attached to oral testimony over purely documentary evidence. In addition, the scope of history had expanded permanently beyond the Prophet and prophetic mission to include the early conquests of Syria, Iraq and Egypt alonside the acts of the first caliphs and so on. The outstanding historian of this period was al-Madāʾinī (d. 225/839).

In the late 3rd/9th century historians of a much broader perspective appeared. They had a wider range of sources at their disposal, but at the same time were much more selective about the material they included in their works. At this point, the writings of the earlier historians had stabilized into definitive versions, and an accepted view of their value as history had emerged, so that authors like al-Balāḏurī (d. 279/892) and al-Yaʿqūbī (d. 284/897) could afford simply to cite a work by an author as the source for an account, or even employ the formula *qālū* ("they said") to refer to the view of earlier historians. The outstanding early example of this new perspective on history is aṭ-Ṭabarī's (d. 310/923) *Taʾrīḫ ar-rusul wa-l-mulūk,* which reveals a vast knowledge and mastery of both historical and legal/juridical sources. Aṭ-Ṭabarī was very careful about his sources, and being well versed in the legal sciences, retained a critically-informed use of *isnād*.

Arabic historiography eventually developed into three basic formats that dominated the writing of history until the middle of the 20th century. Alongside the *sīra,* we find histories based upon biographical accounts of the notable figures in a given place, the best-known example being *Taʾrīḫ Baġdād* by al-Ḫaṭīb al-Baġdādī (d. 462/1071). This kind of "history" is really a special variety of *ṭabaqāt* literature, which collects biographical material on famous figures in a given field such as law or poetry. A second variety of historical work is annalistic, presenting the history of a dynasty arranged by successive years. Ibn Ḥayyān's *al-Muqtabis* belongs generally to this category, though he also includes chapters on topics such as a given ruler's clients, his ministers, the women in his life, and so on, all of which supplements the succession of year narratives. The third variety arranges its material in narrative form but does not adhere to a rigidly chronological framework. Rather, we find a narrative that does not shrink from digressing into details or events and then returning to the larger narrative. Even though historians writing in this narrative style often abandoned older conventions associated with *ḫabar* accounts in order to produce more coherent narratives, such histories still comprise in their essence a series of subjects strung together episodically that are functionally indistinguishable from one another. Thus in each of these formats, the basic building block remained the *ḫabar*-like account that emphasized the lives and deeds of important people.

Throughout the following millennium, *ḫabar*-based history remained the dominant mode of historical narrative. Ad-Dūrī observes that the basic formats and themes laid down in the first three centuries of Arabic historiography were not affected by the later emergence of sciences like geography and philosophy, so that "no change worthy of note overtook the early historical ideas and methods." (75) Even al-Maqqarī in the 17th century, though his *Nafḥ aṭ-ṭīb* takes account of geography, political factions, tribes and so on, still emphasizes accounts of great men as the substance of history. The implication that history comprises Great Men and their Great Deeds was never seriously challenged, for the great Arab historians never developed a critical perspective that would have allowed them to organize history in any other way or to consider other subject matter as proper for history itself.

Even Ibn Khaldun in the late 8th / 14th century, despite his reputation in the West as inventor of a sociological theory of history, did not depart from the fundamental tools and contents of history as they were known up to his day. Indeed, for all the attention justifiably devoted to its introduction, the main body of his great work, *Kitāb al-ʿIbar,* reads very much like conventional history: an assemblage of *aḫbār* strung together to mark out the passage of time, the cyclical progression of one dynasty to the next and the course of empire expressed in terms of great leaders and their successes and defeats. Aziz Al-Azmeh (1981) has argued that the principal subject matter of the *ʿIbar* is not, as some have suggested, a history of "group feeling" (*ʿaṣabiyya*), but simply the rise and fall of states and the collectivities which establish them, "a narrative of human aggregation" as Al-Azmeh phrases it. (9) Ibn Khaldun's achievement in the *Muqaddima,* according to Al-Azmeh, was not a sociology of history founded upon *ʿaṣabiyya,* but rather the notion of *ʿumrān,* organized habitation, which he conceived as an organizing principle in the phenomenal world that in turn would act as a frame within which to measure the plausibility of specific *aḫbār*: Ibn Khaldun's stated purpose in the *Muqaddima* is to provide criteria for doing away with the implausible material which had been handed down as history.

Rather less attention usually is given to the significance of the main body of the *ʿIbar* itself. However Al-Azmeh (1979) argues that to understand the *Kitāb al-ʿIbar* properly, we must read the two parts as forming an analogical argument about the nature of history and of historical relevance (hence the full title of the work, *Kitāb al-ʿIbar wa-dīwān al-mubtadiʾ wa-l-ḫabar,* which might be translated as: *The Book of*

Instructive Examples and the Register of Premise and Evidentiary Conclusion). The relationship between the *Muqaddima* and the rest of the *ʿIbar*, Al-Azmeh suggests, is metaphorically like that of *mubtadiʾ* ("a subject, having logical as well as ontological anteriority") and *ḫabar* (used here in the sense of a "conclusion of a logical relation"). (17) In the main part of the *ʿIbar*, Ibn Khaldun presents numerous narratives of the history of both the Arabs and the Berbers, examples of the proper elucidation of history. On the one hand, he is simply presenting a history of the world as he knew it in his time; but in the context of the introductory material, the narrative section of the *ʿIbar* becomes, not the application of a new historical theory, but the presentation of history in light of new criteria for plausibility. Indeed, the alleged "sociological principle" of *ʿaṣabiyya* appears only rarely in the main body of the *ʿIbar*. Its "theoretical" uses are reserved to the *Muqaddima* alone. In Al-Azmeh's view, there is no need to see in *ʿaṣabiyya* an overriding theme or organizing principle in history, posited first in introductory material and then abandoned in the execution of the history itself. He regards this as an ahistorical view that imposes modern preoccupations upon this late medieval text. It is more appropriate to see *ʿaṣabiyya* simply as a means to an end: the author's explanation for how people link together to produce a state, that is, through genealogy of one form or another.

This is not to say, however, that classical, *ḫabar*-based historiography was devoid of artifice or literary device. On the contrary, from an early stage historians took care in weaving discrete accounts into narratives that were informed by particular thematic structures or incorporated didactic perspectives present in earlier sources. Stefan Leder (1989, 1990) has shown the value of studying the literary features of Arabic historical texts, which reveal the textual histories behind *aḫbār* in these works. Many if not most of the later historians used *aḫbār* in ways intended to create a coherent, didactic narrative, but they also incorporated layers of thematic and schematic development from previous generations of historical writing. These techniques tended to obscure their own contributions to the narrative structure through their attribution to earlier authorities. Leder's discussion of these narrative features makes clear the importance of what today might be described as literary considerations in the construction of *ḫabar*-based Arabic historiography.

In a similar vein, Albrecht Noth (1994) draws attention to themes and topoi present in early Arabic historiography that helped to shape later historical narratives of early Islam. The preoccupation of early historians with the *ridda* wars, the military conquests in Syria and Persia, and so on, established the thematic conventions taken up by later historians. In the same way, topoi such as individual combat, conversion leading to conquest and control from the political center in Medina provided the early historians with narrative building blocks that became standard literary elements in later historians' versions. Like Leder, Noth offers an analysis that underscores the problems with literal understandings of *ḫabar*-based histories while at the same time revealing the significance of didactic and literary intentions in the genesis and dissemination of these historical traditions.

Literary devices like these played an important part in the composition of later historical narratives and in framing their underlying aesthetic-instructive characteristics. Tayeb El-Hibri (1999) points out that narrative histories of the Abbasid dynasty were constructed with an eye to commenting on the personal qualities of the caliphs, to illuminating the moral lessons of the civil war between al-Amīn and al-Maʾmūn, or to casting the conflict in terms of religious themes such as the story of Ibrāhīm, Ismaʿīl and Isḥāq. Though the annalistic histories, like that of aṭ-Ṭabarī, may seem to the modern reader to be relatively plain and realistic, El-Hibri draws attention to the play of topoi and intertextual references that they employ in framing social, political and religious commentary through the structure of the narrative. The aim, argues El-Hibri, was not merely to disguise criticism of the ruling dynasty with literary artifice, but also to engage in an erudite "game" by showing one's skill in weaving subtle references into the narrative.

> The message of the text lay in the very encoded structure of symbolism, allusion, innuendo, symmetry, and intertextuality that governed the make-up of the historical text. If the message does not seem readily accessible to the reader, this only serves to highlight the artistic quality of these rhetorical techniques and the elusiveness of the esoteric method of historical writing.[39]

Classical Arabic historiography, then, took the basic building blocks of *aḫbār* and used them in literary-like ways to construct narratives that nevertheless generally emphasized important individuals over larger social context, and privileged episodic exposition of important events over synchronic analysis of causes through comparison across cases. Modern historians of the Andalusi musical heritage have taken up these characteristics of their sources, even deploying the material itself in a broadly similar way for rhetorical purposes. The standard narrative, written as it is with an eye only for the people and things of that history, corresponds well with the overt methodology of the sources: ideas, acts and actors all are already in focus and so transfer easily into the modern narrative. Moreover, the larger aim of the modern histories seems to be to

---

[39] El Hibri (1999), p. 217.

affirm the "Andalusian-ness" of the musical tradition, a theme that dovetails very well with the expositional technique borrowed from the sources.

Just as aṭ-Ṭabarī, for example, made use of *ḫabar*-based accounts that carried with them the thematic and ideological preoccupations of his sources, so the standard narrative of the Andalusian music as found in authors like Chottin and Guettat imports an array of thematic focal points and beliefs about the nature of history generally (and *this* history in particular). They emphasize the overarching premises that a) the only important music is elite music; b) the only important contents of the history are the Great Deeds of Great Men; and c) the tradition is in its birth and essence chiefly and most importantly Andalusi. This is not to say that writing such history is without its challenges, especially in interpreting linguistically ambiguous passages, the meanings of particular words in context and so on. Yet, the techniques of inference, interpretation and exposition are much less complicated than they might be if the orientation of source and scholar were not so similar.

Circumscribing history with a narrowly focused concern for great men and important acts unfortunately tends to obscure a number of elements that do not fit well into the thematic paradigm, but which nevertheless have helped to shape the larger context surrounding the events described. Too often, the focus on Great Men and Great Deeds erases the common man and the common woman, who provide the labor and economic energy for every society. Equally obscured in the classical model of history are the non-physical aspects of culture, such as ideologies. In fact, ideologies quite often are taken for granted within the frame of standard histories, with little in the way of real analysis offered.

For example, the Shiite slogan *damm ʿAlī* ("the blood of ʿAlī") as found in the Shiite histories of an-Nawbaḫtī (d. ca. 310/922) and al-Qummī (d. 381/991-2) constitutes an acknowledgement of the role played by an ideology in historical events. Yet these authors apply the slogan itself to a number of very different groups, without comment as to its meaning (or appropriateness) in each case. They leave it to the reader to infer the slogan's true significance. Indeed, one finds in these histories that the ideology itself takes second place to the men and the deeds described and serves merely as a marker to distinguish one group (whether "Shiite" or "non-Shiite") from others. The ideology which stands behind the marker is not itself analyzed beyond simple description of particular cases. The authors of these *firaq* histories present ideology, not as a coherent matrix from which political actions arise, but simply as a justification for the aligning of poles for or against the Great Man in his cause. This is one reason why these historians devote so much energy to cataloguing minute distinctions between the beliefs of various groups that are themselves identified simply by an adjective derived from the name of an eponymous figure: the historian's aim was to categorize, not to explain.

If we look again at Ibn Khaldun's *Kitāb al-ʿIbar*, we find a very similar situation. In his account of the Almohad dynasty, he presents first the story of the founder, the Mahdī Ibn Tūmart. Ibn Tūmart was born in the south of Morocco, but traveled to the Middle East where he received training in both law and disputation. Returning to the west inspired with a pious dislike of the worldliness of his era, the Mahdī rallied the Masmuda Berbers to overthrow the degenerate and materialistic Almoravid dynasty based in nearby Marrakech. The historian presents Ibn Tūmart's religious training in the Middle East, his travels, his preaching and teaching methods among the Berbers, and accounts of the early battles against the Almoravids. Ibn Tūmart died early without naming another guide in the religious mission. Ibn Khaldun describes the transfer of power from the religious leader to the secular dynasty in only the briefest of terms, with no reference at all to the religious mission one assumes was taken up by Ibn Tūmart's successor, ʿAbd al-Muʾmin. The remainder of Ibn Khaldun's account treats only the dynasty's fortunes in war and politics. The historian who devoted so much attention to cultural matters in the *Muqaddima*, including the allegedly sociological concept of *ʿaṣabiyya*, ultimately offers no framework within which to analyze the role of religious ideology in historical events, not even in this case, when it could easily have provided an explanation for the *ʿaṣabiyya* of the Almohads after Ibn Tūmart.

Traditional historiography also tends to downplay the underlying institutions – especially the informal institutions – which give support and shape to the careers of so many of history's Great Men. The formal institutions of the past often do find their way into the history books: governments, schools, political and religious parties, businesses, guilds and so on. Yet formal institutions depend upon social conditions and arrangements that are taken for granted, even when they provide the unspoken rationale for the formal institution.

Taking the example of the Almohads in *Kitāb al-ʿIbar*, it is precisely the peculiarity of the transmission of authority outside the expected familial framework in this case (ʿAbd al-Muʾmin and his successors did not hail from the dominant Masmuda tribe) that seems to the modern scholar to call out for a systematic, conceptual explanation. What did the Mahdī's death mean to his followers and their religious mission? How were the Mahdī's religious teachings deployed by the dynasty to legitimize itself after his death? Did the ideology become weaker, or more rigid? Ibn Khaldun might have addressed such questions using his alleged "sociological principle" of *ʿaṣabiyya*, but in fact they received no answer at all in the *ʿIbar* because they fell outside the purview of Ibn Khaldun's concept of history. Yet questions like these direct our attention toward the ideological frameworks and social relationships that exist parallel to and interpenetrate with the political institution of *dynasty*, encompassing rules of succession, cultural norms for the expression and exercise of power, and a host of other details which people of the time simply took for granted. The effort to identify and describe these more cultural-ideological facets of history is all the more difficult for the modern historian confronted with sources that provide only the barest information on such topics.

Only in the middle of the 20th century, under the influence of Western interest in the economic and social aspects of history, did the substance of historical writing in the Arabic-speaking world begin to change. Following early Western efforts to reframe the history of al-Andalus in social terms, such as E. Levi-Provençal's *L'Espagne musulmane au Xème siècle: Institutions et vie sociale* (1932) and *Conférences sur l'Espagne musulmane* (1951, based upon a series of lectures given in 1947 and 1948 at the University of Farouk I in Cairo), scholarly attention in the Arabic-speaking world turned to the literary and social aspects of the history. Jaafar Soulami and M'hammad Benaboud (1994) describe the voluminous attention devoted to the Ṭā'ifa era in al-Andalus, and include several works by Arab authors from a variety of perspectives. Significantly, all these works date from after 1960. A notable example is Ṣalāḥ Ḫāliṣ' literary history of Seville, *Išbīliyya fī l-qarn al-ḫāmis al-hijrī* (1961, French translation *La vie littéraire à Séville au XIe siècle*, 1966), which begins with a Marxian analysis of the economics and class structure of Seville before turning to the famous literary figures and their social networks. Similarly, Abdallah Laroui has contributed socio-economic studies of North African history, such as *L'histoire du Maghreb* (1970, English translation *The History of the Maghrib, An Interpretive Essay*, 1977).

This movement away from traditional *ḫabar*-based history has yet to touch historical accounts of the Andalusian musical tradition, whether in al-Andalus or in North Africa. The standard narrative remains founded upon the same model as its sources, the *ḫabar*-based narrative composed of a succession of essentially interchangeable accounts strung together on the thread of a temporal progression. The subject is, of course, the music of al-Andalus, but the *theme* of the narrative is in fact the Great Deeds of Great Men acting within the bounds of the topic. As with the examples of traditional historiography noted above, the social elements that provided the foundations for elite musical culture in al-Andalus and North Africa do not enter the historical frame.

There is some use, then, in revisiting the standard narrative in hope of teasing out economic and social details that lie in the background of the sources and only surreptitiously find their way into the narrative itself. The next chapter is devoted to reassessing Ziryāb and Ibn Bājja, the two most important figures in the standard narrative prior to al-Ḥāʾik, with the aim of suggesting a fuller and more nuanced narrative that situates them within the social institutions that made their careers possible.

The accepted biographies of Ziryāb and Ibn Bājja present us with a certain complication. If we take the sources at face value, we must ignore an important fact about music and the arts in general: that innovations and revolutions in the arts never occur in isolation from the social and cultural context which surround them. On the contrary, great innovations and innovators in music always draw upon pre-existing matrices of symbols, practices, political developments, social relationships, and cultural and inter-cultural frames of reference. No new style of music ever emerges fully formed without borrowing something of what came before, often including other artists working along similar lines. To accept the notion that Ziryāb "invented" the Andalusian music of his day would be comparable to believing that Beethoven alone was responsible for romanticism in Western orchestral music, or that rock and roll was invented by Elvis Presley, like Athena springing fully-armed from the thigh of Zeus.

Unfortunately these contextual factors rarely are obvious because they never were the subject of histories written before the twentieth century; instead they lie hidden between the lines of conventional historiography, as we have seen. And because the mode of reportage bears the stamp of antiquity, it becomes very easy to regard the sources as brilliant beacons from the past, rather than seeing them as they are: imperfect and partial tales whose conventions and assumptions often obscure details that today seem worthy of consideration. How can one sift these accounts and pull out the meaningful contexts that they conceal? In recent decades a number of methods have been applied to both history and literature in the West, including deconstruction, feminist critiques, Marxist analysis and others. Taken as a group, these methods involve various ways of redefining what is meaningful in history, and each has its merits that derive from what it holds as important for understanding history.

Part 2 of this work develops a theoretical framework for situating *al-Āla* within its social context, a framework that defines *tradition* in terms of the meaningful social relationships that inform it. The present discussion pursues two aims, first, to show how the standard narrative limits our understanding of the music's history, and second, to develop data that can be analyzed within the framework proposed in Part 2. To do this, we will look beyond the main figures of Ziryāb and Ibn Bājja themselves, beyond the assumptions that surround them in the accounts, and instead turn our gaze toward the "unimportant" people and social relationships that the sources take for granted.

Chapter 2
Beyond Ziryāb and Ibn Bājja

Given the limitations of the Andalusian music's standard narrative described in Chapter One, we may wonder about those aspects of the history that have been obscured in the narrative. In particular, we are interested here in the social factors surrounding the elite music of al-Andalus that formed the context for the many individuals who appear in the narrative. Although we cannot retrieve every social detail of an historical moment centuries later (especially true considering the often narrow focus of the Arabic sources available to us), we certainly can cast some light in that direction by taking a careful look at the evidence that has survived, even when the sources themselves take little note of the kinds of details we are interested in. The present chapter now turns to the two founding father figures of the tradition's Andalusian era, Ziryāb and Ibn Bājja, in search of details that the sources may not give much weight to, but which make a more complete picture possible. We will find that doing so allows some people who have previously been largely overlooked to share some of the spotlight. Not coincidentally, this also produces a more subtle and satisfying narrative.

The standard narrative of *al-Āla*'s history begins with Abū l-Ḥasan ʿAlī b. Nāfiʿ, the musician and composer better known to history as Ziryāb. The narrative describes him as a young apprentice to the great composer in Baghdad, Isḥāq al-Mawṣilī, who was a leading light at the court of the Abbasid caliph, Hārūn ar-Rašīd (r. 170/786-193/809). In his one and only appearance before the caliph, Ziryāb so impressed the ruler that he inspired his teacher's jealousy. Faced with a choice put to him by Isḥāq, to stay and face the wrath of the leading court muscian of his day, or to flee at once from Baghdad and never return, Ziyāb chose to leave. He fled westward, where he was invited to al-Andalus by the Umayyad emir of Cordoba, al-Ḥakam I. He arrived with his family at al-Jazīra al-Ḫaḍrā' (modern Algeciras) on the Iberian coast near the end of the Islamic year 206. However he learned upon his arrival that while he was traveling, the emir had passed away. Fortunately, he was met by an envoy from the court in Cordoba, another musician named al-Manṣūr the Jew, who reassured Ziryāb that like his father, the new emir, ʿAbd al-Raḥmān II, was a great lover of music as well. In the end, Ziryāb was indeed welcomed in Cordoba by the new prince around the beginning of the month of Muharram 207 AH (the end of May 822).

Thus began the career of the most illustrious musician and composer in the history of Islamic Spain, according to the standard narrative. Ziryāb is believed to have brought about dramatic changes in the musical culture of Umayyad Spain. His teaching methods, repertoire and musical philosophy are said to have influenced musicians for generations afterward and created almost at a stroke a sophisticated courtly musical tradition in Cordoba. The list of accomplishments and contributions attributed to Ziryāb is astonishing and touches upon many areas beyond music: among other things, he is said to have introduced wearing bangs on the forehead instead of long hair parted in the middle, wearing different colors of clothes with the seasons, the delights of asparagus, gold and silver table service instead of glass, and leathern tablecloths and bedspreads.

In this way, the standard narrative presents a grand view of Ziryāb, not only as the one fount from which all the elite music of al-Andalus flows, but also as revolutionizing courtly culture itself. Moreover, he does not seem to have exhibited any human foibles or weaknesses, nor to have met any opposition in his role as the arbiter of taste among the aristocracy of early-ninth-century Cordoba. This account of his life, presented most famously by al-Maqqarī, has been adopted whole cloth into the modern history of the Andalusian music traditions.

However, if we take a wider range of sources into account, a more interesting and complex image of Ziryāb emerges, and more importantly, the revised biography of Ziryāb that results also allows us to highlight more of the social and economic circumstances that shaped the courtly musical culture of al-Andalus. In particular, it becomes clear that the careers of men like Ziryāb and Ibn Bājja stood upon two social institutions: elite patronage of the arts and what we shall refer to here as "artiste slavery", that is, the use of highly trained slave women as musicians and entertainers. This reevaluation of the careers of Ziryāb and Ibn Bājja does not merely revise important elements in the early history of the Andalusian music tradition. It also represents a first step toward reorienting the entire history of the tradition in terms of its social foundations, a move that will ultimately reveal a great deal about the tradition as it exists in Morocco today.

1. *Ziryāb: Context, images, sources*

Most of what we know about Ziryāb's life and career derives from seven sources: *Nafḥ aṭ-ṭīb min ġuṣn al-Andalus ar-raṭīb wa-ḏikr wazīrihā Lisān ad-Dīn ibn al-Ḫaṭīb* ["The Waft of Perfume from the Fruitful Bough of al-Andalus, and Remembrance of Its Vizier, Lisān al-Dīn ibn al-Ḫaṭīb"] by al-Maqqarī, who depends to a great extent upon *al-Muqtabis fī aḫbār balad al-Andalus* ["Plucking the Firebrand (of Knowledge) in the Accounts of the Land of al-Andalus"] by Ibn Ḥayyān; the *Kitāb al-ʿIbar* of Ibn Khaldun; *Mutʿat al-asmāʿ fī ʿilm as-samāʿ* by Aḥmad b. Yūsuf at-Tīfāšī; *Taʾrīḫ iftitāḥ al-Andalus*[1] ["The History of

[1] This work is known as both *Taʾrīḫ iftitāḥ al-Andalus* and *Taʾrīḫ fatḥ al-Andalus*.

the Conquest of al-Andalus"] by Ibn al-Qūṭiyya (d. 366/977); *al-ʿIqd al-farīd* ["The Unique Necklace"] by Ibn ʿAbd Rabbih; and *Kitāb Baġdād* ["The History of Baghdad"] by Ibn Abī Ṭāhir Ṭayfūr (204/819-280/893). In addition, indirect references to Ziryāb figure in three other sources: *Kitāb al-Aġānī* ["The Book of Songs"] of Abū l-Faraj al-Iṣfahānī (d. 355/967), *Ṭawq al-Ḥamāma* ["The Neckring of the Dove"] by Abū Muḥammad ʿAlī Ibn Ḥazm (394/994-456/1064), and *Jaḏwat al-Muqtabis fī taʾrīḫ ʿulamāʾ al-Andalus* ["The Firebrand of *al-Muqtabis* in the Biographies of the Erudite Men of al-Andalus"] by al-Ḥumaydī (d. 488/1095). Figure 2.1 arranges these authors in chronological order and illustrates their temporal relationships to one another. It shows that the principal source for the standard biography of Ziryāb, Ibn Ḥayyān, died a little more than two centuries after the musician, and that several other sources lie a century or more closer to him.

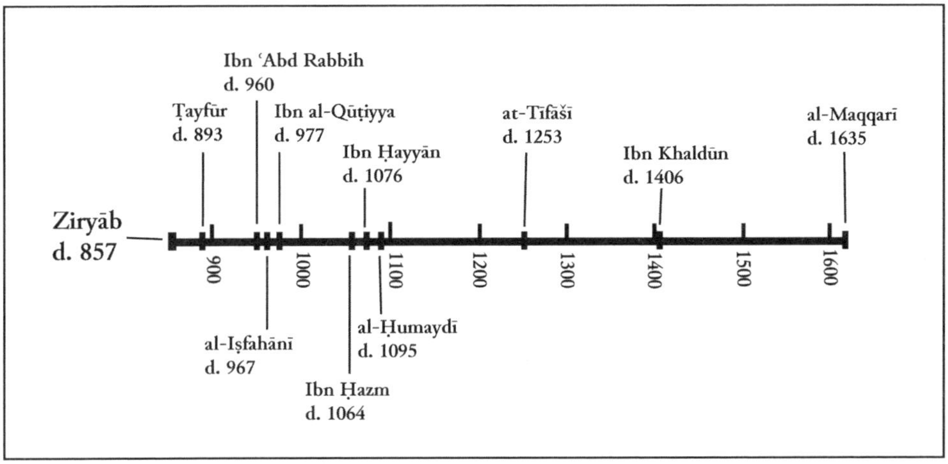

Figure 2.1: *Timeline of sources for the life of Ziryāb*

This chapter examines these accounts in reverse-chronological order from most recent to earliest. Although his is the most recent source for Ziryāb, al-Maqqarī's account will be examined later, because his principal sources are Ibn Ḥayyān and Ibn Khaldun. When we have seen what the other sources tell us, we will be in a better position to evaluate *Nafḥ aṭ-ṭīb* as a source for Ziryāb.

1.1. *Ibn Khaldun and Aḥmad at-Tīfāšī*

Ibn Khaldun and at-Tīfāšī together mention Ziryāb three times. Although Ziryāb's appearance in these two sources is noteworthy by itself, neither gives a great deal of detail about him. Instead both present schematic versions of what has become the accepted narrative of Ziryāb's life, with some of its essential features already in place.

He appears twice in *Kitāb al-ʿIbar*: in the 32nd *faṣl* of Chapter 5 of the *Muqaddima*[2] and in the section of the *ʿIbar* itself entitled *Wafāt al-Ḥakam wa-wilāyat ibnihi ʿAbd ar-Raḥmān al-Awsaṭ* ("The death of al-Ḥakam and the reign of his son, ʿAbd ar-Raḥmān II").[3] The latter account states that Ziryāb arrived from Iraq in the year 207/822, that he was a client (مولى) of the Abbasid caliph al-Mahdī, that he was a student of Isḥāq al-Mawṣilī, that his name was ʿAlī b. Nāfiʿ, and that he traveled to meet ʿAbd ar-Raḥmān and lived well under his patronage. He brought the craft of song (صناعة الغناء) to al-Andalus, and his eldest son, ʿAbd ar-Raḥmān, took up his legacy.

Ibn Khaldun's account of Ziryāb in the *Muqaddima* is more significant, especially when read in its context, at the end of the last *faṣl* of the *Muqaddima*, on the art of song. This *faṣl* includes a lengthy discussion of the Muslim philosophers of music and what they owed to the Greeks, the nature of musical composition and the various sorts of musical instruments in use in his day. Immediately before Ziryāb, the author returns to the larger theme of his *Muqaddima*, that is, civilization (or "organized habitation", العُمران). He describes the austerity of the desert Arabs and their abstinence from ease and pleasure until Islam made them powerful. Then, writes Ibn Khaldun, they came under the influence of the Persians and the Byzantines, whose musicians came to Arabia and became clients of the Arabs.

Thereafter, a number of famous musicians (including Ibrāhīm al-Mawṣilī, d. 188/804, and his son, Isḥāq) "devoted themselves to entertainment and play"[4] (أمعرو في اللهو واللهب). This passage sets the stage for Ziryāb, the only musician whose career is discussed in this section, and who therefore embodies the impetus within العُمران to promulgate the finer things of civilization, according to Ibn Khaldun's argument.

> وكان للموصليين غلام اسمه زرياب أخذ عنهم الغناء فأجاد فصرفوه إلى المغرب غيرة منه ، فلحق بالحكم بن هشام بن عبد الرحمان الداخل أمير الأندلس فغلب في تكرمته وركب للقائه وأسنى له الجوائز والإقطاعات والجرايات وأحلّه من دولته وندمائه بمكان ، فأورث بالأندلس من صناعة الغناء ما تناقلوه إلى أزمان الطوائف ، وطما منها بإشبيلية بحرٌ زاخرٌ وتناقل منها بعد ذهاب غضارتها إلى بلاد العدوة بإفريقية والمغرب ، وانقسم على أمصارها وبها الآن منها صبابة على

2 2004 edition, p. 396.
3 1992, v. 4, section 2, p. 153.
4 p. 396.

تراجع عمرانها وتناقص دولها ، وهذه الصناعة آخر ما يحصل في العمران من الصنائع لأنها كمالية في غير وظيفة من الوظائف إلا وظيفة الفراغ والفرح ، وهو أيضا أول ما ينقطع من العمران عند اختلاله ، والله أعلم .

> The Mawṣilīs had an apprentice[5] whose name was Ziryāb, who learned (the craft of) song from them and excelled (in it). So they sent him away to the west, out of jealousy. Then he reached al-Ḥakam b. Hišām b. ʿAbd ar-Raḥmān ad-Dāḫil, emir of al-Andalus, who did the utmost to honor him. (al-Ḥakam) traveled to meet him and gave him considerable rewards, lands, and stipends. And he invested him with a rank in his state and boon companions. And thus did Ziryāb pass on to al-Andalus the craft of song which they handed down until the time of the Ṭāʾifa states. An abundant sea of it brimmed up in Seville, and it spread from there after the departure of Seville's prosperity to the lands on the opposite shore in Ifrīqiya and the Maġrib. It dispersed throughout their cities, but in them now is (only) a remnant of it, due to the decline of their civilization and the waning of their states. This craft is the last of the crafts that appear in civilization, because it is a sign of refinement in what serves no purpose but leisure and enjoyment. And it is also the first of what is cut off from civilization when it deteriorates and declines. And Allāh is Most Knowledgeable.[6]

Ibn Khaldun's two Ziryāb accounts contain an inconsistency. The main body of the *Kitāb al-ʿIbar* indicates that Ziryāb's patron in al-Andalus was ʿAbd ar-Raḥmān II, while in the *Muqaddima* version, it is not ʿAbd ar-Raḥmān, but his father, al-Ḥakam. However in other respects, Ibn Khaldun broadly agrees with Ibn Ḥayyān's longer and more detailed account, so it is likely that the inconsistency is the result of an error by a copyist of the *Muqaddima* manuscript, possibly simply leaving off the first item in the genealogical chain of Ziryāb's patron's name, ʿAbd ar-Raḥmān.

The *Muqaddima* account obviously operates on a rhetorical level. Ibn Khaldun uses Ziryāb as part of his larger argument in the *ʿIbar*: that civilization (العُمران) develops from poverty and austerity, to wealth and leisure, and then declines. Ziryāb serves as the last and most outstanding musician following the late emergence of music as an art among the Arabs. So the figure of Ziryāb provides an occasion to summarize the place of music within the development of civilization.

---

[5] غلام also means "servant".

[6] p. 396.

This version of the Ziryāb story contains essential elements found in the standard narrative. Ibn Khaldun uses Ziryāb to discuss only one kind of music: elite and refined music, which appears under the rubric of صناعة الغناء . What we might call popular music does appear briefly in this *faṣl*, but Ibn Khaldun devotes little attention to it: he discusses only elite music as "the music of the Arabs." Moreover, the Ziryāb story is rendered here in summary: his tutelage in Baghdad and expulsion by Isḥāq al-Mawṣilī; his arrival in al-Andalus and patronage by ʿAbd ar-Raḥmān; his single-handedly introducing elite music to al-Andalus and thereby initiating a musical culture that dominated al-Andalus until the era of the Ṭāʾifa states. Ziryāb thus serves in the *Muqaddima* as the one important cultural link between Arab east and west, a topos that is also a central feature of the standard narrative.

Ibn Khaldun does not reveal his sources for the life of Ziryāb, but one of them might have been at-Tīfāšī, who hailed from Tunis like Ibn Khaldun, and who compiled an encyclopedia entitled *Faṣl al-ḫiṭāb fī madārik al-Ḥawāss al-ḫams li-ulī l-albāb* ["On Perceiving with the Five Senses, for Those Who Have Intelligence"]. Most of it has been lost, except for a manuscript of volume 41 preserved in Tunis, which contains Chapters 10 and 11 of his essay *Mutʿat al-asmāʿ fī ʿilm as-samāʿ*.[7]

Ziryāb appears near the end of Chapter 11, after the author has concluded a careful description of "the songs of the Andalusis" (أغاني الأندلسيين) that he himself had heard.[8] A new section on the evolution of (elite) music in al-Andalus follows with an *isnād* that begins with one Ibn Durayda and concludes with Ibn al-Ḥāsib of Murcia (d. early 13th c.?).[9] At-Tīfāšī's ultimate source for Ziryāb, then, is Ibn al-Ḥāsib al-Mursī, an Andalusian who wrote an encyclopedia of music that has been lost. Here is at-Tīfāšī's version of Ibn al-Ḥāsib's account:

---

[7] The manuscript is held in the private library of Muḥammad aṭ-Ṭāhir b. ʿĀšūr. E. García Gomez first drew attention to it in two articles, "La lírica hispanoárabe y la aparición de la lírica románica" (*Al-Andalus* 21, 1956, pp. 303-338) and "Una extraordinaria página de Tīfāšī y una hypótesis sobre el inventor del zéjel" (*Études d'orientalisme dédiées à la mémoire de Lévi-Provençal*, 1962, v. 2, pp. 517-523). Muḥammad b. Tāwīt aṭ-Ṭanjī edited and published the text of these two chapters as "aṭ-Ṭarāʾiq wa l-alḥān al-mūsīqiyya fī Ifrīqiya wa l-Andalus" in *Al-Abḥāṯ* 21: 1, 2, 3 (1968), pp. 93-116. Liu and Monroe (1989, pp. 35-43) produced an English translation, omitting at-Tīfāšī's poetic incipits.

[8] p. 114. On p. 110 (Liu and Monroe, 40), at-Tīfāšī presents the text of a specific song (a *našīd* in the mode *mazmūm*) that he says actually was composed and sung by Ziryāb and was later elaborated by Ibn Bājja. The text was written by Abū Qaṭīfa, and is mentioned in *Kitāb al-Aġānī* (see aṭ-Ṭanji, p. 110 n. 2).

[9] Abū l-Ḥasan ʿAlī b. Abī ʿImrān Ibn Saʿīd al-Andalusī, the author of *al-Muġrib fī ḥulā l-Maġrib*, was at-Tīfāšī's immediate informant for this story. Aṭ-Ṭanjī, in his preface (p. 94), informs us that at-Tīfāšī and Ibn Saʿīd were members of a literary circle in 13th-century Tunis.

اخبرني ابن الحاسب ان اهل الأندلس في القديم كان غناؤهم إما بطريقة النصاري وإما بطريقة حُداة العرب ، و لم يكن عندهم قانون يعتمدون عليه إلى ان تأثلت الدولة الأموية وكانت مدة الحكم الربضي فوفد عليه من المشرق ومن إفريقية من يحسن غناء تلحي المدنية فأخذ الناس عنهم إلى ان وفد الإمام المقدم في هذا الشأن علي بن نافع الملقب بزرياب غلام إسحاق الموصلي على الأمير عبد الرحمان الأوسط ، فجاء بما لم تعهده الآسماع واتخذت طريقته مسلكا ونسي غيرها إلى ان مشأ ابن باجة الإمام العظيم ...

> Ibn al-Ḥāsib informed me [Ibn Durayda] that the songs of the Andalusians in ancient times were either in the manner of the Christians or of the Arab camel-drivers [*al-ḥudāh*]. They had no rules which they relied on until the Umayyad dynasty had taken root, which was in the era of al-Ḥakam I, when some who sang well the melodies of Medina came to the emir from the Middle East and Ifrīqiya. And so the people learned from them until the foremost master in this area ʿAlī b. Nāfiʿ, nicknamed Ziryāb, an apprentice of Isḥāq al-Mawṣilī's, came to the emir ʿAbd ar-Raḥmān II. He brought what ears were not familiar with (before), and his style was adopted methodically and all others forgotten, until Ibn Bājja, the supreme master appeared...[10]

Here in Tunis, a century and a half before Ibn Khaldun, we have the essential elements of the Ziryāb story, attributed to someone who had lived in al-Andalus, presumably presented in the form in which it was circulating at the time. Moreover, this account shares certain features with that of Ibn Khaldun. As in the *Muqaddima*, the music of the commoners vanishes from the narrative once the elite music arrives, because it was not governed by rules and therefore did not fit the expectations of proper music as craft (صناعة). Also like Ibn Khaldun, at-Tīfāšī's version uses the same term (غلام) to describe Ziryāb as an apprentice of Isḥāq al-Mawṣilī. According to at-Tīfāšī it was ʿAbd ar-Raḥmān II who welcomed Ziryāb, but (unlike in the *Muqaddima*) the elite music of the Middle East actually arrived *before* Ziryāb, whose style represented a firm break with the past that lasted until Ibn Bājja.

Ibn Bājja lived during the middle years of Almoravid rule (he died in Almoravid Fez in 1139, 114 years before at-Tīfāšī himself). At-Tīfāšī's claim that Ibn Bājja made important innovations in the music of al-Andalus harmonizes reasonably well with Ibn Khaldun's assertion that the musical style of Ziryāb lasted in al-Andalus until

---

[10] pp. 114-115.

the Ṭāʾifa era, which was brought to an end by the Almoravid intervention after the conquest of Toledo by Alfonso VI in 1085. However, Ibn Khaldun does not mention Ibn Bājja in connection with Ziryāb. So although he lived in Ifrīqiya just a century and a half after at-Tīfāšī, and may well have read his work, it seems unlikely that Ibn Khaldun relied upon at-Tīfāšī as his only source for the music of al-Andalus. Yet Ziryāb's role in firmly establishing the music of the Middle East in al-Andalus is common to both accounts, and in both versions of the Ziryāb story, the musician also serves a rhetorical purpose for the author: for Ibn Khaldun, Ziryāb provides a link to the discussion of العمران; while for at-Tīfāšī, he sets the stage for the more important figure in the narrative, Ibn Bājja.

Although Ziryāb's biography is sketchy in these later sources, one detail common to these two accounts speaks to our larger purpose here, namely the emir ʿAbd ar-Raḥmān's patronage. Patronage by members of the aristocracy was a very important feature of life for a cadre of fine poets, musicians and composers in al-Andalus who are prominent in several of the sources even though their numbers were relatively small. The next section will show how thoroughy this informal institution was taken for granted in the Middle Ages, and that its importance could extend far beyond the economics of survival. Ibn Ḥayyān's account of Ziryāb shows that patronage – and the social relationships it implies – was the most significant factor shaping Ziryāb's career.

1.2. *Ibn Ḥayyān*

Abū Marwān Ḥayyān b. Ḫalaf b. Ḥusayn Ibn Ḥayyān was born in Cordoba in 377/987-8, and died in 469/1076. The foremost historian of Islamic Spain, and our principal source for the Umayyad era, Ibn Ḥayyān produced two books, *al-Muqtabis*, which deals with this period, and *al-Matīn*, which covers more recent history up to the author's death during the Ṭāʾifa period. *Al-Muqtabis* is composed of accounts from numerous other authors, and Ibn Ḥayyān usually notes his source for each. It preserves a wealth of material that otherwise would be lost, including the most detailed biography of Ziryāb extant, based largely (but not exclusively) upon a work Ibn Ḥayyān refers to as *Kitāb Aḫbār Ziryāb* (The Book of Ziryāb Stories). No other work preserves this book, and its authorship is uncertain. Maḥmūd ʿAlī Makkī, editor of the 2003 edition that contains the Ziryāb biography, suggests that *Kitāb Aḫbār Ziryāb* is the book about Ziryāb associated with Aslam b. Aḥmad b. Aslam b. ʿAbd al-ʿAzīz (d. 318/931), which is mentioned by two contemporaries of Ibn Ḥayyān, Ibn Ḥazm and al-Ḥumaydī. Al-Maqqarī relies on *al-Muqtabis* for his biography of Ziryāb and draws primarily from the *Aḫbār Ziryāb* material, which has important implications for the resulting biography.

Al-Muqtabis, in essence an annalistic history of the Umayyads, gives year-by-year accounts of each ruler in the format typical of this style of historical writing. However, the author also appends material on the personality and courtly life of each prince. The passage on Ziryāb appears within Ibn Ḥayyān's account of the reign of ʿAbd ar-Raḥmān II, following a chapter about the emir's fondness for women, entitled *an-Nisā'* ("Women"). That chapter concludes with a passage of a little more than one printed page in length concerning three female slave singers owned by ʿAbd ar-Raḥmān, named Faḍl, ʿAlam and Qalam, referred to as "the Medinans." This passage will be of interest in §1.2c, once we have established the career of Ziryāb as context.

Ibn Ḥayyān presents substantial material on Ziryāb, covering about 28 printed pages (307-335 of Makkī's 2003 edition). It comprises 12 distinct accounts drawn from a variety of sources. Ziryāb's biography commences under the chapter heading, "Song", and the subheading, "The Account of Ziryāb, Foremost of the Singers in the Lands of al-Andalus". This biography covers a very broad range of topics, beyond Ziryāb's musical talents and contributions. Here we will only summarize the main themes as they relate to the point at hand, namely, how Ibn Ḥayyān's biography of Ziryāb, in its original form before it was edited by al-Maqqarī, reflects significant aspects of the institutions that shaped both his career and the courtly musical culture of ninth-century Cordoba.

1.2a *Ziryāb and his patron*

The first selection comes from one ʿĪsā b. Aḥmad ar-Rāzī[11] and relates that the emir ʿAbd ar-Raḥmān II was very fond of music, to the extent that he kept at least four salaried musicians and singers at court whom he was very close to. These singers were named Abū Yaʿqub al-Muġannī ("the Singer"), "the two Ḥasans" Ḥasan al-Ḥillī and Ḥasan al-Qarawī, and Manṣūr al-Yahūdī ("the Jew"). Prior to Ziryāb's arrival each of these men received ten dinars each lunar month, in addition to regular awards of gifts and clothing.[12] The emir also took advantage of his musician-courtiers in improving the artistry of his private ensemble:

---

[11] Son of the geographer and historian Aḥmad b. Muḥammad ar-Rāzī (d. 344/955), who wrote an influential description of al-Andalus that included some historical information. The elder ar-Rāzī's work has been lost, except for a handful of references in other works, including a lengthy citation in Yāqūt's *Muʿjam al-Buldān*, and a Castilian translation of a Portuguese rendering from the 13th century. See the brief notice in Levi-Provençal's article "al-Rāzī" in the first *Encyclopaedia of Islam*, which alas gives no dates for ʿĪsā.

[12] p. 308.

ضمته ستارته من محسنات قيانه ومبرزات جواريه ، نازعاً عنهن إلى من اصطنعه
من الرجال أئمتهن في الصناعة ...

His musical ensemble included his most excellent female singers and outstanding female slaves. He eschewed them for the men whom he made their models in the craft (of song)...[13]

This account is one of the most significant passages in *al-Muqtabis* for the purpose of placing the career of Ziryāb in its proper social and economic context. Here we see three central elements of the courtly culture surrounding music and musicians in ninth-century Cordoba: the elite patron, the (male) client/musician (مغنٍّ, pl. مغنّون), and the orchestra (ستارة , pl. ستارات) composed of female slaves.[14] The emir's patronage of music and musicians could be substantial, for not only did his musicians receive a stipend, but a number of them received gifts of housing, clothing and other needs as well.

The informal institution of elite patronage of the arts had already had a long history in the Mašriq before the arrival of the Umayyads in al-Andalus. No sources for al-Andalus compare with the depth and breadth of *Kitāb al-Aġānī* of Abū l-Faraj al-Iṣfahānī in the east, but the basic format of the courtly assembly (*majlis*) and the aristocratic patronage that surrounded it resembled in its essential details that described a century later by al-Iṣfahānī in Baghdad. Indeed, the courtly milieu of al-Iṣfahānī's time was built upon a pattern adopted nearly three centuries earlier during the Umayyad caliphate in Damascus, drawing on even earlier Sassanid and Ghassanid practices. The Umayyads brought this same set of courtly social norms west with them after their expulsion from Damascus, and this in turn formed the basis for such practices among aristocrats in al-Andalus. Al-Iṣfahānī illustrates with many examples the competition among composers and musicians for caliphal favor and the rewards in money, clothing and prestige that came with it.[15] Some of the Umayyad and Tā'ifa patrons of al-Andalus created a similarly competitive (if perhaps less opulent) environ-

---

[13] p. 307.

[14] In this passage Ibn Ḥayyān uses both the specific term for female slave singers, قيان (s. قَيْنة), and the more general term for a female household servant, جواري (s. جارية). This latter term appears in similar contexts throughout *al-Muqtabis*, perhaps signifying a distinction between slave musicians and slave singers as such. Probably in Ibn Ḥayyān's time (if not in ʿĪsā's, as well), جارية in such a context indicated a female slave who performed various household duties, of which playing music was one. According to the *Lisān al-ʿArab*, notwithstanding the fact that قَيْنة originally signified a woman who was *adorned* (التزيّن), perhaps by clothing given by men, the basic meaning was "a female slave singer", and that is how it is used universally in classical literature (cf. al-Jāḥiẓ's epistle, *Qiyān*).

[15] Sawa's study of the *Aġānī* (1989) explores in great detail the practices associated with the courtly *majlis* under the Abbasids, developing a coherent and fascinating picture of courtly musical culture as al-Iṣfahānī characterizes it. On these practices as heritage of the Umayyads, see pp. 111-112.

ment for musicians and composers. Taken together, Ibn Ḥayyān and the other early historians present ʿAbd ar-Raḥmān II as the first of the Umayyad emirs to take a serious interest in courtly high culture.

The *sitāra* (lit. "curtain") was an orchestra of women.[16] The name derives from the curtain behind which such an orchestra performed during the *majlis*, when men who were not members of the patron's household were present. The curtain of course was not needed when the master alone was present. This practice remained part of the aristocratic musical milieu as late as the Ṭāʾifa period, and beyond. For example Ribera, and Guettat following him, mention accounts of *sitāra* performances in Seville, some of which indicate that the *sitāra* concept extended beyond the court to the upper ranks of the aristocracy, where such an orchestra might be composed of members of the host's family and would perform (sometimes without the curtain) at social gatherings.[17]

The members of ʿAbd ar-Raḥmān's *sitāra* were slaves, women captives at least some of whom had been trained in music (and other refinements of culture and entertainment), though some probably were more like household servants who also had musical talents. The best of them had been bought for the emir, sometimes for a very high price, in markets as far away as Medina in Arabia.[18] The institution of slavery was an important feature of the economic and cultural life of al-Andalus. *Muḥtasib* manuals yield evidence of markets for domestic servants that shows they provided significant domestic labor for the aristocratic class. The *qayna*, however, was in a category by herself. No scullery maid, she was a highly trained artist, whose service chiefly involved the entertainment of her owner and his friends (entertainment that could lead in some cases to the birth of future princes, as well). Her value was determined by her beauty and finishing, that is to say, her command of both music and poetry, as well as her wit and skill in courtly manners and repartee.[19]

---

[16] On *sitāra*, the courtly orchestra of women, see the entry in Faruqi's *Annotated Glossary*. See also: García Barriuso, p. 43; Guettat (2000, p. 110 n. 19) says that a similar orchestra composed of men was known as *nūbat al-muġannīn*.

[17] Ribera (1922) pp. 58, 59, Guettat (2000) p. 110. Ribera finds recorded in Ibn al-Qūṭiyya that "Otmán, hijo del emir Mohámed [Muḥammad I, son of ʿAbd ar-Raḥmān II], solía reunir en su casa a los literatos de Córdoba, y en esa tertulia se dejaba oír cantar, tras de la citara o cortina, la célebre Bazea, apodada la Imam por ser la mejor cantora de su tiempo." (58)

[18] Ribera (1922, p. 60) relates the story of a slave singer purchased for 3000 gold dinars by a certain Hudayl b. Raṣīn, master of "Santamaría (región de Teruel)," who regarded the woman worth the price, because she possessed an extraordinary voice, was very well educated (in medicine, as well as the refinements of culture) and possessed a refined sense of grace and elegance.

[19] Levi-Provençal (1932) notes the importance of the Jews of 10th-century Cordoba as "businesssmen specialized in the traffic in slaves and luxury items." (38) He also provides material from the *muḥtasib* manuals (pp. 192-193). See also the economic analysis in Ḫāliṣ (1966), Chapter 2. For more contemporary perspectives, see Lachiri (1993) and Cohen (2002).

According to ʿĪsā b. Aḥmad, the emir ʿAbd ar-Raḥmān expected these female singers and musicians to perform the songs created by his cadre of male client-composers. In other words, they often were the means by which a composer's work found expression before the patron, and thus the client's reward (indeed, his continued sustenance) depended upon their talents and skills as musicians. Far from being simply footnotes in the history, these women were of central importance to the development of the music of al-Andalus, and the informal institution of artiste slavery was a keystone which supported the whole structure of courtly music in this period. §1.2c below deals in more detail with this institution as presented by Ibn Ḥayyān.

Further on, Ibn Ḥayyān presents a short passage from Abū Bakr ʿUbāda Ibn Māʾ as-Samāʾ (d. Malaga after 421/1030)[20] which states that the emir ʿAbd ar-Raḥmān set for Ziryāb a stipend of 200 dinars each lunar month. ʿUbāda also notes that three of Ziryāb's sons, ʿUbayd Allāh, Jaʿfar and Yaḥyā also received monthly stipends of 20 dinars each, so that providing for them would not detract from Ziryāb's own earnings (لألا يرزؤوا أباهم مما يرتزقه قلامة).[21] Ibn Ḥayyān later lists the names of Ziryāb's sons,[22] and the three presented by ʿUbāda come second, third and fourth in the list. ʿAbd ar-Raḥmān, who ranks first in the list and was the eldest (according to Ibn Khaldun as well), apparently was also paid the stipend, and so ʿUbāda's account may be defective in this respect.

Ibn Ḥayyān's fourth selection on Ziryāb, from *Kitāb Aḫbār Ziryāb*, is also the longest Ibn Ḥayyān chose to include in *al-Muqtabis*. It presents the musician's life in some detail, including extensive material on his non-musical contributions to high society in Cordoba, all of which forms the basis for al-Maqqarī's biography of Ziryāb. Here, we will delve into only those passages that touch on our main objective.

As elsewhere, the institution of elite patronage figures strongly in the *Aḫbār Ziryāb* material. The passage commences with the musician's proper name and his status as *mawlā* to the Abbasid caliph al-Mahdī (as indicated also by Ibn Khaldun),[23] and then presents the circumstances of Ziryāb's falling out with his master, Isḥāq al-Mawṣilī: Ziryāb exceeded his master's skill in singing and playing but hid this from Isḥāq himself, until the caliph, Hārūn ar-Rašīd, insisted Isḥāq bring him to be heard. He

[20] This poet was author of the lost book, *Ṭabaqāt aš-šuʿarāʾ* ["The Ranks of the Poets"], which Ibn Ḥayyān consulted from a manuscript written in the poet's own hand. (327 and 328) See Granja (1986).

[21] p. 309

[22] p. 325

[23] مولى here may have one of two meanings. If understood as "client," it would suggest that Ziryāb's family converted to Islam in the time of al-Mahdī who served as their patron. This was a principal means by which non-Arab converts could gain access to elite circles. However, given Ziyāb's likely ethnicity, the word in this context probably means "freedman" and indicates that his family were slaves whom the caliph manumitted.

impressed the caliph with his manners, speech and knowledge of singing, and cleverly piqued the caliph's curiosity:

نعم أحسن ما يحينه الناس ، وأكثر ما أحسنه لا يحسنونه مما لا يحسن إلا عنك ولا
يُدّخر إلا لك فإن أذنتَ غنيتك ما لم تسمعه أذن قبلك!

> "Yes, I do well what (other) people do well. But more of what I do well, they do not do well, which will be beautiful only if it is about you, and kept only for you. So if you desire it, I shall sing for you what no ear has heard before you!"[24]

The caliph agreed and offered Ziryāb his master's *ʿūd* to play. Ziryāb asked for his own instrument instead, claiming he could only play his special compositions on the instrument he made himself, whose strings were of special materials. He then sang a song with the line (*basīṭ*)

ياايها الملكُ الميمونُ طائرُه إليك راح جميعُ الناس وابتكروا

> O ye monarch, whose omen-bird is fortunate,
> to you all the people come in evening and morning.[25]

Powerfully moved by the song, the caliph commanded that Isḥāq provide for the young singer until he called him to him again. This turn of events stirred envy in Isḥāq, and afterwards he offered Ziryāb a choice: either leave Baghdad immediately, with Isḥāq's help, and never return; or stay and face the wrath of his former teacher. Ziryāb took the first choice immediately and fled the city. When the caliph requested another performance from Ziryāb, Isḥāq told him that his student was mad and claimed that *jinn* communicate with him. He left, said Isḥāq, and no one knew his whereabouts. Ar-Rašīd was relieved to be rid of the insane Ziryāb, and in this way his name was forgotten in the Middle East, according to *Aḫbār Ziryāb*.

However, again according to *Aḫbār Ziryāb*, some of Ziryāb's compositions reached al-Ḥakam in al-Andalus, and he sent for the musician. Ziryāb hastened to al-Andalus with his belongings and dependents, but when he arrived in al-Jazīra al-Ḫuḍarā', he learned of al-Ḥakam's death. Manṣūr al-Yahūdī, al-Ḥakam's messenger, described ʿAbd ar-Raḥmān's generosity and refinement, so Ziryāb wrote to the new emir, citing his father's promise, and seeking his protection (إيواءه إلى ظلّه). Manṣūr

[24] p. 310
[25] p. 311

brought the letter to the emir, who was pleased receive the musician. He ordered the governor of Algeciras to accompany the singer to the next town, and each local official likewise, until Ziryāb arrived in Cordoba in the month of *muḥarram* in the year 207/822. The emir ordered a splendid welcome for Ziryāb to the city, and gave him a finely appointed house with its stores of food and supplies.

After three days of rest, Ziryāb was summoned to meet the emir. They conversed at length, and the emir was impressed with Ziryāb's manners and the breadth of his knowledge in many fields. The emir "honored him by sharing his meal with him and his eldest sons" (فشرّفه بالأكل معه هو وأكابر ولده). Before they left, the emir lavished Ziryāb and his sons with gifts, including 1000 dinars.[26]

Thus the *Aḫbār Ziryāb* material recounts Ziryāb's search for patronage, in a form that has become enshrined in the standard narrative. All the key elements are present: Ziryāb's tutelage by and falling out with Isḥāq al-Mawṣilī at the Abbasid court in Baghdad, his arrival in al-Andalus at the beginning of the reign of ʿAbd al-Raḥmān II, and his acceptance by the latter as a client. As I have written elsewhere,[27] there are serious problems with the chronology of this account, which in turn undermine much of this version of the story. For the moment, what matters is the importance of aristocratic patronage to one such as Ziryāb – a fact simply taken for granted in the *aḫbār Ziryāb* account.

Aḫbār Ziryāb gives further, lavish details about the great favor shown to Ziryāb by his patron. It is said he received a monthly income of 200 dinars, and each of his *four* sons (not three, as ʿUbāda would have it) received 20 dinars a month as well. In addition, *Aḫbār Ziryāb* states that "it is generally known" (من المعروف العام) that Ziryāb received gifts totaling 3000 dinars each year: a thousand for each Muslim ʿĪd, and 500 for each *mahrajān* ("festival," presumably meaning one of the Christian holy days, possibly Easter) and New Year celebration. Moreover, he received 300 measures each of various kinds of foodstuffs from the region around Cordoba each lunar year, a sum *Aḫbār Ziryāb* reckons as being worth 40,000 dinars. Even more, the emir was very fond of Ziryāb (فأحبّه جدا شديدا) (314), and loved to converse with him on many subjects at all hours, according to *Aḫbār Ziryāb*. He even installed a special door beneath his palace near Ziryāb's house, so that the musician could come and go discreetly. In addition to

[26] p. 314. It seems that at least four of Ziryāb's sons made the voyage with him to al-Andalus: ʿAbd ar-Raḥmān, Jaʿfar, ʿUbayd Allāh and Yaḥyā. This is consistent with Ziryāb having eight sons, the youngest being Ḥasan, as Ibn Ḥayyān indicates. (Note Ziryāb's *kunya*, Abū l-Ḥasan: does this reflect the name of his youngest, instead of his eldest son, or was there an older son who perhaps died before Ziyrāb's arrival in al-Andalus?). At least three of his sons were old enough to eat with the adults at the time Ziryāb arrived in al-Andalus.

[27] Davila (2009).

private sessions with the prince, Ziryāb participated in drinking and music sessions with his patron in the *majlis*: ... فبدأ بمجالسته على النبيذ وسماع غناءه.[28] (Material supplied by Ibn al-Faraḍī [see below §1.2d] later shows Ziryāb accompanying his patron on a hunting trip.)

We see here Ziryāb assuming the role of *nadīm* ("boon companion") to the emir, though this particular term does not appear in Ibn Ḥayyān's biography of him. *Nadāma* (*nadīm*-friendship) was an intimate, male friendship between patron and client, that included the sharing of wine, song, conversation, games and other kinds of entertainment. The selections from *Aḫbār Ziryāb* in *al-Muqtabis* portray the prince and the musician as unusually close, compared to other relationships at court, indicating that ʿAbd ar-Raḥmān preferred him over his other musician courtiers.

Another feature of *Aḫbār Ziryāb* is the extent of ʿAbd ar-Raḥmān's generosity in supporting not only Ziryāb, but also his elder sons. In this the emir evidently wanted to spare his client from distractions or financial worries. Yet, if ʿĪsā b. Aḥmad ar-Rāzī's account of the court musicians prior to Ziryāb is correct, Ziryāb's sons received a stipend twice that of the court musicians! And Ziryāb's own monthly salary came to 20 times that of the other musicians at the emir's court, in addition to huge annuities granted at festivals. If taken at face value, these figures represented a phenomenal amount of money in the context of the time, particularly when we consider that the emir gave control of the produce of certain farms in the area to Ziryāb, in effect making the musician a landowner and vaulting him into the aristocracy of Cordoba. It is hard to imagine something like this happening without inspiring some resentment, if not outright resistance, among the other musicians or the men with an eye on the prince's purse.

And indeed, *Aḫbār Ziryāb* says that jealous voices were raised at the time:

> وقد صرّح الفقيه عبد الملك بن حبيب بغبْط زرياب بجزيل حباء الأمير عبد الرحمن له عند إطرائه إياه وتمناه لنفسه ثواباً على فضل جدّه هو في صناعته ، فقال أبياته المشهور :

> The jurist ʿAbd al-Malik b. Ḥabīb [d. 238/852] spoke openly about the prosperity of Ziryāb because of the size of the gifts given him by the emir ʿAbd ar-Raḥmān in praising him, for he wanted it for himself as a reward for the excellence of his efforts in his profession. And so he spoke these famous lines:

---

[28] p. 315

Three verses in the meter *sarīʿ*[29] follow:

صلاح أمري والذي أبتغي   هَيْنٌ على الرحمان في قُدرتهْ
ألفٌ من الصفر وأقلل   بهالعالم أرْزَى[30] على بغيته
زرياب قد يأخذها قَفلة   وصنعتي أشرف من صنعته

My proper state and what I desire
are no difficulty for the Merciful, in his power.
A thousand pieces of gold, how little it is
for a scholar who blames his own pleasure.
Ziryāb may take them as a one-time gift
but my profession is more honorable than his![31]

1.2b *Ziryāb as* ẓarīf

Following the discussion of the musician's relationship with his patron, Ibn Ḥayyān/ *Aḫbār Ziryāb* offers an account of his brilliance as a composer. We will take this passage up in the next section, but after this, the historian continues with material from *Aḫbār Ziryāb* featuring an account of Ziryāb's musical and cultural innovations. This long passage describes the musician as a master of taste and refinement. In this he fits well the description of a *ẓarīf*, that is, an aesthete. More than simply a musician or literatus, the *ẓarīf* embodied all that was elegant, tasteful and sophisticated in society.

Aḫbār Ziryāb attributes to Ziryāb an astonishing variety of contributions to Cordoban high society: In music, he is said to have added a fifth string to the *ʿūd*, but Ibn Ḥayyān goes further in describing the entire system of *ʿūd* cordature and its relationships to the body humors, implying that Ziryāb was responsible for introducing these ideas to al-Andalus.[32] Ziryāb is also said to have known 10,000 songs, and to have mastered various sciences (including astrology), to the extent that his oeuvre "was to those learning (music) as geometry was to philosophy, or grammar to rhetoric" (غناء

[29] Makkī (v1, p. 534, n. 37) notes that these verses are found in az-Zubaydī's *Ṭabaqāt al-luġawiyīn*, pp. 260-261.

[30] This construction / أرْزَى / appears in the manuscript, as well as in az-Zubaydī's version (see endnote 21). I read it here as / أزْرَى /.

[31] p. 315

[32] Although other musicians have also been credited with devising this fifth cord (along with its associations), Ziryāb certainly would have been aware of the whole system, which was current in Baghdad at the time. The philosopher famous for writing it down, Yaʿqūb al-Kindī, who died in -874, was a younger contemporary of both Ziryāb and Isḥāq. Guettat (2000, pp. 60-61 and especially Chapter 4) provides a very thorough discussion of al-Kindī's contributions to musical theory.

زرياب للمتعلمين كالهندسة للفلسفة وكاللحو للبلاغة).[33] Also from *Aḫbār Ziryāb*'s enumeration of Ziryāb's innovations comes a much-discussed passage that suggests to some a primitive ancestor of today's North African *nūba*.[34]

This section from *Aḫbār Ziryāb* also extols his exemplary personal qualities and his contributions to hairstyles, hygiene, the culinary arts and clothing fashions. All these innovations allegedly became as popular among the cognoscenti as Ziryāb's musical talents were among musicians. And it concludes with a thorough description of Ziryāb's eight sons' and two daughters' talents and their places in Cordoban society in the next generation.

Broadly speaking, this extended passage (deriving mostly from *Kitāb Aḫbār Ziryāb* but occasionally supplemented and amplified with short insertions from other sources, such as ʿUbāda Ibn Māʾ as-Samāʾ) serves to cast a halo around the figure of Ziryāb. Although this material contributes little to the larger aim of this chapter, it is significant because it lies at the root of the modern standard narrative of the history of *al-Āla*. The lionization of Ziryāb has become part of the mythos of the tradition, to the extent that its historical foundations have rarely been questioned, even by the most careful historians. The fact is that all the most significant contributions and innovations commonly attributed to Ziryāb come from this one passage in *al-Muqtabis* – even worse, from this passage as edited and presented by al-Maqqarī half a millennium later. It is appropriate to wonder, then, how this glowing (but rather one-dimensional) image of the great musician-composer compares with material from other sources, and in light of that, to speculate on its historiographical significance. These questions we will take up near the end of this chapter.

1.2c *Ziryāb and the singing slaves*

In the midst of the previously discussed selection from *Aḫbār Ziryāb* we find a very interesting passage on Ziryāb's fame as a brilliant composer. Comparing this with a later passage (also from *Aḫbār Ziryāb*) opens a window on the importance of artiste slavery to the production of elite music in Ziryāb's era.

Aḫbār Ziryāb indicates that Ziryāb's compositional ability excelled in

حجابه ... الكشف لما غُمّ على المتقدمين من دقائقه بمنزلة لا يفوقه فيها احد من
اهل صنعته [ف] يخبطون عشواء فيما كُشف له هو

[33] p. 315

[34] This problematic passage is discussed in detail with respect to the history of the *nūba* in the Introduction, §4.

revealing details obscured to those who came before his time, in a station not surpassed by any of his peers in the craft, for they trample in a darkness whose veil was lifted for him.[35]

What Ziryāb created thus was handed down from one fine musician to the next, for he was unparalleled in the art of composition. He was so brilliant, in fact, that

ذُكر عنه أن الجن كانت تعلّمه كل ليلة ما بين نوبة إلى صوت واحد فكان يهب من نومه سريعا فيدعو بجاريتيه المحسنتين ، غزلان وهُنيدة ، تأخذان عوديهما ويأخذ هو عوده فيطارحهما ما لُقن في ليلته ، ويكتب لهما الشعر ، ثم يعود عخلا إلى مضجعه . فإذا استوى قيامه بالغداة لم يذكر الشعر ولا لحنه ولا يعرف من أنساه ذلك لسكره ، إذ لم يكن يتلقف ذلك إلا في غمرته ، فتخبره قينتاه تانك بما يطرحهما منه ، فيأمرهما تغنياه إياه فإذا فعلتا ادّكر الخبر ، فأخذ عوده فثقف صنعة الصوت وكمّل لهما ما قصرتا فيه من علمه ، فكانتا تسميان ماسكتي زرياب . وقد دخلتا بعده إلى القصر لتعليم الجواري ، فأشاعتا ثَم بهذا الحديث عن مولاهما بما كان يعتريه من ذلك المناجيات وصححتاه عنه .

وهذا شبيه بما يحمل عن إبراهيم الموصلي في لحنه البديع المعروف بالماخوري ، من أن الجن طارحته إياه ، فطار في الناس يومئذ مطاره حتى قال فيه الشاعر :

لا جزى الله الموصلي أبا إســـ حاق خيرا عنّا ولا إحسانا
جاءنا مرْسلا بوحي من الشيـــ طان أغلى به علينا القيانا

It was said of him that the *jinn* used to teach him every night one *ṣawt* from a *nawba*.[36] He used to rise quickly from sleep and call

[35] p. 316

[36] The two terms here, *ṣawt* and *nawba*, are problematic and have been the subject of some discussion. Part of this debate is dealt with in the Introduction §4, concerning the meaning of the term *nawba* (or *nūba*, in Moroccan usage) and its contents in 13th-century al-Andalus according to at-Tīfāšī. One might assume in this case that, as in at-Tīfāšī's time, *ṣawt* was one component of Ziryāb's *nawba*, a sung composition without *istihlāl* (an instrumental prelude that characterized the other song form, the *našīd*). In any case this passage does raise questions about at-Tīfāšī's data, given that it derives from a source nearly two centuries closer to Ziryāb. Does Ibn Ḥayyān imply here that the *jinn* taught Ziryāb *ṣawt* because it was the only component of a *nawba* in Ziryāb's time? Or is *nawba* used here in a more generic sense to mean a musician's "turn" to perform, as al-Iṣfahānī used the term in the *Kitāb al-Aġānī*? (Perhaps the *jinn* know only songs and no instrumental passages?) This passage and its possible

his two excellent female slave musicians,[37] Ġizlān and Hunayda, who took up their *ʿūd*s, and he took his. Then he communicated to them what was taught in his sleep, and he wrote the poetry for them. Then he hastened back to his bed. And when he arose in the morning, he remembered neither poem nor melody, nor did he know who made him forget that because of his stupefied state, since he was only grasping (the music) in his inebriation. Those female singers of his[38] informed him of what he had communicated to them, and he ordered them to sing it for him, and when they did that, he memorized the information. Then he took his *ʿūd* and corrected the composition of the *ṣawt*, and completed for them what they had missed in it. And so they were called "Ziryāb's two (song-) holders".[39] Afterwards, they went into the palace to teach (it to) the female slave musicians[40] (there), and thus they made this information about their master known there, these communications which he was revealing, and verified it about him.

This is like what is handed down about Ibrāhīm al-Mawṣilī[41] concerning his marvelous tune known as "*al-Māḫūrī*" ("The Brothel Song"), which is that the *jinn* communicated it to him. This story spread among the people when it was made known, to the point that a poet[42] said of him:

May Allāh not reward al-Mawṣilī, Abū
Isḥāq, with good from us, nor grace.
He came to us as a messenger with a revelation from Satan
by which he raises the value of the singing girls[43] to us.[44]

This passage usually attracts attention because of Ziryāb's association with *jinn*, though it is rarely mentioned that such claims about other musicians were not unknown. (Recall as well that earlier in the *Aḫbār Ziryāb* material, Isḥāq al-Mawṣilī uses the accusation of communicating with the *jinn* to defame Ziryāb before Hārūn ar-Rašīd.) More importantly, this passage underscores the role of female slave singers in the

implications have not yet entered the discussion on the *nawba* / *nūba* and its history.

[37] Here, *al-Muqtabis* uses *jāriyatayni*, not *qaynatayni*, suggesting musicians (not necessarily singers) and possibly women who had other duties than just music.

[38] Here, *qaynāhu*, the dual of *qayna*.

[39] *māsikatay* (in construct), lit. "two (f) who hold tight (to something)".

[40] *al-jawārī*

[41] The famous court musician of Baghdad and father of Isḥāq, who was Ziryāb's teacher.

[42] Abū ʿUyayna b. Muḥammad b. Abī ʿUyayna al-Muhlibī, who is known from the *Aġānī*. See Makki p. 534 n.39.

[43] القيان

[44] pp. 361-317

development of the music of al-Andalus, especially their participation in the composition process. Leaving aside the supernatural aspects of this story, these women certainly played an important role in assisting composers who could afford to keep them. This is shown also in the almost casual treatment they receive in the verses about Ibrāhīm al-Mawṣilī (in which they serve to emphasize the dismissive view expressed in the poem). That artiste slaves were active participants in the composition process has the ring of truth to it, the sense that it represents a casually observed fact, rather than an imaginative detail.

Later, another section on the artiste slaves associated with Ziryāb follows, also deriving from *Aḫbār Ziryāb*.

It begins with three names: Ġizlān and Hunayda ("Amorous" and "Little Hind", identified as before as Ziryāb's "song-holders"), and ʿUtba ("Good Pleasure"), described as their friend. The three of them together were known as the Medinans because they specialized in the "Medinese trilling" (هزج المدني) style of singing, but the narrator says he does not know if Ziryāb specialized them in this, and that was why they were known this way, or if they were brought from Medina to the emir and so were connected to that city for that reason.[45] A list of 34 female singers follows, among them colorful names like Nūr ("Light"), ʿIṭr ("Perfume"), Sabā ("Sheba"), Ṣubḥ ("Morning"), Rayyān ("Fragrance"), Ṭarūb ("Merry") and Amal ("Hope"). ʿĀj ("Ivory") is said to have been given by Ziryāb to the *wazīr* Hāšim b. ʿAbd al-ʿAzīz, husband of Ziryāb's daughter, Ḥamdūna. She was a main transmitter of Ziryāb's work.

The 35th singer, Šanīf ("Delightful"), was a *jāriya* who belonged to Ziryāb and outlived him. Her story deserves close attention:

فلما اضطرب المغنون في غنائه واختلفوا في كثير منه ، احتاجوا إليها واقتبسوا
منها وسمعوها فوجدوها أقدم طريقة فيه وأصح نقلا له ، فسمّوها الإمام وانثالوا
على الأخذ منها ، ورجعوا فيما أشكل عليهم إليها ...

> So when the singers became unsure of (how to sing) his songs, and disagreed on many of them, they had recourse to her. They sought knowledge from her, listened to her and found her more advanced in style and sounder as a transmitter for it. So they

[45] The two main schools of singing in the Arab world were that of Medina in Arabia and that of Baghdad, with Baṣra also a significant source of *qiyān*. Ziryāb represented Baghdad, of course, so one would not expect to find him training singers in a Medinan style of singing. The Medina school was influential, partly because so many female slave singers were trained there.

> called her the Imām, and they flocked to learn from her and deferred to her in what was unclear to them.[46]

This passage shows that Ziryāb's songs survived him and continued to be performed more or less faithfully for a generation or more afterwards. (It also implies that other styles of singing existed and competed with Ziryāb's for the patron's ear.)

After the passing of Ziryāb's sons, three *jawārī* named Maṣābīḥ ("Lamps"), Ġulām ("Servant") and Waṣīf ("Servant") belonging to one Ibn Qalqal, taught many of the best female slave singers (أخذ كثير من مجودة القيان عنهن).[47]

These three passages clearly indicate the prominence of the *jāriya* / *qayna* in the elite musical arts of the era. Šanīf played a very important role in perpetuating Ziryāb's work long after his death, being regarded as the most reliable reference for his songs. Likewise, ʿĀj was also an important figure in the perpetuation of Ziryāb's legacy. The latter passage suggests that Ibn Qalqal's three *jawārī* also belonged to the Ziryāb school, and so they, too preserved the master's oeuvre. Given the absence of practical musical notation at this time, the living memory of an oral transmitter was essential for the survival of a composer's work.

Ibn Ḥayyān / *Aḫbār Ziryāb* next discusses the male composers whom Ziryāb taught, and who abandoned their own styles when they heard his work. It is strikingly brief compared with the accounts of the women. Only three names are mentioned, all of them mentioned before: the "two Ḥasans" and Manṣūr al-Yahūdī. Of the three, only Manṣūr seems to have distinguished himself in Ziryāb's style.

Ibn Ḥayyān summarizes by saying that these are the singers, men and women, who distinguished themselves by carrying on the style of Ziryāb (الحاملين لطريقة زرياب) after his death. Then an account taken from ʿUbāda Ibn Māʾ as-Samāʾ relates that the first of those who came to al-Andalus with the music of the Middle East were the two male singers ʿAllūn and Zirqūn in the time of ʿAbd ar-Raḥmān's father, al-Ḥakam. They were excellent singers, he says, but their singing was no longer influential after Ziryāb's arrival.

Thus far, Ibn Ḥayyān's account of Ziryāb has mentioned six men (Abū Yaʿqūb, the "two Ḥasans," Manṣūr al-Yahūdī and the two singers before Ziryāb, ʿAllūn and Zirqūn) as outstanding singers during or after Ziryāb's era, apart from his own sons. If we include the six men in Ziryāb's family (Ziryāb, plus five of his eight sons), the tally of outstanding male singers rises to twelve.

---

[46] p. 329

[47] p. 329

By comparison, the number of female singers mentioned for this era is more than three times as large, all but one of them artiste slaves. In addition to Ziryāb's elder daughter, Ḥamdūna (the only freewoman singer mentioned), we find Ziryāb's two song-holders (Ġizlān and Hunayda), their companion ʿUtba, Šanīf (the long-lived master-teacher of his school), ʿĀj (Ziryāb's transmitter who was owned by Ḥamdūna's husband), Ibn Qalqal's three singers (Maṣābīḥ, Ġulām and Waṣīf) who also preserved his work, and more than 30 others known only by their names (Nūr, Sabā and the others). Altogether nearly 40 women are said to have played a role in the musical culture of Cordoba from the arrival of Ziryāb through the following generation, several of these women being at least as important to the development and preservation of Ziryāb's music as were his male colleagues and emulators, if not more so.

In addition, there is Ibn Ḥayyān's account of the three *qiyān* mentioned earlier, which precedes his account of Ziryāb. As reported by Muʿāwiya b. Hišām aš-Šabīnsī,[48] their names were Faḍl ("Grace"), ʿAlam ("Embroidered Hem") and Qalam ("Reed-Pen"). All three singers, in this order, were ʿAbd ar-Raḥmān's favorites, according to aš-Šabīnsī, and all three were trained in Medina. Faḍl, from Baghdad, had been owned by one of Hārūn ar-Rašīd's daughters but completed her training in Medina,[49] while Qalam was from Iberia but also was sent to Medina to be trained in music.[50] Faḍl bore the emir his youngest son, Abū l-Qāsim ʿUmar b. ʿAbd ar-Raḥmān. Because these three singers sang in the Medinan style, they were known in their time as the "Medinans", and the emir housed them in a special pavilion in his palace that came to be known as Dār al-Madaniyyāt ("the House of the Medinans").[51]

---

[48] This is Muʿāwiya b. Hišām b. Muḥammad b. Hišām aš-Šabīnsī. His dates are uncertain, but his father is known to have died in 300/912. A direct descendant from the Umayyad emir Hišām I (r.168/788 - 176/796), he was a noted historian and literatus during the reign of the seventh Umayyad emir of Cordoba, ʿAbd Allāh b. Muḥammad (grandson of Ziryāb's patron). His work survives only in citations by other historians, most significantly in *al-Muqtabis*. See entry #1741 in the *Takmīla* of Ibn al-Abbār (1955-56, v. 2 p. 692), *Una Crónica...* (1950, pp. 20-21), de la Granja (1970, p. 214) and Marín (1988, pp. 92, 151).

[49] If Ibn Ḥayyān is correct about this, Faḍl represents another link between the Abbāsid court of ar-Rašīd and Umayyad Cordoba, one that has largely been overlooked by modern authors.

[50] She was a Latin-speaker (رومية) from among captives taken from بَشْكُنْس – the land of the Basques (that is, the Kingdom of Pamplona, which since Roman times had featured a largely Basque-Iberian population ruled by a Latin-speaking aristocracy). *Nafḥ...* v. 3 p. 140.

[51] If *Aḫbār Ziryāb* as quoted in *al-Muqtabis* is to believed, there were two triads of artiste slaves bearing this appellation "the Medinans": Ġizlān, Hunayda and ʿUtba were so named somewhat later, though without reference to a special home for them in the palace – indeed, the first two clearly belonged to Ziryāb, as the *jinn*-and-*jawārī* story indicates. This may well be a confusion on Aslam's part, because it seems illogical that Ziryāb, whose career was founded partly on bringing the Baghdadi musical style to Cordoba, would have taught his slave-students a competing singing style. Moreover, aš-Šabīnsī enjoyed a high reputation as historian; simply put, Aslam did not.

After ʿUbayda's discussion of ʿAllūn and Zirqūn, three more *qiyān* appear in a passage signaled by *qālū* ("they said" – indicating that Ibn Ḥayyān incorporated material from several sources). Muḫtāla, Muḫāriq and Muʿallila ("Proud," "Unusual, Extraordinary" and "Entertaining", all names found among the 30-odd women in the group mentioned earlier) were excellent singers who also taught other female slaves in the emir's palace. ʿAbd ar-Raḥmān gave them as a gift to Ziryāb after he used nine songs they had just performed to demonstrate his own skill and knowledge of different singing styles.

The significance of these portions of *al-Muqtabis* should not be underestimated. Little of Ibn Ḥayyān's material on the artiste slaves found its way into *Nafḥ aṭ-ṭīb*, a fact which has tended to reduce their presence in the standard narrative. While it is true that the bulk of this material derives from one source – *Kitāb Aḫbār Ziryāb*, about which we will have more to say later – nevertheless, the numbers of individuals involved, and the nature of the stories reported about them, strongly suggest that the institution of artiste slavery was not merely a secondary curiosity but was almost as central to the production of elite music as the institution of patronage itself.

If it seems peculiar to compare this particular kind of slavery (which would seem after all to be mainly a function of the patron's taste in music) with the more obviously economic (and therefore, apparently more fundamental) system of patron-client relations, we should keep two points in mind. First, slavery was itself a significant part of the larger economy of Islamic Spain, artiste slavery being just one small but expensive subset of that larger institution that was deeply implicated in the production of high culture and by no means limited to ninth-century Cordoba. A more central point, however, is that every economic system is conditioned by its cultural and social frameworks. Elite patronage may look *structurally* similar in its fundamentals from one place to another and from one era to another, but the details of its content, its form, always reflects local social values, mores and tastes. Moreover, the people who participate in any given patronage system rarely if ever question the seemingly "natural" character of the details of that system – any more than most people in the modern world reflect upon the culturally constructed value systems that lie behind market economies. Artiste slavery, which seems to modern sensibilities to be a time-bound curiosity, would have seemed at the time to be simply a natural component of the larger taken-for-granted elite cultural system, including the patronage that sustained male artists like Ziryāb.

1.2d *Ziryāb and life at the court of ʿAbd ar-Raḥmān II*

Ibn Ḥayyān concludes his chapter on Ziryāb and his music with an account taken from *Ṭabaqāt al-udabāʾ bi-Qurṭuba* ("The Ranks of the Literati of Cordoba") by Ibn al-Faraḍī (351/962-403/1013), and he follows this with a chapter on other leading lights at the court of ʿAbd ar-Raḥmān II. Taken together these sections allow us to construct a more elaborate picture of how the patronage system shaped the social life of an artist like Ziryāb.

Ibn al-Faraḍī describes the troubles between Ziryāb and the poet, ʿAbd Allāh b. aš-Šamir b. Namīr. Ibn aš-Šamir had a strong fondness for Ziryāb (كان كثيرة التولع بأبي الحسن زرياب),[52] to the point that he could not stop praising him and telling stories about him. When Ziryāb complained to the emir, he imprisoned the poet, promising not to release him except at Ziryāb's request. Eventually a friend intervened, asking Ziryāb to release the young man, and Ziryāb obliged. Later, during a hunting trip with the emir in search of magpies, the emir despaired of finding any prey and asked whether anyone had seen one. Ibn aš-Šamir rode forward and told the prince of one quite nearby. When asked where, the poet said

زرياب يطلي استه وابطيه بقليل شرار فيجيء عقيفا لا تنكره

> "Ziryāb: for he daubs his ass and armpits with a bit of curd[53] and comes like a magpie, which you cannot mistake!"

The emir burst out laughing at this bon mot, praised the poet, and asked Ziryāb for his opinion of him. Ziryāb replied:

هو ما قاله سيدنا ، وأنا أشهد الله ومن حضرنا ألا أعدد عليه شيئا ، فليقل ما بدا له
وساما فيما بعد على الاستصحاب وحسن المعاشرة .

> "It is as our master said. I swear by Allāh, and all those present, that I do not reckon anything against him, so let him say what he pleases."[54]

[52] p. 332
[53] The word here, شرار is problematic. Makkī suggests that it is a miscopy from شيرار ("congealed milk"), which at least has the virtue of being white, which is what is implied here.
[54] p. 333

Ibn Ḥayyān ends by adding that the two agreed to be friends and good companions afterwards.

Mutual satirizing may well have been just banter and not taken seriously. For after three poetic insertions relating to the two men (deriving from Ibn al-Faraḍī) Ibn Ḥayyān offers a passage from ʿĪsa Ibn Aḥmad ar-Rāzī that portrays the two boon companions of ʿAbd ar-Raḥmān as good friends who enjoyed one another's company. ʿĪsa Ibn Aḥmad allows that Ibn aš-Šamir's irrepressible nature created problems, for though he was of good character, he could not refrain from telling amusing stories about people in the company of the emir, which sometimes crossed the line of good taste.

The following chapter, about the emir ʿAbd ar-Raḥmān's entourage at court (entitled *Ḏikr al-julasāʾ*, "Mentioning the Courtiers"), includes the poets and other literati. Ziryāb figures in two of these accounts. The first, regarding Ibn aš-Šamir, relates that Ziryāb set to music a number of the poet's love poems and praise poems dedicated to their patron.[55] Ibn Ḥayyān's account of the poet Abū ʿUthmān ʿUbayd Allāh Ibn Qarlumān features an episode in which the poet improvises upon a song Ziryāb is singing, showing that others besides the famous musician earned praise and rewards in the *majlis* of ʿAbd ar-Raḥmān. (The source for this account is Ibn al-Qūṭiyya, and we shall examine it in §1.3 below.)

The sometimes vivid images Ibn Ḥayyān presents of the courtly life surrounding the emir ʿAbd ar-Raḥmān II with which he concludes his account of Ziryāb, offer us some insight into the norms surrounding the patronage system which made Ziryāb's career possible. The anthologist especially emphasizes Ziryāb's social and intellectual refinement. The ability to make stimulating conversation was a highly valued skill, quite apart from an individual's specialized talent in music or poetry. At the same time, the emir enjoyed a good wit as well, while Ziryāb comes across as somewhat humorless and unmoved by jokes (at least those told at his expense). At a minimum, however, he was gracious in such situations.

We may note here, as well, that this latter, somewhat less celebratory rendering of Ziryāb comes not from Aslam's *Aḫbār Ziryāb*, but from Ibn al-Faraḍī, a point that will take on some significance when we take up al-Maqqarī's *Nafḥ aṭ-ṭīb* in §1.4. The contrasting views Ibn Ḥayyān presents of the relationships between Ziryāb and Ibn aš-Šamir, and between Ziryāb and Ibn Qarlumān, suggest at least that, whatever his contributions to aristocratic culture in Cordoba of the 9th century may have been, he certainly was not the only memorable figure at the emir's court; and whatever influence he may have had, he did not always have the last word.

---

[55] p. 337

1.3 *Ibn al-Qūṭiyya and Ibn ʿAbd Rabbih*

Two sources for Ziryāb that fall earlier than Ibn Ḥayyān contain fragmentary but important accounts of the famous musician. The timeline in Figure 2.1 shows Abū ʿUmar Aḥmad b. Muḥammad Ibn ʿAbd Rabbih and Abū Bakr Muḥammad b. ʿUmar Ibn al-Qūṭiyya were rough contemporaries living in Cordoba approximately a century after Ziryāb.

Ibn al-Qūṭiyya[56] was best known in his time as a poet, lexicographer and grammarian. His historical work, *Ta'rīḫ iftitāḥ al-Andalus* (The History of the Conquest of al-Andalus) comprises a collection of narratives dictated in a somewhat disorganized way to one of his students. As the oldest surviving historical work from al-Andalus, it has the significance of preserving for us accounts and perspectives not found anywhere else, and in particular, two brief stories involving Ziryāb, both of which appear in the chapter entitled *Min aḫbār ʿAbd ar-Raḥmān b. al-Ḥakam*. The chapter begins (p. 75) with a passage concerning ʿAbd ar-Raḥmān's appreciation of the arts and letters, and follows with an enumeration of a series of men the emir appointed and removed as *qāḍī* (judge). Ziryāb appears next in a seemingly unrelated story. The passage deserves quoting in full:

وكان أخص الناس بعبد الرحمان من أهل الأدب عبيدُ الله بن قرلمان ابن [sic] بدر الداخل . وغنّى زرياب عنده يوماً وعبيد الله حاضر أبيات العباس ابن [*sic*] الأحنف :

(الكامل)

قالت ظلوم سمِيّةُ الظُلم   ما لي رأيتُك ناحلَ الجسمِ
يا من ومى قلبي فأقصده   أنت العليم بموقع السهمِ

فقال عبد الرحمان : إن البيت الثاني منقطعٌ من الأول غير متّصل به وأوجب أن يكون بينهما بيتٌ يتصل به المعنى ، فقال عبيد الله بن قرلمان بديهةً :

قالت ظلوم سمِيّةُ الظُلم   ما لي رأيتُك ناحلَ الجسمِ

---

[56] Lit. "Son of the Gothic woman," a reference to one of his ancestors, who married the daughter of the next-to-last Visigoth king in Iberia. Fierro (1989) offers a study of his career and the propagation of the *Iftitāḥ*; James (2009) provides an English translation and commentary on Ibn al-Qūṭīyya's place in Cordobn society.

فأجبتُها والدمعُ منحدرٌ مثل الجُمان جريمن النظمِ
يا من ومى قلبي فأقصده أنت العليم بموقع السهمِ

فسرّ بذلك عبد الرحمان وحباه وكساه .

ʿUbayd Allāh Ibn Qarlumān b. Badr ad-Dāḫil was the member of the literati closest to ʿAbd ar-Raḥmān. One day, when Ibn Qarlumān was present, Ziryāb sang the verses of al-ʿAbbās Ibn al-Aḥnaf[57]:

Said Ẓalūm ["tyrant"], the one named after injustice:
Why do I see you wasting away?
O you who shot at my heart, and aimed at it,
you know well the place to hit with an arrow.

Then ʿAbd ar-Raḥmān said: But the second line is disconnected from the first, without any link to it. There has to be a line between the two of them by which the meaning connects. So ʿUbayd Allāh Ibn Qarlumān said, improvising:

Said Ẓalūm, the one named after injustice:
Why do I see you wasting away?
I replied to her with tears descending
like silver beads falling off a necklace:
O you who shot at my heart, and aimed at it,
you know well the place to hit with an arrow.

ʿAbd ar-Raḥmān was pleased with this and rewarded him with money and clothes.[58]

Ziryāb here seems almost irrelevant to the story. The musician could be anyone. This is hardly the erudite Ziryāb we met in *al-Muqtabis*, who knew 9000 songs, could converse on a host of subjects, and who had a door to the palace for his own use. Indeed, the relationship between the musician and the emir does not appear particularly close in this account. Nothing indicates Ziryāb's favor by the prince, nor that he was the greatest musician of his time. The emphasis is rather upon Ibn Qarlumān, instead, who is introduced as the leading literary figure at court.

[57] ʿAbbās Ibn al-Aḥnaf (b. 133/750, d. after193/808), Iraqi poet and a favorite of Hārūn ar-Rašīd, was also connected to the Barmakid aristocracy. He was noted for *ġazal* only. The two verses are found in *Dīwān al-ʿAbbās b. Aḥnaf* (1978 reprint) ed. Karam al-Bustānī, Beirut. The interpolated verse in the next passage does not appear in the *Dīwān*, nor in other sources for this poet.
[58] p. 76

An expanded version of this story from Ibn al-Qūṭiyya reappears a century later in the chapter of *al-Muqtabis* following "Song," wherein Ibn Ḥayyān relates stories of various figures at the court of ʿAbd ar-Raḥmān II, including Ibn Qarlumān.[59] Based on material from ʿĪsā Ibn Aḥmad ar-Rāzī and ʿUbāda Ibn Māʾ as-Samāʾ, Ibn Ḥayyān reports on pages 344 and 345 of *al-Muqtabis* that his full name was *Abū ʿUṯmān* ʿUbayd Allāh b. Qarlumān b. Badr ad-Dāḫil. His father, Qarlumān, had been a client (مولى) of ʿAbd ar-Raḥmān I (r. 138/756-171/788) and served as his falconer. He fled Damascus with his patron (hence his epithet, which he shared with his patron: *ad-Dāḫil*, "the one who entered (al-Andalus)"), and served him in Cordoba. Ibn Ḥayyān tells us that ʿUbayd Allāh Ibn Qarlumān knew his father's patron and that he died an old man in the year 233/847-8. This made him a senior figure at the court of ʿAbd ar-Raḥmān II, and so his high status compared to Ziryāb is understandable.

Once, when the emir was angry with Ibn Qarlumān and banned him from his presence (وأقصاه عن قربه), Ziryāb interceded on behalf of the poet. Four verses by the poet in praise of Ziryāb's kindness follow.

The story of the verses from Ibn al-Aḥnaf is told with slight variations in the wording.[60] In light of the additional details about the poet in *al-Muqtabis,* we may suppose that despite his fame and allegedly close companionship with the emir, Ziryāb was not above deferring to an elder figure at the court.

Ibn al-Qūṭiyya's second account of Ziryāb, which comes later in the same chapter of *Taʾrīḫ iftitāḥ*, gives a glimpse of his patron's character: One day Ziryāb sang a *ṣawt* which the emir ʿAbd ar-Raḥmān enjoyed greatly. So he ordered the treasury to give Ziryāb 30,000 dinars. A messenger brought the note to the treasurers, who stared at one another in disbelief. Having never seen such an order before, they deferred to their chief, who sent a message back to the emir saying that they were the emir's treasurers, but also the treasurers of the Muslims, levying taxes on their property and spending these for their benefit. He was thus unwilling to give 30,000 dinars from the property of the Muslims to a singer because he sang a song. The treasurers did not

[59] pp. 343-347 of Makkī's edition.

[60] Ibn Ḥayyān supplies this slightly different, more sensible middle line:

فأجبتها والدمعُ منحدرٌ　　　مثل الجُمان وهي من النظم

I replied to her with tears descending
like silver beads burst from a (broken) necklace.

Bosch-Vilá (1971) points out that an earlier edition of *Iftitāḥ* contains many variant readings, suggesting that a number of copies were made from the original. We should not be surprised, then, that the version in *al-Muqtabis* differs somewhat from that in the recent edition of the *Iftitāḥ* by Ibrāhīm al-Abyārī, which supplied the version cited above.

want this irresponsible act on their "heavenly record". The emir, he wrote, should reward him from his own property. Hearing this, Ziryāb responded by saying, "What kind of obedience is this!" The emir, however, defended the treasurers and rewarded Ziryāb from his own wealth.[61]

An indication of the logic behind this account lies in the career of Ibn al-Qūṭiyya. J. Bosch-Vilá (1991) writes that the grammarian was actually best known in his day as a jurist,[62] and María Isabel Fierro (1989) describes *Iftitāḥ al-Andalus* as "una obra escrita, con intenciones moralizantes, por un ulema de origen no árabe...",[63] Ibn al-Qūṭiyya intended this second story to illustrate the ethically correct attitude of a ruler towards the money derived from taxes levied on his subjects.

The figure of Ziryāb we find in Ibn al-Qūṭiyya's *Iftitāḥ al-Andalus* differs strikingly from that in Ibn Ḥayyān's lengthy account. In the first story, Ziryāb sits in the background, while the poetic talents of Ibn Qarlumān, a senior courtier, are on display. The second story does give him more importance, but even that serves mainly a didactic purpose: the emphasis is on the proper conduct of the prince, not Ziryāb's genius. If anything, Ziryāb comes across in the second account as rather ungracious – perhaps even impious – in being focused only on the reward for his song. It is striking that this source, so close to Ziryāb's lifetime, should present the famous musician in this light. If his image had already acquired the glowing character that comes through a century later in Ibn Ḥayyān, Ibn al-Qūṭiyya seems uninterested in it.

Ibn ʿAbd Rabbih's *al-ʿIqd al-farīd* is one of three other sources that fall even closer to Ziryāb's lifetime and complicate the picture of him even further. Ibn ʿAbd Rabbih conceived of this encyclopedia as a string of precious jewels on a necklace, 25 in all (hence the title): pearl (*lu'lu'a*), emerald (*zabarjada*) and so on symmetrically from one end of the necklace through the center to the far end. Thus the first twelve gem names are repeated (*al-lu'lu'a aṯ-ṯānī*, etc.) in reverse order in the final twelve books, with the middle book called simply *al-wāsiṭa* ("the central (jewel)"). The range of topics found in *al-ʿIqd* includes government (Book 1), proverbs (Book 7), the virtues of poetry (Book 18), and music (Book 20). A striking feature of this *adab* manual from al-Andalus is the rarity of material from al-Andalus in it, which led one ruler in the Middle East to exclaim, "This is our merchandise, which has been returned to us!"[64]

Ziryāb appears in three places, two of them in *Kitāb al-yāqūta aṯ-ṯānī* (The Second Ruby), which is devoted to knowledge of music and singing: various opinions about music's permissibility and what is good and bad in it, the voice, the *ʿūd*, the

[61] p. 84
[62] p. 848
[63] p. 585
[64] Brockelmann, 1971, p. 677.

subtleties of appreciating music, and so on. In one case (v. 7 p. 79) Ziryāb's name is simply deployed in the last verse of a poem about the *ʿūd* as an emblem of master musicianship. Earlier in the same book, however, we find an account of Ziryāb that enriches his image:

وكان لإبراهيم الموصلي عبد أسود يقال له زرياب وكان مطبوعا على الغناء علّمه إبراهيم ، وكان ربما حضر به مجلس الرشيد يغني فيه ، ثم إنه انتقل إلى القيروان إلى بني الأغلب ، فدخل على زيادة الله بن الأغلب ، فغناه بأبيات عنترة الفوارس حيث يقول :

فان تَكُ أُمّي غُرابيةً — من أبناء حامٍ بها عِبْتَني
فإني لطيفٌ ببيض الظُبا — وسمْر العوالي إذا جئْتَني
ولولا فرارُكَ يوم الوغى — لقُدتُك في الحرب أو قدتَني

فغضب زيادة الله ، فأمر بصفع قفاه وإخراجه وقال له : إن وجدت في شيء من بلدي بعد ثالث ايام ضربت عنقك ! فجاز البحر إلى الأندلس ، فكان عند الأمير عبد الرحمان بن الحكم .

Ibrāhīm al-Mawṣilī had a black slave who was named Ziryāb, and who was naturally gifted in singing.[65] Ibrāhīm taught him, and at times he was present with him in the *majlis* of (Hārūn) ar-Rašīd, singing for him. Then he moved to al-Qayrawān[66] to the Banī l-Aġlab, and he entered into (the service of) Ziyādat Allāh b. al-

[65] كـان مـطبوعـا على الـغناء — Note that earlier, in his biography of Ziryāb (p. 317), Ibn Ḥayyān offers a comment from ʿUbāda: "The singer ʿAlī b. Nāfiʿ Ziryāb was a natural-born poet" (كان على بن نافع زرياب المغني شاعرا مطبوعا). He then comments: "I have certainly not found this said by anyone else" (ما إن وجدت هذا لغيره). By Ibn Ḥayyān's time, the idea of the natural-born poet (الشاعر المطبوع) was already a familiar trope in Arabic poetics. From the early 2nd/8th century on, a debate turned around the relative merits of craftsmanship (الـصنعة) versus spontaneous composition arising from inborn talent (المطبوع). Early advocates for the primacy of المطبوع included Muʿtazilī circles of Baṣra, among them Bišr b. al-Muʿtamir (d. before 226/840) and especially al-Jāḥiẓ (d. 255/868 – see his *Bayān wa-tabyīn*), for whom the overworked, overly polished poem was not bad poetry, but simply disagreeable. See: A. Arazi et al. (2008).

[66] A city near present-day Tunis, capital of the Aġlabid dynasty in 9th-century Ifrīqiya.

Aġlab.[67] He sang for him the verses of ʿAntara the Knight,[68] where it says:

Even if my mother is raven-black
from the sons of Hām, by which you blame me,
I am skilled with the edges of swords
and brown high spears when you come to me.
And if you had not fled on the day of battle,
indeed I would lead you to war, or you would have me.

Ziyādat Allāh became angry. He ordered him struck on the back of the neck and expelled. And he said to him: "If I find you in any part of my realm after three days, I will behead you!" So Ziryāb passed over the sea to al-Andalus, and then he was with the emir ʿAbd ar-Raḥmān b. al-Ḥakam.[69]

This account presents an image of Ziryāb as a clumsy courtier who offended his patron, an image which is difficult to reconcile with the well-spoken musician who cleverly captivated the attention of first Hārūn ar-Rašīd and then ʿAbd ar-Raḥmān II with his erudition and courtliness.[70] These are two very different historical characters. Given the the myth-like tale of Ziryāb's departure from the court of ar-Rašīd, the vast range of innovations attributed to him by Ibn Ḥayyān and his sources, and then the absence of this material from works by two authors writing a century earlier than Ibn Ḥayyān, it is easy to suppose that the material preserved in *al-Muqtabis* combines historical fact with a certain amount of legend.

The third and most peculiar appearance of Ziryāb in *al-ʿIqd al-farīd* occurs in the final book, *Kitāb al-lu'lu'a aṯ-ṯānī* (The Second Pearl), which contains jokes and witty repartee. A certain Muḥammad b. Maṭrūḥ al-Aʿraj was known for his biting sense of humor. Ibn ʿAbd Rabbih gives several examples, including the following involving Ziryāb:

وكان يجلس إليه خصي لزرياب ، قد حج وتنسك ولزم الجامع ، فيتحدث في مجلسه
بأخبار زرياب ويقول : كان أبو الحسن رحمة [sic] الله يقول كذا وكذا . قال له

[67] This is Ziyādat Allāh I, ruler of Ifrīqiya from 816 to 837.

[68] ʿAntara is the subject of a cycle of stories recounting his heroism and honorable character as models of the masculine Arab ideal. According to the stories, his mother was a black slave.

[69] v. 7, p. 37

[70] On the other hand, had Ziyādat Allāh himself been less sensitive (or perhaps better educated) and recognized the compliment Ziryāb intended by singing of the famous ʿAntara, things might have gone better for the musician.

الأعرج : من أبو الحسن هذا ؟ قال : زرياب . قال : بلغني أنه كان أخرق الناس
لايتِ خصيّ !

> A eunuch belonging to Ziryāb, who had performed the Pilgrimage, was pious and attended the mosque, was sitting with him and relating stories about Ziryāb, saying, "Abū l-Ḥasan, may Allāh have mercy upon him, used to say such and such..."
> Al-Aʿraj said to him: "Who is this Abū l-Ḥasan?"
> He said: "Ziryāb."
> (Al-Aʿraj) said: "I heard that he was the *aḫraq an-nās* for an anus of a eunuch!"[71]

The joke here turns on the word أخرق, which might suggest two ideas in this context. The word means "awkward, clumsy," but it comes from the verb *ḫaraqa*, which means "to pierce or penetrate." By saying that Ziryāb is "the most *aḫraq of the people* for the ass of a eunuch" al-Aʿraj is poking fun at both men by evoking the image of awkward sexual relations between master and eunuch.

Humor of this sort says as much about the humorist as about the victim of his wit. Nevertheless in these two stories Ibn ʿAbd Rabbih presents us with a very unglamorous image of Ziryāb, one that contradicts the other accounts examined so far in both spirit and substance. Certainly Ibn ʿAbd Rabbih's purpose in writing *al-ʿIqd al-farīd* was to provide a catalog of useful knowledge, clever anecdotes, cautionary tales and models of erudite behavior for men aspiring to appear learned and clever. In this context, Ziryāb served mainly as a vehicle for material the anthologist regarded as instructive in one way or another. Given his apparent disregard for examples drawn from his own country, such treatment of one of its leading lights of the previous century is not too surprising.

At the same time, Ibn ʿAbd Rabbih's attitude toward Ziryāb cannot stem from a negative attitude toward music in general, as some scholars have claimed,[72] since the material on music in *al-ʿIqd al-farīd* as a whole does not reflect such a view. Moreover, an account found in *Jaḏwat al-muqtabis fī taʾrīḫ ʿulamāʾ al-Andalus* by Abū ʿAbd Allāh Muḥammad b. Abī Naṣr al-Ḥumaydī (a contemporary of Ibn Ḥayyān's) reveals Ibn ʿAbd Rabbih expressing a rather different sentiment toward Ziryāb. In al-Ḥumaydī's biography of Ibn ʿAbd Rabbih there is a story in which the author, walking in the

[71] v. 8, pp. 138-139
[72] See for example Ribera (1922) p. 57.

streets of Cordoba, overhears someone singing beautifully, and then pens a poem that includes the following line:

لو كان زريابُ حيّا ثم أسمِعه لذاب من حسد او مات من كسد

If Ziryāb were alive, and made to hear it
no doubt he would waste away from jealousy, or die of grief[73]

Like the first appearance of Ziryāb in *al-ʿIqd al-farīd* mentioned above, the rhetorical significance of Ziryāb here is clear: he is the image of the most accomplished of musicians[74] More importantly, it shows Ibn ʿAbd Rabbih again deploying one of the main rhetorical themes attaching to the figure of Ziryāb, that of Ziryāb as the exemplary musician. There is nothing here that reflects a particularly negative view, either of Ziryāb or of music generally.

It is quite likely that the decades after Ziryāb saw the consolidation of various accounts about the emergence of the Cordoban school of music that came to be focused on the founding father figure, Ziryāb. A century later Ibn Ḥayyān had access to these accounts, many of them collected in Aslam b. Aḥmad's *Aḫbār Ziryāb,* and he drew upon them in portraying the famous musician, to the exclusion of other images of him presented by other well-known Cordobans, including Ibn ʿAbd Rabbih and Ibn al-Qūṭiyya. Aslam thus seems to have played a important role in the process that transformed the image of Ziryāb, as will be seen below.

The traditional emphasis of Arabic historiography on serial accounts of Great Men and their Great Deeds also lent itself as well to reducing the emergence of the Cordoban school of elite music to the innovations of a single individual. The actual process may well have been more complicated than the biography of Ziryāb indicates. Artistic movements rarely if ever emerge from a single source, and always involve complex interactions with social and economic conditions. These factors hardly figure at all in the Arabic historiographical tradition, a fact which also contributed to the survival of the glorified image of Ziryāb found in the most commonly cited source for Ziryāb, al-Maqqarī's *Nafḥ aṭ-ṭīb min ġuṣn al-Andalus ar-raṭīb.*

1.4 *Ṭayfūr and al-Iṣfahānī: further challenges to the biography*

Before taking up the image of Ziryāb as presented in *Nafḥ aṭ-ṭīb*, two other sources can be brought to light that make the version of his biography presented by al-Maqqarī and

[73] 1997 edition, Bāb alif, entry #172, pp. 89-91.

[74] This same entry, with minor variations, is also found in *Buġyat al-multamis fī taʾrīḫ rijāl ahl al-Andalus* by Abū Jaʿfar Aḥmad b. Yaḥyā b. ʿAmīra aḍ-Ḍabbī (d. 599/1203), Bāb alif, entry #328, pp. 139-142.

the standard narrative even more problematic. These sources cannot be overlooked because, although they derive from the Middle East, and the information they provide on Ziryāb is fragmentary, they present similar stories that constitute the material closest in time to him. The central story in *Kitāb Baġdad* and *Kitāb al-Aġānī* is the earliest reference to Ziryāb with a verifiable source that has survived into the present day. It seems to have been current in Baghdad within a generation or two of the people involved, including Ziryāb himself, because it appears first in *Kitāb Baġdād* by Abū Faḍl Ahmad b. Abī Ṭāhir Ṭayfūr, who we recall died in 280/893.

Ṭayfūr's book is an annalistic history of Baghdad during the Abbasid period, not unlike Ibn Ḥayyān's *al-Muqtabis*. Only a fragment has survived, dealing with the era of the caliph al-Maʾmūn. Ṭayfūr devotes a whole chapter to a visit by al-Maʾmūn to Damascus, in which a certain singer, ʿAllūyah, recalls accompanying the Abbasid caliph on a trip to the mountains nearby ("جبل الثلج" lit. "Snow Mountain"). When they come upon a lake that once belonged to the Umayyads surrounded by four hills, the caliph likes the place and calls for food and drink. After a meal and wine, the caliph asks the singer to sing something beautiful, but the only verses that come to his mind reminisce about the vanished Umayyads. The mention of their name angers the caliph, who curses the singer. ʿAllūyah excuses himself by saying that the song was written by Ziryāb, who used to be a client of the Abbasids. Now, however, Ziryāb is living a life of luxury among the Umayyads in al-Andalus while ʿAllūyah himself is starving. The caliph remains angry at the singer for nearly a month afterwards

Since Ṭayfūr died less than forty years after Ziryāb, this story shows that, far from being forgotten in Baghdad after his departure (as Ibn Ḥayyān/Aslam maintains), Ziryāb was still famous enough to be used rhetorically in a gibe at the caliph, and it underscores yet again the significance of patronage to Ziryāb's career, since patronage is in fact what is at issue in the story.

Two other instances of this story occur in *Kitāb al-Aġānī*. *Kitāb al-Aġānī* ["The Book of Songs"] of al-Iṣfahānī needs no introduction, being the single most important surviving source for early Abbasid music and poetry, and for a wealth of historical and biographical anecdotes of courtly life in the century or so prior to its author. It is not surprising, then, that Ziryāb should be mentioned in the *Aġānī*, though he does not appear in person. The name Ziryāb is found in several places, but four of these refer to a different singer, a woman named Ziryāb al-Wāthiqiyya. In Book 5 of the Būlāq edition, she is said to have owned a fine *jāriya* who was bought by the caliph al-Muqtadir (r. 295/908-320/932).[75] In Book 7, Ziryāb al-Wāthiqiyya is mentioned in a

[75] There appears to be some confusion among various editors of the *Aġānī* about which Ziryāb this account refers to: some claim this is ʿAlī b. Nāfiʿ, which is impossible, since he was more than 50 years in the grave when al-Muqtadir attained the caliphate.

section on the sons and daughters of caliphs who were musicians. She is described as following the style of the Abbasid prince, Ibrāhīm b. al-Mahdī, because she sang songs according to her own feeling (rather than following longstanding stylistic conventions as did the prince's rival, Isḥāq al-Mawṣilī). Finally, two interactions with ʿAbd Allāh, son of the caliph al-Muʿtazz, are described in Book 9: on one occasion she gives an account of his composing and singing a song for her, and on the other occasion she sang beautifully a song he had composed.[76]

The Ziryāb who departed Baghdad for al-Andalus appears in three places (though the name ʿAlī b. Nāfiʿ does not), two of them in connection with retellings of ʿAllūyah's rebuke. The first, in Book 4, proceeds very much as the version in *Kitāb Baġdād*, but with more details: the caliph was hunting, and the natural setting is more finely portrayed; the caliph himself regards with wonder the handiwork of the Umayyads, and the singer begins without being asked. The verse that ʿAllūyah sings is rather different, though with the same import, and his reply to the caliph is substantially the same. The caliph calls the singer *son of a whore* (يا ابن الزانية), and is only reconciled with him after the intercession of ʿAbbās Abū Baḥr. In the end, ʿAllūyah receives 20,000 dirhams from the caliph. The story is retold yet again in Book 10, in a chapter of stories about ʿAllūyah. In this case the singer recounts the story himself, supplying still more details about the setting and a slightly different banter between himself and the caliph. But his rebuke is essentially the same, though a bit longer: "Do you blame me for remembering the Banū Umayya? Your *mawlā*, Ziryāb, is with them, riding amongst a hundred servants who are his property. And he owns 300,000 dinars given to him in horses, and luxuries and slaves, whilst I with you am dying of hunger." The caliph's response is much the same, though in this version, he was not reconciled with the singer until he was on his deathbed.[77]

Apart from the fact that this early story about Ziryāb, in all its forms, reflects the patronage system that supported him, the key point to be raised here is the rhetorical use of his image, a tendency that recurs throughout the sources. We have already seen it in a more sophisticated form in the accounts by Ibn Khaldun and at-Tīfāšī, and in the poem found in Ibn ʿAbd Rabbih's *al-ʿIqd al-farīd*, but a similar intention lies behind the figure of Ziryāb in the standard narrative, wherein he supplies a cultural-historical link between the Middle East and al-Andalus for modern scholars like Muḥammad al-Fāsī and others.

---

[76] I know of no other sources for Ziryāb al-Wāthiqiyya, nor of any other information on her in the *Aġānī*. This is a pity, for it appears she was a freewoman (she owned at least one *jāriya*), and thus provides a contrary example to those discussed by Ibn Ḥayyān. Her story would be an interesting one for this reason alone.

[77] Ziryāb is mentioned once more in the *Aġānī*. See §1.5b, below.

1.5 *al-Maqqarī and the lionizing of Ziryāb*

Having traced *aḫbār* about Ziryāb in reverse chronological order, peeling back the layers of his literary persona, as it were, it is now time to study his most recent and most famous biographer, Šihāb ad-Dīn Abū l-ʿAbbās Aḥmad b. Muḥammad b. Aḥmad b. Yaḥyā at-Tilimsānī al-Fāsī al-Maqqarī. His *Nafḥ aṭ-ṭīb min ġuṣn al-Andalus ar-raṭīb wa-ḏikr wazīrihā Lisān ad-Dīn Ibn al-Ḫaṭīb*, has served as the main source for the standard narrative of Ziryāb's biography. Like Ibn Khaldun, al-Maqqarī makes brief mention of Ziryāb at the beginning of his biography of ʿAbd ar-Raḥmān II, following closely Ibn Khaldun's wording, but the main part of al-Maqqarī's account of Ziryāb comes directly from *al-Muqtabis*.[78] The final three printed pages of this material add brief accounts from other sources, as well.

Most of the passages in *Nafḥ aṭ-ṭīb* deriving from *al-Muqtabis* are paraphrases of the *Aḫbār Ziryāb* material. Al-Maqqarī stays reasonably close to the original, but in several places he omits details and repetitions. We also find interesting variations in wording. For example, the verse that Ziryāb sings to ar-Rašīd has a different second hemistich (compare the version in §1.2a above):

ياايها الملكُ الميمونُ طائرُه　　　هارون راح إليك الناس وابتكروا

O ye monarch, whose omen-bird is fortunate,
Hārūn, to you the people travel in evening and morning

Al-Maqqarī also edits the *Aḫbār Ziryāb* material, as for example the *jinn*-and-*jawārī* story (see above, §1.2a). Ibn Ḥayyān begins the story by stating

ذكر عنه أن الجن كانت تعلمه كل ليلة ما بين نوبة إلى صوت واحد ...

It was said of him that the *jinn* used to teach him every night one *ṣawt* from a *nawba*...

Al-Maqqarī turns this slightly, indicating some reservation by putting the assertion in Ziryāb's mouth:

---

[78] 1988 v. 3, pp. 122-130.

ذكر أن زريابا ادّعى أن الجن كانت تعلمه كل ليلة ما بين نوبة إلى صوت واحد ...

It was said that Ziryab claimed that the *jinn* were teaching him every night one *ṣawt* from a *nawba*...

He also reduces the role of the slave singers, Ghizlān and Hunayda, in the composition process, and also in the story of the *jinn* and Ibrāhīm al-Mawṣilī.

Ziryāb's knowledge of astrology, his having memorized 10,000 songs, his personal qualities, and his various contributions to fashion and elite culture all survive in condensed form, though precisely in the order they appear in *al-Muqtabis*. The material on Ziryāb's sons and daughters also has been reduced, and his two youngest sons, Aḥmad and Ḥasan do not appear at all. Also missing is Ibn Ḥayyān's presentation of the female slave singers and the male musicians Ziryāb taught. Al-Ḥakam's two singers, ʿAllūn and Zirqūn, survive in *Nafḥ aṭ-ṭīb*, as do the two verses in praise of Ziryāb by Ibn aš-Šamir (though al-Maqqarī gives the poet's name as ʿAbd ar-Raḥmān, not ʿAbd Allāh).

Except for a short passage concerning Ziryāb's two daughters, summarizing the information on page 328 of *al-Muqtabis*, the remainder of al-Maqqarī's account derives from sources other than Ibn Ḥayyān. He presents a quatrain sung by Ziryāb, whose source he gives as Ibn Saʿīd, with no further information (possibly Muʾmin b. Saʿīd al-ʿIrrīḍ, whose poem about Ziryāb is among those cited in *al-Muqtabis* on the authority of Ibn al-Faraḍī; see above §1.2d). We find also a beautiful *jāriya* owned by Ziryāb, named Mutʿa ("Pleasure"), who worked for the emir ʿAbd ar-Raḥmān as a singer and wine-server. He was fond of her, and when she realized his regard for her, she sang four verses revealing her desire for him, as well. When Ziryāb learned of it, he gave her to the emir.

The *jāriya* Maṣābīḥ (one of Ibn Qalqal's three singers, see §1.2c above) also appears in *Nafḥ aṭ-ṭīb*, though said here to be owned by Abū Ḥafṣ ʿUmar b. Qalhīl and not accompanied by her two companions, Ġulām and Waṣīf. Al-Maqqarī says she learned to sing from Ziryāb, and describes her as a model of courtesy and noble character with an excellent voice. He presents two verses in praise of her, which he attributes to *al-ʿIqd al-farīd* (though neither she nor either of her supposed masters are to be found in Ibn ʿAbd Rabbih's book today).

Al-Maqqarī concludes with a series of stories that illustrate well the image of Ziryāb being used for rhetorical purposes. It begins with the story of the singer ʿAllūyah's retort to al-Maʾmūn. In the first version, the caliph's party visits a palace in

Damascus formerly owned by the Umayyads. The caliph's objection to ʿAllūyah's song and the singer's retort are essentially the same as in *Kitāb Baġdād*.

Two other, slightly different versions of this story follow. Both begin with al-Maʾmūn and his entourage in the mountains, as in Ṭayfūr's version. As in Ṭayfūr and the *Aġānī*, the caliph admires the surroundings and calls for food and drink. He then requests a song, and ʿAllūyah sings two different lines referring to the Umayyads, arousing the caliph's anger. Al-Maqqarī presents two versions of the singer's, both of them in broad agreement with the first version, and again, the caliph remains angry at the singer for nearly a month afterwards.

After the story of ʿAllūyah's retort, Ziryāb appears in one other place in *Nafḥ aṭ-ṭīb*, later in the same volume.[79] Al-Maqqarī presents several short anecdotes about singers, among them another (unattributed) version of the Ibn Qarlumān story found in *Iftitāḥ al-Andalus*. This time, the poet who supplies the verse called for by the emir is one "ʿUbayd Allāh b. Firnās,"[80] and the original poet's name is given anomalously as Abū al-ʿAtāhiya.[81] The wording of the account is neither Ibn al-Qūṭiyya's nor Ibn Ḥayyān's; it is likely that al-Maqqarī was relying upon yet another, intermediary source from between his time and Ibn Ḥayyān's. Apart from this, and one variation in the text of the poetry,[82] the story is otherwise the same in all its details as that given by Ibn al-Qūṭiyya.

This survey of al-Maqqarī's version of Ziryāb's biography illustrates the problem inherent in relying upon *Nafḥ aṭ-ṭīb* as a single source for the singer. Al-Maqqarī depends primarily upon Ibn Ḥayyān, but while he does not misquote the Andalusian historian, he edits out some very important information *al-Muqtabis* has to offer: the rich detail about the *jawārī/qiyān* singers who contributed so much to the musical culture of Cordoba in the 3rd/9th century. Moreover, al-Maqqarī makes a passing reference to *al-ʿIqd al-farīd* and yet does not include the two most important references to Ziryāb found in that work, in which Ibn ʿAbd Rabbih offers a contrasting

[79] 1988 v. 3, p. 615.

[80] The editor of the 1988 edition has "corrected" the courtier poet's name to ʿUbayd Allāh from ʿAbd ar-Raḥmān, which itself is probably an error: the original story as we have it both from Ibn al-Qūṭiyya directly, and via Ibn Ḥayyān, gives the name ʿUbayd Allāh b. Qarlumān (see above, §1.3), but in addition, Ibn Ḥayyān mentions ʿAbbās b. Firnās, who also was a courtier of ʿAbd ar-Raḥmān II. See: *al-Muqtabis* (2003) p. 347.

[81] Abū Isḥāq Ismāʿīl b. al-Qāsim b. Suwayd b. Kaysān Abū l-ʿAtāhiya ("father of craziness"), b. Kūfa 130/748 and d. 210/824 or 211/826. He was a pauper who gained the attention of the caliph Hārūn ar-Rašīd, though he remained an outsider to aristocratic circles all his life. He was a friend of Ibrāhīm al-Mawṣilī's, and so some of his verses were set to music. His poetry was known for its simple language and unaffected, spontaneous style, which earned him the admiration of the common people.

[82] The verses are similar to Ibn Ḥayyān's version, except al-Maqqarī gives us الخبير ("cognizant, aware") for العليم ("knowing") in the second line of Ziryāb's song.

image of the great composer, as we saw in §1.3. In short, over-reliance on *Nafḥ aṭ-ṭīb min ġuṣn al-Andalus ar-raṭīb* as a source has encouraged an incomplete and shallow impression of Ziryāb that obscures the significance of the institution of artiste slavery that made his career possible.

1.6 *Ziryāb reconsidered*

This review of the sources for the musician and composer, Abū l-Ḥasan ʿAlī b. Nāfiʿ Ziryāb, highlights some of the problems in the standard narrative of his career. A critical perspective on the sources shows that Ziryāb became a larger-than-life figure in Cordoba in the decades after his death. Even Ibn Ḥayyān offers one or two contrary voices, such as that of the jurist ʿAbd al-Malik b. Ḥabīb, who objected to the huge rewards from Ziryāb's patron. But it was the glorified version of him that was selectively taken up by al-Maqqarī in the 17th century, providing the model for the modern narrative. In addition, just as the standard narrative deploys Ziryāb to link the modern tradition to the Golden Age of Baghdad, the sources also show Ziryāb deployed in various contexts to serve rhetorical purposes. This phenomenon begins within his lifetime (as Ṭayfūr's story of ʿAllūyah's retort shows) and continue in all the sources that have survived.

Finally, careful attention to the most abundant source we have for him, *al-Muqtabis*, allows us to nudge the Great Man from center stage and to view his Great Deeds in the light of historical conditions that informed them. The result is a surprisingly rich array of accounts that highlight two social institutions that were crucial to Ziryāb's success: patronage and slavery.

1.6a *Ziryāb as rhetorical figure*

An overlooked aspect of the Ziryāb biography is the ways in which various perspectives on him are deployed for rhetorical purposes. Of course, Ziryāb is today very much a rhetorical figure within the standard narrative, representing both the emergence of the Andalusian musical heritage from the Abbasid golden age, as well as the elite qualities that characterized it from that time until the present. As was observed in Chapter 1, he represents both foundation and continuation. Yet Ziryāb is deployed to rhetorical effect in the old Arabic sources, as well. The differences between the Ziryāb of Aslam / Ibn Ḥayyān / al-Maqqarī and that of the early accounts by Ṭayfūr, al-Iṣfahānī, Ibn al-Qūṭiyya and Ibn ʿAbd Rabbih suggest that already in the 9th and 10th centuries, very shortly after his death, Ziryāb had become a complex figure noted as a successful musician and at times an exemplary one. Ṭayfūr's and al-Iṣfahānī's story of ʿAllūyah's retort to the caliph al-Maʾmūn shows that Ziryāb was not forgotten in Baghdad, and that even during his lifetime his image could be summoned rhetorically to make a point about princely patronage. But in this case Ziryāb served not as a figure of musical or cultural excellence, but merely as a symbol of success and affluence.[83]

The Ziryāb figure in the west was more complex, with contrasting images of him circulating in Cordoba of the early 10th century. For literati like Ibn ʿAbd Rabbih and Ibn al-Qūṭiyya, he was a model of the successful musician who nevertheless could be shown displaying flaws in character that complicate (and enrich) his image as *nadīm*. At the same time, other stories were circulating that portrayed him in a very different light. In the material collected by Aslam, Ziryāb was a paragon of culture and taste who had brought not only fine music but also a host of cultural refinements to Umayyad Cordoba. The success of this image of Ziryāb can be measured by the other sources that make reference to it. For example the book *Ṭawq al-ḥamāma fī ilfa wa-l-ālāf* by the Andalusian intellectual Abū Muḥammad ʿAlī Ibn Ḥazm refers to Aslam and his collection of Ziryāb stories, calling it a very remarkable anthology (*dīwān ʿajīb jiddan*).[84] Similarly, the biographer al-Ḥumaydī also found Aslam's work notable. That both Ibn Ḥazm and al-Ḥumaydī were rough contemporaries of Ibn Ḥayyān suggests that by the mid-11th century Ziryāb-as-*ẓarīf* had taken precedence over the less exciting (but perhaps more realistic) image that predominates in the sources of a century earlier. It is the former image, passing through Ibn Ḥayyān to al-Maqqarī, that has been selectively summoned as Ziryāb in the standard narrative.

1.6b *From Baghdad to Cordoba*

The standard narrative has it that Ziryāb upstaged his master, Isḥāq al-Mawṣilī, before the caliph, Hārūn ar-Rašīd. As a result, Isḥāq forced Ziryāb to choose between facing the wrath of the most influential musician at the caliph's court, or fleeing Baghdad permanently. Ziryāb chose the latter, according to the narrative, and fled to al-Andalus, arriving there just after the death of the emir al-Ḥakam I and at the beginning of the reign of his son and successor, ʿAbd ar-Raḥmān II. As Hārūn died in 809 and al-Ḥakam died in 822, Ziryāb would have to have traveled for more than a decade from Baghdad to Cordoba. These dates are reasonably certain, as all existing accounts of the two men agree on them, and moreover, there is general agreement that the career of Ziryāb was linked to ʿAbd ar-Raḥmān II (not, for example, to his father, al-Ḥakam I). So, how long would such a trip, from one end of the Mediterranean to the other, have taken?

While Ziryāb's mode of travel is not known exactly, the *Aḫbār Ziryāb* narrative refers to ships (سُفُن , p. 313), and he almost certainly traveled overland, as well. In either case, we can be sure that the entire trip should not have lasted more than a few weeks,

[83] The image of Ziryāb as an exemplary musician seems to have been confined to al-Andalus. At least, no accounts have survived from the Mašriq portraying him as such.
[84] 2001, pp. 247-248.

if accomplished in one continuous trip by the shortest practical route (i.e.: west from Baghdad, not south and all the way around the Arabian peninsula via the Persian Gulf and Red Sea, for example). Proof of this may be found in similar journeys around the medieval Mediterranean: accounts of travel by such figures as Muḥyī d-Dīn Ibn al-ʿArabī (d. 638/1240) and Ibn Baṭṭūṭa (d. 770/1368 or 779/1369), and accounts of pilgrimages by Ibn Tūmart (d. ca. 523/1130) and others. This is incompatible with the minimum span of perhaps 12 or 13 years that the *Aḫbār Ziryāb* account implies. There are three possible ways to reconcile this difference. Either the standard narrative is wrong, and Ziryāb left Baghdad much later than *al-Muqtabis* indicates (and therefore was not driven out by Isḥāq al-Mawṣilī); or he spent a significant amount of time somewhere in between; or perhaps both.

Thus the version of Ziryāb's biography put forward by *Aḫbār Ziryāb* via *al-Muqtabis*, and which reappears later in schematic form in at-Tīfāšī's *Mutʿat al-asmāʿ* and Ibn Khaldun's *Kitāb al-ʿIbar* cannot be the complete story. As I have argued elsewhere (2009), two earlier accounts of Ziryāb, suggest a solution.

Ibn al-Qūṭiyya's second account of Ziryāb contains a passage cited by Bennūna (1994) in calculating the date of Ziryāb's arrival in Cordoba:

وقدم زرياب على عبد الرحمان بن الحكم ، رحمه الله ، وكان بالمحلّ القديم من الأمير محمد بن هارون الأمين وكان المأمون الوالي بعد الأمين ، فعدّد عليه أشياء فلما قُتل الأمين فرّ إلى الأندلس ، فحلّ من عبد الرحمان بن الحكم بكل محلٍّ وكان أهلا لذلك في أدبه وروايته وتقدمه في الصناعة التى كانت بيده .

> Ziryāb reached ʿAbd ar-Raḥmān b. al-Ḥakam, his previous position having been with the emir Muḥammad b. Hārūn al-Amīn. Al-Maʾmūn was the ruler after al-Amīn, and he reproached him for certain things; and when al-Amīn was killed, Ziryāb fled to al-Andalus. He occupied a high station with ʿAbd ar-Raḥmān b. al-Ḥakam, and he was worthy of that with his refined manner, his eloquence, and the eminence in the art (of music) that he had at his fingertips.[85]

This passage refers to the Abbasid caliph al-Amīn (r. 193/809-198/813). After Hārūn ar-Rašīd, died, there was a struggle for power between two of his sons, al-Amīn and al-Maʾmūn (r. 198/813 to 218/833). The former, the elder and favored by his father though he was not of pure Arab blood, held power in Baghdad for about four years before being assassinated, probably by agents of his brother, who then claimed the

[85] p. 83

caliphate for himself. As Bennūna has observed, this account is completely incompatible with the standard narrative. Nothing indicates a conflict with Isḥāq al-Mawṣilī, and Ziryāb does not leave Baghdad during the reign of Hārūn ar-Rašīd, but at least four years later, after the death of al-Amīn in 198/813.

The pronoun referents in the above passage are somewhat ambiguous: *whom* did al-Maʾmūn reproach, al-Amīn or Ziryāb? If the latter, Ziryāb's flight from Baghdad would be quite understandable. But even if Ibn al-Qūṭiyya intended that al-Amīn was the object of al-Maʾmūn's criticism, reasons for Ziryāb's departure after al-Amīn's death are not hard to find. The struggle between the two sons of Hārūn had been bitter. Ziryāb, as an associate of al-Amīn's, may well have felt ill at ease with the new caliph, who furthermore imposed a ban on music at court after his arrival from Khurasan. This also would not have encouraged Ziryāb to stay. And yet, Bennūna argues that Ziryāb lingered six or more years in Baghdad under al-Maʾmūn's reign, which seems unlikely. Indeed the verb Ibn al-Qūṭiyya uses to describe Ziryāb's departure, *farra,* means "to flee, to run away", which suggests that the musician left Baghdad more or less urgently – and therefore probably soon after al-Amīn's death. However that may be, Ibn al-Qūṭiyya places Ziryāb in Baghdad as late as the ascension of al-Maʾmūn, son of Hārūn, which took place in 813.

In the passage quoted earlier, Ibn ʿAbd Rabbih tells of a falling out between Ziryāb and Ziyādat Allāh I, the Aghlabid ruler of Ifrīqiya between 816 and 837. Neither that account, nor the material in *Taʾrīḫ iftitāḥ* hint at all of a falling out with Isḥāq al-Mawṣilī (the only reason given for Ziryāb's departure from Baghdad in the standard narrative), and they offer evidence of Ziryāb's whereabouts during the long gap in the usual chronology: he stayed longer in Baghdad than the standard narrative allows, and he spent time in Ifrīqiya.

Both Ibn al-Qūṭiyya and Ibn ʿAbd Rabbih were writing about a century after Ziryāb and therefore may have had access to eyewitness accounts about him transmitted by oral tradition. On the other hand, although Aslam b. Aḥmad, author of Ibn Ḥayyān's main source for Ziryāb, *Kitāb Aḫbār Ziryāb,* was a contemporary of Ibn ʿAbd Rabbih's, his book contains a number of passages that hang such marvels on him that we would do well to approach his material with some caution. Indeed, Ibn ʿAbd Rabbih seems to have ignored Aslam's book completely.

Ibn al-Qūṭiyya's wording suggests that Ziryāb fled Baghdad very soon after the death of al-Amīn, but Ziyādat Allāh did not become emir until 816, about three years after the death of Ziryāb's patron. It is possible that Ziryāb arrived in Ifrīqiya before Ziyādat Allāh came to power, but the three-year gap between the two dates can in fact be filled by Ṭayfūr. The account of ʿAllūyah in *Kitāb Baġdād* concludes thus:

زرياب مولى المهدي صار إلى الشام ثم صار إلى المغرب إلى بني أمية هناك .

> Ziryāb, a *mawlā* of al-Mahdī[86], betook himself to Syria, then to the West, to the Banū Umayya there.[87]

Ṭayfūr thus gives the musician a stopover of undetermined length in Syria that complements the other sources for Ziryāb's biography, filling a gap in the chronology between his departure from Baghdad after the ascension of al-Maʾmūn and his arrival in Ifrīqiya during the reign of Ziyādat Allāh I. Note that he does not say when Ziryāb left Baghdad, nor why; he merely indicates that Ziryāb traveled first to Syria (*aš-Šām*) before traveling on to the West (*al-maġrib*) to the Umayyads there.[88] Life in Abbasid Syria may not have been particularly attractive to Ziryāb (after all, he had just fled the imperial capital after the murder of his patron). One can understand that he might not be comfortable settling in a city ruled by his patron's antagonist. Neverthelesss a sojourn of three years or perhaps more would not be unreasonable, and a further move to North Africa remains quite understandable whenever he actually did it.[89]

For his part, Ibn Abī Ṭāhir Ṭayfūr was a younger contemporary of Ziryāb's, living in Baghdad, the city he left behind. His account of ʿAllūyah's rebuke of al-Maʾmūn lends plausibility to the idea that Ziryāb lingered in Baghdad through the reign of al-Amīn and was known to al-Maʾmūn (he is notable in this story, not just as a famous singer of al-Andalus, but also as a former client of the Abbasids). (Moreover it underscores yet again the significance of patronage to Ziryāb's career, since patronage is in fact what is at issue in the story.) Thus Ṭayfūr also supports the somewhat different, more logical chronology that emerges from the accounts by Ibn al-Qūṭiyya and Ibn ʿAbd Rabbih.

Putting all the pieces together, the account of Abū l-Ḥasan ʿAlī b. Nāfiʿ Ziryāb's migration to al-Andalus is complete in the sense that there are no logical gaps in the story. Ziryāb evidently stayed in Baghdad much longer than the standard

---

[86] Abbasid caliph, r. 775/158-785/169, father of Hārūn ar-Rašīd and grandfather of al-Amīn and al-Maʾmūn.

[87] p. 153

[88] According to anthropologist Jonathan Shannon, Andalusian musicians in Aleppo to this day still say Ziryāb lived in that city.

[89] 'Abd al-Wahhāb (1966, 178) points out that Qayrawān in Ifrīqiya was a logical stopping-over point for travelers headed westward from the Mašriq toward al-Andalus. He speculates – based upon *Nafḥ al-ṭīb* – that Ziryāb arrived late in the year 205 of the Hijra and left some time during the year 206, thus allowing for just a few months' travel between Qayrawān and Cordoba.

narrative allows. Whether or not there was an actual falling out with Isḥāq al-Mawṣilī is a moot point: Ziryāb was on good terms with the caliph al-Amīn while he was alive, and left Baghdad only after his death in the year 198/813. Probably he did not linger long in Baghdad after his patron's death, because he had been a client of the new caliph's rival and was therefore vulnerable. Moreover, as was often the practice with succession of the caliphate,[90] the new caliph imposed a moratorium on music. In such a situation, with his patron dead and his patron's rival now in power, and with no chance of earning courtly favors because his livelihood was barred from court, what reason would Ziryāb have had to stay in Baghdad?

Ziryāb traveled first to Syria, a move that was noted in Baghdad at the time and is still remembered in Aleppo. He may have stayed in Syria at least three years and possibly longer, moving on and arriving in Qayrawān, the seat of the Aghlabid emirate in Ifrīqiya, some time after 816. He may have lived in there for as long as five years (ca. 201/816-206/821), serving as a court musician to Ziyādat Allāh I until approximately 821. It may well have been during this period that Ziryāb's fame reached Cordoba (as suggested, though never explained, by the standard narrative). Some exchange between the musician and the emir of Cordoba, al-Ḥakam I, probably took place at this time, since Ziryāb seems not to have arrived in al-Andalus completely unannounced. However that may be, in 821 Ziryāb offended Ziyādat Allāh, and was forced to leave Ifrīqiya. He seems to have departed al-Qayrawān headed more or less directly for al-Andalus and arrived in Algeciras just after al-Ḥakam's death. Abū Naṣr Manṣūr b. Abī l-Bahlūl al-Yahūdī ("Manṣūr the Jew", al-Ḥakam's go-between) may have traveled with Ziryāb all the way from Ifrīqiya, or he may have been awaiting him in Algeciras, but in any case he was present in Algeciras when Ziryāb learned that al-Ḥakam had died. Manṣūr convinced Ziryāb to seek the new emir's patronage, which he did. ʿAbd ar-Raḥmān invited Ziryāb to Cordoba, and he arrived there in the month of *Muḥarram*, 207/822.

2. *Music and informal institutions in 9th-century Cordoba*

According to Ibn Ḥayyān, when Ziryāb arrived in Algeciras he received news of al-Ḥakam's death and considered leaving. Al-Manṣūr al-Yahūdī convinced him to wait and appeal to the new ruler of Cordoba. The suggestion that the prince's successor might be willing to sponsor him did not come as a great surprise to Ziryāb, and in fact, no interest on the part of ʿAbd ar-Raḥmān in music as such was necessary to change Ziryāb's mind:

---

[90] See Sawa (1985), 72-73.

وعرفه في زيادته في كرم الخلال على أبيه وشبهه به في ثقوب معرفته ونصاعة ظرفه وقوة أدبه واطمأنت مفسه إليه ...

> [Manṣūr] informed him of [ʿAbd ar-Raḥmān's] exceeding his father in notable characteristics, and compared him to his father in the acuity of his knowledge, the purity of his elegance, and the strength of his education [in the refinements of culture]. [Ziryāb] was put at ease about him...[91]

To judge from the story as we have it, the issues involved the prince's generosity and overall refinement, not just his interest in music. The discussion between the two musicians takes for granted an institution of patronage in which princes naturally expected (and were expected) to support musicians, poets, literati and other boon companions, both for their own entertainment and as a sign of their erudition, and that such artists could reasonably expect to earn a living at their hands. The informal institution of patronage thus was a given in the interaction between al-Manṣūr and Ziryāb; and all our sources on poetry and music in the medieval Islamic world provide abundant evidence that the distribution of money and other means of livelihood through patronage was a cultural element that al-Andalus, North Africa and the Middle East held in common. This should come as no surprise, since the Umayyad princes of al-Andalus descended from the family that had helped to set the tone for this social institution during the early phase of the Arab-Islamic empire.

The Abbasids inherited this system and developed it for themselves in Baghdad, where Ziryāb became familiar with it. However, the fundamental elements traced back to the Umayyads a century earlier, and before that to the ancient Arab tribal patron-client system. The Umayyads had exploited this tribal ethos in their bid for power in the 1st/7th century, but as caliphs ruling in Damascus, they had adopted the courtly norms of the Sassanian empire, thus giving a new, more elaborate form to the early Arab-Islamic dynastic style.

Aristocratic patronage fits the definition of an informal institution set out the Prologue to Part 1. Two of the conditions are met clearly: it certainly carried prestige; and it was not associated with particular individuals, but persisted over time. The third condition (being *legally constituted*) must be understood in terms of the legal system which prevailed in al-Andalus at the time. Except for those areas of life covered specifically by the religious law (chiefly prayer and fasting, marriage, divorce, inheritance, taxation and relations with non-Muslim subjects), a prince like ʿAbd ar-Raḥmān was reasonably free to do as he pleased, as long as he defended the practice of the

---

[91] p. 313

religion and carried on the *jihād* (which meant making at least a token effort to spread the domains of Islam and protect them from its enemies). To the extent that he could resist limitations on his authority from outside the palace, so to speak, the prince *was* the government. His hold on power depended in large part on the ability of his family and clients to control influential groups in various areas of society. Tribal affiliations were one example of power groups in the society at large that played a significant role in the maintenance of dynastic power[92]; the community of legal scholars and jurists was another.

While patronage of artists for the emir's personal entertainment may not have been defined in a legal sense that we would recognize today, the practice had limits with legal implications in the context of the religious law. The incident of the 30,000 dinars retold by Ibn al-Qūṭiyya illustrates one such limit: the emir could not simply dispense favors to his entourage out of the public coffers. The emir's behavior was circumscribed in this case by a kind of moral sanction that might easily have erupted into opposition from the religiously-led legal community if violated or taken too lightly. If moral arguments did not suffice to change the prince's behavior, legal opinions could have been issued against it. A prince who confronted the stream of religious-legal consensus too directly risked alienating one or more parts of his power base. This could have important repercussions, given that the history of Umayyad al-Andalus is replete with insurrections by various local head men, which had to be put down with force. Any crack in the Umayyads' perceived legitimacy would have compromised their ability to suppress these rebellions.[93]

Princely patronage survived at the whim of the patron himself, but the history of the Umayyads in al-Andalus also reflects a shifting balance of power between religious conservatism and princely permissiveness. Farmer (1929) traces the fortunes of music at the hands of various Umayyad princes with respect to the restraints imposed by religious orthodoxy, showing that the ruler was not always free to act without regard to the opinions of the legal scholars. Music, in particular, was considered by the orthodox to be a questionable enterprise because the Prophet Muḥammad was said to have frowned upon it, and because of the activities (such as wine-drinking) it was thought to encourage. A number of the Umayyad rulers depended heavily on

---

[92] The classic work on the history of al-Andalus that takes account of the tribal divisions in the society is Levi-Provençal's *L'Espagne musulmane au Xème siècle: Institutions et vie sociale* (1932). An overtly anthropological view of the subject is taken by Pierre Guichard in *Structures sociales "orientales" et "occidentales" dans l'Espagne musulmane* (1977), while Muṣṭafā Aḥmad explores the political dimensions of tribalism in al-Andalus in *al-Qabāʾil al-ʿarabiyya fī l-Andalus* (1983). But see M'hamed Benaboud's critique of scholarship on ethnicity in al-Andalus (2003).

[93] Safran (1999, 2001) discusses the Umayyad state's ritual, rhetorical and political projections of legitimacy during the caliphate after 929.

the religious establishment in maintaining their hold on power. In several cases cited by Farmer, religious authorities were able to impose limits on princely patronage of the arts, especially music.[94] In this way the system of patronage was indeed legally constituted in a sense that was meaningful in that era. To the extent that patronage of the arts fell within sensitive areas of the religious law, the opinions of jurists could exercise a great deal of influence on it.

We cannot overestimate the importance of patronage to Ziryāb's career. For an artist like Ziryāb, support from a prince like ʿAbd ar-Raḥmān II was the pinnacle of success in his field. He lost lucrative positions like this on two occasions (al-Amīn died; and he inadvertently offended Ziyādat Allāh), with the result that in each case he was forced to travel abroad in search of another patron. All the details presented in the sources need not be accepted uncritically: the startling sums of money ʿAbd ar-Raḥmān allegedly paid to Ziryāb are wildly out of proportion to the economy of the day, and in particular to the stipends paid to other musicians at the court.[95] What matters is that the patronage system was taken for granted by all concerned, and that it supported Ziryāb (and his family) while binding him to the prince (and his entourage) in socially meaningful ways.

Not only did patronage index the patron's prestige (and that of his client, as well) in the context of the time, it also implied a set of social relationships that entailed certain kinds of behavior, norms of dress and personal presentation. The prince did not merely expect Ziryāb to perform music at his command, but as his *nadīm* he was to provide companionship and stimulating conversation. Moreover, the anecdotes about Ziryāb and Ibn aš-Šamir show that *nadāma* also thrust the *nadīm* into the company of others like himself, bound to the prince, dependent on his pleasure, and constrained by the norms of behavior, courtesy and wit that held sway in the prince's retinue. Thus it is no exaggeration to say that the system of patronage was the single most important factor in shaping Ziryāb's career, as well as his social life in al-Andalus.

Slavery also shaped the life of a court musician in 9th-century Cordoba. Though some of Ibn Ḥayyān's accounts stretch credibility, they show clearly the importance of female singers and musicians, all but one of whom (Ḥamdūna, daughter of Ziryāb) were slaves.[96] They outnumber the male musicians by three to one in the era covered by Ibn Ḥayyān's biography of Ziryāb – roughly from the end of the reign of al-Ḥakam I, through Ziryāb's time, to the reign of Muḥammad I, son of ʿAbd ar-Raḥmān

---

[94] pp. 98-99

[95] Ṣalāḥ Ḫāliṣ (1961, 1966) presents a carefully-researched and fascinating analysis of the economics of the arts and music in 11th-century Seville, even making reference to Ziryāb and his patron.

[96] Lachiri (1993) finds that Ziryāb's daughters, Ḥamdūna and ʿUlayya, are the only examples of free women who achieved any recognition as singers in al-Andalus.

II (r. 852-886) – a span of six or seven decades. Before Ziryāb arrived, these women received their training abroad. Some, like Faḍl and ʿAlam, were born abroad, trained in Medina, and sold to the ruler of Cordoba. Others, like Qalam, were born in Iberia, sent abroad for training, and then brought back to al-Andalus. Unlike other domestic servants, they do not figure in the *muḥtasib* manuals, and thus were not bought and sold in the slave markets of the inland cities. More likely they were marketed as luxury items directly to members of the aristocracy who alone could afford their expensive services. Some accounts from this period and after indicate that they were purchased more or less directly from the schools where they were trained.[97] Ziryāb, however, seems to have created his own school for training these artiste slaves. No doubt circumventing the traffic coming from Medina augmented his personal means, but it also contributed to the influence of his stylistic school in the generations that followed.

The contributions of female artiste slaves were irreplaceable. These women often served as the vehicles for composers to be heard at court. ʿAbd ar-Raḥmān maintained a *sitāra* composed of these performers and expected them to know the latest works by his favorite composers. Even the curious story of Ziryāb and the *jinn* shows the role of the two female slave musicians in helping Ziryāb preserve the music he heard in his sleep. Whatever the source of the music, some assistance like this would have been needed, since musicians of the era lacked a practical means for notating music. If Ziryāb found himself prone to receiving inspiration in the middle of the night, it seems logical that he might need help to remember the music the next day. This service, that would have been by provided for a less wealthy musician by a (male) apprentice, was provided in Ziryāb's case by *his* apprentices: the artiste slaves. Moreover, the story shows the two "song-holders of Ziryāb" taking the new compositions to the emir's own *jawārī* in the palace, thus providing the necessary link between Ziryāb, the male courtier, and female performers in the emir's harem. Finally, in the generation after Ziryāb five of his sons distinguished themselves as musicians, ʿUbayd Allāh being the foremost. But several female slave singers also served as authoritative transmitters of Ziryāb's music, especially Maṣābīḥ, Ġulām and Waṣīf (the three slaves of Ibn Qalqal), ʿĀj (Ḥamdūna's slave), and the *imām* of that generation, Šanīf.

These artiste slaves and music teachers provided an incalculable service to the elite musical culture of their day.[98] The absence of most of Ibn Ḥayyān's material on the

---

[97] For example there is the case of Ibrāhīm b. al-Ḥajjāj, the master of Seville between 286/899 and 298/911, who purchased the artiste slave Qamar directly from Baghdad (al-Maqqarī *Nafḥ al-ṭīb* vol. 3 130-131). Similarly, Ḥasan Ḥusnī ʿAbd al-Wahhāb (1966, v. 2 p. 196) finds in Ibn ʿAsākir's *Ta'rīḫ madīnat Dimašq* that Ziyādat Allāh (Ziryāb's former patron) sent an envoy to Baghdad with 30,000 dinars for the purpose of buying artiste slaves.

[98] Whether any of them actually composed music of their own is not clear from the sources, but can we doubt that at least some of them did? The story of Mutʿa, the student of Ziryāb, seems to suggest that

slave singers in al-Maqqarī's version obscures the extent of their influence upon Ziryāb's career, but we cannot fully appreciate the career of a distinguished composer and musician like Ziryāb without recognizing the role that the social institution of slavery played in supporting, preserving and perpetuating his music. Both princely patronage and artiste slavery formed part of the web of social and economic relationships that gave shape to Ziryāb's career.

3. *Ibn Bājja: patronage and slave singers in the Almoravid era*

Having reworked Ziryāb's biography into a form that illustrates how two social institutions defined and circumscribed his life, let us look now at another representative of the elite Andalusi music tradition: Abū Bakr Muḥammad b. Yaḥyā aṣ-Ṣā'iġ Ibn Bājja. Ibn Bājja serves the standard narrative as a second founding father after Ziryāb, a composer who initiated a clear break with the music of the Middle East (and thus of Ziryāb himself) by reworking the elite music of his day into a distinctively Andalusi style. Although he is better known today as a philosopher, the accounts of Ibn Bājja's musical career reveal that he depended upon the same informal institutions that served Ziryāb some three centuries earlier.

Ibn Bājja fills the role of founder-innovator just as well as Ziryāb does, though for different reasons. Ziryāb, the former client of the Abbasids and student of the great musician and composer Isḥāq al-Mawsilī, appears in Ibn Ḥayyān, at-Tīfāšī and Ibn Khaldun as bearing the cachet of cosmopolitan Baghdad to an apparently backward corner of the Arab-Islamic world. Ibn Bājja, a *wazīr* and philosopher during Almoravid rule in al-Andalus, was an intellectual giant in a society already marked by its cultural sophistication. His philosophical views inspired admiration in some quarters, and disgust in others. What concerns us here is how patronage and slavery helped to shape his role in the development of the music of al-Andalus.

Born in or near Saragossa sometime in the second half of the 5th/11th century, Ibn Bājja grew up in that city and apparently was well known there, for after the Almoravids took it in 503/1110, he became the *wazīr* of the Almoravid governor, Ibn Tīfalwīṭ (d. 510/1117). While representing Ibn Tīfalwīṭ in a delegation to Saragossa's former ruler, ʿImād ad-Dawla b. Hūd (d. 524/1130), Ibn Bājja was imprisoned for several months (possibly for treason against the former ruler of his native city). After leaving prison, he traveled to Valencia, where he was living when he learned of the death of his former master, Ibn Tīfalwīṭ, and later the fall of Saragossa to King Alfonso el Batallador of Aragon in 1118. He departed from Valencia for western al-Andalus.

she, at least, was capable of improvising a song to suit a particular occasion. Such a talent must have pleased the emir immensely, and so would have been a valuable skill for Ziryāb to cultivate among his students.

However, when passing though Šātiba (Játiva), he again was imprisoned, this time by the Almoravid governor, Ibrāhīm b. Yūsuf b. Tašūfīn (on a charge of heresy, according to Ibn Ḫāqān). Freed once more, he reached Seville, where he served for somewhat less than 20 years as *wazīr* to Yaḥyā b. Abī Bakr b. Yūsuf b. Tašufīn. He was there as late as 1135 but left Seville for North Africa, and died in Fez in 533/1139.

Ibn Bājja was born into tumultuous times. Umayyad rule from Cordoba had slipped in the early 11th century, allowing the emergence of independent principalities across al-Andalus, the so-called Ṭāʾifa (pl. *ṭawāʾif*, "party" or "faction") States. This political shift had a surprisingly positive affect on the patronage system that sustained the poets and musicians of the day. Ṣalāḥ Ḫāliṣ (1961, 1966) points out that the collapse of the caliphate gave local overlords increased autonomy in political and economic affairs. One effect of this was to free up resources that had been held and distributed from the center in Cordoba, and this resulted in increased support of artists, especially writers and poets, whose presence brought prestige to local princes. Accordingly poetry and music flourished in the era of Ṭāʾifa States. At the same time, competition among the petty kings weakened them as a group and allowed the Christian states to make inroads from the north.

Ibn Bājja grew up under Almoravid rule. Military support from this North African Berber dynasty had been invited to al-Andalus in 1086 in the hope of stemming the tide of Christian conquests after the fall of Toledo. But the Almoravids went on to reunify al-Andalus under their own banner. His home region, Saragossa, was a frontier in the struggle. It had remained an autonomous kingdom hostile to the Almoravids after their arrival, but in 503/1110 they finally conquered the city. This power struggle marked Ibn Bājja's early career, for not only was he imprisoned (and thus denied patronage) by the former ruler, but the contest eventually led to the fall of Saragossa to the Christians in 1118, after the death of Ibn Tīfalwīṭ. Ibn Bājja's travels across al-Andalus in search of patronage led him back to prison again, and then finally to security as *wazīr* to the Almoravid governor of Seville.

The earliest account of Ibn Bājja's life, and one of the more complete, may be found in the biographical dictionary, *Qalāʾid al-ʿiqyān fī maḥāsin al-iʿyān* by al-Fatḥ b. Muḥammad Ibn Ḫāqān, a contemporary of Ibn Bājja's (he died in 528/1134).[99] Ibn Ḫāqān criticizes Ibn Bājja severely, accusing him of being the "disease on the eyelid of religion and the sorrow of well-guided souls" (رمد جفن الدين وكمد نفوس المهتدين.).[100] Yet despite

[99] 1966 edition by Muḥammad al-ʿInābī. Ibn Ḫāqān was a courtier in Šātiba at the time and something of a nemesis to Ibn Bājja. He may have played a part in his imprisonment.

[100] p. 346. Ibn Saʿīd summarizes Ibn Ḫāqān's characterization, and also presents an opposing view of the philosopher (1977, v. 2 p. 94).

his abhorrence of the philosopher, Ibn Ḫāqān provides a detailed account of his life, including the following passage:

> واقام سوق الموسيقا وهام بحادي القطار وسقا ، فهو يعكف على سماع التلاحين ويقف عليه كل حين …

> He frequented the music *sūq*, and he loved the camel-driver songs and drinking. He indulged in listening to songs, and devoted all his time to it.[101]

Ibn Ḫāqān also says he composed praise poems to the emir (Yaḥyā b.) Abū Bakr b. Yūsuf b. Tašufīn in Seville:

> ودهيه في ذلك واضح مستبين ، فانه وصل بهذه النزعة من الحماية إلى حرم وحصل في ذمة ذلك الكرم واشتمل بالرعي وامن من كل سعي ، فاقتنى قينات ولقّنهن الأعاريض من القريض وركّب عليها ألحاناً أشجى من النوْح ولطف بها إلى أشادة العلان باللوعة والبوْح ، فسلك بها أبدع مسلك وأطلعها نيرات ما لها غير القلوب من فلك …

> …and his cunning in that is clearly evident. So he came, by this route of protection to a sanctuary, and he remained in the shelter of this generosity, and he surrounded himself with men's authority and was safe (there) from any defamation. Then he acquired female slave singers, and he taught them the prosody of poetry for which he composed melodies which were sadder than lamentation. And he crafted them to pain and self-revelation. And he followed with them a most novel path, and he raised them up as luminaries of a celestial sphere, which for them were not hearts...[102]

So once again we find a link between the two institutions explored in the career of Ziryāb. For Ibn Bājja, the cunning apostate in Ibn Ḫāqān's view, patronage (here: الحماية , "shelter") represented protection (ذمّة) from calumny. Shielded by patronage, he found the means to pursue his musical interests, relying upon female slave singers (قينات here,

[101] p. 347
[102] p. 352

as an alternative plural to قيان) as the vehicle for his compositions, just as they did for Ziryāb three centuries earlier.

In contrast to the image presented by Ibn Ḫāqān, Ibn Bājja appears a century later as a true musical innovator in at-Tīfāšī's *Mutʿat al-asmāʿ*.[103] This passage is very important for the standard narrative, because it provides the most significant link connecting the philosopher, poet and *wazīr* to the evolution of Andalusi music. Following immediately after at-Tīfāšī's reference to Ziryāb (§1.1 above), the anthologist presents Ibn Bājja in the passage cited earlier, in Chapter 1 §2:

> Ibn Bājja , the greatest master, appeared and devoted himself for some years (to working with) expert female slave musicians.[104] He improved the *istihlāl* and the *ʿamal*; and he combined the songs of the Christians with those of the Middle East, inventing a style found only in al-Andalus. The temperament of the people (there) inclined to it, and they rejected everything else.

What Ibn Ḫāqān regarded as a vice, at-Tīfāšī presents as a virtue, showing once again the role played by female slaves in the production of elite music in al-Andalus, three centuries after Ziryāb, even though neither at-Tīfāšī nor Ibn Ḫāqān explains their exact role in Ibn Bājja's composing and performing. Given the importance of Ibn Bājja to the music of al-Andalus according to at-Tīfāšī, the contribution of these artiste slaves must have been substantial.[105]

A third account of Ibn Bājja may be found in Ibn Khaldun's *Muqaddima*. In his *faṣl* on "*muwaššaḥāt* and *azjāl* of al-Andalus"[106] the historian speaks of the poetic innovations that took place in al-Andalus and provides short accounts of several leading lights, including some interesting insights into their lives. For example, one passage describes a circle of Sevillan literati during the Almoravid era. As Ibn Khaldun relates the story (on the authority of "more than one of the masters" – وذكر غير واحد من

[103] p. 115.
[104] جوارٍ
[105] Indeed, we might almost read *Mutʿat al-asmāʿ* as at-Tīfāšī's argument for Ibn Bājja's significance to the music of al-Andalus in the century preceding him. He presents a series of 44 songs he says were sung in al-Andalus at the time (pp. 103-114). Of these, Ibn Bājja had a hand in composing 15 (either poetry, music or both), more than any other artist represented in the list. Moreover, elsewhere in the same chapter, at-Tīfāšī mentions two other composers, Ibn Jūdī and Ibn al-Ḥammāra, who "came after him … and expanded his melodies by refining [or: improving] them" (جاء بعده ابن جودي وابن الحمارة ... فزادوا ألحانه بهذيبا). The suggestion seems to be that these two composers (and others like them) represented a sort of stylistic school that stemmed from Ibn Bājja himself. The two younger composers together were responsible for 11 more of the 44 songs at-Tīfāšī lists. Altogether, this "Bājjan school" was responsible for nearly sixty percent of the songs at-Tīfāšī attributes to al-Andalus.
[106] The final *faṣl* of the *Muqaddima*, beginning on p. 542 of the 2004 edition.

المشايخ , p. 543) Ibn Baqī[107] and the other *muwaššaḥ*-writers (وَشّاحون) present threw away their own compositions after hearing one read out by al-Aʿmā aṭ-Tūṭīlī.[108]

The following passage from this part of the *Muqaddima* tells us about Ibn Bājja's pragmatic side:

وكان في عصرهما أيضا الحكيم أبو بكر بن باجة صاحب التلاحين المعروفة . ومن الحكايات المشهورة أنه حضر مجلس مخدومه ابن تيفلويت صاحب سرقسطة ، فألقى على بعض قينات موشحته :

جَرِّرِ الذَّيْلَ أَيُّما جَرِّ   وصِلِ السُّكْرَ مِنْهُ بِالسُّكْرِ

فطرب الممدوح لذلك لما ختمها بقوله :

عَقَدَ اللهُ رايةَ النصْرِ   لِأَمِيرِ العُلا أَبِي بَكْرِ

فلما طرق ذلك التلحين سمْع ابن تيفلويت صاح واطرباه وشقّ ثيابه وقال : ما أحسن ما بدأتَ وختمتَ . وحلف بالأيمان المغلّظة لا يمشي ابن باجة إلى داره إلا على الذهب ، فخاف الحكيم سوءَ العاقبة فاحتال جعل ذهبا في نعله ومشى عليه .

In the era [of two poets previously mentioned] also was the sage Abū Bakr Ibn Bājja, the master of the well-known musical compositions. One famous story is that he attended the *majlis* of his patron, Ibn Tīfalwīṭ, the master of Saragossa, and handed one of the female slave singers[109] his *muwaššaḥ*:

Trail the hem (of your robe), wherever it trails
and put drunkenness from him with drunkenness

And the object of praise was delighted by this, when he concluded by saying:

Allāh has bound the banner of victory
to the prince of the high deeds, Abū Bakr

---

[107] Abū Bakr b. Aḥmad Ibn Baqī aṭ-Ṭulayṭulī was born at the end of the 5th/11th c. and died in Seville in 545/1150-1.

[108] Abū ʿAbbās Aḥmad b. ʿAbd Allāh b. Hurayra al-ʿUtbī al-Aʿmā ("the blind") aṭ-Ṭūṭīlī died in Seville in 525/1130-1.

[109] قِيَنات

> So when this [last verse] reached the ear of Ibn Tīfalwīṭ, he exclaimed, "Oh, what rapture!" and tore his clothes, and said: "How beautiful what you began and ended!" And he swore that "Ibn Bājja shall not walk home except upon gold." But the sage feared an unfortunate outcome of this, so he ingeniously put gold in his sandal and walked home on that.[110]

The *Muqaddima* again links the two central institutions of the court musician/composer's life: princely patronage and the artiste slave. The slave singer is shown as the composer's musical interpreter, realizing the composer's inspiration within a context where his work can produce material results: the princely *majlis*. In this account the emphasis is not on the opulence and generosity of the patron, but rather on his parsimony and the poet/composer's modesty. Assuming there is some truth in it, it reflects the constrained means (or the frugal attitude) of the Saragossan court, which lay near the frontier of a border war between two hostile states, Christian Castile and Almoravid al-Andalus. This amusing and poignant story also underscores a major theme in Ibn Bājja's early career: his quest for a patron that would guarantee his livelihood and allow him the means to produce his poetic, musical and philosophical works.

4. *Institutions and innovation in the music of al-Andalus*

For Ibn Bājja, just as for Ziryāb, the standard narrative tends to obscure significant details. The modern historian's version does not really tell us much about the conditions that shaped the careers of these two men and made their contributions possible. We have seen in this chapter that the historical, biographical and literary sources for both Ziryāb and Ibn Bājja contain clues to a much richer picture of these two men. Each of them, in his own time and in his own way, depended for his livelihood upon networks of people and the informal institutions that shaped society.

Beyond the legend-like halo that surrounds Ziryāb's biography in the principal source, Ibn Ḥayyān's *al-Muqtabis*, the evidence suggests that artiste slaves served him as a tool for both composition and presentation. These women were accomplished musicians in their own right, for not only did they execute his compositions in performances for the patron, but some of them were required to act as living recorders of his nascent compositions and preservers of his works-in-progress who could faithfully reproduce what they had been given, assimilate the composer's corrections, and then

---

110 p. 543. Al-Maqqarī presents this story, as well (with an indirect reference to Ibn Khaldun), but its origins may lie with Ibn al-Ḫaṭīb. See v. 7, pp. 7-8.

pass the finished works on to others who ultimately would have to perform the material for the emir.

If we read between the lines of the *jinn*-and-*jawārī* tale, we see that this community of women (for clearly there were several of them at court and in Ziryāb's entourage at any one time) had its own internal structure and probably its own internal politics, as well. Ziryāb's "song-holders" served as teachers within the emir's harem. What status did Ziryāb's own *qiyān* hold with respect to those of the emir? The "Medinans" (Faḍl, ʿAlam and Qalam) had their own quarters, separate from the other members of the emir's *sitāra*. Obviously this meant higher status within the palace. Faḍl bore her master a son; this, too, would have had important social ramifications within the slave society, not to mention with respect to the rest of the emir's family. We can only speculate on questions like these, for the sources remain silent in such areas. Simply put, artiste slavery, like the institution of princely patronage, entailed a variety of social relationships, networks and statuses that shaped the lives of both slave and slave owner.

Ibn Bājja's story is less rich in detail concerning his musical career. Yet the fundamental social institutions (and the meaningful relationships implied in them) retained the same basic format, despite the three centuries that lay between the two men. Even this brief survey of accounts of the philosopher-composer shows that his career was shaped by his search for patronage, and his life highlights dramatically the fundamental relationship that existed between patronage and artiste slavery. The accounts tell us less about Ibn Bājja's servants as people: we have no names, and few details. Yet women like these appear to have played much the same role in his artistic production as they did for Ziryāb. Access to such well-educated and accomplished performers was possible for a man like Ibn Bājja only through the means provided by a wealthy patron. Moreover, their services surely would have been meaningless without the *majlis* that served as the performance milieu within which the arts were received, appreciated and rewarded.

The most difficult aspects of the standard narrative to evaluate in the sources are Ziryāb's and Ibn Bājja's artistic innovations, which cannot be defined with much precision. *Al-Muqtabis* tells us that Ziryāb was not the first musician to come from the Middle East to al-Andalus; and there is evidence of a distinction to be drawn between the "school" of Medina (where a number of artists surrounding the emirs of Cordoba received their training) and that of Baghdad.[111] Ziryāb does appear to be the first

[111] Those two schools were also recognized in the Middle East. In addition, two competing styles of singing in the 9th century are mentioned in the *Aġānī*: the conservative style of Isḥāq al-Mawṣilī and the freer, more inventive style of his rival, Ibrāhīm b. al-Mahdī. See the *Aġānī* (1989, v. 5, p. 290; Bulaq v. 9, p. 35)

important musician to arrive having been trained by the Mawṣilīs in Baghdad. According to Ibn Ḥayyān only one of the (male) court musicians Ziryāb trained, al-Manṣūr, ever excelled in Ziryāb's style, so perhaps his style was distinctive enough that a musician trained in what came before might have difficulty in mastering it. They also imply that Ziryāb's was not the only style of music at the court of ʿAbd ar-Raḥmān II, that the emir's taste was not limited to the Baghdad school. Even if Ziryāb's compositions did represent a substantial departure from what had been performed before his arrival, clearly other styles continued to be performed in Cordoba after his arrival.

Claims for Ibn Bājja's originality rest entirely upon at-Tīfāšī's brief account (though we might infer something similar from Ibn Ḫāqān's diatribe against the philosopher). In essence, Ibn Bājja combined two existing kinds of music into a new kind that was unlike either. At first glance, this seems plausible enough: both "the music of the Middle East" and "the music of the Christians" were alive in many regions of al-Andalus, so that Ibn Bājja could certainly have heard both performed, particularly (it would seem) in Saragossa, which lay close to the frontier. Yet it is unlikely that these two kinds of music existed as bounded entities, each an island unto itself. At the level of courtly music, such a firm distinction might be tenable. An Almoravid governor like Ibn Tīfalwīṭ might well have disdained "Christian music" for ideological reasons alone. A distaste for the music of the Christian adversary in an area of direct military confrontation between their respective societies would not surprise us: in times of conflict, cultural boundaries often become less permeable.

However Ibn Ḫāqān's account indicates that the philosopher-composer's musical innovations took place after his second imprisonment, when he was *wazīr* to (Yaḥyā b.) Abū Bakr b. Yūsuf b. Tašufīn in Seville. There, more removed from the atmosphere of open hostilities with the Christian states, a synthesis of the kind suggested by at-Tīfāšī certainly seems more plausible. And therein lies the difficulty, for if the arts in the present day are any indication, multicultural societies (like that of 10th- and 11th-century al-Andalus) seem to produce hybrid arts quite naturally and spontaneously through the interactions of artists from diverse backgrounds. Can we really believe, then, that Ibn Bājja was the first – the very first – to combine two musical styles present in his environment ("Christian" and "Middle Eastern") into a new one? Did he never hear Christian and Muslim musicians playing together in tea shops as he walked the streets of Seville? Did he never attend a social affair at the house of some Christian friend where musicians from the two communities performed together? Did he never stroll past a house where a marriage was taking place uniting a Muslim family to a Christian one, with all the musical possibilities such an occasion might suggest? While we have no firm evidence to address such questions at this time, to answer them firmly in the negative seems premature at least.

The sources for the lives of Ziryāb and Ibn Bājja demonstrate clearly that patronage and artiste slavery characterized the social and economic framework within which the elite music of al-Andalus developed. Viewed from a distance of some centuries, these institutions show a feature that typifies informal institutions, which is the personal quality of the relationships enacted through them. Formal institutions like those of the modern world may at times encourage a certain conviviality in the social interactions that surround them (as when "customer service" is emphasized at a bank), but this takes place despite the general character inherent in the institution, which has a life and aims of its own, apart from those of the people who participate in it. Indeed, the "faceless institution" has become an axiom of the modern world because in general, formal institutions rely to one degree or another on their *im*personal nature to accomplish their aims. To act "personally" in the sense we are speaking of here, to treat each and every case as unique, would paralyze a formal institution, because it depends upon standardization and the efficiencies and aura of fairness that that makes possible.

In contrast, not only do informal institutions like those of 9th-century Cordoban courtly life depend upon personal, one-on-one relationships, but such relationships are their raison d'être. Informal institutions exist to provide roles and norms for organizing personal social and economic relationships in a meaningful way. For example, the patronage system that supported composers and musicians in al-Andalus may be seen as merely the format by which resources held by the ruler were distributed to a class of artists. Yet such a view ignores the fact that these were human beings, not "rational actors" operating in an idealized economic system. The *form* of these economic relationships carried meaning for the people involved; it gave them a means of orienting themselves in society and with respect to one another. The patronage system created for all its participants a field for meaningful action that allowed them to actualize their abilities and satisfy their needs within a culturally constructed system of relationships. Such relationships may or may not have existed without the patronage institution that organized them, but the institution certainly could not exist without them.

The same argument can be made for the female slave system. It comprised far more than a set of economic relationships. Like princely patronage, it also served as an expression of beliefs and values that gave meaning to action and informed personal relationships. The role of artiste slave was the vehicle for a handful of talented and highly trained women singers and musicians to bring their talents to fruition through meaningful action in a social setting, and even more, this role involved a set of statuses and norms that both expressed and embodied the place of women, music, poetry and so on in that society. The system provided the framework for all its participants to orient themselves with respect to one another and to the economic system within which they lived. This is not to deny the oppressive aspect of these relations. It is natural nowadays to regard any form of slavery as morally reprehensible. But we should not lose sight of the fact that even oppression can be socially meaningful for both oppressor and oppressed.

A key feature of these relationships was their intimate quality. An informal institution perpetuates itself by establishing roles for the people interacting within it, while not depending directly upon particular individuals to fill these roles; it exists to organize personal relationships with respect to an accepted system constituted in one way or another through legal means. Just as with marriage, another kind of intimate relationship constituted in part through legal means, particular instances of patronage depended upon the patron and client knowing one another well: the terms of the patronage (rewards dispensed, honors bestowed and punishments meted out) depended on the patron's pleasure and the client's ability to satisfy that pleasure, and even to anticipate it. It was crucial that the composer know his patron's taste, lest he prepare something that found disfavor with the prince or even offended him. Ziryāb showed himself surprisingly adept at this when he met Hārūn ar-Rašīd and in effect made a bid for patronage at the caliphal court. Later, ʿAbd ar-Raḥmān found his personal qualities appealing, and they made his presence at court a pleasure for the emir. Obviously, the concept of *nadāma* itself implies personal contact with the patron while sharing his entertainments. The personal quality of such relationships is precisely why the account of Ziryāb at the court of Ziyādat Allāh is so surprising: a skilled courtier should have been aware that Ziyādat Allāh's mother was African (as was the case with ʿAntara) *and* that he was sensitive to that fact. Ziryāb failed to anticipate the patron's taste, and paid a heavy price as a result.

Similarly, the personal qualities of the *qayna* herself permeated the institution of female artiste slavery, which depended upon her ability to meet and anticipate her master's tastes. Ziryāb's "song holders" were involved in their master's career and his creative process in a very intimate way. Their working relationship surely had a personal dimension: Ziryāb probably selected Ġizlān and Hunayda for their skill in swift and accurate memorization, as well as their musical talents. Moreover, they were in close contact with their master and had to be on call at all hours of the night; he taught them his songs personally and prepared them to teach his compositions to other female slave musicians. As for those belonging to the prince-patron, their relationship to their master was no less personal (even speaking now only of the musical functions the *qayna* fulfilled and setting aside the special case of Faḍl, whose relationship with her master was obviously even more intimate). They served the tastes and whims of their master and were selected and purchased precisely for whatever qualities they possessed which he liked.

Like all of us, Ziryāb and Ibn Bājja were the products of their times. Their lives and careers should be read with appropriate attention to the social and economic contexts within which they worked, performed, traveled and composed songs. Perhaps the most remarkable fact is how similar their respective eras were in terms of the informal institutions that shaped them, despite the three centuries that lay between. However brilliant these two Great Men must have been as artists and personalities, we need not let the glare from their light obscure the very important role played by the people and social frameworks surrounding them in shaping their careers and providing meaningful context for their Great Deeds as musicians and composers.

Chapter 3
al-Āla in the Modern Era

The social basis of *al-Āla* today differs substantially from that of the elite music of al-Andalus from which it appears to have evolved. Gone are the ancient forms of personal relationship which the music served (patrons and clients, masters and slaves), for the music has moved out of the aristocratic *majlis* and onto the concert stage and radio, the cassette deck and CD player. It now reaches a wider audience than ever in its history, both in real numbers and in terms of the variety of social classes and even nations that now have access to it. These changes, of course, reflect the vast changes in society and economy that have taken place over the past thousand years. Hand in hand have come shifts in the meaning the music holds within Moroccan society. This chapter describes the emergence of various formal institutions in the modern context, which support and perpetuate *al-Āla* today. In this way, it attempts to show how these modern institutions embody important changes in the social and economic environment surrounding the music since the time of Ziryāb.

First, though, it is important to mention a term that will be used throughout this chapter: the concept of *modern*. Largely unexamined and generally assumed to be "good," modernity was once a given in intellectual discourses in the West and an important rhetorical marker that served as a synonym for "Western" in order to distinguish that from the non-Western in teleological terms. Modernity, by this line of reasoning, was both inherently Western and that which the whole world was (and should be) striving toward. Happily, most Western scholars have turned away from the idea that there exists one uniform modernity that is an exclusive characteristic of the West, and they now recognize that the issue of what constitutes "modern" is subject to diverse interpretations. Far from being either universal or uniform, modernity has been borrowed and manifested in numerous ways to serve local needs and to reflect local realities. It is no longer possible to speak of *a* modernity, but rather of *modernities* that must be viewed as culturally specific and economically informed.

Nor does the word *modern* as used here imply any sort of all-encompassing reality that distinguishes West from East or *developed* from *developing*, or any other similar dualism. Although some of the "modern" phenomena described in this chapter appear to be characteristic of larger trends taking place in the contemporary world (in particular the growth of formal institutions acting as agents in society), the term serves here only as a convenient way of talking about economic practices and social relationships that have appeared in recent times and are distinct in various ways from those of the more distant past.

1. *1100-1800: "Decadence," "degeneration" and "loss"?*

Between Ibn Bājja in the first half of the 6th/12th century and al-Ḥāʾik at the end of the 12th/18th century lies a gulf of nearly seven centuries in the history of the music of al-Andalus in Morocco. The timeline of the standard narrative (Figure 1.1) contains a large gap in the latter half of this era, between approximately 1500 and the appearance of al-Ḥāʾik at the end of the 1700s. Modern histories commonly describe this period after the fall of Granada in negative terms. For Chottin it was an era of "décadence" in which the greater part of the "glorieux édifice" of the music of al-Andalus was lost and only the "débris" conserved, an era in which the music was uprooted and "détachée de ses foyers d'inspiration, de ses jardins, de ses villes et surtout de contact d'une race pleine d'allant et vibrante d'un amour passsionné de la vie...."[1] Only ʿAbd ar-Raḥmān al-Fāsī's[2] and ʿAllāl al-Baṭla's contributions animate this otherwise moribund period, according to the standard narrative. For his part, García Barriuso regards the music's life in Morocco as totally dependent upon that of al-Andalus:

> La música ... ha penetrado en Africa en los tiempos del apogeo del reino musical hispano-árabe. En el Magrib se ha mantenido floreciente o decadente, según las vicisitudes por que ha pasado en la Península ... Las sucesivas readas de moriscos no pudieron aportar tampoco apreciables sedimentos artísticos. Su influencia desde este punto de vista sería muy semejante a la que ejercerían en un país los gitanos, pongo por ejemplo, que en el mismo se establecieran.[3]

Of course this implies that once al-Andalus fell to the Christians, so too must the music have fallen into decay in the Maġrib.

Even as sympathetic an author as Guettat repeats Chottin's undocumented claims regarding al-Baṭla and al-Fāsī, but then writes of the "decline" of the cultural life of North Africa in general, and of Morocco in particular. Guettat attributes it neither to the "Arab race" nor "Muslim fatalism" but to "les conflits politiques et les systèmes culturels qui ont plongé la population maghrébine durant plus que quatre siècles dans

[1] 1939, p. 98.
[2] Or his nephew, Abū l-ʿAbbās Aḥmad al-Fāsī – see Chapter 1 n. 14.
[3] 1940, p. 90

une longue et affreuse nuit de 'domestication', de désarroi et de résistance passive."[4] For Guettat, it is as if the sun never rose on the Maġrib in these three centuries. Rather, he maintains that religious brotherhoods harbored the music and safeguarded it from the French colonial project, though as noted in Chapter 1 §2, his discussion of Sufism and its role in Islam fails to offer much evidence to support this idea with respect to Morocco.

It does appear that much of the musical material known in al-Andalus has disappeared.[5] The surviving fragment of at-Tīfāšī's encyclopedia alone lists no less than 100 poems (selections from monorhymed poems, one to six lines in length) that were sung in al-Andalus and the Maġrib in the 13th century, of which exactly two lines appear in *Kunnāš al-Ḥā'ik*.[6] On the other hand, the very title of Guettat's book (*La musique arabo-andalouse: l'empreinte du Maghreb*) seems to belie his own dire assertions of benighted North African culture in this era. The sun did indeed rise occasionally during the long Moroccan night: a new *nūba* (*al-Istihlāl*) was composed, a specifically Moroccan genre of poetry (the *barwala)* was incorporated, and a fifth *mīzān* (*ad-darj*) was added. Moreover, the structure of the Moroccan *nūba* probably was a North African creation of this era. So the post-Andalusi history of *al-Āla* deserves a much more careful examination than it has received in the standard narrative.

Just as with the two founding figures of the Andalusian music, Ziryāb and Ibn Bājja, a view into the history of Moroccan literary and artistic life through the lens of the institutions and social frameworks which surrounded and to some degree shaped that life can point toward a richer narrative of the music's development during this difficult era. One advantage of this approach over that taken by Guettat and others is that it does not require a mechanical relationship between political and economic vicissitudes on one hand, and poetry and music on the other, for the main developments in the history of the tradition show that no simple correspondence exists between the two.

A case in point is the career of al-Jāmiʿī, who created a supplement to the *Kunnāš* and established the first conservatory for the music in Fez in the 1880s. If a direct relationship between political or economic turmoil and neglect of the tradition

[4] 2000, p. 219.

[5] But the written dimension of the tradition reveals more than simple loss. See Chapter 5.

[6] Lines 1 and 3 from the poem by Ibn az-Zayyāt al-Wazīr (aṭ-Ṭānjī p. 106) *Sal diyāra l-ḥayyi man ġayyarahā* (a *ṣawt* in the mode *al-Ḫusrawānī*) is found in the *Kunnāš* manuscript #144 at the Dāwūdiyya library in Tetuan (Bennūna 1999, #313, p. 332 – Quddām Ramal al-Māya), though with significant variations in the text. Bennūna notes the *ṣanʿa* appears in three other *Kunnāš* manuscripts, and he suggests (in part following at-Tīfāšī) that the text appeared in al-Andalus originally with a melody that Ibn Bājja later revised, as did his student Abū ʿĀmir b. al-Ḥammār al-Ġarnāṭī, as well; and it remained an active part of the tradition until at least the time of the Moroccan sultan Mūlāy ʿAbd al-ʿAzīz (r. 1894-1908). (n. 1098) This *ṣanʿa* does not appear in the modern songbooks by Ibn Manṣūr, Ibn Jallūn and ar-Rāyis.

existed, al-Jāmiʿī's anthology surely would never have been created, for the end of the 19th century was a time of intense political pressure on Morocco from the European states. The monarchy was engaged in a desperate effort to preserve its autonomy, while at the same time attempting to manage unruly tribes in the countryside. The official correspondence collected by Khalid Ben Srhir (1992) shows clearly both the internal turmoil confronting the monarchy and its simultaneous preoccupation with fending off the aggressive European powers. Al-Jāmiʿī's anthology and conservatory project appeared in the midst of these crises, despite these ongoing political and economic problems.

Furthermore, it is important to keep in mind that Morocco historically could be described as two "nations" coexisting within the confines of one country. A pronounced division between urban and rural society has persisted for most of Moroccan history, and so one should not assume a direct correspondence between rural economy, for example, and urban life. Section 1.3 below will examine some of the data concerning environmental and other crises that took place in this era, as a background for the discussion, but in general it is wise to avoid blanket statements about the role of large political, economic or even environmental conditions in shaping the history of *al-Āla*.

Contrary to the notion that the tradition's history in North Africa has been simply one of decay and loss, there exists substantial evidence that the tradition's structure and many of the *ṣanāʾiʿ* performed today are in fact North African creations. §4 of the Introduction, for example, explores the historial references commonly cited to discuss the development of the *nawba*/*nūba* and comes to the conclusion that there is no evidence that a suite form like the modern *nūba*, juxtaposing (theoretical) modal unity with rhythmic variation, existed prior to the music's establishment in North Africa. The *mayāzīn* of the Moroccan *nūba* (for example) are plainly North African creations, and indeed, one of them (*mīzān ad-darj*) did not exist as a separate element until the end of the 19th century at the earliest.[7] Thus renarrating the history of *al-Āla* requires setting aside the simplistic notion that the Andalusian musical heritage knew only degeneration during most of its North African history. Instead a fresh view of this history is needed.

Chapter 2 approached the standard narrative with the underlying assumption that an overwhelming emphasis on Great Men and Great Deeds obscures the significant role social institutions played in the music's history. In fact, the sources for two great men in the history, Ziryāb and Ibn Bājja, provide a considerable amount of information revealing the institutions that made their contributions to the tradition possible and wove their careers into the social fabric of the time. The rich sources

[7] Further evidence for this, as well as for the North African origins of much of the poetic material, may be found in *Pen, Voice, Text*.

available for this period made this retelling relatively easy. Historians and other literati of both al-Andalus and North Africa of the 10th through the 14th centuries devoted considerable attention to important poets and musicians. This, combined with the remarkable florescence of poetry and music in al-Andalus, left a sizable written legacy to draw from.

The same cannot be said for Morocco between 1500 and 1800. The effort to explore the history of *al-Āla* through formal and informal institutions during the era in question faces substantial difficulties, because resources for the cultural life of Morocco between the 16th and 20th centuries are rare and concerned primarily with famous people in a limited number of fields. Music is not one of these, as it had been for Ibn ʿAbd Rabbih and Aḥmad at-Tīfāšī. Poetry, too, while not completely neglected, did not receive as much attention from anthologists and other literati as during its florescence in al-Andalus. Certainly Moroccans of this era wrote poetry, but the surviving examples in general it do not compare in vitality and originality with that produced earlier in al-Andalus. Apart from poetry used as a teaching or mnemonic aid in academic subjects, themes included primarily religious odes, praise of the Prophet Muḥammad, and to a lesser extent celebration of rulers. Elegant verses on nature, for example, so familiar from the poets of al-Andalus, seem not to have flourished.[8]

In a similar vein, we find indications that while music was regarded with suspicion by many in both al-Andalus and North Africa, this seems to have been much more deeply woven into the fabric of religious law and society in North Africa, which could well have inhibited the creativity of musicians in Morocco in this period. An Andalusi account cited in Ribera, for example, tells of a certain jurist of Cordoba who could not resist rewarding a woman singer with a discrete donation of money.[9] In contrast, Moroccan poets and musicians seem to have felt the need to defend their work by adducing legal arguments in favor of poetry and music as entertainment. The influential Maliki jurist Aḥmad b. Yaḥyā al-Wanšarīsī (d. 911/1508) summarized the arguments surrounding the legality of music in his compendium *al-Miʿyār al-muʿrib wa-l-jamīʿ al-muġrib ʿan fatāwā ʿulamā' Ifrīqiya wa-l-Andalus wal-l-Maġrib*. In general, he disapproved of mixing music with the spiritual practices of the Sufis, as was done in some brotherhoods of his day, and overall he viewed music as allowable but "disliked" (مكروه).[10] Similarly, at the end of the 18th century al-Ḥāʾik devoted a portion

[8] See for example, Laroui's (1977) comments on North African Literature of the period, p. 212. Benchekroun (1974) provides a very thorough study of literary life in the 13th-16th centuries in Morocco. See especially pp. 455-469 for an outline of poetic production in this era. Chapoutot-Remadi (1997) summarizes well the state of historiography of the various nations of North Africa.

[9] 1922, p. 58. See also Ribera's discussion of the acceptance of music by the jurists of al-Andalus, pp. 53-54.

[10] 1982 edition in 13 volumes published in Beirut by Dār al-Ġarb al-Islāmī. On music, see v. 11, pp. 73-80.

of the introduction to his *Kunnāš* to a defense of music as a licit pastime, showing that in his day music still was regarded with misgivings by religious orthodoxy.[11]

A socially-informed retelling of the North African period of *al-Āla*'s history must begin at a much more basic level and draw much more upon speculation and inference. This should not discourage us, however, from exploring as well as we can the social environment which fostered the Moroccan Andalusian music in its earliest stages of development, for evidence suggests that the tradition experienced a significant shift in its social base in this period. An effort to address this shift can cast a different light on later developments, for which we have more detailed information.

1.1 *From al-Andalus to Morocco*

The standard narrative relates the transplantation of the Andalusi musical tradition to North Africa directly to the migrations connected with the Christian conquest. However a number of other migrations took place, which were not related to the conquest, and which the standard narrative overlooks. Moreover, since it does not concern itself with the music's audience, the narrative also ignores the effects of these migrations upon the social environment surrounding the music.

1.1a *Other migrations*

The role of the Reconquista in the migrations of Andalusis to North Africa cannot be ignored. In each of them, tens of thousands of people, whole families from all walks of life, uprooted and traveled to North Africa in search of a new life. They tended to settle together, forming communities in cities like Fez and Tetuan that had an important impact on the local social environment. Yet other types of migration appear in the historical record which likewise influenced the social context in which the music was performed.

For example, we know of certain individual poets and poet-composers who either emigrated to or passed through North Africa during their lives. An early case was Ibn Bājja of Saragossa, who died in Fez in 1139. The 13th-century mystics Ibn al-ʿArabī and aš-Šuštarī, both of whom composed strophic poems that probaby were set to music in their lifetimes (and certainly were sung later), each passed through Morocco on his way eastward in the 13th century. Another important figure was Ibn al-Ḥāsib al-Mursī (d. early 7th/13th c.?), who brought to Ifrīqiya songs by Ibn Bājja and

[11] All this evidence, of course, comes from writings by educated men. Just as the medieval authors ignored "folk" music entirely as being not worthy of discussion, so one should not assume that Moroccans universally "disliked" music in this era. On the contrary, Wanšarīsī's comments suggest just how prevalent music actually was in the 16th century...as it has been for every human society in every era we know of.

others current in 13th-century al-Andalus.[12] These well-known individual migrations may represent the visible tip of a larger iceberg of artist migrations taking place throughout this period.[13] Such migrations may have been very significant to the tradition's history, because we see indications that already in Ibn Bājja's time, the princely *majlis* was not the only venue for propagating the poetic-musical art. In North Africa as well as in al-Andalus literati gathered to appreciate one another's works. Examples from the sources include Ibn Khaldun's story of Ibn Baqī's literary circle in Seville, roughly contemporary with Ibn Bājja,[14] as well as aṭ-Ṭānjī's evocation of the literary circle in 13th-century Ifrīqiya that included Ibn Saʿīd and at-Tīfāšī, and was connected through Ibn Saʿīd's father to Ibn al-Ḥāsib al-Mursī.[15] In these literary salons an eminent poet or poet-musician, like Ibn al-Ḥāsib, could find a venue for his work, quite apart from patronage by the local prince. Just as important, members of the circle were brought in contact with talented individuals in their community. A newcomer's presence thus could gain notice, and he might contribute something to the local poetic-musical environment. The lack of accounts like these for Morocco should not be taken as evidence that such literary-musical salons did not take place.

In addition, group migrations from al-Andalus were not limited to those stimulated by the Reconquista, but also included migrations for other purposes. Muḥammad Razzūq (1996) finds that the first important migration of Andalusis to the Maġrib took place as early as the reign of Idrīs II (r. 187/803-213/829), and comprised some "8000 houses" from the area around Cordoba.[16] These people established the Andalusian quarter in Fez, on the so-called ʿUdwat al-Andalusiyyīn ("The Andalusians' Side") of the River Fez, and brought with them skills in agriculture and important crafts like leatherworking, which contributed to the city's economic life. Andalusi migrants also helped to build the region's infrastructure. The Almoravid sultan, Yūsuf b. Tāšufīn (453/1061-500/1107), brought a group of Andalusi artisans to Fez in the late 11th century to work on construction projects, including public baths and mosques.[17]

---

[12] See Chapter 2 §1.1.

[13] Guettat (2000) argues (from no clearly stated evidence, unfortunately) that such migrations belong to a process of cross-fertilization between the Maġrib and al-Andalus, by which he implies the presence of a pre-existing North African genre of Arabic music that provided one source for al-Āla.

[14] See Chapter 2 §2.

[15] See Chapter 2, n. 7.

[16] pp. 17-18.

[17] Razzūq (1996), p. 19.

1.1b *A wider audience*

We do not know whether any of these early migrants had knowledge of courtly music. It is possible that at least some brought by Idrīs II did, since this was around the time when Ziryāb arrived in Cordoba. But they were for the most part from the working classes and had little if any link to the Umayyad court. More importantly, as a group, they provided support for the later, larger migrations. When later waves of migrants arrived from Valencia, Seville and Cordoba, and eventually Granada, the earlier migrants were already in Fez to receive them. Over time, communities of Andalusi immigrant families became a political and cultural force in Fez and other cities such as Tetuan and Salé. On the Atlantic coast, Andalusi settlers in Salé formed a statelet in the 16th century as a basis for continuing the *jihād* in the form of piracy against European ships, while Andalusi settlers fleeing Granada ahead of the Reconquista were responsible for the refounding of the town of Tetuan in the late 15th century.[18]

The Andalusians of northern Morocco eventually proved to be a formidable power group whose actions could have serious repercussions beyond their communities. This became apparent in the 16th century in the patterns of ethnic group relations after the battle of al-Qaṣr al-Kabīr in 1578 and the internal political turmoil that followed the accession of the Saʿadī sultan, Aḥmad al-Manṣūr (r. 1578-1603). In this era, the army was divided into three contingents: a northern group composed of tribal recruits from northern Morocco, a Sūsī group comprising recruits from southern desert areas, and a separate Andalusian contingent. In addition, the previous sultan, ʿAbd al-Malik (r. 1576-1578), had created a corps of Turkish mercenaries that he hoped would provide a stable center to help balance political rivalries among the native contingents. Up to that time, the Andalusian communities in the north of Morocco had been loosely allied with the northern Arab tribes and with the urban elites of cities like Fez and Tangier. All of these groups had supported ʿAbd al-Malik against his competitor for the throne, al-Ġālib, who had refused to intervene in a Morisco rebellion in Spain, thereby earning the enmity of the Andalusian émigrés.

In the power struggle that followed ʿAbd al-Malik's untimely death at al-Qaṣr al-Kabīr, the Andalusians withheld their support from al-Manṣūr. Dahiru Yahya (1981) suggests that the Andalusians felt no connection to al-Manṣūr and believed that he was not able to govern Morocco.[19] They staged a short-lived mutiny in September of 1578. This was rightly regarded by al-Manṣūr as a serious threat to his legitimacy, and so he commissioned members of the northern military contingent to assassinate the leaders of the rebellion. This shrewd response on the young sultan's part not only decapitated

[18] On the "Andalusian republic" of Salé, see Razzūq (1998) pp. 210-221. On the refounding of Tetuan, see Latham (1965).
[19] p. 96.

the Andalusian resistance to his authority, but also put an end to the understanding that had existed between the tribes and the Andalusians and thereby reduced the Andalusians' ability to oppose him.

A later example of the influence ethnic Andalusians exerted both in Fez and the larger political landscape was the rebellion of 1820-1822 against the sultan Mūlāy Slīmān. El Mansour (1990) notes that the city had always had a separate governor (*qaid*) for each of its three major ethnic components: al-ʿAdwa, al-Lamṭiyīn and the Andalusians. Mūlāy Slīmān imposed a single governor, but as long as his government was able to ensure order this was accepted. However, after the sultan's defeat and capture by the Ait Oumalou in May of 1819, internal order in the city broke down. The city fathers eventually rebelled and appointed a new sultan. Mūlāy Slīmān laid siege to the city, which finally yielded in 1822. According to El Mansour, the Andalusian community played an important role in organizing and promoting the rebellion.[20]

Such cases illustrate the Andalusians' capacity for collective action and thus their awareness of themselves as a distinct group within Moroccan society. Probably the first arrivals had developed a sense of ethnic identity in the new setting, but certainly the later immigrants contributed to Andalusian solidarity within their community, for in later generations the Andalusians of Fez formed a power group that exerted considerable influence on political developments in the country. Given the advanced state of both music and poetry in the culture of al-Andalus they had left behind, can one doubt that either of these arts played some role in these migrants' cultural identity?

1.2 *A shifting social basis: the zāwiya as meeting ground*

One of the most important vehicles for solidarity among the leaders of the Andalusian community in Fez was the *zāwiya* (pl. *zawāyā*), the religious brotherhood focused around an eponymous saint. Fernando Mediano's study, "L'élite savante andalouse à Fès (XVème et XVIème siècles)" (1996) reveals the *zāwiya*, as a meeting place for the Andalusian intellectual, economic and social elite in Fez that provided a social space for creating links that helped them take a leading role in the governance of the city. Membership in the Jazūliyya *zāwiya* in particular constituted a social network for a number of important figures among the Andalusians of Fez in the 16th and17th centuries. Indeed, according to Mediano, the Moroccan historian al-Qādirī says that not a single member of the intellectual and social elite of Fez could be found who was not a member or a disciple of a member of this influential brotherhood.

[20] See Chapter 6, especially p. 202.

The key figure in Mediano's account is the Andalusian Sufi, ʿAbd ar-Raḥmān al-Fāsī.[21] ʿAbd ar-Raḥmān's great-grandfather, Abū l-Maḥāsin, had established a branch of the Jazūliyya *zāwiya* in Fez around 988/1580. ʿAbd ar-Raḥmān was himself an important religious figure, musical theorist and poet who played a leading role in several political crises in the city. This is the same ʿAbd ar-Raḥmān al-Fāsī who is said by some to have redefined the theme of *Nawbat Ramal al-Māya*. Mediano also provides a series of short biographical sketches for saintly figures of Andalusian origins in this and other *zawāyā* of Fez in the late 16th and early 17th centuries,[22] and he concludes with observations about how the various Andalusian families of Fez (the al-Fāsīs chief among them) used the social networks articulated in the *zawāyā* to further their social and political hegemony in the city.

The *zāwiya* thus lay at the intersection of social, political and religious affairs in Fez (and likewise other cities in northern Morocco) and as such has played a significant role in the tradition up through the modern era. Even today, leading musicians of *al-Āla*, such as the singer ʿAbd al-Fattāḥ Bennīs, are *zāwiya* members and perform both the sacred and the secular Andalusian repertoires. The brotherhoods have served *al-Āla* not because the music was one of their central concerns, but rather as a byproduct of their primary function as a focus of religious activity for community members who also had some interest in the music.

However, it is unlikely that the tradition depended solely upon the *zāwiya* for its survival, either before or during the Protectorate. Two lines of evidence support this conclusion. First, *al-Āla* contains far more secular than religious material, nearly all of it organized into *nawbāt* and *mayāzīn*, which the modern *zawāyā* do not use to organize performances. The preservation of the *nūba* as a performance unit must therefore include other factors than the *zāwiya* alone. Furthermore, neither repertoire – neither *al-Āla* nor the religiously-focused *as-Samāʿ* – contains all the material of "Andalusian" origin (that is, performed in "Andalusian" *ṭubūʿ* and *īqāʿāt*): the Sufi repertoire in particular contains *ṣanāʾiʿ* that do not appear in the *Āla* repertoire, as well as additional verses of *ṣanāʾiʿ* that do; and *Āla* musicians organize their *mayāzīn* performances differently, making use of different performance units. In addition, the Sufi *Samāʿ* repertoire is largely (not not exclusively) performed a capella. Thus the *zāwiya* did not play a significant role in preserving the instrumental aspect of *al-Āla*, especially the *buġya* and *tūshiya*. Even given the common Sufi practice of redefining profane imagery in esoteric terms, how could the *zāwiya* been a venue for preserving material that was not used there?

---

[21] On the life and works of ʿAbd ar-Raḥmān al-Fāsī, see: Lakhdar (1971) pp. 88-95; Levi-Provençal (1991/1922) pp. 266-269.

[22] pp. 90-94

Second, despite Guettat's suggestions to the contrary, the Protectorate governments (both French and Spanish) actively supported study and preservation of the tradition in Morocco. On the Spanish side both Patrocinio García Barriuso and Fernando Valderrama Martínez, two scholars who contributed important research on the tradition in the 20th century, worked for Protectorate-related educational institutions. On the French side, the very conservatory system that today serves to ensure the survival of *al-Āla* owes its birth and early development to Alexis Chottin and the Service des Arts Indigènes. While the Protectorate governments did adversely affect many aspects of Moroccan cultural life, *al-Āla* probably was not one of them. In fact, scholars like Chottin and García Barriuso placed their primary emphasis on the secular repertoire, which seems to have survived well enough outside the *zāwiya*. Thus, the social roots (and performance contexts) of *al-Āla* almost certainly were much broader than the *zāwiya*, even if the brotherhoods did contribute important figures to it.

The Andalusian music's links to the Sufi brotherhoods extend back at least to the 17th century. This in turn suggests one way that the tradition's audience had expanded. Michaux-Bellaire's study (1921) finds that the first religious brotherhoods (*zāwiya* in the Maġrib, *aṭ-ṭarīqa aṣ-ṣūfiyya* in the Mašriq) came into existence in Morocco in the 11th century (he counts the Almoravid dynasty of the 11th and 12th centuries as the first of these).[23] Marzano's research indicates that by the 16th century the *zawāyā* had come to play a major role in social networking and ethnic association in Morocco. Not all these brotherhoods used music in their meetings, but of those that did, some probably drew upon the elite musical tradition of al-Andalus in their rituals since we still find *zawāyā* that do so today. The Moroccan *zāwiya*, then, acted not simply as one repository of the tradition during the Protectorate (as Guettat argues), but also as a link binding ethnic identity, political influence and musical performance in a culturally-informed web of associations during the three centuries in question.

From these various pieces of evidence a hypothetical picture emerges of how the musical heritage of al-Andalus might have served as a vehicle for social solidarity among the Andalusians of Fez in the three centuries after the fall of Granada. Andalusian ethnic identity, exemplified in the leading social and political roles played by prominent members of the Andalusian community, and in the role of Andalusian communities in the country's political life, appears to have been connected with the *zāwiya* and the networks of relationships that centered upon that social institution. Is it

[23] The doctrinal and intellectual pattern for the *zāwiya*/*ṭarīqa* was established in the Mašriq between the 9th and 11th centuries, but quickly spread to the west, and there was a certain amount of interchange thereafter. For example, the eponymous source of the Šādhuliyya, Abū l-Ḥasan aš-Šādhulī, was a disciple of the North African descendant of the Prophet, Mūlāy ʿAbd as-Salām Ibn Mšīš. Abū l-Ḥasan died in Egypt while returning from the Ḥajj, and thus his *ṭarīqa* spread across North Africa and into the Mašriq.

too great a leap to suppose that the Andalusian musical tradition served as a marker of social identity / solidarity outside the *zāwiya*, in the non-sacred domains of social life, as well? The innovation attributed to ʿAbd ar-Raḥmān al-Fāsī (changing the theme of *Ramal al-Māya*) implies precisely such a profane use of the music, one that signals a connection to musical performances among the aristocracy in Seville and other cities of al-Andalus five centuries earlier. In the new setting, however, the music very likely took on much broader social significance as an emblem of the lost homeland, and therefore of a shared heritage. In such a situation, performance of the music of al-Andalus at weddings or circumcision parties, in private soirees and on public occasions, could have come to carry powerful symbolic meaning for people beyond the elite of the Andalusian community. It became the music of Andalusian identity, and it survived as such because of the social prestige attaching to this community and its cultural products.

This hypothesis is consistent with the available historical evidence, and it complements the suggestion put forward by Guettat regarding the importance of the Sufi brotherhoods in maintaining the musical heritage of al-Andalus. Chottin too, in a negative way, suggests the affective power of the lost Andalusian homeland in the immigrants' "regrets inutiles et dissolvants."[24] Thus this hypothesis offers a concrete explanation for the observed fact that a musical tradition that is held to have begun its history in aristocratic circles today reaches musicians and audiences at many levels of society; what was once the province of the elite has become the "property" of the whole society. This question is entirely overlooked by the standard narrative, but it lies at the heart of this renarration of the music's history.[25]

1.3 *Cyclic crises and social stability*

One line of argument sometimes put forward to explain the alleged "decay" of the tradition during the four centuries after 1492 has to do with a series of economic and environmental difficulties the country experienced in this period. Certainly Morocco's economy in this era suffered from a cluster of weaknesses. Environmental instability in the region combined with both internal political disorder and increasing pressure from foreign incursions to produce a cycle of economic crises that intensified after 1750. However, given the role *al-Āla* played in Andalusian group identity, as well as the fact that it is and always has been an urban art form, we should not leap too quickly to the conclusion that these factors affected the tradition dramatically in quite the way implied by Chottin and others.

---

[24] 1939, p. 98.

[25] The book, *Aġānī as-sīqā fī ʿlm al-mūsīqā* by Ibrāhīm at-Tādilī (d. 1894), offers a similar argument for the role of music Andalusian identity in this period.

Already in the time of Leo Africanus (ca. 1494 - ca. 1554), we find evidence of persistent poverty that touched many levels of society. Born in Granada as Ḥasan b. Muḥammad al-Wazzān, he spent his youth in North Africa, mostly in Fez. He was captured by Christian pirates while returning from Mecca in 1520 and taken to Italy where he converted to Christianity and composed his famous *Description of Africa*. Despite some fantastical aspects, it does offer a remarkable depiction of "the kingdom of Fez" (meaning the Wattasid dynasty during the early 16th century) whose detail (lengthy descriptions of the layout of the city, the various crafts and manufactures found there and the ruler's military deployments) strongly suggests its considerable value as a source. Leo comments on the simplicity of the ruler's entertainments and the general poverty of his court and makes similar reference to the reduced splendor in ceremonies honoring poets.[26]

The precise extent of this penury is difficult to verify, but it does seem that the wealth of the earlier Marinid dynasty had largely vanished from Fez by the early 16th century. On the other hand, as the musical forms of al-Andalus were perforce already somewhat removed from the social-economic milieu that had sustained them in Iberia, the transition to a wider audience had already begun, so that the survival of the tradition in its North African milieu was perhaps not so depndent upon elite patronage of the sort that it had previously known.

In the countryside, erratic climatic changes resulted in periods of relative ease punctuated by extremely bad years of agricultural shortfalls. Nicolas Michel (1997) and Daniel Schroeter (1988) have documented these cyclic crises and present a grim picture of rural Moroccan life in this period. At the same time, the hardships that resulted from these agricultural shortfalls were not felt equally by all Moroccans. Urban dwellers and those connected to foreign trade were insulated to some degree from the perennial food shortages in the countryside. This was particularly true for the coastal trade centers, and so it is likely that many in Fez, a city connected to Mediterranean trade through Tetuan and Tangier, were spared the lesser vagaries of moderate agricultural downturns.

However, the worst years affected nearly everyone to some degree, and one especially pernicious effect of persistent malnutrition is susceptibility to disease. Those whose economic or social connections protected them from outright starvation might still succumb to the plague (outbreaks occurred in 1750, 1799-1800 and 1818), cholera (which ravaged the countryside in 1834-5, 1855-56, 1868-69 and 1878), or smallpox, which could arrive by any of several routes and once established, could devastate the

[26] See for example his discussions of the kingdom's tax revenues (p. 163 in John Pory's English translation of 1600) and of the simplicity of the king's ceremonies (p. 164). Page 147 contains a remarkable description of an annual competition to name the best poet in praise of the Prophet.

population.[27] Michel underscores this problem, noting that the era just prior to the Protectorate was marked by four to six grave crises per century.[28]

The agricultural and health crises just described were exacerbated by political pressures from within and without. Dynastic struggles took place repeatedly over the three centuries in question, as first the Sa'dis in the first half of the 16th century, and then the Alawites in the middle of the 17th, wrested control of the country. Yet even long after a new dynasty had established its legitimacy in urban areas, a newly-anointed sultan might have to demonstrate his military power in order to enforce taxation in uncooperative areas. Sometimes a sultan's rule was contested even in urban areas or by other members of his family. Failure to meet such defiance with sufficient strength invited even further rebellion and the collapse of the sultan's authority. This was true even for the relatively stable and successful Alawite dynasty, which has ruled Morocco since the mid-17th century. Mūlāy Slīmān had to devote much of the years 1792 and 1793 to defending his position against two of his brothers, Maslama and Hišām, who were elected sultan in different parts of the country in defiance of Slīmān's claim. In addition to the Fez rebellion of 1820-1822 mentioned earlier, a similar revolt took place in Fez in 1727 after the death of Mūlāy Isma'īl, during the struggle for power that finally brought Mūlāy 'Abd Allāh to the throne.

Alongside these problems, increasing pressure from European states also strained the resources of the realm. The sultans of Morocco were expected to carry on the *jihād* against the Christian states, and failure to do so could severely undermine their prestige and thus their authority, especially among the Andalusian communities. Incursions by the Portuguese in the 16th century, and later by Spain and France presented a persistent threat that had to be met using income from either taxation or trade. Taxation posed difficulties because it often had to be collected by force of arms, and trade likewise had its pitfalls, leading eventually to an erosion of the monarchy's economic base.

These internal and external political contests during the 18th and 19th centuries compounded the problems caused by environmental and economic difficulties, and diverted resources that might have been spent on ameliorating these crises, not to mention patronage of musicians and other artists. If earlier centuries are even remotely similar, the survival of *al-Āla* in this period testifies indirectly to its valued status among certain urban communities, foremost among them being the Andalusian families of Fez, Tetuan and Rabat.

---

[27] Renaud (1921, 1925) presents the plague of 1799 in some detail, and likewise for the subsequent plague of 1818 (1923).

[28] 1997. p. 41

1.4 *al-Āla in its social frame between 1500 and 1800: preservation, development and loss*

A more complex picture of the state of the Andalusian music tradition in its early North African social context may now be drawn. Nourished by both large-scale migrations as well as the arrival of individual musicians, composers and poets from al-Andalus, the tradition probably first took root among families of Andalusi origin and served as a marker of their ethnic identity. Over time the *zawāyā*, especially those connected with such socially important Andalusians as ʿAbd ar-Raḥmān al-Fāsī, played a significant role as institutions that helped integrate the music into the social milieu of the time. Non-sacred branches of the tradition also served the community in a similar fashion at weddings and other social occasions.

At the same time, the social foundations of the *Āla* tradition experienced long-term economic pressure. Life could be precarious at times, even in a city like Fez, when cycles of famine and disease took a heavy toll. Dynastic struggles and foreign intervention also disrupted the situation, exacerbating problems arising from the cyclic health crises, especially after 1750. In such circumstances, enjoyment of music and attention to tradition must yield to the demands of basic survival, and yet to the extent that *al-Āla* carried significant social meaning, it could be maintained to some degree despite adverse conditions, because there is also survival value in preserving group membership and solidarity.

Within the boundaries of the social milieu just outlined, *al-Āla* developed in some areas but experienced loss in others. Some of the developments have already been mentioned: the emergence of the *ṭab*ʿ-based *nūba* in its modern form, the assigning of *Nawbat Ramal al-Māya* to praise of the Prophet, and the composition of *Nawbat al-Istihlāl*. These three, at least, must have been in place before al-Ḥāʾik, since we find them represented in his *Kunnāš*.[29] A fourth development, introduction of the *barwala* song form into the *nūba*, probably took place in stages around the end of the 19th century (and perhaps much earlier). On the other hand, it is virtually impossible now to know precisely the extent of the loss experienced by the tradition in these three centuries. Since no comprehensive collections have survived from before al-Ḥāʾik, there is no way to know how many compositions might have existed. Nor is there any clear evidence of how many *nawbāt* actually had been composed prior to his time.

There is no doubt that the North African period prior to al-Ḥāʾik was a time of multiple economic and political pressures on Moroccan society. It would be of no surprise to find that there was significant loss of material from the *nūba* tradition as the communities upon which it depended were wracked by disease and economic

[29] Another characteristic of *al-Āla* as found in *Kunnāš al-Ḥāʾik*, the rhythm-based *mīzān*, may owe its ultimate origins to an emphasis on rhythm as an organizing principle in Andalusi courtly music. See the discussion of references to song sequences by Ibn Ḥayyān and at-Tīfāšī in the Introduction, §4.

hardship. However, these crises were in some ways rather less severe in the urban environment that was home to *al-Āla*, as compared with life in the countryside. For despite these challenges, this was also the period in which the tradition was adopted as a marker of social identity by the Andalusian communities in the north of the country, so that on the whole, it was much less dependent upon aristocratic patronage in this era of increased privation. As a result, although an unknown number of compositions probably were lost, the exact extent of that loss cannot be determined, and set against that we must consider that several important additions and developments also took place that made this era much more than simply one of loss and decay.

2. *al-Ḥāʾik: a step toward standardization*

Modern authors frequently cite the reduction of the *nawbāt* from 24 to 11 as evidence of the tradition's decay, part of the standard narrative. Yet the claim for 24 ancient *nawbāt* stands upon the assumption that the *nūba* based on a single mode dates all the way back to al-Andalus. Chottin wrote that there once were 24 *nawbāt*, though he presented no evidence supporting this idea.[30] García Barriuso discussed this idea based upon a manuscript dating from 1717,[31] which Shiloah describes in some detail.[32] It appears that García Barriuso confounded the issue by assuming that whenever this manuscript says that someone composed a certain *ṭabʿ*, this refers to the composition of an entire *nūba*. Shiloah finds that the portions referring to *nawbāt* in this manuscript are only fragmentary and written in a different hand from the references to *ṭubūʿ* that comprise the bulk of the manuscript. Shiloah concludes that the *nūba* sections of this document are later additions. This confusion of *ṭabʿ* with *nūba* and the later date of these additions cast doubt on García Barriuso's argument. Apart from accounts like these, I have found no firm evidence that 24 *nawbāt* as such existed in al-Andalus. At best, one finds lists of *ṭubūʿ* in various manuscript sources and the inference by later authors that these represented *nawbāt* as well, a speculation based perhaps upon the idea that there were 24 *ṭubūʿ*, or upon the North African tradition itself. As argued in the Introduction §4, there is little firm evidence at this time to say much definitively about the Andalusi *nawba* after at-Tīfāšī in the 13th century, and even the *nawba* he describes is not clearly defined in terms of modal unity. Reynolds' work (2013) offers some tantalizing possibilities that may point toward a mode-based *nawba* in al-Andalus before the fall of Granada. However, the idea of 24 Andalusian *nawbāt* appears to be an argument made after the fact based upon the notion that the creator of a melodic mode is the same as the composer of a suite.

---

[30] 1939, p. 98.
[31] 177-179.
[32] 1979, #314 pp. 406-407.

Nowadays Moroccan musicians recognize 25 *ṭubūʿ*, but only eleven *nawbāt*, and this system commonly is attributed to al-Ḥāʾik. If the standard narrative is true, we are given to believe that al-Ḥāʾik single-handedly redefined the idea of a *nūba* itself, apparently violating one of its basic characteristics by combining multiple *ṭubūʿ* into one *nūba*. A strong argument against this is that an earlier work that combined a treatise on the modes with an anthology of texts, Muḥammad al-Būʿaṣāmī's (d. 1151/1738?), *Īqād aš-šumūʿ li-laḏḏat al-masmūʿ bi-naġamāt aṭ-ṭubūʿ*,[33] contains portions of six *nawbāt* (*al-Iṣbahān*, *al-Ḥijāz al-Kabīr*, *al-Ḥijāz al-Mašriqī*, *al-ʿUššāq*, *al-Māya* and *ar-Raṣd*), two of which (*al-ʿUššāq* and *ar-Raṣd*) comprise more than one *ṭabʿ*.[34] So it seems that the notion of a *nūba* having more than one *ṭabʿ* did not originate with al-Ḥāʾik at all. The principal of theoretical modal unity (perhaps *modal uniformity* would be a better expression) that distinguishes the Moroccan *nūba* probably was a North African invention, but one that has not been carried out consistently since at least the first half of the 18th century.

Al-Ḥāʾik himself remained silent on the number of ancient *nawbāt* in al-Andalus. He wrote simply:

ولما كانت الطبوع أربعة وعشرين وطبع الصيكة جرت عادة أهل زماننا أن
يستعملوا أحد عشر نوبة يضيفون إلى كل نوبة ما يناسب من نغمتها .

> Whereas the *ṭubūʿ* were 24, as well as *aṣ-ṣīka*, the people in our time customarily use eleven *nawbāt*, to each of which they attach its note which is appropriate to it.[35]

This is not a claim for the number of *nawbāt* at any other time than his own, nor for any particular date when the present *nawbāt* came into being. Rather, al-Ḥāʾik simply states what he witnessed: that people still used the 24 *ṭubūʿ* associated with al-Andalus (as

---

[33] 1995 edition by ʿAbd al-ʿAzīz b. ʿAbd al-Jalīl. On the problematic biography of al-Būʿaṣāmī, see Ibn ʿAbd al-Jalīl's introduction, pp. 9-12.

[34] This manuscript is incomplete: material clearly has been lost from the *muqaddima*, and only portions remain of *al-Māya* and *al-Ḥijāz al-Mašriqī*. Given the thorough way that the author details the modes in his introduction, it is quite likely that the book at one time contained more than six *nawbāt*, but the actual number will probably never be known.

[35] This version of the passage comes from Valderrama Martínez (1953, p. 54). Essentially the same text may be found in Ibn Jallūn (p. 40), who adds in a footnote that this proves that al-Ḥāʾik himself was not the person responsible for the eleven modern *nawbāt*, as Chottin (1939, p. 98) claims. Ibn Manṣūr's introduction, on the other hand, makes reference to 24 ancient *nawbāt*. Since he paraphrases al-Ḥāʾik in several places and does not always quote verbatim, it is safe to say that this detail was added to his edition by Ibn Manṣūr himself.

opposed to other *ṭubūʿ* which he enumerates elsewhere[36] and says are not part of the *nūba* tradition), but they customarily insert *ṣanāʾiʿ* that belong to some of these *ṭubūʿ* into *nawbāt* belonging to other *ṭubūʿ*, combining these modes in harmonious ways. (which is precisely what we find in the *nūba* system today). Al-Ḥāʾik thus did not claim to create new *nawbāt*, nor any innovations in their structure. Nor is it certain how well al-Ḥāʾik preserved material that was disappearing from the tradition, since he says nothing on this subject, either. Finally, there is no information at all about al-Ḥāʾik that might help us understand his work, apart from what he says of himself in his introduction.

Nevertheless *Kunnāš al-Ḥāʾik* was indeed an important milestone in the tradition's development, and not only because it is the earliest surviving comprehensive anthology. The fact that it was compiled at all suggests a certain level of awareness of the distinctiveness of the Andalusian music tradition, an awareness that spurred the standardization and canonization of the tradition and its contents over the subsequent two centuries. Moreover, the format al-Ḥāʾik used in the *Kunnāš* reaffirmed the traditional format for representing song texts, a format more characteristic of Arabic poetry anthologies than of songbooks as we think of them in the West today, and one that has persisted into the 21st century.

We do not know whether Muḥammad b. al-Ḥusayn al-Ḥāʾik at-Tiṭwānī al-Andalusī was aware of al-Būʿaṣāmī's work of a half-century earlier. (Versions of the *muqaddima* found in some *Kunnāš* manuscripts present much of the same information on the *ṭubūʿ*, though that by itself is not conclusive proof.) When he assembled his anthology of *al-Āla* in the late 18th century, he may perhaps have thought that he was the first to attempt a comprehensive collection. It is unlikely, though, that he foresaw the full impact of his project on the tradition. The standard narrative holds that he wanted to collect what was being lost in his time, but that does not gibe with what the anthologist himself actually says about his own motives.

Published texts of al-Ḥāʾik's introduction (*muqaddima*) vary somewhat. Ibn Jallūn and Ibn Manṣūr, each working from more than one manuscript, include in their songbooks a statement in al-Ḥāʾik's *muqaddima* about himself and his reasons for compiling his anthology. Bennūna's manuscript edition contains only a fragment of the introduction that does not have this statement. Ambīrkū's edition begins like the versions in Ibn Jallūn and Ibn Manṣūr, though it does not contain the statement in question, either. Valderrama Martínez appears to have been working from an incomplete manuscript as well,[37] which follows Ibn Jallūn's/Ibn Manṣūr's version

---

[36] Valderrama Martínez (1954), pp. 52-53; Ibn Jallūn, p. 39.

[37] Recently published (2003) in facsimile form, with a preface by Manuela Cortés García.

closely, but is missing about one page of text, the page that includes the following passage:

وقد كنت زمن الشبيبة مولعا بحفظ الأشعار ، وأطلبه من الأجلة الأخيار ، إلى أن
بلغت فيه ما يؤنس الخاطر ويسليه ، واعلم أن من دخل هذا البحر غرق في ساحله
فطلب مني بعض الإخوان أن أجمع له ما حصل عندي حفظه من فن الموسيقى
زجلا وتوشيحا ، وأوضحه له إيضاحا مبينا صحيحا ليكون ذلك عونا للتعليم ...

> In the time of my youth, I loved memorizing poems, seeking it from the best and most distinguished (people), until I attained in it [a level] that pleases the mind and entertains it. Know that anyone who enters this sea founders by its shores, so one of my friends asked me to gather together for him the art of music as far as I have memorized it, the *zajal* and *tawšīḥ*, and to present it clear and correct for him, so that it will be an aid in teaching...[38]

This is almost all the information al-Ḥāʾik provides on his life and purpose in creating the *Kunnāš*, and by itself it does not give any hint that the musical tradition was endangered in his time. Rather the anthologist says he found in his youth experts in the tradition from whom he learned the material. Moreover, he indicates here that in his time, study of *al-Āla* (at least its poetic contents) was a profound undertaking. Neither of these statements implies loss or decadence in and of themselves, quite the contrary. Finally, he indicates he is answering a request for a teaching aid. Thus *Kunnāš al-Ḥāʾik* comprises the poetry he found was "used" (مما يستعمل فيها , as he indicates at the beginning of each *mīzān*) in each of the eleven *nawbāt* performed in his era, amounting to texts of more than 700 *ṣanāʾiʿ*. Significantly, this passage seems to focus upon the poetry as much as on the musical aspect of the tradition.[39]

In addition to the above statements, the Dāwūdiyya library #144 manuscript of the *Kunnāš* contains another possible clue. The *muqaddima* to this manuscript is only a fragment, an unknown number of pages having been lost. What remains begins with a passage apparently not found in other manuscripts, in which the anthologist praises his patron, the prince Mūlāy ʿAbd as-Salām, son of the Sultan Sīdī Muḥammad b. ʿAbd Allāh and continues as follows:

---

[38] Ibn Jallūn, p. 38. Ibn Manṣūr's version (pp. 10-11) follows this very closely, differing only in omitting the case indications from زجلا, توشيحا and صحيحا and in giving أفيد ("more useful") for عونا.

[39] The anthologist also provided in his introduction a legal argument in favor of music as a legitimate pastime, explained the musicotherapeutic ideas attaching to the various ṭubūʿ, and summarized the modal and rhythmic contents of the tradition.

> وقد أمر أيّده الله بكنّاش يحتوي لِما يُستعمل من الطبوع على الصنائع والأزجال والتوشيحات والأشغال . فامتثلنا أمره من غيرِ ونا ، وأخذنا في جمع هذا الكناش باعْتنا ، واعتمدنا على ما جمعه من قبلنا ، أساتيذُ الغنا [sic] ، فانتخبنا من ذلك ما وضعنا هنا ، وهو إن شاء الله وضع عجيب ...

> He (may Allāh support him) ordered a handbook, which comprises the *ṭubūʿ* which are used for *ṣanāʾiʿ*, *azjāl*, *tawšīḥāt* and *ašġāl*. We followed his command without slackening, and set about collecting this notebook painstakingly. We relied upon what the masters of song before us collected, and we chose from that what we (have) put here, which is, Allāh willing, a remarkable work ...[40]

This statement is somewhat problematic. The Dāwūdiyya manuscript in which it is found has certain features that distinguish it from other *Kunnāš* manuscripts, so that some scholars (notably Cortés García, 1996) have argued that it does not belong to the main stream of the *Kunnāš* manuscript tradition, and therefore is not, properly speaking, an exemplar of *Kunnāš al-Ḥāʾik*. Be that as it may, the statement above does not significantly contradict statements found in other versions of the *muqaddima*: it is not a statement about loss or decay, but rather an explanation that the anthologist's patron had requested the work, and that the project was carried out diligently, based upon knowledge held by contemporary experts.

The idea of a comprehensive anthology of *al-Āla*, such as *Kunnāš al-Ḥāʾik*, may have represented a departure from the musical tradition as it had been understood. The aim was to gather all the poetry available relating to the *nūba* format as a way of making the *ṣanāʾiʿ* more easily transmittable. With so little information available it is difficult to be too precise, but according to its introduction, the *Kunnāš* was simply an effort to pull together what al-Ḥāʾik himself had memorized at the hands of an older generation of *al-Āla* aficionados[41] and present it in the form of a teaching reference manual. But what exactly did al-Ḥāʾik think he was collecting? What categories did he have in mind, and what were the criteria that allowed him to define the scope of the *Kunnāš* and compile it? Although he does distinguish between Andalusi *ṭubūʿ* and others that he does not regard as Andalusi, nowhere does al-Ḥāʾik use the expression *al-mūsīqā l-andalusiyya*, which would signal that such a category existed. Moreover, he

---

[40] 1999, pp. 119-120.

[41] Versions of the standard narrative often suggest that the anthologist consulted a variety of experts in compiling his anthology (e.g.: Guettat, 2000, p. 248). The foregoing should make clear the chronology: the statements above imply that al-Ḥāʾik had already mastered the poetry of the tradition before he was asked to write it down, that in this project he consulted mainly his own prodigious memory.

purports in his *muqaddima* to be presenting the *azjāl* and *muwaššaḥāt* he has memorized, which would suggest some connection to al-Andalus, and yet his anthology also presents not a few selections from non-strophic poetry, too. To judge from the contents of the *Kunnāš* and its *muqaddima*, the principle that binds these *ṣanā'iʿ* together seems to be that each is performed in one of the 25 *ṭubūʿ* that had been organized into the eleven *nawbāt* he presents. Thus, al-Ḥā'ik understood his subject as *ṭabʿ*-based *nūba* music, potentially (but not necessarily) *Andalusian* music as such.

Beyond this, the anthologizing project itself implies that the musical-poetic *nūba* corpus represented an art form, an artistic unity distinct from others, available to be recorded and thus legitimized as a cultural artifact. This thought did not originate with al-Ḥā'ik. Al-Būʿaṣāmī's earlier, anthology-treatise on the *ṭubūʿ* shows that the model *nūba* existed for at least half a century before al-Ḥā'ik (and of course probably longer). Moreover, it was regarded as embodying music *par excellence* in that era. Al-Ḥā'ik's "innovation" was merely in attempting a more-or-less comprehensive collection of what was then performed in his region under the *nūba* rubric. These were simply the *ṣanā'iʿ* that al-Ḥā'ik regarded as belonging together. This cluster of issues will be revisited briefly in Chapter 5. The point at the moment is that such questions simply underscore how little is known about the anthologist and the tradition as it existed in his era. Knowingly or not, in producing his *Kunnāš* al-Ḥā'ik took an important step toward standardizing the contents and organization of the tradition and therefore consolidating the idea of *al-Āla* as an object of study and ultimately, of organized teaching. The very existence of the anthology provided the first prerequisite for the emergence of the formal institutions that now surround the tradition.

Moreover, not only did *Kunnāš al-Ḥā'ik* define the boundaries of the tradition, but it also reaffirmed the format in which the tradition was to be represented in writing. *Kunnāš al-Ḥā'ik* is not constructed as a practical guide for singing. In fact, it is not much use as a songbook in the sense we use this word today, because it does not represent the *ṣanā'iʿ* as they are sung, but simply as poetry, with all the appropriate conventions, leaving out the repetitions and *tarāṭīn* that characterize so many of the *ṣanā'iʿ*. Al-Ḥā'ik's time knew no practical method for representing songs as such, which is precisely the point: these conventions serve as part of the discursive frame surrounding the tradition that shapes how the anthology is used and therefore binds it in a certain relationship to the social milieu surrounding the tradition. Al-Ḥā'ik's anthology made tangible and underscored what had existed up to then largely as a generalized belief, namely, that the *nūba* (and all that came with it: *mayāzīn*, *ṭubūʿ*, *ṣanā'iʿ* and *īqāʿāt*) represented a distinct art form. The act of collecting it and writing it down was, in a sense, a statement that *al-Āla* was in fact worthy of enshrining in written form. Al-Ḥā'ik's aim had less to do with presenting the lyrics of *songs* than with *representing the tradition according to an established set of conventions* of a highly-valued form of discourse, namely, poetry. Representing the contents of *al-Āla* in this format situated the literary dimension of the tradition within the prestigious domain of Arabic poetry. To have done otherwise, to have included the repetitions and *tarāṭīn,* would have accomplished exactly the opposite.

3. *al-Jāmiʿī and the first conservatory*

Near the end of the 19th century another attempt was made to assemble the poetry in *al-Āla* into an anthology, this one apparently driven by an entirely different agenda from that inferred from al-Ḥāʾik's *muqaddima*. This second anthology of *al-Āla* is attributed to the son of a government official, the *faqīh* Sīdī Muḥammad b. al-Wazīr as-Sayyid al-ʿArabī b. al-Wazīr as-Sayyid al-Muḫtār al-Jāmiʿī.[42] Cortés García, in her introduction to the recent facsimile edition of the *Kunnāš* (2003) gives his death date as 1885, which fell within the reign of the Alawite sultan Mūlāy al-Ḥasan I (r. 1873-1894). According to Benmūsā, in addition to creating the new anthology, al-Jāmiʿī also participated in founding the first bona fide conservatory of *al-Āla,* which was located in the old governor's palace in the al-Baṭḥāʾ neighborhood of the Fez Medina (a building now known as the Musée Batha).[43] It appears that the impetus behind al-Jāmiʿī's compilation was to provide written teaching materials for a centralized effort at teaching the tradition. This apparently unprecedented step deserves closer examination in its historical context.

3.1 *al-Jāmiʿī in historical context*

The hundred years following al-Ḥāʾik, the 13th/19th century, were marked by the hardships documented in the evidence collected by Michel and Schroeter. Unfortunately, Morocco's weakened internal condition coincided with increasing aggressiveness on the part of the European states. The end of the Napoleonic wars produced a newly stabilized Europe in which Great Britain and France especially prospered. These two states began creating spheres of influence in Asia and Africa, and in particular, they divided Africa between them in this colonial competition. In this scheme, eastern and southern Africa fell to Britain, and western Africa and the Maġrib (Tunisia, Algeria and Morocco) fell to France.

---

[42] This is the most complete version of the anthologist's name available. It appears on the cover of a manuscript facsimile deposited at the Ḫizāna al-ʿĀmma in Rabat (ms. 1327). The cover of this manuscript gives its title as: تاليف في الموسيقى مما جمعه واختاره ورتّبه الفقيه ("A collection of music, which [the above named al-Jāmiʿī] gathered, selected and arranged"). This manuscript has no *muqaddima,* and contains elements of *mīzān ad-darj* written in the margins of *al-bṭāyḥī* in each *nūba*.

[43] 2001a, p. 26.

Spain was one of France's competitors for Morocco. France gained the upper hand in this contest after first taking control of Algeria in 1830, and then crushing the Moroccan army at Isly in 1844 thereby effectively limiting Spain's sphere of influence in the region. This military disaster severely damaged the Moroccan monarchy's credibility, especially when it was learned that Sultan Mūlāy ʿAbd ar-Raḥmān had begun negotiating with the French even while the army was being decimated in the field. The tribal rebellions that ensued further weakened the monarchy's position and effectively left it with only one diplomatic option: to play France and Spain against one another. The documents collected by Khalid Ben Srir (1992) show the sultans Muḥammad IV and al-Ḥasan I in the last decades of the 19th century trying to enlist Britain as an ally in the diplomatic maneuvering. They did not have much success with this ploy, but they did manage to put off complete colonization for a while. Finally, in 1906, the French crossed the Algerian border in force. In 1912 Morocco was divided into French and Spanish Protectorate zones, and four decades of foreign domination ensued.

3.2 *The al-Jāmiʿī corpus*

Al-Jāmiʿī appeared during this complicated period. Less is known about him even than al-Ḥāʾik, because not only does he not appear in historical sources, but the manuscripts of his anthology contain no introduction that might provide clues. What information is found in secondary sources today like Cortés García (1996) and Guettat (2000) derives from oral tradition and from titles added to later copies of manuscripts containing his anthology, such as that held by the Ḫizāna al-Waṭaniyya in Rabat.

The manuscript basis for the al-Jāmiʿī corpus is also somewhat problematic. ʿAbd al-Fattāḥ Benmūsā expressed skepticism that an actual al-Jāmiʿī anthology ever existed.[44] Indeed, in his introduction to *Min waḥy ar-rabāb* (1982), ʿAbd al-Laṭīf Aḥmad Ḫāliṣ tells us that in that book, ʿAbd al-Karīm ar-Rāyis presents the al-Jāmiʿī corpus based upon two sources: handwritten notebooks circulating among musicians, and his own deep knowledge of the tradition. Yet the manuscripts attributed to al-Jāmiʿī which I have examined (all of them 20th-century copies) are similar enough to one another to suggest strongly a single, common source document which probably is lost.[45] At the same time, they differ in several ways from the modern "edition" of the al-Jāmiʿī

[44] Interview, October, 2004.

[45] Cortés García, in the introduction to the *Kunnāš* facsimile edition, mentions the existence of an "original" al-Jāmiʿī manuscript. See also *Pasado...*, p. 49. However, since she neither describes this manuscript nor gives any information on its location, there is no way at this point to discover whether this "original" manuscript differs in any way from others available for scrutiny in public and private libraries in Morocco.

corpus, *Min waḥy ar-rabāb*. Given Ḫāliṣ' comments, it may be that in al-Jāmiʿī's case, the anthology was not disseminated at first as a single, definitive document. Rather, it may have begun only, or primarily, as a notebook teaching aid at the newly-established conservatory from which informal copies were made that served as the ancestors of the manuscripts available today. Certainly al-Jāmiʿī's anthology has nothing like the notoriety and emblematic status that *Kunnāš al-Ḥāʾik* enjoys. The idea of a *Kunnāš al-Jāmiʿī*, or even of an anthology bearing his name is almost unknown. For this reason, we will refer to his collection as the al-Jāmiʿī corpus.[46]

Nevertheless the al-Jāmiʿī corpus is significant because it differs in important ways from al-Ḥāʾik's anthology. It is shorter than the *Kunnāš* and contains *ṣanāʾiʿ* that appear in the *Kunnāš* (often shortened or altered in some way), as well as a few that do not appear in the *Kunnāš*. Curiously the Moroccan colloquial song form *barwala*, whose introduction Cortés García attributes to al-Jāmiʿī does not appear in any of the manuscripts I have examined. Likewise *mīzān ad-darj* as a distinct element in the *nūba*, appears only as marginalia, and therefore is a later addition.

3.3 *al-Jāmiʿī's conservatory*

ʿAbd al-Fattāḥ Benmūsā describes al-Jāmiʿī's "first conservatory" as simply a central location where masters of the tradition could meet with students in an environment conducive to teaching and practice. According to Benmūsā, in the beginning there was neither a fixed curriculum nor a systematic program for teaching, other than (1) adherence to the *ṣanāʾiʿ* as they were performed in Fez at the time (what Benmūsā calls *al-madrasa al-muḥāfiẓa*, "the conservative school") and (2) use of the al-Jāmiʿī corpus and *Kunnāš al-Ḥāʾik* as reference materials.[47] In the late 19th century the conservatory moved from the al-Baṭḥaʾ neighborhood to the building known today as Dār ʿAdīl, also in the Fez Medina, though the organizational structure remained the same. This second location served as the principal site in Fez for organized teaching of *al-Āla* in the 20th century up to the present. Even after the National Conservatory was established and assumed responsibility for this instruction, Dār ʿAdīl continued to operate as the Medina branch of the Conservatory.

Unfortunately, as with so many areas of the tradition's history in the last two centuries, relatively little is known about al-Jāmiʿī and the institution he helped to establish. His biography derives from oral tradition, which relates nothing about precisely in what way al-Jāmiʿī actually was involved in the day-to-day operation of

[46] A brief study of these manuscripts is found in Chapter 5, along with an analysis of their intertextual relationships to *Kunnāš al-Ḥāʾik*.
[47] Benmūsā interview, 2/14/2004.

the conservatory. It seems unlikely that al-Jāmiʿī alone could have been responsible for the conservatory. At the very least, the master musicians who taught there must have played an important role in establishing the curriculum, arranging lesson times, selecting students and so on.

3.4 *The significance of al-Jāmiʿī*

From the point of view of the standard narrative, which ignores the social frame surrounding *al-Āla*, it is easy to underestimate al-Jāmiʿī's importance to the tradition as it exists today. He appears simply as an anthologist who followed in al-Ḥāʾik's footsteps but included *mīzān ad-darj* in the *nūba*. Yet the al-Jāmiʿī corpus preserves *ṣanāʾiʿ* and performance units (that is, sequences of *ṣanāʾiʿ*) that differ from those in *Kunnāš al-Ḥāʾik* and that have proven to be popular with musicians and audiences. Moreover, since the early 1980s the al-Jāmiʿī corpus (in its published form, *Min waḥy ar-rabāb*) has become the most widely available canonical text for *al-Āla* and as such, serves as a standard teaching reference at the National Conservatory.[48] Equally important for the tradition's survival, the al-Jāmiʿī corpus (side-by-side with *Kunnāš al-Ḥāʾik*) contributed to standardizing the contents of the tradition, thereby making the idea of a conservatory possible.

Al-Jāmiʿī's conservatory had an important impact on the social relationships surrounding the music, simply by bringing students and masters together in a central location with the aim of facilitating the teaching process. This itself may have helped to reshape the status of the tradition in its social environment. By creating a more-or-less public space for teaching the music, al-Jāmiʿī's conservatory moved the tradition out of the master's private salon and placed it in a more detached environment ("professional," in contemporary terms) within easier reach of the public. This shift also contributed to formalizing the relationships between an elder generation of master musicians and their students, creating a nexus from which a living memory of master-disciple links, a clear genealogy of masters, could emerge. Figure 3.1 represents a genealogy of masters connected to the Dār ʿAdīl conservatory, based upon

[48] Whereas both the Ibn Jallūn and Ibn Manṣūr songbooks based upon the *Kunnāš* have gone out of print, *Min waḥy ar-rabāb* continues to be reprinted and can be found in many bookshops around the country. See the discussion of teaching methods at the National Conservatory of Music and Dance in Chapter 4 §5. Note, however, that *Kunnāš al-Ḥāʾik* retains an iconic significance as the indespensible urtext for the tradition (a topic discussed in Part 2), and it remains a very important source for *ṣanāʾiʿ* and performance units among professional musicians and *ajwāq*. The al-Jāmiʿī corpus does not by any means define the extent of the tradition as it is performed today.

conversations with Benmūsā and his knowledge of the relationships among masters of the five most recent generations.[49]

Benmūsā placed the first three individuals, al-Fāsī, al-Bū'aṣāmī and al-Ifrānī, in the genealogy as early exemplars of the tradition, men who made important contributions even though they predated the conservatory and so cannot be linked directly with the rest of the genealogy.[50] The generation of at-Tahīfa, al-Jābarī and az-Zemmūrī participated in al-Jāmi'ī's conservatory at the end of the 19th century as either teachers or students, or perhaps both. The next generation, al-Būsdarāwī, aṭ-Ṭanjī and 'Abd as-Salām al-Brīhī, were all students at Dār 'Adīl, the latter being the father and teacher of the great master from Fez, Muḥammad al-Brīhī. Benmūsā notes a stylistic division in the generation after Muḥammad al-Brīhī, as al-Wakīlī, a student of al-Brīhī's, also received training from masters who studied outside the Dār 'Adīl lineage (al-Mṭīrī and Kurīš). Larbī at-Temsemānī was taught by al-Wakīlī, but also taught himself a great deal of the tradition. Al-Wakīlī and at-Temsemānī developed a highly respected stylistic school in the second half of the 20th century (Benmūsā calls it *al-madrasa at-ta'bīriyya* — "the expressive school" — and identifies two sub-schools within it: *al-wakīliyya* and *at-temsemaniyya*) that introduced innovations into the tradition, distinguishing them from *al-madrasa al-muḥāfiẓa* of Fez. In the same generation as al-Wakīlī and at-Temsemānī, 'Abd al-Karīm ar-Rāyis inherited the mantle of the conservative school from Muḥammad al-Brīhī.

[49] Benmūsā interview, 3/10/2004.

[50] Note that he places 'Abd ar-Raḥmān al-Fāsī here, and not his nephew Aḥmad.

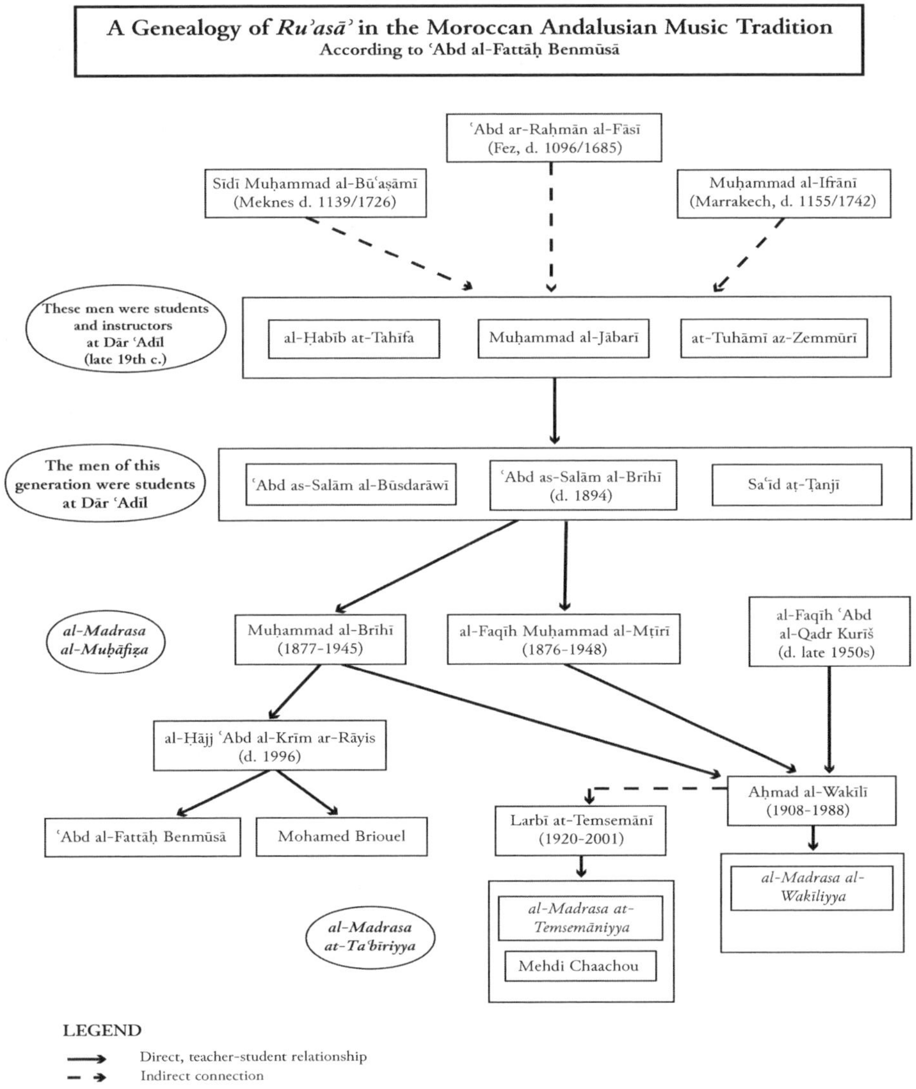

Figure 3.1 *A genealogy of al-Āla masters*

The al-Baṭḥāʾ/Dār ʿAdīl school thus exerted an important influence on *al-Āla* in the generations following al-Jāmiʿī. While Figure 3.1 does not take account of masters outside the Dār ʿAdīl genealogy, it illustrates the impact on the music as it is known today of this early effort at institutionalized teaching, for not only did it contribute to perpetuating *al-madrasa al-muḥāfiẓa* in Fez (the main lineage on the chart, passing through the al-Brīhīs, ar-Rāyis and Benmūsā), but more than one of its alumni taught the music in other cities (for example, al-Mṭīrī, who taught in Rabat and Tangier[51]). Moreover, both al-Mṭīrī and Muḥammad al-Brīhī influenced al-Wakīlī, who was an important innovator in *al-madrasa at-ta ʿbīriyya*, as well.

The al-Jāmiʿī school's importance extends beyond issues of style, for even though it was not a fully modern institution in the sense of having completely standardized all aspects of the teaching that took place there, it nevertheless represented a significant step toward formalizing and canonizing *al-Āla*. This and its seemingly sudden appearance at the end of the 19th century raise the question of what purpose lay behind it. Possibly, as Cortés García suggests, al-Jāmiʿī (or the sultan, Mūlāy al-Ḥasan I) was spurred on by a perceived decay of the tradition in the century after al-Ḥāʾik.[52] The economic, political and environmental crises that shook Morocco in the 19th century certainly support this notion. Yet such decay cannot have been total, since a century later musicians still perform material found only in *Kunnāš al-Ḥāʾik* and not in the al-Jāmiʿī corpus. Therefore the aim was not merely to capture what was left of a dying tradition, and so some other agenda also was at work.

The audience for *al-Āla* came to extend beyond the aristocratic classes as it became an emblem of Andalusian ethnic identity among 16th- and 17th-century descendents of Andalusi immigrants. The music may still have been largely associated with these communities as late as the end of the 18th century. Al-Ḥāʾik himself bore the name *al-Andalusī*, indicating his émigré Andalusi descent. He does not mention in his *muqaddima* the ethnicity of the friend who asked him to commit his knowledge to writing, but he identifies the contents of the *Kunnāš* as *muwaššaḥāt* and *azjāl* (forms of strophic poetry originating in al-Andalus) while overlooking the non-strophic poems also present in his anthology. These clues support the possibility that *al-Āla* still spoke largely to ethnic Andalusians up through the 18th century.

Whatever social-ethnic associations attached to *al-Āla* in al-Ḥāʾik's time, by the middle of the 20th century at least, the audience had expanded from the confines of the Andalusian community to include a wide range of people in urban Morocco. Al-Jāmiʿī's conservatory probably played a part in this. Most likely the process started in the 19th century, if not before, and may have involved the *zawāyā* that had already incorporated much of the Andalusian repertoire into their rituals. Membership in these brotherhoods was by no means limited to Andalusians, so it is reasonable to suppose that the Andalusian music began to acquire a non-Andalusian audience at least in part through exposure in the *zāwiya*.

[51] Benmūsā, 2001a p. 26.

[52] 1996, p. 48.

Possibly sponsorship by the monarchy played a role, as well. The standard narrative tells us that Sultan al-Ḥasan I commissioned al-Jāmiʿī's conservatory.[53] No specific documentation has surfaced yet to support this, but such a project would not be out of character for the Alawite sultans, who certainly were familiar with the power of ritual and performance as tools of self-promotion. M. Elaine Combs-Schilling (1999) has argued that, from the middle of the thirteenth century onward, ruling dynasties in Morocco increasingly deployed public display on carefully selected and orchestrated occasions to reinforce their legitimacy and to underscore the communal foundations of the state. The Alawites, she says, became particularly adept at this form of cultural propaganda, making use of the Prophet's birthday celebrations to enhance their own image as descendants of the Prophet and as patrons. Given the nexus of social relationships and religious practices embodied in the *zāwiya*, and the musical dimension we have already noted in it, it is quite plausible that the ruling dynasty promoted *al-Āla*'s associations with these public religious festivals. Al-Jāmiʿī's project may then have grown out of a further Alawite effort to enhance social and political solidarity by promoting *al-Āla* as a common musical heritage for all Moroccans.

Far more than merely a preserver of the tradition, al-Jāmiʿī actually continued a process that had begun a century earlier with al-Ḥāʾik. Al-Ḥāʾik established the boundaries of the tradition by gathering what he had memorized and presenting it in an organized fashion, but he did not express any interest in the larger implications of committing the tradition to writing. By writing the *ṣanāʾiʿ* down in one volume, he also created a canon by which future masters would define the tradition. Rather, it was al-Jāmiʿī who deliberately moved the tradition toward the next step of deploying the standardizing power of the written text for an organized teaching enterprise. However al-Jāmiʿī's school still did not realize a modern formal institution's full potential to iron out irregularities and impose order, for the tradition was still dominated by the individualized master-student bonds. (We know nothing at all of the economic relations that existed between masters and students at the al-Jāmiʿī conservatory, but it is unlikely that they were fundamentally different from those that came before.)

This is where the tradition stood on the eve of the Protectorate: a threshold had been reached beyond which the tradition would never be quite the same. The formal institutions which emerged in the 20th century have successfully preserved the tradition and enshrined it as a facet of the Moroccan cultural patrimony, but at the same time, they have depersonalized the social relationships which surround the music in ways

[53] E.g.: García Barriuso (1940) p. 256, Cortés García (1996) p. 48. Curiously, Chottin seems to have overlooked al-Jāmiʿī's work entirely. Was this because he was based primarily in Rabat and had limited contact with other branches of the tradition? This raises the question of just how widespread the al-Jāmiʿī corpus really was prior to the publication of *Min waḥy ar-rabāb*.

that are characteristic of modern economic relationships. The effects of these changes have been profound.

4. *The modern institutions and their social conditions*

As with colonial encounters throughout the developing world, the Protectorate era (from 1912 until 1956) left deep impressions in many areas of Moroccan social and economic life, not least in terms of the changes wrought by Morocco's entry into the modern international market economy defined largely in and by the West. After decades spent struggling to engage with this international system on its own terms, the country was at last forced to cope with wholesale integration according to the demands of foreign powers. This process varied in different areas of the economy, but socially it forced a realignment in relationships as they came to be expressed more clearly in economic terms. As a result of the colonial encounter, the music has expanded beyond the private domain of the princely *majlis*, the aristocratic soiree, the *zāwiya* or social occasions within the Andalusian community and has been thrust into a different set of economic relationships and the social frameworks that they imply. These changes can be seen at work in the emergence of conservatories and private associations of music lovers, and in the indirect role played by the government as well. Less personal, but also more universal in scope, modern institutions have brought the tradition into a new kind of relationship with both its past and its audience, and this can be seen clearly in the crucial role in preserving *al-Āla* played by the two most important types of formal institution associated with the tradition today: the National Conservatory of Music and Dance, and the *jamʿiyya* (the private association of music lovers), which reflect the profound changes that have affected the social environment surrounding the music.

4.1 *al-Maʿhad al-Waṭanī*

In 1917 the French Protectorate government established the Service des Arts Indigènes au Maroc as way of promoting local industries and adapting them to the demands of a European-style market economy. At first, the musical arts were not considered relevant to this project because, as Prosper Ricard (1932) points out, the field of music seemed to be healthy enough: each city and tribe had its cadre of musicians, and others toured the countryside; and the sultan himself was supporting orchestras which entertained on both public and private occasions. Yet Ricard maintains that beneath the surface, the musical arts had not escaped "la décadence générale":

> Faute de directions, faute de maîtres, faute d'un enseignement approprié, faute de documents écrits (la transmission orale fut de tous temps la seule pratiquée), faute de générosité aussi, car les

> professionnels, avares de connaissances lentement, difficilement et incomplètement acquises, se souciaient fort peu de léguer à d'autres, en qui ils ne voyaient que de futurs concurrents, faute de tout dela et d'autres choses encore, la musique marocaine s'appauvrissait chaque jour.[54]

This blanket statement points to an absence of organization and institutionalization that he would recognize as constituting a "healthy" musical culture. To be sure, Ricard speaks here of all varieties of music, not just *al-Āla*, and it is likely that particularly Moroccan forms of organization were serving *al-Āla* in ways that Ricard could not see. (That *al-Āla* was without masters is particularly difficult to believe since Muḥammad al-Brīhī and Muḥammad al-Mṭīrī were both active at the time.)

Nevertheless, this was the view of the Protectorate when in 1927 a music section was incorporated into the Service under Ricard's direction. Using a grant of 5,000 francs, the Service brought together musicians and singers from Rabat, Fez and Marrakech, and sought out accomplished Berber musicians. The following year, a series of concerts in Rabat presented these musicians from diverse backgrounds to an audience of Protectorate officials and French residents. More important, however, was the foundation these contacts laid for the work of a new specialist assigned to study and promote indigenous music, Alexis Chottin.

Under Chottin's guidance, the Service established a conservatory-research center in the French quarter of Rabat in October of 1930. The field of study for this laboratory included both the Arabic *al-Āla* and Berber musical forms. The following year, the organization moved to the Rabat Medina, to a building on Rue Taht al-Hamam that formerly had been part of a palace belonging to the Alawite prince Mūlāy Rašīd. This location, now known as Maᶜhad Mūlāy Rašīd, still serves as a conservatory of the Andalusian music. Operating from this location with an annual budget of some 20,000 francs, Chottin's laboratory, known at the time as Dār aṭ-Ṭarab ("The House of Music"), embarked on the first systematic, Western-style study and teaching of *al-Āla*. From the scholarly point of view, this conservatory produced important results, including Chottin's own works on *al-Āla*, notably *Tableau de la musique marocaine* (1939) and the first known attempt to transcribe the music of *al-Āla* into Western notation, *Corpus de musique marocaine, fascicle 1, Nouba de Ochchak* (1931).

Alongside Chottin's academic achievements, his laboratory established an organizational infrastructure from which sprang the contemporary al-Maᶜhad al-Waṭanī li-l-Mūsīqā wa-r-Raqṣ (National Conservatory of Music and Dance). By 1952 Dār aṭ-Ṭarab had given birth to several branches of a conservatory system, operating

---

[54] p. 2

under Chottin's leadership, which eventually came to include all the major cities of Morocco.[55] In addition to offering programs in Western and Middle Eastern music performance and theory, al-Maʿhad al-Waṭanī today bears primary responsibility for teaching the Andalusian music tradition. Chapter 4 looks closely at the techniques employed in teaching at al-Maʿhad, revealing a mixture of oral and written transmission that reflects a complex web of social meanings attaching to these two channels of interaction.

The social relationships that obtain within the teaching program are of primary concern here. In his article, "Music Education in Morocco: Three Models" (1979), Philip Schuyler examined the process of music education in Morocco in terms of the social relations that are served by them, arguing that the social factors of a musician's training are crucial to his or her success as a public performer. With this in mind, he outlined the social-cultural dimensions of three avenues to becoming a musician in Morocco: inspiration from a saint, personal apprenticeship and formal institutional training. Both apprenticeship and institution-based training are at issue here. The former represents what we might call the traditional process of training, while the latter embodies the conservatory system as it has emerged in the 20th century. Schulyer's observations on the social rationale behind each are therefore significant.

Apprenticeship, according to Schuyler, involves association from youth with a master musician, just as with any other trade such as carpenter or tailor. Through the processes of oral transmission, rote memorization, and close participant observation of performance and the teaching of other students, the young student develops the musical skills and knowledge required for musicianship, the social connections necessary for success in the trade, and (perhaps most significant) a lifetime relationship with a living resource for the music. The master essentially passes on proprietary knowledge which constitutes his own repository and license, as it were, to perform. It is a trust which offers the elder musician some hope of security in his old age when his student would be expected to include him in his work opportunities as repayment for years of training. Violation of this trust can have consequences, because it represents a subversion of the social and economic arrangements that define the master-student relationship. The student risks alienating his clientele, other musicians and potential students by damaging his own reputation. Though the apprenticeship system still persists, Schuyler says, it does not thrive, partly because of mutual distrust between students and masters.

[55] Much of this history is taken from a pamphlet entitled "On the History and Activities of the Mūlāy Rašīd Conservatory for Andalusian Music" (*Nubḏa ʿan tārīḫ wa-našāṭ Maʿhad Mūlāy Rašīd li-l-Mūsīqā l-andalsusiyya*), published by Maʿhad Mūlāy Rašīd.

The conservatory format has placed greater distance in the relationship between student and master, because the student selection process and financial arrangements now fall into the hands of the institution: "The student who neither serves nor pays his master has made no commitment. An important safeguard against betrayal has been removed."[56] Moreover, rewards and punishments have been removed from the master's hand. To these factors that Schuyler recognizes could be added the demystification that can occur when a trade that was once controlled by a cadre of masters becomes more widely available beyond their reach. The availability of *al-Āla* in the conservatory has eroded whatever mystique of exclusivity that may have surrounded *al-Āla* and its performers. By these means, the social frame supporting the music has shifted toward the impersonal.

Even so, the traditional relationship between master and student had not completely disappeared in Schuyler's time (just as it continues among *Āla* musicians today). Teachers typically withheld everything beyond the most basic lessons until the conservatory student demonstrated sufficient seriousness to merit a deeper level of training:

> As the years go by, the new relationship takes on more and more resemblance to apprenticeship. A small group of students may begin to gather at a master's house, to work and study privately. Some of the most successful pupils are conservatory students in name only, learning music as apprentices to the master and returning to the conservatory only for examinations and student performances.[57]

Schuyler's study illustrates the central issue in the transition to conservatory training in *al-Āla*, which concerns the format of the actual teaching and the nature of the social relationships operating within the teaching framework. Even in al-Maʿhad al-Waṭanī, an institution built upon a European model of organization, oral transmission remains the dominant mode of teaching because the teaching process itself is highly dependent upon the living memory of the master. For various reasons, which will be examined in Chapter 4 and further explored in Chapter 8, rote memorization by oral repetition at the hands of a master musician remains the preferred teaching method for *al-Āla*. Thus, the relationship between master and student remains a central element, perhaps the crucial one, in determining the course of the teaching process.

The student-teacher relationship is at the same time linked to the economic relationships upon which the conservatory system stands. Though the personal and the

---

[56] p. 29
[57] p. 30

informal have persisted, especially in the higher levels of teaching, the formal institution sits always in the background, demanding acknowledgement even when it is effectively irrelevant to the actual teaching process. The institution embodies the economic dimension of the relationship between master and student as the middleman and guarantor of the master's salary on one hand and of the student's curriculum on the other. Therefore the modern master-student relationship must negotiate a careful path between the impersonality inherent in the institutional framework and the highly valued personal relationships upon which the music has always depended. As a result, the introductory levels of teaching become commodified and impersonalized through the institution, while the intimate, personal dimensions emerge over time as the student demonstrates increasing commitment to the music and the master, just as Schuyler notes in his article.

Oral versus literate transmission, apprenticeship versus conservatory training, personal versus impersonal relationships, all these polarities intersect in the modern Moroccan Andalusian music tradition. The next chapter will bring them into sharper focus by examining the teaching process within the *Āla* tradition at all levels, and Part 2 will develop a framework for bridging these various polarities by showing how the connections between them may be explained in terms of the values operating within the social context. The present renarration of *al-Āla*'s history underscores the fact that the modern conservatory system, as a formal institution, depends upon a uniformity and impersonality that reflects a profound change from what we might call the "traditional" master-student relationships surrounding the music.

4.2 *The jamʿiyya*

Personal relationships between musician and employer characterized the music's economic base throughout much of its history, whether the employer was an aristocratic or royal patron or a Moroccan Andalusian family holding a wedding party. The personal quality of these relationships were related to the economics of the situation: when the compensation offered to the musician came from the employer's own resources, he or she was more likely to take a personal interest in the performer. The careers of Ziryāb and Ibn Bājja suggest that in the era when aristocratic patronage dominated the music's social landscape a patron's personal involvement with the musician was the very raison d'être for the economic relationship. Much the same could be said in the middle period, in North Africa after the fall of Granada. Aristocratic patronage continued, of course, but even as the music's audience expanded (thanks to new social meanings that became attached to it, connected with Andalusian ethnic identity), the social relationships underlying the economic arrangements probably remained personal, since the sponsor of a performance continued to be personally responsible for compensating the musician.

To the extent that Andalusian ensembles today perform for private parties, *al-Āla* still embodies similar relationships. Yet, it is difficult to judge how pervasive such performances are nowadays, particularly since numerous musical groups in a city like Fez combine *al-Āla* material with various other genres, so that composite musical events like these should be distinguished from performances of Andalusian music as such. Performances in which *al-Āla* is merely one style among many place it in a social-economic context that has to do with the social meanings attaching to all the various styles of music performed.

My own research suggests that purely Andalusian performances at private parties in Fez are becoming rare. *Al-Āla* simply is not as popular for these events as it once was. The colloquial *Malḥūn* genre is more in vogue for wedding parties, for example, than *al-Āla*. Furthermore, the advent of electronic instruments has made less erudite styles of music more readily accessible, allowing a small ensemble of two or three people to sound like a much larger group. *Al-Āla* cannot be performed in this way; it is far less expensive to hire a smaller ensemble that makes use of electronic instruments than to hire a larger Andalusian ensemble with live musicians, each of whom must be paid. Most importantly, the very popularity of these other styles suggests that the social meanings they embody speak directly to many people in ways that *al-Āla* does not.

The chief venues for *al-Āla*, and the most common contexts in which the music is performed today for its own sake (and not mixed with other styles), are two kinds of showcase concerts, the public *ḥafla* and the *mahrajān*. A *ḥafla* (pl. *ḥafalāt*, "party, concert") is devoted to a performance by one *jawq* at a public venue, often a large salon in a private house with room enough for the performers and an audience of one hundred to three hundred people.[58] A *mahrajān* (pl. *mahrajānāt*, "festival") usually features more

[58] Moroccans use the word *ḥafla* also for a private party or soiree. Circles of friends, some of whom are Andalusian musicians, hold such private *ḥafalāt* where they gather to enjoy the music in an informal setting. I was invited to one such evening in Tetuan in January of 2003. Sī Mehdi Chaachou and several of his friends gathered at the apartment of one member of their circle for several hours of music, tea and conversation. I counted about a dozen men, including several from Mehdi's *jawq*. (The women of the household were absent, except when serving refreshments; and no female friends of the musicians were present, either.) Apart from the warmth and intimacy of the occasion, I was struck by the absence of a clear boundary between audience and performer. Since everyone present was an aficionado of *al-Āla*, everyone participated on one way or another in the music. Some who were not themselves professional musicians took turns playing along with some *ṣanāʾiʿ*, and of course, everyone was singing. At one point in the evening, everyone in the room took a turn at *baytayn*. While the playing did not follow the usual *mīzān* or *nūba* organization, I did observe that performance units — sequences of particular *ṣanāʾiʿ* that customarily go together — gave shape to the music. Some of these obviously had been decided in

than one *jawq*, as is the case with the major national festivals held each year in major centers like Fez, Chefchouen and Tangier. A program like this can span up to three evening performances, either in a large hotel ballroom, a public auditorium or plaza.

These showcase concerts are supported by a new kind of formal institution dedicated to promoting and presenting only the Andalusian music, one that was born during the Protectorate and came into its own in Morocco after independence. The *jamʿiyya* (pl. *jamʿiyyāt*), or association of music-lovers, has largely taken the place once occupied by the various forms of personal support or patronage. Responding to the sweeping changes that have overtaken Moroccan society and economy in the 20th century, the modern *jamʿiyyāt* have served the tradition well by providing a coordinated and organized economic basis for the music, without which the tradition might not have survived into the 21st century. A brief survey of their history reveals their importance to *al-Āla*.

4.2a *Roots and roles*

Both Prosper Ricard[59] and J. Gotteland[60] mention the first such private society dedicated to music in Morocco, founded in the mid-1920s in Oujda by a Mr. Ben Smaïl, and named L'Andalousia. To judge from its name, this association was wholly or chiefly focused around the Andalusian music, though neither author is explicit about this point. Both authors write that L'Andalousia did not accomplish much for lack of funds, though it did sponsor an ensemble that gave a well-received performance in Paris. Guettat mentions two other early *jamʿiyyāt*: al-Jamʿiyya al-Idrīsiyya, founded in Fez in 1930 by ʿAbd ar-Raḥmān aṭ-Ṭāhirī, "mais qui fut rapidement dissoute"; and Jamʿiyyat Iḫwān al-Fann ("The Association of the Art Brethren"), founded in Tangier in 1940 by Muḥammad Larbī at-Temsemānī and Aḥmad al-Wakīlī.[61]

Since the 1950s *jamʿiyyāt* have provided an increasingly significant share of the organizational and financial backing for the major Andalusian *ajwāq* in Morocco. Performance programs deposited at the Ḫizāna Dāwūdiyya in Tetuan reveal that Jamʿiyyat Hawāt al-Mūsīqā l-Andalusiyya (aka L'Association des Amateurs de la Musique Andalouse) played a leading role during the 1950s and 1960s in organizing both private *ḥafalāt* and public *mahrajānāt* (such as those held in the 1950s to celebrate Throne Day, the national holiday commemorating the king's accession). Today, the

advance, but it was clear that the players were improvising in places, as well. For example, during one *baytayn*, a singer deliberately shifted the *ṭabʿ* with a subtle inflection of his singing and then began to sing a *ṣanʿa* from the *nūba* thus "suggested." The other musicians, delighted at this bit of artistry, joined in enthusiastically.

[59] 1932, p. 2.

[60] See his Preface to Chottin (1939), p. 8.

[61] 2000, p. 236 and n. 51.

major *ajwāq* benefit from similar support from these institutions, which operate much like similar societies in the West: members pay an annual subscription fee which entitles them to attend a number of *ḥafalāt* organized and presented by the *jamʿiyya*. In some cases, the *ḥafalāt* are closed to the general public, but in others, the public may pay a fee to attend individual performances.

Sometimes the association selects a special location for a series of concerts – a *mahrajān* – by one *jawq*. In the spring of 2003, the Fez *jamʿiyya*, L'Association des Melomanes de Fès (founded in 1974), sponsored a weekend "retreat" in the resort town of Īmmūzār Kandar featuring Jawq Benmūsā li-Baḥth al-Mūsīqā l-Andalusiyya. For a special premium, association members could purchase a package that included hotel, meals and a series of afternoon and evening performances spread over three days. (Unfortunately, when the war in Iraq started, the event was cancelled. However, a similar program was held in the spring of 2004.) L'Association des Melomanes patronizes a number of *ajwāq*, providing a varied menu of performances for its members, though it maintains a close relationship with Jawq Benmūsā. Sī Benmūsā serves as artistic director for the association.

Ḥafalāt typically are staged so as to project an aura of affluence and exclusivity. The salon, usually in a private house but sometimes in a hotel, will have been chosen to evoke the classically Moroccan: laid out in the traditional style with a large central court and alcoves on all sides, the room will be ornately decorated with geometric tile and plaster work, perhaps carved woodwork in the ceiling, traditional carpets, and often traditional couches along the walls (though folding chairs are always needed to accommodate the audience). Coffee, tea, orange juice and water circulate periodically, as do trays of sweets and pastries, all served by waiters in uniform. The audience, having paid well for the privilege of attending, always arrives elegantly dressed, the women often in formal evening attire and the men in suits, though many of both sexes prefer the traditional *jallaba*. Though presented very much in Moroccan style, the atmosphere recalls the elegance of a classical music concert in the West, summoning the aura of what would be described in the West as upper-class privilege.

In cooperation with the Ministry of Cultural Affairs, certain *jamʿiyyāt*, notably Jamʿiyyat Hawāt al-Mūsīqā l-Andalusiyya, help to organize the major *mahrajānāt*. For example, members of this *jamʿiyya* provide important organizational infrastructure for the National Festival in Fez, especially with respect to the academic conference that takes place in tandem with the musical performances. Moreover, the *jamʿiyyāt* provide the crucial link between the government sponsor and the musicians. Association members are involved in selecting the *ajwāq* and coordinating their program selections. With respect to the musicians, one might say that *jamʿiyya* members serve as the face of the *mahrajān* organization.

Like arts associations in the West, the *jamʿiyyāt* contribute to the music in more ways than by organizing concerts. They often undertake educational and other activities, either on their own or in combination with performances. L'Association des Melomanes often includes a short lecture during the intermission of a *ḥafla* on a subject connected to the history of the music. Jamʿiyyat Rabaṭ al-Fatḥ has sponsored scholarly conferences such as the one in May of 1995 that led to the publication of a volume of articles, *Taqālīd al-Mūsīqā l-andalusiyya fī duwal ḥawḍ al-baḥr al-abyaḍ al-mutawassiṭ*. In addition, associations frequently use *ḥafalāt* to honor well-known musicians in the tradition, presenting each with an award and usually a brief dedicatory address on his or her life and career.

Associations of Andalusian music lovers thus play a key role in the social and economic environments that surround *al-Āla* today. They serve as the channel through which most of the money flows that perpetuates the music as a performed art in Morocco, and at the same time they mediate between audience and performer by creating a shared public space. In this they represent and enact the impersonal, commodified kinds of relationships that characterize many areas of public life in the modern world. The members of a *jamʿiyya* share the cost of organizing and presenting Andalusian music concerts with their membership dues, but through this arrangement, they also participate in a culturally informed rite that at once makes the music available and yet embodies a specific social distance between them and the musicians. This does not mean that the musicians are inaccessible, but only that their relationship with the audience is commodified, being relatively indirect and mediated by the institution. Individual audience members need not have any particular relationship at all with them: they have paid collectively for the opportunity to enjoy the music performed live.

In contrast, the *jamʿiyya* officers who deal directly with the *jawq* often take a more personal interest in the musicians. In seeing to the practical arrangements and coordinating services for the group (such as food, lodging and transportation to and from the concert), these individuals usually develop friendships with the *ruʾasāʾ* and the leading musicians they work with. They fill the role of patron in the dual sense of both providing a human face for the *jamʿiyya* (serving and eating the obligatory pre-concert meal with the musicians, for example) and in acting as the intermediary through which services are provided. Given the particular blend of institutional and personal dimensions in play, these men act neither as impresarios interested only in the performance, nor as "roadie" or "gopher" figures merely catering to the musicians' needs. They see themselves as providing the necessary personal link between the patron-like association and the client-like performers.

The intimate and profoundly personal dimension of classical aristocratic patronage (in which the musician lived within a complex web of personal relationships involving patron, various members of the patron's entourage, and female slave musicians) has vanished, as have the communal meanings and identities which bound the music to the Andalusian immigrant families in the middle period in North Africa. Instead the Andalusian music's dependence upon private *jamʿiyyāt* betrays the degree to which is has become a commodity, one variety of music among many that must compete for resources, as well as the ears and loyalties of Moroccan audiences. At the same time, the elite values evoked by the way the *ḥafla* is staged suggest that association members view the music as part of what would be called highbrow culture in the West.

4.2b *Jamʿiyyat al-Hawāt li-l-Mūsīqā l-Andalusiyya*

By far the most important *jamʿiyya* in Morocco is Jamʿiyyat Hawāt al-Mūsīqā l-Andalusiyya, which is based in Casablanca but has members in major cities around the country. Everywhere one looks in the Andalusian music community one sees evidence of this organization and its works. From its inception in 1957 under the leadership of Idrīs Ibn Jallūn (whose songbook/anthology of *al-Āla* is discussed in Chapter 5), it has boasted a highly visible and influential membership, involving many of the most important figures in the Andalusian music community, including not least the scholar Muḥammad al-Fāsī and Ibn Jallūn himself, as well as notable figures in the business community in Casablanca and certain government officials.

Founded to support the Andalusian music in various ways, the association presents in its bylaws eight principal goals, among them: to preserve the music by various means (including sound recordings), to restore (إصلاح) the poetry of the tradition, to perpetuate traditional instruments used in the music as well as introduce new ones (!), to participate in performances of various kinds both in Morocco and outside the country and to publish *Kunnāš al-Ḥāʾik*. The bylaws further contain a list of specific means to accomplish these goals, including establishing local conservatories, a museum and a library; and encouraging the use of Western tools in the teaching of the music.[62] In placing items like these explicitly in the association's bylaws, the founders set the association on a modernizing path that has proven to be somewhat controversial over the years. The introduction of non-traditional instruments, and whether and how to record the music, have been particularly contested by advocates of a more

[62] From the undated pamphlet, *Qānūn Jamʿiyyat Hawāt al-Mūsīqā l-Andalusiyya*, published by the association.

conservative view, as Ibn ʿAbd al-Jalīl describes in Part One of his book, *Al-Mūsīqā l-andalusiyya al-maġribiyya* (1988).[63]

Nevertheless, recording the tradition has been one of the association's chief contributions and most thorough successes. During the 1990s, the association cooperated with the Ministry of Cultural Affairs and the French music company Éditions du Monde to produce a set of some 75 compact disks covering all eleven *nawbāt*, performed by a wide range of *ajwāq* from around the country representing a variety of regional performance styles. In addition, each *ḥafla* presented by the association is recorded, committed to CD and distributed to association members. Over the years, the association has placed in circulation an impressive array of live recordings featuring all the major *ajwāq* currently performing in Morocco. Some of these recordings offer unique and fascinating glimpses of both traditional and modernist interpretations of the music.

In addition, programs from association *ḥafalāt* always give substantial information on the featured *jawq* and its *raʾīs*. For example, the program for the *ḥafla* that took place in March of 2004 featuring Jawq al-Brīhī under the direction of Anas ʿAṭṭār contains a history of the *jawq*, which naturally includes biographical information on its founder, Muḥammad al-Brīhī. When a *ḥafla* is dedicated to one of the important figures in the Andalusian music community, his biography is included, as well. While the information in these programs is often anecdotal and unverifiable, at the very least they represent a substantial and largely untapped library of data reflecting contemporary perspectives on the music, its most important *ajwāq* and leading lights.

The importance of Jamʿiyyat Hawāt al-Mūsīqā l-Andalusiyya is further reflected in its co-sponsorship of the National Festival of Andalusian Music in Fez, in cooperation with the Ministry of Cultural Affairs, attendance at which is (theoretically) by invitation only and therefore restricted to association members, influential figures in the arts and academic communities, and their guests.[64] Association members like ʿAbd al-Malik aš-Šāmī also are prominent in the academic conference that accompanies the festival.

---

[63] More on this debate can be found in Benmūsā (1998) and as-Srāyrī (1998).

[64] In practice the invitation system seems designed primarily to protect the elite atmosphere of the event by discouraging potentially "disruptive" lower-class folk from attending: invitations are readily available to foreigners acquainted with any of the *ru'asā'* involved (and foreign students connected to established educational institutions), and they appear not to be necessary once the performance is underway. Rather, ushers stationed at the door deny entry to people deemed inappropriate to the atmosphere of the event. Students and well-dressed individuals are always admitted. Furthermore, at least one free concert is always held in a public venue in the Medina. In contrast, the summer *mahrajān* in Chefchaouen, which not connected to jamʿiyyat Hawāt al-Mūsīqā l-Andalusiyya, is held in the town square and is completely open to the public.

In the summer of 2004, the association realized one of the goals stated in its bylaws when it opened the first museum of Andalusian Music in Morocco. In cooperation with Fondation Reso, an organization devoted to financing educational projects in Morocco (including grants for low-income students), association members restored Dār Bennānī in the Place Rcif neighborhood of the Fez Medina, which had been donated by the Bennānī family for the purpose. The building now houses a display of old instruments, a collection of photographs dating back to the early 20th century, a small library of reference works and recordings, and a handful of old manuscripts. The museum's opening included a brief performance by Farqa Šīkī and speeches by several participants in the project.[65]

Finally, the association has staged a series of three-day events, known as the Rencontre Internationale des Musiques Andalouses, in Casablanca starting in November of 2004. The first of these brought together a selection of Moroccan *Āla* ensembles, as well as a *Ġarnāṭī* group from Tlemcen, a *Mālūf* ensemble from Tunis, a flamenco ensemble from Spain and a Portuguese *fado* group. Six concerts were held at four different sites around the Casablanca area, and an academic conference convened as well. Subsequent editions have been held annually since then.

Support for all these activities comes from three principal sources. Members of Jamʿiyyat Hawāt al-Mūsīqā l-Andalusiyya pay an annual subscription of 1400 Mdh (about $170) per couple. In return they receive tickets to six *ḥafalāt* spread across a concert season from October to May. According to association officials, memberships of this kind hover around 600 couples at the moment. Simple arithmetic thus yields a potential budget of about 840,000 Mdh (about $101,000). This is not a large sum in American terms to operate an arts organization of this scale, but in the Moroccan context it is a considerable amount, especially given that the association runs primarily on volunteer labor and donated services.[66] In addition, the association sells advertising space in *ḥafla* programs, which also contributes to the budget. Finally, the association also receives occasional lump-sum donations from wealthier members, adding substantially to the association's budget. On occasion the association can muster considerable resources for a particular project. According to the Moroccan daily *Le Matin*, the budget for the first Rencontre came to 1.3 million Mdh (more than $150,000 – 150% of annual receipts from memberships), from which the association realized some 200,000 Mdh ($24,000) in profit.[67]

---

[65] In 2010, the museum, along with its collection of books and manuscripts, was moved to Dār al-Āla in the Habous neighborhood of Casablanca.

[66] Printing and catering services for *ḥafla* programs, for example, come courtesy of association members. Renovations to Dār Bennānī were donated by an association member who is a professional architect.

[67] 12/22/04, p. 9.

4.3 *Government participation*

The government, at both national and local levels, plays a significant but indirect role in support of *al-Āla*. At the national level, the Ministry of Education subsidizes the National Conservatory, permitting students of modest means to receive a very good education in *al-Āla*. Similarly, the Ministry of Cultural Affairs supports the national festivals, tellingly described on concert programs as "sous l'haut patronage de S.M. le roi..." As noted above, such "patronage" operates in support of another organization (such as the jamʿiyyat Hawāt al-Mūsīqā l-Andalusiyya in the case of the festival in Fez) and not entirely as an initiative of the Ministry itself. Local government also occasionally plays a role. For example, the city government in Chefchouen co-sponsors the festival there, providing security services and the concert site (a large plaza in front of the town hall). These government contributions, while significant in themselves, stand one step removed from the tradition: their support is generic and not concerned with needs or issues peculiar to *al-Āla*, its musicians or audiences. The government's role is even more impersonal than either the Conservatory or the *jamʿiyya*

In Fez, participation by the local government recently has proven rather contentious. A new city government was elected in 2003, which has been reluctant to invest in the National Festival there. The festival preparations cannot go forward without the active support of the city, so the affair has led to a series of proposed dates being cancelled by the city government, to the frustration of members of the Andalusian music community. No festival at all was held in 2004, and dates were set for the spring of 2005 and again for November of that year. The *mahrajān* was finally held in January of 2006, more than two years after the previous one.

Until very recently, the medina section of the Fez city government sponsored a weekly *ḥafla* series entitled Ḥafalāt Ḫamīs at-Turāth ("The Thursday Heritage Concerts"). Each week a free soiree featuring *al-Āla*, *malḥūn* or Sufi music was held in the large auditorium of the town hall (just across the street from Musée Batha, original home of al-Jamiʿī's conservatory), complete with a printed program and a short lecture covering historical or other topics relating to the music performed that week. Unfortunately, support for these concerts (funds to pay the musicians) was cut off by the local government in 2002, despite protests from community leaders who had been donating their time and business resources to the project.

It comes as no surprise that the larger Andalusian music events depend to some degree on government support and participation, since the logistics involved and the financial demands would tax the resources even of the Jamʿiyyat Hawāt acting alone. Moreover government policy, as expressed in the policies of the Ministries of Cultural Affairs and Education, treats the Andalusian music like a national classical music for Morocco. This shows in the financial support from the Ministry of Cultural Affairs and also in the emphasis the Ministry of Education places on *al-Āla* in the National Conservatory system: encouraging traditional teaching methods, hiring traditionally-trained instructors, and actively discouraging private conservatories from teaching *al-Āla*.[68]

5. *al-Āla as emblem of tradition*

The various forms of institutional support for *al-Āla* described above of course operate within a social-cultural environment in which the music carries signficant symbolic meaning (just as was the case in the "middle period" among Andalusian migrant communities). In the modern context, the underlying symbolism may at times surface and manifest on public occasions when the the Andalusian heritage is on display. For example, the king's patronage of the major festivals is always prominently noted, thus implying a link to discourses of national heritage and cultural tradition. Similarly, portions of the tradition figure in general music classes in primary schools and academies. Just as grade school students in the United States might learn to sing the famous Ode to Joy from Ludwig van Beethoven's Eroica Symphony, so certain *ṣanāʾiʿ* from the *Āla* tradition (and others from the *Samāʿ/Madīḥ* tradition) find their way into general education, especially if the music teacher has had some formal training in the tradition. This is the case with Omar, who regularly teaches *Āla* and *Madīḥ* songs in his classes at both a public and a private school.

A year-end school recital can be revealing. In June of 2001, I attended one that combined students from Omar's school with those of another school. The program opened with the youngest, beginning-level students, demonstrating their proficiency with the song flute. They were followed by the older instrumental-music students playing excerpts of Western classical pieces on piano and violin.

Next came the vocal music students of a French-trained teacher. They presented a few solos and duets, followed by a couple of choral numbers. These students sang European popular songs (all of them French except for one Beatles song and the ubiquitous Eagles pop hit, "Hotel California" which seemed to be in vogue everywhere that year). The teacher herself accompanied her students on piano, and they were dressed in typical Western evening wear, just as one might see in any high school or conservatory recital in the U.S. Throughout these performances the audience of family members, friends and fellow students waiting to perform was restless and talkative, like most Moroccan audiences I have observed. Families did make their way

[68] See Chapter 4 §5.The Tunisian government has taken a similar attitude toward the *mālūf*, the Tunisian Andalusian music, though with very different aims and results. See Davis, 1986 and 1997a.

to the front to listen attentively when their loved ones performed, however much of the audience's energy was spent milling around and socializing.

Omar's students followed, comprising a chorus of perhaps a dozen, all wearing the traditional Moroccan musician's garb (white *jallāba*s, red *tarbushes* and yellow *darbushes* for boys; ochre *jallāba*s, headscarves and white *darbushes* for girls) and accompanied by a small Moroccan-style *farqa* featuring *ʿūd*, *darbūka* and *ṭār*. They performed two songs from the Andalusian tradition. The recital then concluded with a well-known Sufi *ṣanʿa* featuring a chorus composed of students from both schools, accompanied by the student ensemble. Not only were the students more animated in performing songs in Arabic from their own heritage, but the audience, too, became more engaged in the performance, clapping and singing along.

On display here were two distinct musical-educational worlds, thrown together by the colonial encounter. In one, the West held sway. Its emblems were the piano, the evening gown and the suit, and its contents were divided and specialized according to two dominant musical forms: for instrumentalists, Western classical music, and for vocalists, the Western popular song. In the other world, the traditional Moroccan, the emblems were the *ʿūd* and the *jallāba*, and the contents were drawn from the Andalusian tradition. In this case, there was no clear division between the vocal and the instrumental, though such a division does exist in the Andalusian tradition (as with the a cappella *Samāʿ/Madīḥ* genre).

Too much might be made of the relations of power in evidence here. It is, after all, only one example played out on a local stage for family and friends. Nevertheless the difference between the two symbolic worlds was quite pronounced, and the two modes spoke to very different affective domains in visible ways. In language and cultural style, the Western mode on display, for all its apparent cultural and economic power, simply could not touch the audience with the same emotional depth as the indigenous mode represented by the Andalusian tradition.

Moreover in the arrangement of the recital program, we see a culturally-informed division of labor. The Andalusian music was separate and reserved for the closing portion of the concert, the point in any performance of the Andalusian tradition where a Moroccan audience would expect to be roused and stirred by the most exciting music of the concert. In the recital, they received the Andalusian tradition presented as a sharp contrast to the Western music that had come before. In its structure, the performance context commented on the significance of the tradition and the social meanings attaching to it.

A similar division of labor occurs at the next higher educational level, al-Maʿhad al-Waṭanī. The larger Moroccan cities are each divided into an older Moroccan section (the medina) and a modern, French- or Spanish-built ville nouvelle. In Fez and

Rabat, where there are two branches of al-Maʿhad, a branch in the ville nouvelle offers the general, Westernized curriculum, while *al-Āla* teaching is focused at the branch in the medina. Thus in Fez, Dār ʿAdīl in the medina is administratively connected with the Conservatory system but offers classes in *al-Āla* and *al-Madīḥ;* and in Rabat, Maʿhad Mūlāy Rašīd in the medina trains Andalusian music students, but no such classes are offered at the branch in the ville nouvelle.[69] There is a certain cultural-historical logic in this. The classical home of the Andalusian music lies not in the modernized, Westernized domain of contemporary Morocco, but in the old city, and so the student entering the ancient Andalusian music stream must approach it in the traditional and historically-identified domain: the medina.

Likewise, the cultural-historical associations attaching to the Andalusian *ṭarab* tradition have promoted a conservative attitude toward teaching and transmission techniques at the conservatory. The philosophical history of the tradition, surviving in name and performance ethos, along with government support of its status as the classical music for the Moroccan nation, have helped to insulate it against the encroachment of Western tools and teaching methods (even within the French-style conservatory system). Yet the teaching system is not wholly an oral one, either. Literacy has been integrated into the process in the form of anthologies and note-taking by students, which itself evokes a longstanding relationship between the spoken and the written in the Arabic literary domain. The meaning of *tradition* and the systems of value that underlie it will be explored in Part 2, in order to show how both orality and literacy have come to serve *al-Āla* as a poetic-musical tradition.

6. al-Āla *in its modern social frame*

As with many areas of modern life, the emergence of formal institutions has profoundly influenced the social relations that surround the Moroccan Andalusian music. Formal institutions, constituted in whole or in part through literate means, have replaced informal ones in organizing how people act and interact through providing a meaningful context in which to enact the tradition. More impersonal than earlier frameworks that shaped the social dimensions of *al-Āla,* institutions like the National Conservatory have provided a basis for expanding access to the tradition to a degree that would have been unthinkable a century ago. As long as the economic foundations of the tradition remained within the confines of personal patronage during the Middle

[69] At the same time, the modernizing trend inherent in the Conservatory system can turn this symbolic structure in interesting directions, as when, for example the examination for the Diploma is held in the ville nouvelle branch of the Rabat Conservatory. This might be attributed to space considerations: Mūlāy Rašīd has no classrooms or performance spaces large enough to accommodate the exam. On the other hand, the inherently modern nature of the examination process itself also resonates with the modern setting in a way that the medina setting would not. See Chapter 4 on the examination.

Ages, the economic resources associated with the music were bound to remain limited within the narrow circle of patrons and musicians.

These limitations on the music's reach began to change as the social meanings attaching to the music expanded among Andalusian immigrant communities in Morocco. From the end of the 15th century on the music became increasingly associated with ethnic identity, and its audience included people from all walks of life. At the same time, the economic relationships surrounding the tradition also changed, as the music came to be performed among the middling classes at weddings and other events. Performers of *al-Āla* could make a living playing for (and being paid by) families at some remove from the aristocratic classes that had originally nurtured the music in al-Andalus.

From the late 16th or early 17th century, the *zāwiya* provided one social focus that brought together *Āla* musicians and others interested in the tradition. It thus helped to enmesh the music in the networks that extended outward from the brotherhoods and touched the larger social environment of Fez. The *zāwiya* itself represents an intermediate type of formal institution, one that combines the formality inherent in its literate dimensions with the personal nature of its aims. Although often constituted through written, legal means (many *zawāyā* branches were established through bequests that fall under the Islamic legal category of *waqf,* and were administered by formal foundation-like endowments called in Morocco *habūs* – all of which falls within the realm of literate, legal practice), the social relationships within the *zāwiya* retain a very personal character. Indeed, the institution's principal function is to organize religious observances and keep alive the doctrines and teachings of the eponymous founder, activities that rely upon intimate familiarity among the group's members. In this sense, the *zāwiya* has much in common with certain kinds of social service and mutual aid societies found in the West, as well as religious orders within the Catholic church. Such groups serve overtly communal purposes, and the written documents that define them reflect this. The point with respect to *al-Āla* is that the *zāwiya* did not represent a significant step away from the personal quality of the social relationships surrounding the music.

Only in the 20th century, with the sudden and rapid growth of modern formal institutions during and after the Protectorate, spurred in large part by the nation's integration into the global market economy (and the attendant adoption of many of the discourses of modernity), has the tradition come to depend, not upon an economic system characterized by familiarity between performer and audience, but upon an impersonal economic framework that places increasing distance between participants in the tradition and simultaneously extends the music's reach and commodifies it, converting it into one "product" among many competing for attention in a marketplace full of musical products. The formal institutions that today protect the musical heritage of al-Andalus in Morocco also help uphold the social and economic distance between the music and its audience. (This distance is also seen in the economics of the recording project: not only do cassettes and CDs contribute to commodification of the tradition as an economic product, but they also increase the distance between the audience and the performance, further abstracting and idealizing the tradition's social frame.)

These developments have not come without a price. While lovers of the Andalusian music may come from all walks of life, live performances are only rarely available to the middle and lower economic strata. These people lack the resources to contribute substantially to the music's preservation; they are enthusiastic but largely passive consumers. As a result, the commodification of the music is complete for most of this audience: the meanings attaching to it have become highly individualized and the communal aspects that once bound the music to a particular social framework (the ethnic Andalusian community) have eroded away. What remains is the sense that *al-Āla* belongs to the Moroccan nation as a whole, as part of its cultural heritage. Active support for the music today seems to be locked into a particular economic and social niche of wealthy aficionados. Yet for these people too, the music has become a commodity, albeit one that combines the sense of national heritage with the highbrow connotations of exclusivity and erudition.

This state of affairs is especially problematic because the doyens of the tradition have carefully defined its boundaries and seem content to contain the music within them. No new compositions have been introduced for more than a century, and even innovations in instrumentation have been contested in some quarters. As a result, *al-Āla* appears to be caught in a predicament created by the clash between the music's highbrow associations and the unwillingness of its aficionados to allow substantial innovation. Outside its immediate community, the music is widely regarded as "bourgeois" and therefore irrelevant to the lives of most Moroccans. Young people I have spoken with in Fez often treat the music as a quaint relic that holds little or no meaning for them personally. It does not "speak" to them of their interests and the issues that affect their lives. The problems *al-Āla* faces in reaching a larger audience reflect the deep gaps between rich and poor, between educated and uneducated, and especially between literate and unlettered, that crosscut Moroccan society.

Like classical music in the West, *al-Āla* has had difficulty bridging the disparate values held dear by its aficionados on one hand and those put forward by the rapid advance of the modern world. Western classical music, however, has to some degree adapted and therefore retains some relevance in contemporary popular culture. Experimentation, new compositions and new aesthetic movements injected vitality into the music through much of the 20th century. Just as important, classical music has become one source for references in popular music, a phenomenon that began in the 1960s and 70s with groups like the Beatles, Emerson, Lake and Palmer, and Queen. Nowadays a pop music reference to Western classical music (whether borrowing a phrase or structural form from a classical composition, or a wholesale rendering of a classical piece in a modern idiom) raises no eyebrows at all. Even if a few aficionados of classical music may disdain works poached from their domain, the fact remains that adventures like these have contributed to classical music's survival and vitality in the West, for they suggest that contemporary musicians still are listening to classical music and deriving meaning from the experience.

The same cannot be said for *al-Āla*. Not only would new compositions be regarded among Andalusian music aficionados as specious, but to perform the tradition in a different idiom or with electronic instruments (for example) would evoke incredulity. The aesthetic clash between the values associated with the ancient music and those evoked by modern instruments could only be viewed as either absurd or irreverently satirical. In short, there exists no space, no aesthetic forum, in which any significant innovation could appear without being contested and ultimately rejected by a substantial part of the music's audience. This is not to say that innovation alone will save *al-Āla* from fossilization, but without it, the tradition will not be able to compete successfully in the marketplace for the active allegiance of more than a thin slice of Moroccan society.

Chapter 4
A Tradition of Teaching a Tradition: al-Āla Between the Spoken and the Written

The social history of *al-Āla* traced thus far reveals a trajectory in the development of institutions that underlay the tradition at various points in its history. The personal character of the informal institutions that supported the musical heritage of al-Andalus (princely patronage and artiste slavery, and later social institutions like the *zāwiya*) has given way in the modern era to the more impersonal quality of the formal institutions that now surround *al-Āla* (the *jamʿiyya* and the conservatory). Superficially, the changes wrought by the Protectorate regime appear to have touched all aspects of the tradition, reshaping the economic and social conditions that surround the tradition and inform the cultural environment in which it is practiced. In this sense, we see *al-Āla* moving in the direction of modernization and institutionalization, driven to a large degree by the discourses of modernity that arrived with foreign domination.

However, the picture is more complex than it first appears. Modernity has taken on a local character within the Moroccan Andalusian music, because although the contemporary context resembles the conditions of modern Western society, in practice the modern institutions that support *al-Āla* are conditioned by cultural norms that draw upon personal qualities like those of the pre-modern informal institutions. The process by which the tradition is taught in the National Conservatory show clearly that *al-Āla* today lies at the intersection of oral and literate modes of transmission, just as it has throughout its history, and especially since *Kunnāš al-Ḥāʾik*. Even more: the combination of oral and literate processes that operates within the tradition contains clues to the values that bind the tradition within its social-cultural milieu, an idea that will be developed more thoroughly in Part 2.

1. *Teaching, oral and otherwise*

> When I asked about other musicians in the *jawq*, Omar replied,
> "No, not all the others went to the conservatory."
> "So," I said, "they learned the music in the *zāwiya*, and so on."
> "That's right," he said.

This interlude from a conversation with my Andalusian music teacher in Fez alludes to several issues which are shaping the preservation and perpetuation of *al-Āla* today. The surface issue in this exchange was the role of the conservatory in training the members of Jawq Benmūsā li-Baḥth al-Mūsīqā l-Andalusiyya, the orchestra Omar performed in. But behind this lie broader questions of how the tradition is conveyed from one generation to the next, and behind that, the role of oral and written methods and the meaning of each in the contemporary context. The relationship between spoken and written language and their respective meanings will be analyzed at length in Part 2 of this dissertation. The present chapter analyzes the techniques by which the tradition is passed on across generations in light of these processes.

The contemporary teaching process, shaped as it is by both ancient practice and modern influences, should be understood in its cultural and historical contexts. Throughout the scholarly literature on *al-Āla*, we find it spoken of as an oral tradition, or at least as having been preserved orally. Sometimes the idea is rendered precisely as *oral tradition*.[1] Elsewhere it is expressed indirectly, in terms of masters and disciples or in expressions like the "practical pedagogy of Ziryāb" (Guettat 2000, 121). To understand fully the contemporary teaching process in Morocco, we should begin by carefully evaluating historical claims for oral tradition in the music's history.

The observation that the Andalusian music has been taught orally throughout its history rests upon three foundations. One is that practical musical notation was unknown for most of that history. Guettat alleges that a system of tablature was fundamental to the teaching of the music that was imported from al-Andalus to North Africa.[2] Indeed, tablature of this kind is to be found in more than one medieval Arabic treatise on music theory, in the Middle East as well as in the Maġrib. Yet Guettat offers no evidence at all that this tablature ever functioned in al-Andalus as a practical method. Some master musicians may well have used a form of shorthand notation like that found in the theoretical treatises of al-Fārābī or al-Kindī, but this would have served at best as a mnemonic device, for the music notation systems to which Guettat refers were descriptive in nature and not well suited to practical applications like teaching. More likely, the music simply was memorized through direct teaching from the master musician, and that written versions of these compositions were idiosyncratic notes that never existed in a form adequate for reproducing them from the page alone.

A second reason to believe that the Andalusian musical tradition depended for centuries on some form of oral teaching or transmission is the old accounts of Ziryāb's teaching methods. In the *jinn*-and-*jawārī* story his first recourse was not to pen and ink but to his students, Ġizlān and Hunayda, who heard and memorized the music directly from him. They in turn brought Ziryāb's finished compositions to the prince's harem, teaching them the same way they learned them. More to the point, Ribera[3] and Guettat[4]

[1] Chottin, 1939, 102; García Barriuso, 1940, 172.

[2] 2000, p. 192

[3] p. 56

make reference to a method in which Ziryāb taught singing first, alongside basic rhythm patterns assisted by a percussion instrument, beginning with simpler songs and then moving on to more complex ones.[5]

Finally, the presence of oral teaching today in the Moroccan Andalusian music tradition strongly suggests an historical role for the method. When we consider that large-scale publication of printed works did not arrive in the Arab world until the early 19th century (and the first press in Morocco was founded in the 1860s[6]), it is not difficult to accept the idea that the technologies of education probably did not change much for centuries before that. So the idea that a poetic-musical genre such as the Andalusian music has retained its ancient teaching methods certainly seems plausible.

2. *What's in a name: the Andalusian* ṭarab

As noted in Chapter 3, §4.1 Philip Schuyler's study of music teaching in Morocco describes an apprenticeship model that emphasizes the personal relationship that evolves from lifelong association between a master musician and his student. Schuyler's work underscores the social conditions that have shaped the production of music in the country, and emphasizes the ways in which the National Conservatory has undermined the traditional master-student relationship. Another scholar, Michel Loopuyt, studied specifically Andalusian music teaching methods. His article on the subject, "L'enseignement de la musique arabo-andalouse à Fès" (1988), remains the only scholarly work to date dealing with Andalusian music teaching methods, establishing an important datum point for a discussion of teaching methods within the tradition today.

Loopuyt studied the Andalusian music at the Fez conservatory in 1972 and 1973. He observed the teaching methods in use there, which were based upon rote memorization "*par coeur*" through repetition of the repertoire. At the first level of instruction, students learned to tap out the basic *īqāʿāt* associated with each set of songs simultaneously with memorizing the text and melody. At the second and third levels, the student's repertoire of songs was expanded, while first percussion instruments and then violin or *ʿūd* were added, according to the desire of the student.[7]

Loopuyt takes the expression *par coeur* seriously. In making a connection between the teaching method at the music school and that used in the Qurʾānic schools

---

[4] 2000, p. 122

[5] Neither author cites a specific source for this account of Ziryāb's teaching method, but it derives from al-Maqqarī's rendering of Ibn Ḥayyān's description of Ziryāb's method.

[6] See for example Oman, 1991.

[7] Echoes of the teaching method attributed to Ziryāb are clear here, though Loopuyt does not recognize them as such.

where young children memorize large portions of the Qurʾān, he argues that the method of rote memorization by oral repetition cultivates the skill of memorization and leads to the material becoming second-nature to the student. In the case of the Qurʾān, this inculcates the Word of God, impressing it deeply upon the student. In the case of *al-Āla,* the student imbibes not only the raw material, but also a certain aesthetic experience associated with the Andalusian music, which becomes deeply ingrained. The method tends to create an emotional affinity with the music that enhances the learning process by engraving the music "on the heart," as it were. Loopuyt's work demonstrates that the ancient method survived into the 1970s, albeit transplanted from the master-student apprenticeship format into the conservatory environment.

Loopuyt makes a telling observation: that part of the importance of the learning method to the student is the deep familiarity with the music's style and nuances it cultivates. On a second visit to the conservatory in 1980, he noted that certain changes to the curriculum had been instituted, including the introduction of written texts and a new emphasis on solfège as a learning tool. In light of the signficance he perceived in the rote learning method, Loopuyt expresses some misgivings about the future of the tradition. Can a tradition like this, he wonders, survive the transition from oral to literate transmission?

Loopuyt further suggests that the rote memorization technique is connected with a name sometimes used for the musical genre. Moroccans apply various names to their Andalusian musical tradition, each reflecting a different perspective on it. In common parlance, one says simply *al-mūsīqā l-andalusiyya,* that is literally, "the Andalusian music." More formally, *al-Āla* signifies that it is performed with instruments and distinguishes it from the a cappella Sufi music *as-Samāʿ*. These two names are the most commonly used today. The former is perhaps more direct, but also more general, and so it serves well for titles of books and festivals (e.g.: *al-Mahrajān as-Sābiʿ al-Waṭanī lil-Mūsīqā l-Andalusiyya bi-Fās,* "The Seventh National Festival of the Andalusian Music in Fez"). The other name, *al-Āla,* belongs largely to academic circles. In contrast to these names, the tradition is sometimes referred to as *aṭ-ṭarab al-andalusī,* as Loopuyt discusses. Even less common than *al-Āla, aṭ-ṭarab al-andalusī* is also more specific. I have found that using it invariably raises a smile on the face of the aficionado because the word *ṭarab* suggests an important facet of the tradition that bears upon the philosophical connections attributed to the music as well as the question of its teaching and preservation.

In classical Arabic, the verb *ṭariba* means to be moved (with either joy or grief), or to be delighted or transported with joy; and the noun *ṭarab* means *joy* or *rapture*. In post-classical usage, particularly in al-Andalus, *ṭarab* came to mean *music*.[8] Thus, the expression *aṭ-ṭarab al-andalusī* suggests something like *the Andalusian musical rhapsody*.[9] There are both philosophical and musicological reasons for this appellation.

The entire Arabic music tradition, both Middle Eastern and North African, has inherited a substantial element of Greek philosophy, and among the notions imported in the Middle East was the idea that musical modes bear a relationship to cosmic phenomena and to human emotions and body humors. Ibn Ḥayyān, drawing on *Aḫbār Ziryāb*, credits Ziryāb with introducing basic elements of this heritage to al-Andalus by changing the cordature of the *ʿūd* in al-Andalus.[10] According to Guettat, each of the four original strings of the Middle Eastern *ʿūd* was attributed a color, a natural element and a bodily humor followin an interpretation set out by Isḥāq al-Mawṣilī (found in *Risāla fī l-mūsīqā* by Ibn Munajjim, d. 275/888) and al-Kindī: *Zīr* (yellow, fire and bile), *Maṯnā* (red, air and blood), *Maṯlaṯ* (white, water and phlegm) and *Bamm* (black, earth and black bile).[11] Ziryāb is said to have added a fifth string between *Maṯnā* and *Maṯlaṯ*, which was dark red and corresponded to life and the soul. This arrangement is presented in Figure 4.1. Whether Ziryāb actually was responsible for this change, and indeed whether these associations were ever put to practical use, are open questions, depending upon how much faith one puts in the old Arabic sources. Certainly he is not the only one said to have made changes like this to the *ʿūd* in this era; these ideas would have been part of the courtly milieu to which Ziryāb was exposed in Baghdad.

***ʿŪd* String**	**Color**	**Element**	**Humor**
Zīr	Yellow	Fire	Bile
Maṯnā	Red	Air	Blood
< Ziryāb's string >	Dark Red	"Life"	"Soul"
Maṯlaṯ	White	Water	Phlegm
Bamm	Black	Earth	Black Bile

Figure. 4.1: *The classical associations of the ʿūd strings, with "Ziryāb's" addition (after Guettat 2000, p. 128)*

[8] See Dozy's *Supplement...* and *The Hans Wehr Dictionary of Modern Written Arabic* 4th ed. (1994) gives this sense of the word for Modern Standard Arabic, as well.

[9] The phenomenon of *ṭarab* has been studied for its physical/gestural and psycho-social qualities, many of which are reflected in *aṭ-ṭarab al-andalusī* as described below. See especially Racy (1991) and Shannon (2003).

[10] Ibn Ḥayyān , *al-Muqtabis* (2003) pp. 317-318.

[11] 2000, pp. 65-72 and 126-128.

Vestiges of these philosophical ideas survive today as part of the Moroccan Andalusian music ideal. According to the modern canon, which draws primarily on the *muqaddima* of *Kunnāš al-Ḥā'ik,* there were 24 *ṭubūʿ* used in al-Andalus, which were held to correspond to specific times of day or to certain astronomical events like the full moon. A mode performed at the appropriate time was thought to have a salubrious effect on the performer and listener. At one time the various modes, like the strings of the *ʿūd,* were associated with the humors of the body. However, although there are still 24 *ṭubūʿ* distributed among the eleven *nawbāt,* the humoral associations are scarcely mentioned nowadays. Nevertheless each *nūba* still is held to be most appropriate for a certain time of day.[12]

For example, *Nawbat Raṣd aḏ-Ḏīl* is said to be most appropriate for the middle of the night, between approximately 11pm and 1am. *Nawbat al-ʿUššāq* is said to belong to the last hours just before dawn. Sī Mehdi Chaachou, *ra'īs* of Jawq al-Hayik al-Tetuani, explained that this is particularly appropriate when one has been up all night singing and playing music: if your *ḥafla* lasts past 4:00 am, and dawn is appearing, that is the time for *al-ʿUššāq.*[13]

In at least some cases, the poetic material of the *nūba* has been selected to reflect the temporal associations of the *ṭabʿ*. *Ṭabʿ al-māya,* is held to correspond to the time of sunset, and so the poetry in *Nawbat al-Māya* focuses upon sunset reveries and evening revelries. In most cases, the correspondence between the poetry and the *ṭabʿ* is more tenuous. Al-Šāmī (1997) says that the mode *al-ʿuššāq* reflects the rise of hope in the heart of the lover when he thinks of his beloved, and this is why *Nawbat al-ʿUššāq* features primarily love poetry.

This is not to say that these suites are actually performed with an eye to the sky or the health of the audience. Modern life being regimented by the clock and the calendar, *Āla* performance practice today takes little or no account of the ancient philosophical ideas. These dimensions of the tradition certainly are talked about among scholars, but I have not witnessed any performance that was deliberately organized around the modal associations. In spite of that, the performance of the music itself is said to produce a certain elevated state. The *ra'īs al-jawq* is expected to understand how to create this effect, which is related to the tempo structure of the *mīzān*, (as outlined in Figure I-2).

The ideal *mīzān* performance proceeds with a rising intensity and emotional pitch, as the *ra'īs* skillfully juxtaposes gradually increasing tempos with *tawāšī* and un-timed vocal interludes (*inšād* and *baytayn*). Beginning in a slow and stately fashion, the

[12] See Appendix 1. Ar-Rāyis (1982) summarizes the virtues of each principal *ṭabʿ* in his brief introductions to each *nūba*. Ibn Jallūn's *muqaddima* provides this material both in the text of al-Ḥā'ik's own *muqaddima* and in his own expansion on it.

[13] Interview, 1/26/03.

music gradually moves on to quicker and lighter tempos, and eventually culminates in a series of quick, lively songs. For shorter performances, this progression moves in a more or less continuous climb until the finale. Longer performances are divided into sections corresponding to the *marāḥil al-mīzān*, each stage being punctuated so as to heighten the sense of dramatic tension. Minor climaxes are built into each *marḥala*, wherein a series of songs in a quick tempo gives way to *inšād* or *baytayn*. Resuming again a little more slowly, the orchestra works once more toward a more lively tempo. Each wave-like climax anticipates the finale, which features the most energetic musicianship in a series of *ṣanā'i'* that are well-known to the audience.

The effect of such a structure on the audience can be impressive. At the beginning, the audience is generally seated and listening attentively, but some still may be milling about and talking amongst themselves. However, by the end of the performance nearly all audience members will be singing and clapping along, and it is not unusual to see young and even old men standing on chairs dancing and encouraging the musicians with shouts and gestures. The typically reserved and composed Moroccan persona will have given way to enthusiastic abandon to the energy of the music. The atmosphere created by the music and amplified by the *jawq*, the audience and the performance, can be infectious. More than once I have left such a concert feeling a gentle upwelling of contentment and joy, as verses of poetry and musical passages wandered in and out of my thoughts.

This is *aṭ-ṭarab al-andalusī*. The idea that the music has a profound emotional, even restorative or tonic, effect on the listener has not been lost by any means. Although the philosophical links between the *ṭubū'* and the temporal and humoral elements are rarely if ever brought into play, performances still are influenced strongly by the belief that the music has a special power to create an elevated, almost mystical state in the listener. This accounts for the smile that usually greets the expression *aṭ-ṭarab al-andalusī*: it is a smile of recognition, of understanding that behind the aesthetic dimension of appreciation lies another, deeper kind of shared experience.

3. *Aṭ-ṭarab al-andalusī as aesthetic ethos*

As noted earlier, the popularization of the expression *al-mūsīqā l-andalusiyya* is a relatively recent phenomenon originating with French scholarship and adopted by Moroccan aficionados, scholars and musicians. The idea of *al-mūsīqā l-andalusiyya* has become so firmly established in common usage, and its roots in al-Andalus defined so convincingly with references to the old Arabic sources, that the cultural-historical rationale behind the adoption of this name is scarcely questioned. Even as observant a scholar as Muḥammad al-Fāsī, in his comments on the composite origins and character of the music (1962), never considers *why* Moroccans have embraced al-Andalus as the source of this highly refined and sophisticated music. To be sure, some Andalusi poets have found their way into the tradition, but the same may be said of North African and Middle Eastern poets, as well. In my study of *Nawbat Ramal al-Māya*, I have identified 28 poets who contributed verses to this *nūba*, only two of whom were confined to al-Andalus, while at least nine spent their entire careers in the Mašriq and several others traveled among the three regions.[14] An entire monograph could be written on the ideological and rhetorical uses of al-Andalus as an historical moment that reaches deeply into aspects of history and cultural ideology.[15] Here I merely offer my own observations of musicians in the tradition and of the music's place in the cultural life of Fez and other cities in Morocco, which are relevant to a fuller appreciation of the mythos surrounding the tradition, which in turn reflects back upon, and is reflected in, the teaching tradition that resides within it.

Al-Andalus is understood today in both the West and the Arab world as a significant cultural and historical moment, frequently regarded in Western cultural discourses as a symbol of benign, even harmonious, coexistence among Muslims, Christians and Jews, three religious-cultural traditions whose followers today find themselves embroiled in conflict.[16] The musical heritage of al-Andalus is a most telling example of this: a visit to any well-stocked music shop in Madrid, New York or London will reveal several CDs of recent vintage, all highlighting in one way or another the respective musical legacies arising from the cultural interactions amongst the three religions in al-Andalus.

The discourses that inform Moroccan views of al-Andalus appear to be rather different. It is not the al-Andalus of the *tres culturas* that speaks most clearly in Morocco, but that of the great *Arab-Muslim* achievements in music, literature and architecture. My conversations with scholars and aficionados of the Andalusian music suggest that, while the presence and important contributions of non-Muslims to the history of al-Andalus are not considered irrelevant, the discourse is always framed in terms of *Arab* dominion, of Arab and of Muslim hegemony, and especially the belief that ideological tolerance characterized Muslim rule and allowed for the contributions of non-Muslim peoples not only to survive but to flourish. In other words, whereas Westerners tend to conceive of al-Andalus as a sort of cultural melting pot analogous to their conception of a modern multiethnic nation-state, Moroccans tend to see it (not

---

[14] See the Appendix to *Pen, Voice, Text....*

[15] In fact, both Dwight Reynolds of the University of California in Santa Barbara and Jonathan Shannon of Hunter College, CUNY, are working on books that touch on these issues.

[16] The actual nature of this *convivencia* has been the object of some discussion. Several scholarly works have been written on the subject over the past decade, a good recent example being Christopher Lowney's *A Vanished World: Muslims, Christians and Jews in Medieval Spain* (2006).

without justification) as a salad featuring one dominant ingredient – Arab-Islamic culture – with important contributions from Jewish and Iberian-Christian societies.

Given the profound impact of colonization and economic hegemony of the West in Morocco, we should not be surprised to find that identifying with the cultural achievements of al-Andalus appeals strongly to musicians and scholars of the music. Perhaps it serves as a reminder that, though the West is at the moment the dominant political and economic (and arguably cultural) influence in the Arab world, there was a time when the roles were reversed, when it was Europe that bowed to the cultural and political influence of Islamic Spain. Moreover, the power of al-Andalus as an emblem of Arab-Muslim greatness contributes further to the modern proposition that the tradition is effectively bounded and closed to further innovation. For many Moroccans, the very idea of an *Andalusian music* itself militates against any tampering with the heritage of that shining moment in history. In this situation, the actual relationship of this tradition to al-Andalus is almost incidental.

There is a profound irony here, for by adopting al-Andalus as the ancestral home of the musical tradition, the Moroccans are in a very real sense ignoring, even denying, the very significant contributions to the tradition's structure and content made by North Africans. In this they mirror Western scholarship's own preoccupation with the poetry of al-Andalus and general disregard for the North African *barwala,* for example. Furthermore, the earliest scholarly works on the music by Chottin and García Barriuso discuss at some length the relationship between the Arab music of al-Andalus and the music of the Christian states of Iberia. In itself, this is a perfectly reasonable inquiry, yet underlying the discussion we find the assumption that, whatever impact the *Arab* music of al-Andalus may have had on the music of Christian lands, that Arab music benefited in significant ways from the contact with Europe and European culture implied in the Muslim conquest. These authors thus suggest that only contact with European civilization made this sophisticated musical form possible. Just as the colonizer sought to attribute the (apparently) most sophisticated facet of Moroccan musical culture to the influence of Europe on Muslim al-Andalus, the Moroccans also appropriated the symbol for themselves in a double movement that affirmed the integrity of classical Arab culture even as it ignored the achievements that came afterward and closer to home.

Chapter 3 addressed the place of the music in the cultural life of urban Morocco as it is sustained by modern institutions that have supplanted the older systems of patronage and ethnic identification. These modern developments represent a significant change in the status of the tradition, that reflects in part the influence of modern economic arrangements which impinge on so many aspects of Moroccan urban life. Yet *al-Āla* survives, in part because of the cultural-ideological formations that it evokes and stands upon. Among these cultural themes, al-Andalus (and the historical hegemonic power it represents) looms large today. This identification with al-Andalus has helped to define the place of the musical tradition in the Moroccan cultural landscape.

The Andalusian music tradition in Morocco is characterized by a set of features which distinguish it from other musical genres in the public eye. On one occasion in Fez a friend of mine introduced me to a young Moroccan woman, describing me as a scholar from the United States. She politely asked me about my field of study, and when I responded that I was studying the Andalusian music, she smiled mischievously and sang a snippet of an Andalusian-sounding melody using *tarāṭīn*, exaggerating the melody and nonsense syllables in a way that showed she recognized something stereotypical in the music and found it humorously archaic. It was a caricature that spoke volumes about the power of the music's aesthetic ethos: certain musical qualities and performance practices that distinguish *al-Āla* and mark it as both sophisticated and arcane. For the aficionado, this aesthetic ethos represents a fundamental, unalienable quality of the music that makes it both traditional and valuable.[17] For many youth today in urban Morocco, who focus on the future more than the past, and on development rather than the status quo, the aesthetic ethos of the Andalusian music marks it as old-fashioned and backward-looking, and therefore obsolete.[18]

In contrast, *al-Āla* aficionados tend to regard the music as a coherent whole, which demands a certain sensitivity from the listener and emotional empathy or attunement from the performer. (One might make an analogy here to American jazz music. Jazz musicians also regard their music as demanding a subtle feel or sensitivity, which they call *swing*, an aspect of both the performance and the audience experience.) The Andalusian music can only be performed properly, it is said, by someone who has deep feeling for its melodic and rhythmic subtleties and its emotional nuances. This only comes from learning the tradition in the classical manner: through repetition and rote memorization, face-to-face with an established master.

4. *Aṭ-ṭarab al-andalusī in the conservatory*

Loopuyt's concerns notwithstanding, the classical method of teaching survives in 21st-century Morocco. Rote memorization by repetition is the only method employed in Andalusian music lessons at al-Maʿhad al-Waṭanī li-l-Mūsīqā wa-r-Raqṣ, the contemporary descendant of the music *laboratoire* and conservatory established by

[17] More on both the terms *tradition* and *value* in Part 2.

[18] What is more, because of the class affiliations of many of its most influential supporters, many refer to it disparagingly as bourgeois.

Alexis Chottin in 1930.[19] This is not to say, however, that the product of this teaching method is, or even could be, the same as it was before the advent of the formal institutions that now support the tradition. Without doubt, some degree of education in *al-Āla* reaches a much greater number of people than ever before, but the depth of that education is limited in most cases.

The Maʿhad has received principal responsibility from the Ministry of Cultural Affairs for teaching the Andalusian music tradition. To be sure, there are opportunities to learn the music at private conservatories, but the resources for such instruction are limited. One reason for this is that the government explicitly discourages Andalusian music teaching in its communications with the private conservatories, thus assigning the preservation of this national heritage chiefly to the various branches of the National Conservatory in Rabat, Casablanca, Tangier, Tetuan, Marrakech, Meknes and of course Fez. In January 2003, I had a conversation with the director of Monde Musicale, a private music conservatory in Tetuan, that clarified this situation.

He explained that education in the Andalusian music tradition takes place almost exclusively in two places. Literary and historical studies are carried out in the universities, he said, and training in the music itself is done at al-Maʿhad al-Waṭanī. The Ministry makes clear that it prefers this arrangement and encourages private schools to teach Western music, and to leave the "classical" Moroccan music to the Maʿhad. For this reason Monde Musicale offers only Western classical music, including solfège, reading and written music. Occasionally, he said, the school does accept a student who wants to learn the *ʿūd*, for example, and so *ʿūd* music of the Middle East can be taught, using the modern methods and tools at their disposal. However since Monde Musicale does not use the traditional method of teaching, it is not possible to satisfy a student who wants to learn the Andalusian repertoire. The written materials for this kind of study are limited, he said, and moreover, such a student generally does not consider it adequate to learn *al-Āla* outside the traditional method. Monde Musicale does have one teacher of violin who is versed in the Andalusian repertoire, however he also teaches primarily at al-Maʿhad al-Waṭanī and only part time at Monde Musicale. In general, a student specifically interested in the Andalusian repertoire is better served at the Maʿhad. He mentioned one student who wrote a special project at Monde Musicale that involved transcribing one *nūba* into Western notation, but he regarded this as an unusual exercise in musical notation, rather than a part of the regular curriculum.

In more practical terms, the government subsidizes music instruction at al-Maʿhad al-Waṭanī, which makes it an inexpensive alternative to the private schools. Whereas tuition at a private conservatory can cost thousands of dirhams a year (8 Mdh

---

[19] See Chapter 3 §4.1.

equaling about US$1), tuition for a year's course in the Andalusian music at the Tetuan branch of al-Maʿhad al-Waṭanī in 2002, for example, was around 160 Mdh (at the time, about US$15). Students have access to loan instruments at the Maʿhad, as well. The economic factor is especially important when one considers the observed fact that for many, if not most of the beginning students, interest in *al-Āla* is more like a hobby than a potential career. Opportunities for performing at the amateur and professional levels are limited, and teaching positions even more so. Only the most gifted and dedicated young musicians have any hope of finding work, and that only after years of study and memorization. The musician who supports himself exclusively by performing *al-Āla* is virtually unknown.

After observing a class at Dār ʿAdīl, the branch of al-Maʿhad al-Waṭanī in the Fez Medina, I took the opportunity to speak with the instructor, Sī Aḥmad Šīkī, who is one of the most respected Andalusian musicians in Morocco. He considers himself fortunate to work at Dār ʿAdīl, but he expressed mild frustration, especially with his first-year students. While he appreciates the enthusiasm most of them show for the music, he is acutely aware that few of them will go on to the second year. They learn a few *ṣanāʾiʿ* and acquire some feeling for the structure and aesthetic of the music, but after only one year they remain far from the heart of the tradition. In his view, they have only just begun to open the book on *al-Āla*. The majority, who leave after one year, receive only a superficial introduction to a tradition to what he considers a profound art form that can be appreciated only with prolonged study. He therefore finds it difficult to be patient with misbehavior or negative attitudes, some of which I had witnessed in the lesson. At one point in our conversation he became quite emotional about the demands placed upon him by his years of training and his work at Dār ʿAdīl. Only his love of the tradition itself and the hope that one or two of his students may choose to continue their studies keep him interested in his teaching.

Because of this, Professor Šīkī did not sound optimistic about the future of the tradition. He said that the subtleties and nuances of performance are slipping away. He demonstrated this by first playing a certain *ṣanʿa* in the "old" style on his *ʿūd* – slower, softer and very sweet in tone – and then playing the contemporary version of the same *ṣanʿa*, which was louder, more aggressive and less nuanced. Professor Šīkī clearly implied in this conversation that, although lessons at al-Maʿhad al-Waṭanī do provide an entry into the tradition, for the majority of students this introduction remains superficial. A proper education in *al-Āla* might begin in this way, but some facets are not taught well in this format and require another level of both interest from the student and commitment by both student and professor.

We see here echoes of Loopuyt's concerns for the future of the Andalusian music, as well as Schuyler's commentary on the problematic relationship between apprenticeship and the conservatory system. Professor Šīkī's passion about his teaching experiences are his own, but his story does underscore the problems that the conservatory system introduces into the master-student relationship and the conundrum that results. Although the number of people receiving formal training in the tradition has grown, this has not necessarily resulted in a higher level of training for the average student, nor has it guaranteed that the refinements of the genre have been well preserved.

An important factor distinguishing al-Maʿhad al-Waṭanī from other music schools is that the Maʿhad employs only specialists to teach the Andalusian music courses, that is, musicians who have memorized a significant portion of the tradition and have been certified as having mastered this material. These men and women, though typically conversant in Western musical tools such as solfège, nevertheless have received the tradition in the same manner that they teach it: rote memorization by oral repetition. Thus the formal teaching of the tradition involves masters who teach only by the traditional method, and mastery itself is defined in part by the method. This particular notion of mastery, at once traditional in its apparent bona fides, and yet modernized (or *professionalized*), is a distinctive feature of the conservatory system noted by Schuyler in the 1970s. At the same time, we may question to what extent this professionalism really serves the tradition, beyond simply perpetuating it in its present, highly bounded form. What is missing from the conservatory system, at least at the lower levels of instruction, is the very element noted by Schuyler as subverted by the conservatory: personal responsibility between the student and the professor. However, a more traditional mode of master-student relationship does hold sway in two other contexts: levels of instruction beyond the second year in the conservatory, and the highest level of training, the *jawq*.

4.1 *The first two years at the Maʿhad*

Al-Maʿhad al-Waṭanī comprises a group of local branches funded by the Moroccan government in all the major cities. Where a particular city has two branches, as is the case with Fez and Rabat, both are under the direction of a single individual so that they operate as a single administrative unit answering ultimately to the Ministry of Education and Cultural Affairs. In Fez a branch in the Ville Nouvelle houses the office of the director, Mohamed Briouel, and deals primarily with modern-style instruction in both Arabic and Western music and instruments. Western musical theory based upon the French notation system (solfège) is taught there, as well. Briouel also oversees the operation of Dār ʿAdīl, which was closed for some years for renovations and had reopened just a few months before my arrival in Fez in the summer of 2000. During the renovations, classes in *al-Āla* were held in the Ville Nouvelle.

I have observed no "typical" profile of a Andalusian music student. The first year of study at al-Maʿhad al-Waṭanī is open to anyone with an interest, which results in a student body composed of a range of ages and backgrounds, from pre-teen up to middle age, male and female, musically-trained and novice. First-year students form classes by age groups, with classes for younger children, adolescents (roughly, junior-high and school ages in the U.S.), and adults. I observed only two common denominators.

First, the student must be literate, because writing and written texts have been integrated into the teaching process. Moreover, the student must have time and resources to devote to study and attending classes. These constraints effectively limit the student body to the urban middle and upper classes.[20] The second common quality shared by all the students is a love and appreciation for the music itself. To be sure, some younger students are present by parental decree, and so may be rather less enthusiastic learners. Yet a palpable level of camaraderie and mutual support prevails in every class I have observed. Conversations with students outside the classroom suggest that most students are enthusiastic, motivated and proud of the tradition they are studying because they regard it as part of the classical heritage of their nation.

The core curriculum for *al-Āla* was standardized among the various branches of the Maʿhad in the early 1980s under reforms instituted by ʿAbd al-Karīm ar-Rāyis.[21] A common program of *mayāzīn* from particular *nawbāt* is taught in the first two years, though there also appears to be some leeway in including portions of other *mayāzīn*, and also in the choice of particular *ṣanāʾiʿ* taught. The first year is devoted to singing only, although the students also learn a traditional technique of hand gestures that correspond to the strong and weak beats of each *īqāʿ*. They are encouraged to practice this style of keeping time as they rehearse the *ṣanāʾiʿ*, thus situating each *ṣanʿa* (or series of *ṣanāʾiʿ*) in the rhythmic context of its *mīzān*.[22] Students who show a serious interest may also be taught to tap out the *īqāʿāt* on the *darbūka* and may learn to tap out

[20] Social barriers against the lower economic classes likely represent an obstacle for many poorer individuals as well, since the cultural distance between the poor and the comfortable is substantial. However, there may be at least some exceptions to this: it is unlikely that the Maʿhad would reject a promising working-class student simply for social reasons. The most difficult challenges in this case would be money for supplies, and then the student's comfort and familiarity with the classroom environment.

[21] Embodied in al-Rāyis (n.d.), *al-Durūs al-awwaliyya fī l-Mūsīqā l-andalusiyya*, a publication found in the libraries of most of the conservatory branches.

[22] This style of keeping time works as follows: strong beats (*dūm*, in the center of the *darbūka* head) are tapped with the open hand on the right thigh or tabletop; weak beats (*tak* on the rim of the *darbūka*) are tapped with the hand closed lightly so that the heel and first knuckles of the fingers strike the thigh, or else with the tips of all five fingers drawn together; open beats (that is, longer rests that fall within the *īqāʿ*) are marked by a sweeping gesture from right to left with the palm open and facing to the left.

the variations of the *īqāʿāt* corresponding to the *marāḥil* of the *mīzān* (*al-muwassaʿ*, *al-qanṭara* and *al-inṣirāf*), though these are not required at this stage.

The first-year curriculum includes *ṣanāʾiʿ* from the *nawbāt Ramal al-Māya* (*mayāzīn* al-basīṭ, al-Bṭāyḥī and ad-Darj) and *al-Iṣbahān* (al-Qāʾim wa-Niṣf, ad-Darj and al-Quddām). I have observed portions of *al-Māya* (ad-Darj and al-Quddām), *Raṣd aḏ-Ḏīl* (al-Bṭāyḥī) and *al-Istihlāl* (al-Basīṭ and al-Quddām) being taught, as well. Thus all five *mayāzīn* are covered in the course of the first year. Altogether, the students are responsible for at least 25 *ṣanāʾiʿ* in the first year, according to the printed curriculum in use at Maʿhad Mūlāy Rašīd, following the outline set down by ar-Rāyis. According to teachers and students I have interviewed, these *ṣanāʾiʿ* are chosen because they are simpler and easier to memorize and sing. *Ṣanāʾiʿ* in the *ṭarab* tradition often have complicated melodies with many turns, repetitions and decorations. Moreover, words and even syllables may be divided according to the demands of the melody in unpredictable ways. These features can be difficult for beginners to master. Of course, *ṣanāʾiʿ* with complicated *tarāṭīn* passages present further problems. All of this has been taken into account in planning the curriculum for the lower levels.

The following *ṣanāʾiʿ* are among those taught in the first year at Maʿhad Mūlāy Rašīd: *Li-n-nabī r-rasūl*, *Yā ʿāšiqīn*, *Šaddu l-ḥumūl*, *Yā Muḥammad*, and *Sayyidu r-rusli* (Basīṭ Ramal al-Māya)[23]; *Muḥammadun ḏū l-mazāyā*, *Ḍaqqānī man hawīt*, *Zāranī badrī*, *Kullu man yahwā*, *Yā zaynu l-ḫalāʾiq*, *Saʾaltu rabbī*, *Iḏā kāna ḥisābuk* (Bṭāyḥī Ramal al-Māya)[24]; *Qad ṭāla šawqī* (Darj Ramal al-Māya)[25]; *Anta aḥlā min al-munā*, *Mā aḥlā r-raḥīq*, *Badīʿu l-ḥusni*, *Bi-llāhi yā zaynu ṣ-ṣiġār*, *Istaġfir Allāh* (Qāʾim wa-Niṣf al-Iṣbahān)[26]; *Law ḏuqta yā ġazālī*, *Yā mudīru l-ḥumāyā*, *Ana l-musīʾu*, *Amlakta ʿaqlī*, *Ġazālu masā* (Quddām al-Iṣbahān)[27]; and *Yā ahlu wuddī* (Darj al-Iṣbahān).[28]

---

[23] See *Pen, Voice, Text...*, Basīt #17. Page references in the modern printed anthologies are given there.

[24] *Pen, Voice, Text...*, Bṭāyḥī #11, 12.

[25] *Pen, Voice, Text...*, Darj #1.

[26] ar-Rāyis (1982) , pp. 61-62; Ibn Jallūn (1979) pp. 67-69; Ibn Manṣūr (1977) pp. 98, 100-101. (*Badīʿu l-ḥusni* is found only in *Min waḥy ar-rabāb*.).

[27] ar- Rāyis, pp. 76-78; Ibn Jallūn pp. 78-79; Ibn Manṣūr pp. 111-113. (*Ġazālu masā* is not found in Ibn Jallūn.)

[28] ar- Rāyis p. 68; Ibn Jallūn p. 72; not found in Ibn Manṣūr.

Figure 4.2: *The exterior of Maʿhad Mūlāy Rašīd in Rabat*

Figure 4.3: *Interior of Maʿhad Mūlāy Rašīd*

Figure 4.4: *Dār ʿAdīl, Fez (interior)*

The lessons I observed with Professor Šīkī at Dār ʿAdīl in Fez included a performance unit from Quddām al-Iṣbahān beginning with *Law ḏuqta yā ġazālī* followed by two other *ṣanāʾiʿ* recommended by ar-Rāyis. The third *ṣanʿa* in the series (the *šuġl*[29] *min basīṭ, Ana l-musīʾu*) contains a complex *tarāṭīn* passage. Indeed, the *ṣanʿa* has what amounts to a kind of refrain of *tarāṭīn* that includes the words *yā mawlāya* ("Oh, my master..."), so that I thought for a moment the lesson had passed on to some other *ṣanʿa* which is not in *Min waḥy ar-rabāb*. Only when the group returned to the text on the page of *Min waḥy ar-rabāb* did I realize the actual form of the *ṣanʿa*. The class worked a long time on this one *ṣanʿa*, with Professor Šīkī breaking it down into short phrases to facilitate memorization and repeating them over and over again with the class. At the end, the students remarked how difficult it was to get the *ṣanʿa* right.

Another first-year lesson I observed, taught by Professor Awatif Bouamar at al-Maʿhad al-Waṭanī li-l-Mūsīqā[30] in Tangier in March of 2003, featured *ṣanāʾiʿ* from the *inṣirāf* of Quddām al-Istihlāl. One of these, *Rīmun ramatnī*,[31] contains the *tarāṭīn*-refrain: *ha-na-na-na ṭāy-ṭiri-rāy*, which is repeated several times with variations in the rhythm in the middle of the *ṣanʿa*. Again, not being familiar with this particular *ṣanʿa* as it is sung, I lost track of the text until one student wrote the syllables into my copy of *Min waḥy al-rabāb*. In this lesson, the students had already learned the *ṣanʿa*, and so were able to perform the entire *ṣanʿa* at tempo with a minimum of refreshment and correction from Professor Bouamar.

These episodes illustrate both the teaching process in action, and the difficulty presented by *ṣanāʾiʿ* that contain long or complicated *tarāṭīn* passages. The printed anthologies of the tradition are inadequate for teaching the texts of *ṣanāʾiʿ* – especially if the student is not well-acquainted with the tradition and its aesthetic ethos, as was my problem on these occasions. On the other hand, even first-year students are rarely complete novices to the tradition. The aesthetic of the tradition (the presence of *tarāṭīn*, the general shape and style of melodies, common musical figures, etc.) is very familiar to most students, for it is part of the musical landscape in which many middle-class children are raised. The music can be heard daily on the radio and television, especially during Ramaḍān, and is played in most neighborhood music shops at one time or another. This explains how the young woman mentioned above was able to parody the music so effectively: many songs from the tradition are widely known, and many in a

[29] See the Glossary: the term *šuġl* has a different meaning in the *Kunnāš* manuscripts than it does in the modern canon and in contemporary usage among musicians. Where once it meant a non-strophic, monorhymed *ṣanʿa*, today it refers to any *ṣanʿa*, whether strophic or not, that has *tarāṭīn*.

[30] *wal-Raqṣ* has been removed from the name (and the facade of the building) in Tangier, presumably because dance is no longer taught there.

[31] ar-Rāyis p. 179; Ibn Jallūn p. 151; Ibn Manṣūr p. 301.

city like Fez or Tetuan will recognize at least one song and can mimic the melodies of several others.

In the second year, the students expand their base of memorized material from the same *mayāzīn* as in the first year, and add songs from *al-Māya* (ad-Darj and al-Quddām), *Raṣd aḏ-Ḏīl* (al-Bṭāyḥī) and *al-Istihlāl* (al-Basīṭ and al-Quddām). Selections from *ar-Raṣd* (al-Basīṭ and al-Quddām), *Ġarībat al-Ḥusayn* (al-Qāʾim wa-Niṣf and al-Bṭāyḥī) and *al-Ḥijāz al-Kabīr* (al-Basīṭ and al-Qāʾim wa-Niṣf) may be taught, as well. In addition, they begin to learn the rudiments of the *ṭār*, which include not only the tapping out of *īqāʿāt*, but also the distinctive technique of playing this instrument. Students who do not already play one of the melodic instruments of the Andalusian orchestra may select one (usually either *ʿūd* or *kamān*) and begin to learn the rudiments in an informal way, using Andalusian songs they have already learned to sing as the principal subject-matter. This training on a melodic instrument, while not part of the formal curriculum at this stage, is all but required for those students who have no previous background in an instrument. Sī Otmane Alami, who performs *qānūn* in Jawq al-Hayik al-Tetuani, assured me that this preliminary training is absolutely essential for the serious student, who will need to be able to play the *ṣanāʾiʿ* while learning them in the third year. There simply will not be time to catch up.[32]

Ṣanāʾiʿ taught in the second year (again according to the curriculum at Maʿhad al-Rašīd) include *Šamsu l-ʿašī qad ġarrabat, Yā šamsu l-ʿašiya, Ana kullī milkun, Ḥubbī maʿī, Yā amlaḥu n-nās* (Quddām al-Māya)[33]; *Wa-ʿašiya samaḥat* (Darj al-Māya)[34]; *Aḥmilu yā ḥamām, Irḥam yā qulayībī, Bušrā lanā, Aḥsanta yā layl, Ḥāṭa l-wajdu bī, Ḥubbukum, Yā l-wālaʿ, In kāna wiṣālak* (Bṭāyḥī Raṣd adh-Dhīl)[35]; and *Wa-law annanī amsaytu* (Darj Raṣd al-Dhīl)[36].

Second-year classes are much smaller. Whereas first-year classes I observed in Fez, Tetuan, Rabat and Tangier ranged from 12 to 25 students, no second-year class exceeded three. Students with only a passing interest in the tradition have fallen away at this point, partly because the large number of *ṣanāʾiʿ* to be memorized represents a

[32] I myself did not meet any second-year students studying *qānūn*, but this instrument certainly is not unknown in the conservatory. Sī Alami is an example. The main difficulty for would-be *qānūn* students at the conservatory (apart from the cost of the instrument) is finding a teacher for the rudiments. The instrument has only recently been added to *ajwāq*, and so the pool of experts in the Andalusian music who are competent to teach the instrument is very small.

[33] ar-Rāyis pp. 108-110; Ibn Jallūn pp. 100-102; Ibn Manṣūr pp. 375-377. (*Ana kullī milkun* and *Ḥubbī maʿī* are not found in Ibn Manṣūr.)

[34] This *ṣanʿa* is mentioned in the curriculum, but curiously it is not found in any of the modern anthologies.

[35] ar-Rāyis pp. 126-128; Ibn Jallūn pp. 112-113; Ibn Manṣūr p. 203. (*Aḥsanta yā layl* and *Ḥubbukum* do not appear in Ibn Jallūn; these two plus *Bušrā lanā, Yā l-wālaʿ* and *In kāna wiṣālak* do not appear in Ibn Manṣūr.)

[36] ar-Rāyis p. 130 only.

significant commitment of time. Moreover, the introduction of musical instruments into the curriculum requires a new level of sophistication and attention from the student, who must devote much more time and effort to study, not just of the *ṭār* and its rudiments, but to the stylistic elements that characterize the aesthetic ethos of *al-Āla*. By embarking upon a second year of study, the student shows a much more serious interest, and the atmosphere in the second-year class is correspondingly more intimate. Without question, entering the second year is an important turning point for the student in terms of effort and personal commitment.

Altogether, students at al-Maʿhad al-Waṭanī are responsible for having memorized the text, melodies and accompanying rhythm patterns of at least 50 *ṣanāʾiʿ* by the end of their second year of instruction. Although this number embodies only a small fraction of the over 700 *ṣanāʾiʿ* in the tradition, it constitutes a respectable amount of memorization nonetheless and forms an essential foundation for study at the third year and beyond. In addition to the *ṣanāʾiʿ*, the student finishes the second year with practical knowledge of all five *īqāʿāt* as they are performed at each *marḥalat al-mīzān*, both as marked by the traditional hand-gesture method, and as performed on the *ṭār*. Finally, those without prior training on a melodic instrument will have learned at least the rudiments of the *ʿūd* or *kamān*.

4.2 *The living tradition of teaching a tradition*

The method of instruction at al-Maʿhad al-Waṭanī, as has been noted, is rote memorization by oral repetition. The professor first dictates the text, and each student copies the dictated text into a notebook. (In every first- and second-year class I have observed some students made use of *Min waḥy al-rabāb* as a reference at this stage, though often there is only one textbook available for all the students; some students have access to photocopied pages, and many use no book at all.) The students will be given any *tarāṭīn* syllables at this point as well (the main purpose behind copying the dictated text). Once the professor is assured that each student has copied the text by hand, he or she plays the song, demonstrating how the melody, text and *tarāṭīn* fit together.[37]

When the students have a sense of how the text and melody work together, the professor and students begin repeating the song, line by line. More complicated *ṣanāʾiʿ* may require the professor to break the melody into smaller pieces and rehearse those before stringing them together to form whole verses and eventually the whole *ṣanʿa*. In effect, the process is one of shaping and refining the students' performance, helping them collectively toward closer and closer approximations of the *ṣanʿa* as the professor

[37] On just one occasion, I saw one of the wealthy students had brought a tape recorder to class to make a teaching tape to practice with.

learned it. As they repeat the *ṣan ͑a*, students tap out the *īqā ͑* in the traditional fashion. Naturally, some students learn more quickly than others, especially if they are already musically trained or very familiar with the tradition. These quick learners soon begin trying out various standard performance techniques within the *Āla* tradition, such as moving between octaves for dramatic effect. In the course of the repetitions, the professor gradually increases the tempo and may emphasize subtle nuances or details of the melody for the sake of the more advanced students.

Periodically, the professor may devote class time to individual audition, giving each student a chance to be heard and corrected, before resuming the group recital. (In addition, students having difficulty or wanting special attention may seek out the professor for private audition time outside the class meetings.) This entire process (including text dictation) may be repeated in later lessons, and over time, as more *ṣanā ͗i ͑* are integrated into the students' repertoire, *ṣanā ͗i ͑* within the same *mīzān* are strung together to form performance units that are then practiced and repeated as a whole. Thus, a typical lesson may involve a combination of text-dictation of new *ṣanā ͗i ͑* (or the re-introduction/re-dictation of a recently-introduced *ṣan ͑a*), rehearsal of previously-learned *ṣanā ͗i ͑* or performance units, and/or review of all the *ṣanā ͗i ͑* covered to date. The process is dynamic and dependent on the professor's mood and evaluation of the class. A good instructor will use this variety of teaching elements to reduce the tedium inherent in constant repetition of the same material.

Thus, the age-old method of study, oral repetition and rote memorization, survives into the 21st century as the principal means by which the *ṭarab* tradition is passed on to the next generation in the National Conservatory. Despite Loopuyt's concerns, solfège, printed texts and written music have not replaced the ancient method. On the contrary, students and musicians alike insist on oral repetition as their preferred teaching method. They feel it is the only way to achieve a proper appreciation of the music.

For example Khalid, a student at the Ma ͑had in Tetuan, learned to play the *͑ūd* and read music, based upon Middle Eastern music theory and solfège, at a private conservatory. He came to al-Ma ͑had al-Waṭanī, he said, because he wanted to study the Andalusian music, which was not possible at the private school. When we spoke, he was in the midst of his fifth year at al-Ma ͑had and looking forward to another three years before taking the national examination that could earn him the first-level diploma in the Andalusian music.

He recalled that in his first classes at al-Ma ͑had al-Waṭanī he found himself at a disadvantage because his previous study had made him dependent on written music. Not used to memorizing large amounts of material, he found the traditional teaching method challenging. Other students seemed to retain the lessons more easily, while he had to work hard at it. However he said that over time his proficiency at memorization improved. Overall, he preferred the traditional method as the proper way to teach the Andalusian music, because it instills a profound intimacy with the music. (At the same time, he found Western tools like solfège and musical script to be helpful in studying the *ʿūd* and does not think they should be discarded in teaching the fundamentals of the instruments, even in the context of studying *al-Āla*.)

Instruction at al-Maʿhad al-Waṭanī is by no means limited to *al-Āla*. The larger branches located in the Rabat, Tetuan and Fez villes nouvelles offer "Arab classical" (that is, Middle Eastern) and Western classical music, taught using modern methods. Students may learn the tools of Western music theory (solfège, reading and writing music) and choose from a variety of instruments (piano, classical guitar, *ʿūd*, violin, *darbūka* and Western percussion are common, woodwinds rarer and brass instruments rarer still). These classes are distinct from the Andalusian music classes, which are open to any interested students, whether they have previous musical training or not. Though students may cross over, the two domains are regarded as separate curricula.

For example, when students in the second year of Andalusian music study take up an instrument, they may be encouraged to learn the fundamentals and tools of Western music theory as part of their training. Students also may move the other direction, as well, as Khalid did. This was the case with Omar my private teacher in Fez, as well. He took up the *ʿūd* when he was a young boy in Fez, learning the rudiments of the instrument from a family friend and imitating the Middle Eastern and Andalusian songs he heard on records and the radio. Later, he continued his studies at the Maʿhad in Fez, developing his skills as a player while learning Western music theory and tools. Only after two years at the conservatory did he take up the Andalusian music. Thus he came to formal instruction in *al-Āla* with a grounding in the Western tools as well as training in his instrument. Eventually he earned a diploma in music teaching, with specialization in *ʿūd*.

In addition to formal teaching of the tradition as such, we must bear in mind that many musicians performing in Andalusian music ensembles do not attend the conservatory at all. One example is Bilāl Biḫāt, who plays *darbūka* in Jawq al-Hayik al-Tetuani. Sī Mehdi Chaachou, *raʾīs* of Jawq al-Hayik, told me affectionately that Sī Bilāl is the best *darbūka* player in Tetuan, but when I spoke to him, I found that he has never had any formal training in the instrument at all. Rather, like so many musicians in the tradition, he first learned the instrument as a child by imitating recordings and the radio. Later, when he began playing in ensembles with friends, he learned not only the basic rhythmic cycles of the *mayāzīn*, but also specific *ṣanāʾiʿ* and *tawāšī*.

Now in his mid-thirties, Sī Bilāl is a fixture in the various formations of Sī Mehdi's Andalusian *jawq*. I have observed him in rehearsals and performances, and there is no obvious difference between his knowledge of the tradition and that of those who have attended the conservatory. What is more, as the core rhythm player, the *ra'īs* must turn to him sometimes in rehearsal to clarify to less-experienced musicians exactly how to execute certain transitions, such as shifting from one *marḥala* to the next, or where exactly to break for *inšād*. Significantly, though Sī Bilāl's knowledge of the tradition is extensive, his study of the text is another matter. On one occasion, I was chatting with some members of Jawq al-Hayik – including Sī Bilāl – about the poetic content of one *ṣanʿa* they were working on. Their comments reflected what I would describe as a gloss on the text, that is, it seemed they were not commenting on the text itself but rather on a received explanation of its meaning. Indeed, many details of the old Arabic poetic tradition may remain rather obscure even to literate native Arabic speakers, unless they have studied it in depth. Sī Bilāl's story illustrates that even though the conservatory is not the only avenue into the tradition, oral transmission is by far the predominant method by which it is learned.

4.3 *Beyond the second year*

Lessons beyond the second year are extremely difficult for outsiders to observe, for several reasons. Instruction is far more personal than at previous levels and generally takes place one-on-one, based upon the student's and professor's schedules. Indeed, while the *site* of higher level instruction in *al-Āla* in theory may be the conservatory, the *context* retains the quality of the old apprenticeship system noted by Schuyler. It is understandable, then that a master might not want to have the lesson disturbed, even out of politeness to a guest.

Nevertheless, the contents of instruction at the higher levels are standardized to some degree. The curriculum at Maʿhad Mūlāy Rašīd lists *ṣanā'iʿ* to be learned all the way through the eighth year. As noted earlier, it is in the third year that the student specializes in one of the melodic instruments. More difficult *ṣanā'iʿ* continue to be added, while the student transfers previously memorized material to his or her chosen instrument. The fourth year completes a level of training for which there is a more-or-less comprehensive examination. This exam takes place at the local conservatory and covers approximately 118 *ṣanā'iʿ*. The successful student receives a diploma that certifies completion of the first level of training in the Andalusian music. (This is the point at which Omar chose to specialize in teaching general music classes, rather than the Andalusian repertoire as such.)

From the 5th year on, the most sophisticated (and the most beautiful) *ṣanā'iʿ* enter the curriculum. The student also is expected to progress in instrumental technique, and to begin to learn *buġayāt* and *tawāšī* alongside the *ṣanā'iʿ*.[38] In this phase of instruction, music reading and solfège enter the student's skill set, though they are treated as general skills not necessarily to be applied to the Andalusian music itself.

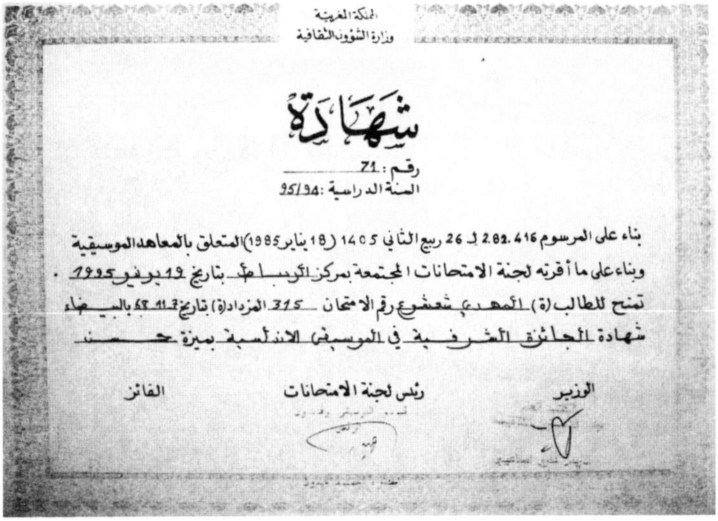
المملكة المغربية
وزارة الشؤون الثقافية

شهادة

رقم: 71
السنة الدراسية: 95/94

بناء على المرسوم 2.82.416 لـ 26 ربيع الثاني 1405 (18 يناير 1985) المتعلق بالمعاهد الموسيقية
وبناء على ما أقرته لجنة الامتحانات المجتمعة بمركز الرباط بتاريخ 19 يونيو 1995 .
تمنح للطالب(ة) المهدي شعشوع رقم الامتحان 315 المزداد(ة) بتاريخ 11-7-62 بالبيضاء
شهادة الجائزة الشرفية في الموسيقى الاندلسية بميزة حسن

الوزير	رئيس لجنة الامتحانات	الفائز

Figure 4.5: *A diploma from the National Conservatory*

5. *The national examination*

The eighth year of instruction completes another level and culminates in a national examination held in June at al-Maʿhad al-Waṭanī in the Rabat Ville Nouvelle. There is no fee for the examination, and it is in principle open to all students who have completed the requisite course of study. In addition to memorized *ṣanā'iʿ* and instrumental passages, and performance on the instrument of choice, the student is tested on detailed knowledge of the tradition itself: which secondary *ṭubūʿ* belong to which *nawbāt*, which *tabʿ* a particular *ṣanʿa* is performed in, how the rhythm of a given *mīzān* changes from *al-muwassaʿ* to *al-qanṭara* to *al-inṣirāf*, and so on. In addition, at the end of the examination, each student is given a short passage of written music (approximately eight bars), which she or he must sing using the French solfège system. Successful students receive a *šahāda* ("diploma," lit.: *witnessing* to one's achievement)

[38] The more advanced students will, as a matter of course, have already begun to learn the instrumental repertoire as early as the third year. The fourth-year exam assumes some knowledge of *buġayāt* and *tawāšī*.

certifying having mastered the Andalusian music sufficiently to teach the tradition at the lower levels.

A second examination, held on the same occasion, is offered for students in their ninth or tenth years of study. The level of performance expected for this second *šahāda* is effectively professional. Indeed, most of the those sitting for the second *šahāda* have already been performing more-or-less professionally.

Figure 4.6: *Driss Barrada sits for the national exam, with Mohamed Briouel second from left and Professor Imlāḥī next to hm in the dark shirt.*

I had the opportunity to observe both examinations (called *mubārayāt*, "competitions") on June 15th and 16th, 2004 in Rabat. The *mubārayāt* were held in a small auditorium on the lower level of the Maʿhad building in the Ville Nouvelle. Present were three judges, Professor Mohamed Briouel, director of the conservatory in Fez and *raʾīs* of Jawq Briouel; Mūlāy ʿAbd al-Salām al-Imlāḥī, a professor at Maʿhad Mūlāy Rašīd across town in the Rabat medina; and a third judge who was present only to examine students for a diploma in *Malḥūn*. These judges were selected by the Ministry of Education and Cultural Affairs for their expertise, Briouel in particular because of his eminence as both a performer and an administrator in the conservatory system. They were assisted by a secretary responsible for managing the examinees' paperwork, and an assistant who escorted examinees to and from the examination room, provided them with water and performed other similar services.

Eight *Āla* students were scheduled for the lower-level *mubāraya* on the first day, and four more for the second level the next day.[39] No women took the *Āla* exam on this occasion. A number of other interested people (mostly friends and families of examinees) also attended. The examination lasted between 45 minutes and an hour for each examinee. The assistant led the examinee in and handed his papers and identity card to the secretary. He then took a seat in the middle of the room facing the judges, who sat at a long table with the secretary. Professor Briouel encouraged each examinee to warm up on his instrument and tune to the piano on the nearby stage.

Once he had been formally greeted by the judges, each examinee was then asked to sing several *ṣanā'iʿ* a cappella while keeping time with his hand in the traditional fashion. Eight to ten *ṣanā'iʿ* were requested, occasionally interrupted by one of the judges, who might ask him to give the *ṭabʿ* or location of the *ṣanʿa* (its *nūba*, *mīzān* and *marḥala*). All the examinees were asked to perform a certain *ṣanʿa* which appears in two different *nawbāt*. The judges took note whether he realized the choice to be made, and in each case they asked for detailed information on the location of both versions. Some were asked to perform both versions. At least one examinee was asked to stop and then resume the same *ṣanʿa* at another point, apparently to see how well he knew the *ṣanʿa*. The choice of *ṣanā'iʿ* was not known to the examinees in advance; the judges chose them from a list of required *ṣanā'iʿ* on a sheet of paper in front of them.

Some examinees were asked to stop and check their vocal intonation against their instruments, and it was evident that Professor Briouel in particular was concerned that the examinee had command of both his singing and the *ṭabʿ*. Judging from his expressions, I did not believe he was always satisfied. More than one examinee was asked to sing more strongly or improve his tone; clearly performance quality was being examined as well as knowledge of the music itself.

Following the a cappella portion of the test, each examinee was asked to perform on his instrument *buġayāt* and *tawāšī* selected by the judges. The examinees played either *ʿūd* or *kamān*. Some candidates were further asked to discuss the instrumental passage in detail: which *ṭabʿ* did he perform it in, how many other *tawāšī* are found in the same *mīzān*, and so on. Then he was asked to accompany himself in a series of four or five selected *ṣanā'iʿ*, and then to perform a *tūšiya* and transition into a *ṣanʿa*. At any point in the instrumental part of the exam, the candidate might be

---

[39] Only two *Malḥūn* students (two women singers) were present for the examination. Only one of them appeared to qualify for the *šahāda*. Neither could read music, though both made reasonable attempts to do so.

critiqued on various aspects of his performance, such as technique, timbre, or intonation.

The exam concluded with the solfège test, which appeared quite perfunctory. Each examinee was asked how long he had studied solfège (most replied between one and two years), and then was given a sheet of paper with a passage of eight bars to sight-sing. Most simply recited the names of the notes on the page (*fa-mi-re-do…*), in rhythm, rather than actually singing the pitches. Only two of the examinees were able to sing the whole selection competently, and only one of them executed it without flaws and without stopping.

Professor Briouel later confirmed my general impression that the majority of the examinees on the first day failed to qualify for the *šahāda*. I thought that perhaps two of the eight had demonstrated adequate control of both material and instrument, and Professor Briouel agreed. He mentioned three criteria for success in the examination: first, accurate memorization of the tradition, both music and text, and the ability to recall specific *ṣanāʾiʿ*; second, a clear and musical voice, accurate singing and good vocal technique; third, good instrumental skills (technique, tone and ability to accompany oneself). Although nearly all the students appeared to know the tradition well from the point of view of memorization and structure (the first part of the *mubāraya*), a number of them had weak voices that left the judges unimpressed. In addition, only two or three were able to demonstrate adequate performing skills on their instruments in accompanying themselves (the second part of the *mubāraya*).

One should avoid focusing on the results of the *mubārayāt* as evidence of limitations in the students' education or abilities; it is important to take into account the larger economic forces in play. To be fair, the exam is very difficult, in that it demands both theoretical knowledge and skills, as well as mastery of scores of *ṣanāʾiʿ* and instrumental passages. True command of this amount of material at this level of competence requires an investment of time and energy that economic circumstances in contemporary Morocco rarely allow: the examinees did not appear to be the sort of professional students one usually encounters at conservatories in the West, who often enjoy financial support from the government or other institutions that allows them to focus on their musical training. Several of the examinees had taken time off from work to attend the *mubārayāt*.

Failure to earn the *šahāda* does not necessarily mean the end of a musician's aspirations to perform the Andalusian music. The ranks of many *ajwāq* and other kinds of ensembles are occupied by musicians who have had no conservatory training at all. In a local context, a skilled musician having any familiarity with the tradition, having memorized even a handful of *ṣanāʾiʿ* and *tawāšī*, could be quite welcome, even in one of the more famous *ajwāq* such as Sī Benmūsā's Jawq li-Baḥth al-Mūsīqā l-Andalusiyya or

Jawq al-Hayik at-Tetuani. Moreover, the *šahāda* (and indeed the whole conservatory-oriented method of training Andalusian musicians) represents a modernizing approach to perpetuating a tradition that faces strong pressures to ensure the *aṣīl* ("authentic") character of the result. Thus, the *mubārayāt* attempt to assess a highly specialized set of skills and competencies informed by tradition. The *šahāda* is best understood as a stepping stone toward *teaching* the tradition, certifying a performer's level of memorization and competence. Given the limited opportunities for teaching in the conservatory or privately, it is not surprising that the standards for this diploma should be high and that few should earn it.

The second-level *mubārayāt* on the following day proceeded similarly to the first. The examination format was identical (except there was no solfège section), but many of the *ṣanāʾiʿ* and *tawāšī* tested were far more difficult. Moreover, questions about the structure and contents of the tradition appeared to be more complex. In short, the 9th-10th year examination tested the examinee as a nascent professional Andalusian musician. The level of the examinees' performances was correspondingly higher. Just as the second year of conservatory separates casual students from those with a serious interest in learning the music, the second *šahāda* is directed at active musicians who have attained a professional degree of control over all aspects of the tradition beyond memorization and instrumental competence. The examinees need to demonstrate that they can perform the music with feeling and attention to the nuances of the *ṣanāʾiʿ* and *tawāšī*.

All four examinees performed very well on nearly all aspects of the exam, though only two of them stood out for their musical expression. Both of these are professional musicians already performing in Andalusian music ensembles. One, Sī Driss Barrada, studied extensively in the conservatory in Fez under the tutelage of Professor Briouel himself. Rumor has it that Professor Briouel considers Sī Driss to be his best student, and is grooming him to become a *muʿallim* himself one day. While his vocal performance was not exceptional, his command of the tradition and the *ʿūd* were impeccable, and his performance was pleasing and musically expressive.

The second outstanding examinee, Sī ʿAzīz al-ʿAlamī has been performing in Fez for years, usually with the various formations of Jawq Briouel and Jawq Fez, but also in *farqāt* with Professor Aḥmad Šīkī of the Fez conservatory and other notable musicians of the tradition in Fez. (He is the *ṭār* player in Figures I-3 and I-4 in the Introduction to this book.) His instrument being the *ṭār* presented a problem for the judges, since he could not be expected to perform on a melodic instrument. (The solution was simply to ignore the second part of the examination altogether.) However, Sī ʿAzīz is known in Fez for his remarkable vocal talents. His *inšādāt* are always featured in Jawq Briouel, and it is said that once, at a performance commissioned by

King Ḥasan II, the monarch singled him out to sing a cappella for him. Thus Sī ʿAzīz's reputation preceded him, and since his knowledge of the tradition and its nuances were indisputable, the judges decided simply to name a dozen or so *ṣanāʾiʿ* for him to perform. They also asked him to sing a *baytayn*. His singing more that met with their approval, and indeed, everyone in the room was moved by the beauty of his performance.

It puzzled me that such an outstanding musician should be sitting for this examination at all, since he clearly is on a par with the best performers of his generation. When I asked him why he had come to the *mubārayāt*, he explained that for him it was a mark of professionalism in keeping with the times, and that he would need this certification in order to teach in the conservatory. Sī ʿAzīz is a product of the juxtaposition between the modern and the traditional in the Andalusian music described in Chapter 3. As Moroccans cope with changes wrought by contemporary economic and institutional relationships, professional musicians like Sī ʿAzīz – some trained in the conservatory and others informally – will have to adapt their careers and their perspectives to a system that seeks to import the methods and standards of modernity into the tradition. Since the rise of the conservatory system and the *jamʿiyyāt* in the first half of the 20th century, the modernizing trend in *al-Āla* has exerted increasing influence on the discourses that shape the tradition. The effort to sustain the tradition in the modern era has led to formalization and commodification within both the teaching system and the performance contexts. For good or ill, the compromises of modernizers like Mohamed Briouel, who are trying to walk a fine line between the demands of tradition and the perceptions of modernity, have come to predominate in the Andalusian music tradition in Morocco.

Likewise, this is not to say that because the method of teaching has been preserved, the result of Andalusian music training today is the same as it once was. We have already seen that the venues for teaching have changed, as have the performance contexts. In general, formal institutions have replaced the older informal ones in support of the music and the social/cultural milieu which surrounds it. It is only natural, therefore, that the product of Andalusian music training has altered, as well. This comes into focus at the third level of teaching in the *ṭarab* tradition, the *jawq*.

6. *Mastery: the* jawq *as teaching institution*

Although we have little specific data from our older sources, it is probable that the *jawq* as we known it today (an ensemble of between seven and 20 musicians) is a relatively new phenomenon. We have photographs from the early twentieth century showing relatively small ensembles centered around a *raʾīs/muʿallim*, such as the well-known photograph of Jawq al-Brīhī with its *raʾīs* (d. 1945) playing *rabāb* and a young ʿAbd al-

Karīm ar-Rāyis at his side playing *ʿūd*. (Figure 4.7). The size and instrumentation is similar to the smaller, less complex *jawq* of the early twentieth century described by García Barriuso (1940, 236) as having 7 to 11 instruments, including up to four *kamānāt* (both violin and viola) and an equal number of *ʿūd*s (a number which would be more typical of a larger ensemble today). Wind instruments were not used at the time, nor piano, nor were the larger strings such as the cello, which is quite common today. García Barriuso also indicates that the *qānūn* had not yet made its appearance in the Moroccan ensemble, stating that in his day it was more common in the Algerian tradition.[40]

Figure 4.7: *Jawq al-Brīhī ca. 1939. Al-Brīhī is playing* rabāb, *with a young ʿAbd al-Karīm ar-Rāyis to his left playing playing the ʿ*ūd

Ajwāq of the decades prior to 1940 did not differ much in composition or size from those of a century or more earlier, with the exception of the *darbūka*, which may not have entered the Moroccan ensemble from the Middle East until the 20th century. Prior to the incorporation of the *kamān* in the 18th century,[41] the ensemble was even simpler, being based upon the *ʿūd* or *suwīsan*, the *ṭār* and the *rabāb* (though no visual representations of this kind of ensemble have come to light). It was only in the

[40] Contrary evidence is offered by the book *Aġānī s-sīqā fī ʿilm al-mūsīqā*, by the Fassi scholar Ibrāhīm b. Muḥammad at-Tādilī (d. 1311/1894), which indicates that the *qānūn* was in use at that time, and indeed, lap zithers were known in both al-Andalus and the Mašriq in the Middle Ages.

[41] García Barriuso 1940, p. 224.

generation after Muḥammad al-Brīhī, with the increased importance of the conservatory system and the stylistic innovations of al-Wakīlī (d. 1988) and at-Temsemānī (d. 2001), that the *jawq* began to expand in size and composition.[42]

Changes in the institutions surrounding the music and the ensembles which perform it also encouraged changes in the size and instrumentation of the Andalusian *jawq*. The expansion of teaching in the conservatory system during and after the Protectorate created a cadre of musicians and aficionados well versed in the tradition, and as noted in Chapter 3, the modern financial support system for many of the modern *ajwāq* (one or more formal associations of Andalusian music lovers, of which the *ra'īs al-jawq* may be an officer) owes its existence to the changes in economy wrought by modernization since the Protectorate. All of these factors also have altered the membership of the *jawq*. Much of the basic training that used to fall to the *muʿallim* in a local, intimate context has in theory been removed to the classrooms of the conservatories. It is in the third-year lessons and beyond at the Maʿhad that preparation for performance in a *jawq* begins. This means that, in theory, the *muʿallim* now can draw upon an external resource of well-prepared musicians who can enter the ensemble without demanding too much training in the fundamentals.

In practice, however, conservatory training in the Andalusian music remains the province of relatively few musicians, and the results of the *mubārayāt* show that even at at the higher levels of instruction, conservatory training does not guarantee complete mastery of the tradition. Some of the most accomplished Andalusian musicians still are trained informally and have only minimal contact with the conservatory. As a result, it is easy to overstate the importance of conservatory training for the Andalusian *jawq*. Omar's, Bilāl's and ʿAzīz ʿAlamī's musical careers are all instructive in this regard. The *jawq* itself, especially one led by a *muʿallim*, offers the highest and most refined stage of education. It is in the context of the professional *jawq* that the novice musician solidifies his or her knowledge of the repertoire, and acquires both experience in the art of performing, and familiarity with its aesthetic nuances. For all but the most accomplished conservatory students (such as Sī Driss Barrada) this refinement is the direct result of instruction from a *ra'īs*. As Omar once said to me: *Al-madrasa al-ḥaqīqiyya hiya l-jawq*. ["The real school is the *jawq*."]

For musicians fortunate enough to earn a place in the *jawq* of one of the recognized masters of the music, it is more than simply an opportunity to perform. It is an environment in which the musician imbibes a complete performance ethos, the stylistic qualities and details that distinguish a local school within the larger *Āla* tradition. The *ra'īs* in this case serves both as exemplar of the whole tradition, and as the model for the *jawq*'s stylistic school. Not only has he mastered his instrument and

[42] See Chapter 3, Fig. 3.1.

learned the music and text thoroughly, but this kind of *raʾīs* will have received the tradition at the hands of a master from the previous generation. This situates him within a genealogy of past masters like that presented in Chapter 3, Figure 3.1. (Once again, an analogy with American jazz music is appropriate. Even today, in an era when jazz is taught at all the major universities and conservatories, an up-and-coming player will be recognized more for the established artists he has played with than for the degree of his formal training.)

The concept of the *muʿallim* implies the idea that not all *ajwāq* and not all *ru'asā'* are equal. Fez, for example, has several *ajwāq* including all-purpose ensembles which can perform some Andalusian music for weddings and private parties, but whose *ru'asā'* may or may not have had formal training in the *ṭarab* tradition. Other *ajwāq* center around a student or recent graduate from the conservatory, or perhaps a musician who also performs with an established master, as well. Such *ruʾasā'* may command the formal aspects of the tradition but lack subtle stylistic skill within the *ṭarab* tradition. They may be respected as musicians but not as true masters. Not having completed an apprenticeship within a genealogy of recognized masters, they do not fully embody the tradition.

In Fez, two men in particular are recognized in the Andalusian music community as masters of the kind just described: Mohamed Briouel and ʿAbd al-Fattāḥ Benmūsā. Both men studied at the conservatory in Fez under the tutelage of the late ʿAbd al-Karīm ar-Rāyis, and both played *kamān* in ar-Rāyis' orchestra, Jawq al-Brīhī (ar-Rāyis himself having inherited the leadership of the orchestra of his own late master, Muḥammad al-Brīhī). These two contemporary masters embody different and perhaps complementary perspectives on the preservation and perpetuation of the Moroccan Andalusian music.

Sī Briouel worked closely with ar-Rāyis in producing a musical score for *Ġarībat al-Ḥusayn*, and today he holds ar-Rāyis' former position as director of al-Maʿhad al-Waṭanī in Fez. He now leads his own ensemble, Jawq Briouel, some of whose members also appear with him as Jawq Fez, which has performed in Europe and the U.S. both on its own and in support of the Sephardic Jewish singer Françoise Atlan, and which often performs on important occasions such as the ʿĪd holiday reception held by the wife of the governor of Fez in December of 2002 described earlier. Sī Briouel does not shy away from engaging the modern institutional system surrounding the music, and he sees the tradition being best served by actively presenting the music in modern formats on as large an international stage as possible.[43]

[43] Similarly, Sī Briouel's performance practice includes some stylistic departures from the conservative school, falling closer to the modern expressive schools identified by Benmūsā and Šīkī (See above, §4).

Sī Benmūsā's career has been quite different. A lawyer by profession, he too studied the Andalusian music with ar-Rāyis, and has made a name for himself in the Andalusian music community as a scholar and writer, as well as *ra'īs*, but he is an educator of a different sort. He participates in conferences on the *Āla* tradition and has written books and articles on formal and historical aspects of the tradition. Whereas Sī Briouel fills an institutional role as musician, administrator and ambassador for the music, Sī Benmūsā, as an independent musician and researcher, addresses himself to an educated Moroccan public and contributes to an historically-informed perspective on the music and its performance ethos. Even the full name of his *jawq* reflects Sī Benmūsā's intellectual commitment: Jawq Benmūsā li-Baḥth al-Mūsīqā l-Andalusiyya, The Benmūsā Orchestra for the Study of the Andalusian Music. His performance practice follows more closely the conservative aesthetic values he attributes to ar-Rāyis as exemplar of *al-madrasa al-muḥāfiẓa* as distinct from the more overtly "expressive" schools of al-Wakīlī and at-Temsemānī (and Briouel, as well).[44]

I have had the opportunity to observe rehearsals of two different orchestras and witnessed the advanced level of teaching that takes place in the *jawq*. In the spring of 2003, Jawq li-Baḥth al-Mūsīqā l-Andalusiyya (or simply, Jawq Benmūsā) was preparing for a weekend concert series in the town of Īmmūzār Kandar, near Fez, sponsored by l'Association des Melomanes, the association which supports Sī Benmūsā's *jawq*. Most of the rehearsals were held in a salon in the complex of Association Fès Saiss in the Baṭḥā' neighborhood of the Fez medina, although at least one took place in an empty hall adjacent to the main courtyard of Musée Batha.[45] Not all the musicians attended every rehearsal, but over the course of five meetings, I saw each rehearse at least once: two *ʿūds*, *rabāb*, *qānūn*, four to six *kamān* (depending upon the occasion), at least two violas and Sī Benmūsā playing *kamān*.[46] All were well-versed in the music, and they clearly have been performing together for some years, for they seemed to be familiar with one another and with the repertoire they were rehearsing on these occasions, primarily from Basīṭ al-Māya and Quddām al-Ḥijāz al-Kabīr. In some ways, these did not differ very much from classical music rehearsals one might see in the U.S., except for issues emerging from the oral aspects of the tradition.

---

[44] *al-madrasa taᶜbiriyya*; see: Benmūsā (2001a).

[45] Formerly the Batha Palace, site of al-Jāmiʿī's Andalusian music madrasa in the late 19th century. See: Benmūsā (2001a) and Chapter 3 §3.

[46] One unusual – dare I say non-traditional? – feature of Jawq Benmūsā is that one of the *ʿūd* players is a woman, and in the 2006 edition of the Fez *mahrajān* he included a chorus of four women singers. The mixing of the sexes in a single orchestra is rare indeed in the otherwise masculine *Āla* tradition. (Integration of the sexes is much more common in the Algerian *Ġarnāṭī* genre.) Over the course of two years of contact with the members of Jawq Benmūsā on both performance and social occasions, I have never seen women treated in any way except as musical and social equals by the other members of the jawq.

Most important of these was that I noted the absence of sheet music, which came as no surprise since such materials are rare (and probably would not be used by Jawq Benmūsā in performance in any case). In general, text and music must be learned together, and they are almost always performed from memory. On the other hand, the relationship between printed and memorized text was complicated and fascinating. It was apparent that most of the material was already well known, though not to everyone. For one series of *ṣanāʾiʿ* two *jawq* members used as a reference *Min waḥy al-rabāb* and a printed text from an earlier *ḥafla* by Jawq Benmūsā. I found it remarkable how easily these musicians picked up the melodies of *ṣanāʾiʿ* they barely knew. In this process there seemed to be a kind of dynamic interplay between the use of written text and memorized material. For example, Omar pointed out that one *ṣanʿa* they were rehearsing in *al-Ḥijāz al-Kabīr* had the same melody as a *ṣanʿa* he knew from *Min waḥy al-rabāb*, but the text was completely different (deriving from *Kunnāš al-Ḥāʾik* only, according to Benmūsā). This similarity was not quite sufficient for memorizing the *ṣanʿa*, however, because of the complicated and unpredictable way that the *ṣanāʾiʿ* of *al-Āla* divide words and phrases across the melody. Omar and the other musicians still needed Benmūsā's help, and reference to the text in the *ḥafla* program, to render the song correctly.

This episode shows that, though *Min waḥy al-rabāb* is used nearly everywhere, it is not the only resource for *ṣanʿa* texts. As in the conservatory, it is used mainly as a convenience because it is readily available and inexpensive. Conversely, the al-Ḥāʾik repertoire is considered fundamental; *jawq* leaders have no qualms about drawing material from it, even if the musicians have only limited access to it because there are no editions currently in print. This is why a *muʿallim* like Sī Benmūsā will often use concert programs he has put together for previous occasions as reference materials: he will have already assembled the *ṣanāʾiʿ* himself from various sources into a performance unit. Some of this material will be unfamiliar to the *jawq*, either because few of the musicians have attended the Maʿhad, or else because the particular *ṣanāʾiʿ* are not taught at the conservatory except perhaps at the very highest levels, when the student is working most closely with his or her master.

I observed a similar practice of a *muʿallim* working with the text of a previous concert in rehearsals of Mehdi Chaachou's Jawq al-Hayik at-Tetuani in Tetuan in the spring of 2004, preparing to perform at a *ḥafla* in Fez. Sī Chaachou was trained by Larbī at-Temsemānī, and is widely respected in the Andalusian music community as a promising young *raʾīs* and arranger. Still in his thirties, he has not yet acquired a status comparable to that ascribed to Sī Briouel or Sī Benmūsā, not having distinguished himself by publishing books or articles, or affiliating himself with a major institution such as al-Maʿhad al-Waṭanī. At this point his fame rests upon his performing and arranging skills. Nevertheless he has already acquired a reputation for innovation, in keeping with his training in the expressive school of at-Temsemānī.

On this occasion, a portion of the program being rehearsed involved, not a *mīzān* or portion of one, but all the *ṣanāʾiʿ* with texts by Ibn Sahl al-Israʾīlī (d. 649/1252), irrespective of their *ṭubūʿ* and *īqāʿāt*. This was a very interesting and unusual concept, and it posed unique musical and textual problems: Ibn Sahl's poems are scattered throughout the tradition. In addition to the problem of shaping these diverse compositions into a musically pleasing arrangement (Sī Mehdi's solution was to give his musicians written transcriptions of the melodies for use in rehearsal), even if all these *ṣanāʾiʿ* were known to the musicians, jumping from place to place among the various *mayāzīn* and *nawbāt* (i.e.: ignoring the usual flow of *ṣanāʾiʿ* as performance units) would have placed an unusual demand upon the memories of those who already knew the texts. Sī Mehdi therefore used the concert program to be handed out to the audience as reference material to help the musicians remember the sequence of *ṣanāʾiʿ* in rehearsal.

Another interesting feature of Sī Benmūsā's rehearsals was his manner of conducting them, which was not so different from a conductor of Western classical music in his efforts to elicit a stylistically pleasing performance from the musicians. Of course, *ṣanāʾiʿ* were rehearsed in blocks, performance units corresponding to portions of *marāḥil al-mīzān*. When the group finished a series of these *ṣanāʾiʿ*, Sī Benmūsā often took time to comment on very subtle aspects of the performance he had just heard. He might comment, for example, on how long to hold a particular syllable or where to "cheat" in the pronunciation of a certain word to create a smooth transition from *ṣanʿa* to *ṣanʿa* in keeping with *al-madrasa al-muḥāfiẓa*. Sometimes he explained how particular changes he was making would distinguish the *jawq*'s performance from that of a more modern-sounding *jawq* or from a *jawq* from another region like Tetuan. On one occasion he was specifically unhappy with some detail in the *ṭār* player's execution of the rhythm. He pointed out that, although the rhythm was technically correct, that particular nuance was forcing the rest of the *jawq* out of the feeling considered natural for the repertoire at hand. After three or four repetitions, he was still not satisfied and took the *ṭar* in hand himself and demonstrated for a minute or so the subtle difference between the sound he desired and the sound he was hearing.

Omar often expressed to me his deep respect for Sī Benmūsā. Sometimes he would only shake his head in wonder at the mention of Sī Benmūsā name. "Nobody knows the music," he once said, "as well as Benmūsā." The examples above illustrate how a *jawq* in the hands of a *muʿallim* like Sī Benmūsā serves as the final *madrasa* for the Andalusian musician. Some members will have had varying degrees of conservatory training, and others will have absorbed a great deal of the tradition from their childhoods and through contact with other musicians. The *mu ʿallim* takes these nascent Andalusian musicians and, in the context of rehearsal and performance, gives them the stamp of the stylistic school he imbibed from a master of the previous generation. This training includes not only stylistic nuances that distinguish the *mu ʿallim*'s school, but also *ṣanā ʾiʿ* and variant texts of *ṣanā ʾiʿ* that he learned from his own master, and which may not be readily available to the musicians otherwise.

7. *Formal and informal, spoken and written*

Part 1 has explored the role informal and formal institutions played in sustaining and perpetuating the Moroccan Andalusian music tradition. The economic arrangements that surrounded the music at its inception were mediated through aristocratic patronage, which provided the social and economic support system for musicians through most of its history in al-Andalus and later in North Africa. The customary separation between the *ḫāṣṣa* ("the elite") and *ʿāmma* ("the common folk") concentrated discretionary wealth in the hands of an aristocratic few, and thereby ensured that music and poetry appealing to educated tastes would find an audience. This wealthy aristocracy expressed its taste (and status) through the institution of patronage, which provided financial support and a competitive environment (the princely *majlis* or the aristocratic salon) for the best poets and musicians to write and compose in exchange for their sustenance. Alongside elite patronage, the institution of artiste slavery provided means for poets and composers to have their works heard in the *majlis*, and provided well-to-do artists like Ziryāb and Ibn Bājja with students able to help with the process of composition.

In North African cities like Fez and Tetuan, Andalusian immigrant families formed new niches in the local aristocracies. Here again, the *ḫāṣṣa-ʿāmma* divide was important in the financial arrangements surrounding the music, though its historical and ethnic associations probably allowed the music to extend its influence beyond the salon and the *majlis* into a wider community of descendants of Andalusi immigrants. The music became an entertainment among families wishing to affirm their solidarity with the community as a whole, even during the periods of dynastic upheaval, when Fez in particular became an important nexus of political influence informed by ethnic allegiances often dominated by the Andalusian community.

Beginning in the colonial period, these informal institutions eventually gave way to modern-looking formal institutions. Today, personal patronage by a prince or a wealthy family has been replaced by royal patronage through the Ministry of Cultural Affairs, and by collective patronage through private *jamʿiyyāt* of Andalusian music lovers. Just as the ancient *ḫāṣṣa-ʿāmma* divide has been redefined in terms of modern economic relations, so support for the music has been reshaped by modern discourses of economy and modernity, and relationships defined by social class.

The complexity of these changes is reflected in the modern process of musical training within the tradition. While the government and certain elements of the Andalusian music community have turned to al-Maʿhad al-Waṭanī as the model to perpetuate the tradition, important elements of the ideology underlying the music (the *aesthetic ethos*) tend to turn the training of musicians back toward personal relationships characteristic of the ancient apprenticeship system. Although the conservatory does support a broader interest in the tradition amongst the general population, as a practical tool for the training of musicians it does no more than lay the most basic groundwork. Training those musicians who will become the exemplars of the next generation still falls to the acknowledged masters of the present generation, who were themselves trained by masters of the past generation: the instructor at the higher levels in the Maʿhad and the *muʿallim*.

The most salient feature in transmitting the Andalusian music tradition in Morocco today is the way in which the spoken and the written word have combined, or we might say, *the way that the spoken word has survived the impact of literacy*. We see this at all levels, from the teaching method in first-year classes at the Maʿhad, to the informal training that many contemporary *jawq* members receive from their peers, to explanatory glosses passed on as poetic meaning, to discourses on stylistic nuance put forward by the *muʿallim* during rehearsal. The system appears at first glance to be a fully institutionalized one, built upon a Western model of "classical" music instruction. However the Western observer, looking at the process through the eyes of teaching practice, is likely to ask, "Where are the textbooks?" Where are the songbooks that tell the student *exactly* what to sing? Where are the written analyses of theory and practice that make the music accessible to a literate audience and student pool, and which are considered essential in the West for a comprehensive understanding of an art form?

A better question would be to ask why oral transmission has proven to be so stable in this context, and why the tradition has evolved, not toward a greater dependence upon written texts and literate analyses, but toward a symbiotic relationship between the spoken and the written word. Part 2 sets out to provide a theoretical framework for addressing these questions. However before exploring that, some account should be taken of the materials that comprise the literary dimension of *al-Āla*. Chapter 5 that follows analyzes their format and what is known of their history in order to illustrate further the role that oral processes have played in the formation of the tradition.

Chapter 5
History and the Oral Tradition

In exploring the cultural and historical foundations of *al-Āla*, we do well to consider the fact that it is both a musical tradition and a literary one. Although it will be argued in Part 2 that the true contents of the tradition are the *ṣanāʾiʿ*-as-sung, since the time of al-Ḥāʾik written anthologies of the song texts have played an important role in defining the boundaries of the tradition and stabilizing it as an art form. Al-Ḥāʾik himself probably did not realize the full implications of his anthology project: to judge from comments in the *muqaddima* of his work, he saw it as an aid for people wanting to teach the songs. Yet without question it was a turning point in the history. Not only did the *Kunnāš* contribute to a sense that this was an art worthy of preservation in literary form (by no means a minor consideration, given the deep respect accorded to literature and especially poetry amongst Arabic speakers), but in time it became an authoritative reference work – an urtext of sorts – against which the authenticity of a given *ṣanʿa* could be measured, and which ultimately provided a key resource for the modern institutional conservatory system.

Moreover, close study of the anthologies and the manuscript traditions that lie behind them reveals traces of oral processes, in particular the presence historically in Morocco of multiple streams of orally-transmitted texts in use parallel to the al-Ḥāʾik anthology and eventually intersecting with it. The textual tradition of *al-Āla* thus provides supporting evidence for the historical importance of oral processes in the tradition's history, and it offers indications of diversity amongst the communities who enjoyed the tradition. This chapter, then, describes the printed anthologies that comprise the textual canon of *al-Āla* today, with reference to the manuscript traditions that lie behind them, in order to illustrate the role of oral processes in the formation of the canon.

1. *The modern canon*

The modern canon of *al-Āla* texts comprises three printed anthologies: ʿAbd al-Laṭīf Muḥammad b. Manṣūr's *Majmūʿ azjāl wa-tawšīḥ wa-ašʿār al-mūsīqā l-andalusiyya al-maġribiyya al-maʿrūf bi-l-Ḥāʾik* (*The Collection of the Zajals,* muwaššaḥāt *and Poems of the Moroccan Andalusian Music Known as al-Ḥāʾik*, 1977, hereafter referred to as IJ); al-Ḥājj Idrīs b. Jallūn at-Tuwaymī's *at-Turāṯ al-ʿarabī al-maġribī fī l-mūsīqā: mustaʿmalāt nawbāt aṭ-ṭarab al-andalusī al-maġribī: šiʿr, tawšīḥ, azjāl, barāwil – dirāsa wa-tansīq wa-taṣḥīḥ Kunnāš al-Ḥāʾik* (*The Moroccan Arab Tradition in Music: The* Nawbāt *of the Moroccan Andalusian*

Ṭarab: *Poetry,* muwaššaḥāt, *Zajals and Barwalas – Study, Arrangement and Emendation of* Kunnāš al-Ḥā'ik, 1979, hereafter referred to as IM); and ʿAbd al-Karīm ar-Rāyis' *Min waḥy ar-rabāb* (*From the Inspiration of the* Rabāb, 1982, hereafter referred to as MW). These works are, in essence, the modern crystallization of the two manuscript anthologies, *Kunnāš al-Ḥā'ik* and the al-Jāmiʿī corpus.

Two earlier scholars, Ambīrkū al-Makkī (see: al-Ḥā'īk, 1935) and Aḥmad b. al-Ḥasan Zuwītin (see: al-Ḥā'īk, 1972), also sought to render the *nūba* tradition of *al-Āla* in print. IM and IJ were landmarks, however, because they augmented the *ṣanā'iʿ* in the *Kunnāš* manuscripts with *ṣanā'iʿ* and other material probably unknown to al-Ḥā'ik, including most of the material from the al-Jāmiʿī corpus, thereby making more comprehensive compilations of the tradition available to a wider audience, most importantly to students and faculty at al-Maʿhad al-Waṭanī.

Indeed, when asked about textbooks, the director of the Rāšidiyya conservatory in Rabat pulled out a very old copy of IJ, saying that it was the source for most of the material taught there. This surprised me somewhat, as I had seen only MW used in actual classroom situations. When asked if there were other textbooks, he handed me an equally worn copy of IM. When I followed up by asking specifically about MW, he said that it is sometimes used by students because it is more readily available (IJ and IM are currently out of print), but that the curriculum was based upon the tradition as presented in IJ and IM.

Both of these anthologists defined their works in terms of the *Kunnāš* (each alludes to the *Kunnāš* in its title, and each contains a version of al-Ḥā'ik's *muqaddima*), but neither volume merely reproduces *Kunnāš al-Ḥā'ik*. Each contains introductory material on musical performance by the modern compilers and adds material not found in the *Kunnāš*: *mīzān ad-darj*, as well as *barāwil* in *ad-darj* and *al-quddām*. Furthermore, details of the *muqaddima* of each and the organization of the two anthologies suggest that they are based upon somewhat different manuscript versions of the *Kunnāš*.[1] Both anthologists have also added a small amount of material from sources outside the standard *Kunnāš* manuscript tradition which they considered appropriate.

ʿAbd al-Laṭīf Aḥmad Ḫāliṣ's introduction presents MW as a supplement to the printed canon of IJ and IM, based primarily upon the al-Jāmiʿī corpus.[2] Quite a bit shorter than either IJ or IM and arranged in the usual order of *nawbāt*, as is IJ, MW offers little material not found in them and makes no pretenses to being a

[1] The two anthologies also differ in containing variant versions of some *ṣanā'iʿ*, and in the fact that IM places *mīzān ad-darj* after *al-quddām*. These differences may not derive from the manuscripts.

[2] pp. 12-14.

comprehensive anthology of the canon.[3] In a few cases material in MW differs from the same material in IJ and IM, especially in the arrangement of some performance units. Finally, instead of presenting al-Ḥāʾik's *muqaddima* as such, MW presents al-Ḥāʾik's material on the *ṭubūʿ* in brief introductory notes to each *nūba*.

The foundations for all three of these modern printed anthologies lie in two somewhat complicated manuscript traditions identified in the present work as *Kunnāš al-Ḥāʾik* and the Jāmiʿī corpus. Taken together, the manuscript traditions and the printed anthologies preserve for us clear traces of the oral processes by which *al-Āla* was maintained and transmitted, both before al-Ḥāʾik's time and after. The logical place to start is with the *Kunnāš* manuscripts and their relationship to the modern anthologies.

2. *Kunnāš al-Ḥāʾik*

According to the standard narrative of *al-Āla*'s history, the textual canon of the Moroccan Andalusian music was first defined near the end of the 18th century by the anthologist, Muḥammad b. al-Ḥusayn al-Ḥāʾik at-Tiṭwānī, whose *Kunnāš* ("handbook") is said to represent the first attempt to create a comprehensive collection of all the *ṣanāʾiʿ* performed in *nawbāt* using the 25 "Andalusī" *ṭubūʿ*. In point of fact, it appears that Muḥammad al-Būʿaṣāmī's *Iqād aš-šumūʿ* may well deserve this honor. Although the only manuscript of this book contains just six *nawbāt*, an unknown number of pages clearly have been lost (for example, three of the four *mayāzīn* in *al-Māya*). In its original state, the book might have encompassed the eleven modern *nawbāt* (and perhaps even more). Yet for reasons that are not entirely clear, al-Būʿaṣāmī's work never acquired the recognition that *Kunnāš al-Ḥāʾik* did, so that the latter work has become part of the mythos surrounding *al-Āla*, while *Iqād aš-šumūʿ* is known today only to a handful of experts in the tradition.

Little is known today about the anthologist al-Ḥāʾik, other than his name and a few clues in his anthology about his purpose in creating the work. His name suggests that he hailed from Tetuan, but his roots there are not recorded by any leading families.[4]

The act of compiling the *nūba* tradition in written form clearly has had a significant effect on the tradition's history by initiating a process that contributed to the music's present status as the classical music of Morocco. The *Kunnāš*, perhaps not at first but certainly over time, came to be regarded as the defining written record of *al-*

[3] In all of *Nawbat Ramal al-Māya*, for example, MW contains only four *ṣanāʾiʿ* not found at all in IJ or IM.
[4] See Chapter 3 §2. Also Valderrama Martínez, 1954, especially pp. 33-34.

Āla. Aficionados now treat it as evidence that the Andalusian musical heritage of Morocco is a identifiable art form worthy of conscientious preservation.

Scholarship on the *Kunnāš* has been rather limited. Valderrama Martínez (1953, 1954) produced the first serious studies of the *Kunnāš* as a document, describing the anthology's basic structure and characterizing its contents, based upon two manuscripts he found in Morocco. His student, Manuela Cortés García (1995, 1996, 2003), has also written on the *Kunnāš*. Among Moroccans, only Malik Bennūna has conducted extensive research on the poetry of *al-Āla*. His edition of the Dāwūdiyya #144 manuscript of the *Kunnāš* (1999) provides a wealth of historical and literary data on the *Kunnāš* in his introduction and footnotes. Cortés García concludes that al-Ḥāʾik was well-educated, being versed in Qurʾān and law, poetry, and music, and that he produced the *Kunnāš* from both oral and written sources. She maintains that he combined material from the Andalusian community in Morocco with material he supplied from Moroccan authors, though she does not indicate her basis for this distinction.[5] The anthologist himself does not make it in any version of his *Kunnāš* that I have encountered.

2.1 *Manuscripts*

An unknown number of manuscript copies of *Kunnāš al-Ḥāʾik* may be found today in archives and libraries scattered across Morocco and Europe. Some undoubtedly were intended for the bookshelf, having been executed in a decorative hand with ornate verse and hemistich markers. Others were reference volumes for performers that include marginalia presenting additional *ṣanāʾiʿ*, alternative verses and annotations on the music. Cortés García mentions some 21 manuscripts identified as "*Kunnāš al-Ḥāʾik*" but defines a "familia al-Ḥāʾik" comprised of only six of these. The data in this chapter are based upon study of eight of the most commonly cited *Kunnāš* manuscripts, using either copies of the manuscripts themselves, summaries found in Shiloah (1979) and Bennūna (1999), or published editions (Bennūna, 1999; Valderrama, 1954, 2003). Those marked with a superscript "f" in the list belong to Cortés García's *familia al-Ḥāʾik*:

1. *Bennīs* – ms. owned by the *wazīr* ʿAbd ar-Raḥmān Bennīs (copy donated to Bennūna for use in his 1999 edition: see p. 17); dated by Bennūna 1881.
2. *Dāwūdiyya* – ms. #144 from the collection of the late Tetuani historian, Muḥammad Dāwūd, now deposited at his private library, al-Ḫizāna ad-Dāwūdiyya in Tetuan (subject of Bennūna edition, 1999); dated 1202/1788.

[5] 1996, p. 89.

3. *Leiden* – Leiden Universiteits Bibliotheek Or. 14100 (Shiloah # 066; Bennūna, p. 17); undated.
4. *London* – British Museum, London Or. 13235 (Shiloah #067); undated.
5. *Raysūnī* – ms. in the library of the ar-Raysūnī family of Chefchaouen (copy donated for Bennūna 1999 edition: see pp. 17, 19 fn.); no date indicated.
6. *Raqīwaq*[f] – ms. owned by al-Ḥājj ʿAbd as-Salām ar-Raqīwaq of Tanger (copy donated to Bennūna for use in his 1999 edition, see p. 17); copied 1325/1907. (This ms. was published as a facsimile edition of 1000 copies in 1981 by Jamʿiyyat Hawāt al-Mūsīqā l-Andalusiyya.).
7. *Valderrama*[f] – Copy of a ms. executed in 1350/1931 for Fernando Valderrama Martínez by as-Sayyid Muḥammad Būʿasal (original now lost, facsimile of copy published in 2003).
8. *Wazzānī* – Copy of a ms. given to Sīdī Muḥammad ar-Raysūnī by al-ʿArabī al-Wazzānī that includes the *Kunnāš* attached to an anthology of poetry associated with the *zawāyā* (photocopy made available by Mehdi Chaachou); undated.

Each of these manuscripts comprises *ṣanāʾiʿ* organized into *ṭabʿ*-based *nawbāt* composed of four *mayāzīn* (al-Basīṭ, al-Qāʾim wa-Niṣf, al-Bṭāyḥī and al-Quddām), and each identifies itself with the anthologist, al-Ḥāʾik. Each contains a mixture of songs labeled *tawšīḥ*, *zajal* or *šuġl*, and each has at least part of the anthologist's *muqaddima*. To this extent, they clearly are related to one another.

2.2. *Problematic origins*

And yet even a superficial comparison of these manuscripts shows that the manuscript tradition behind the modern canon is far from simple. Some "al-Ḥāʾik" manuscripts contain *nawbāt* not recognized in the modern canon, and even contain multiple versions of individual *nawbāt*. Figure 5.1 compares these various structures with one another.

This table reveals that only the four manuscripts in the first column have all eleven contemporary *nawbāt*, and only those *nawbāt*, in their modern canonical order. Structurally speaking, *Leiden*, *Raqīwaq*, *Wazzānī* and *Valderrama* clearly are related to one another and embody the al-Ḥāʾik canon more or less as it is recognized today. While *Wazzānī* and *Leiden* are not dated, *Raqīwaq* and *Valderrama* are 20th-century copies of older manuscripts and may be much later than the other two (though this is not absolutely certain: it may be that all four are very late copies). *Wazzānī* is also obviously late because the manuscript is appended to another anthology of non-*Kunnāš* material. *Leiden* could be the source for the others in this group, but is most likely a copy descended from a lost original and not the "original *Kunnāš*" (for reasons that will be discussed below). Indeed it is equally likely that all four are descendants of a lost fifth manuscript and/or that any one could be a source for one or more of the others. Their contents, particularly those of the "familia al-Ḥā᾿ik", are so similar that even a careful comparison of the specific *ṣanā᾿iʿ* and details of the *muqaddima* each contains might not reveal which of these possibilities is true.

	Leiden, Raqīwaq, Wazzānī, Valderrama	**Bennīs, London**	**Raysūnī**	**Dāwūdiyya**
1	*Ramal al-Māya*	*ar-Raṣd*	*al-Ḥusayn*	*al-Istihlāl* (1)
2	*al-Iṣbahān*	*al-Ḥijāz al-Kabīr*	*al-Iṣbahān* (1)	*al-Istihlāl* (2)
3	*al-Māya*	*ʿIrāq al-ʿAjam*	*ar-Raṣd*	*ʿIrāq al-ʿArab*
4	*Raṣd aḏ-Ḏīl*	*Ġarībat al-Ḥusayn*	*ʿIrāq al-ʿAjam*	*al-Māya*
5	*al-Istihlāl*	*al-Māya*	*Ġarībat al-Ḥusayn*	*al-Ḥusayn*
6	*ar-Raṣd*	*al-ʿUššāq*	*al-Māya*	*Ramal al-Māya*
7	*Ġarībat al-Ḥusayn*	*Raṣd aḏ-Ḏīl*	*al-ʿUššāq*	*al-Iṣbahān*
8	*al-Ḥijāz al-Kabīr*	*al-Istihlāl*	*Raṣd aḏ-Ḏīl*	*al-Ḥijāz al-Kabīr*
9	*al-Ḥijāz al-Mašriqī*	*Ramal al-Māya*	*al-Istihlāl*	*ar-Raṣd*
10	*ʿIrāq al-ʿAjam*	*al-Iṣbahān*	*Ramal al-Māya*	*Raṣd aḏ-Ḏīl*
11	*al-ʿUššāq*	*al-Ḥijāz al-Mašriqī*	*al-Iṣbahān* (2)	*al-Ḥijāz al-Mašriqī*
12			*al-Ḥijāz al-Mašriqī*	*aṣ-Ṣīka*
13				(*Ġarībat al-Ḥusayn*)
14				[*al-ʿUššāq*?]

Figure 5.1: *Arrangement of nawbāt in eight Kunnāš manuscripts (based upon Shiloah, 1979, and Bennūna, 1999)*

Of the other manuscripts, only *Bennīs* and *London* contain all the contemporary *nawbāt*, though not in the modern order. Their contents suggest that these two are related as well, perhaps via a third copy as their common source.[6] Because they contain the same *nawbāt* but differ only in the order, these two manuscripts clearly relate in some way to

[6] Bennūna (interview, 10/14/2005) believes that London is a copy of Bennīs.

the first four. Possibly they represent a variant on the now-canonical order, either as a corruption of the "standard al-Ḥāʾik," or as an alternative arrangement that was considered acceptable at one time.

The origins of these various arrangements of *nawbāt* remain unexplained. In the absence of clear dates for so many of the *Kunnāš* manuscripts discussed here, it is conceivable that the modern canonical order of *nawbāt* did not come into full acceptance until well into the 20th century. Indeed, an examination of the al-Jāmiʿī manuscripts suggests that this order only became canonical *after* al-Jāmiʿī's time.[7] Thus it could well be that any number of equally valid arrangements circulated in various parts of Morocco in the last two decades of the 18th century, and that what is recognized today as standard was an outgrowth of non-canonical arrangements such as those in the second, third and fourth columns of Figure 5.1. This raises questions about the idea of a single "*Kunnāš al-Ḥāʾik*" as canonical urtext and stretches the anthologizing project over a much wider time and space than the standard narrative allows. This simple comparison at the level of structure suggests that Muḥammad b. al-Ḥusayn al-Ḥāʾik could be seen as something other than the mastermind of a unique reformulation of the Andalusian corpus; rather he may have been an eponymous figure who initiated (or perhaps merely participated in) a complex process that resulted at some later point in the modern canon that is now attributed to him.

The remaining two manuscripts – *Raysūnī* and *Dāwūdiyya* – depart even further from those in the first column:

1. They contain *nawbāt* not found in the modern canon (*Raysūnī*: *al-Ḥusayn; Dāwūdiyya*: *ʿIrāq al ʿArab, al-Ḥusayn* and *aṣ-Ṣīka*).
2. They lack *nawbāt* that are found in the modern canon (*Raysūnī*: *al-Ḥijāz al-Kabīr; Dāwūdiyya*: *ʿIrāq al-ʿAjam* and *al-ʿUššāq*[8]).

[7] See §3b below.

[8] Bennūna points out (1999 p. 15) that the *Dāwūdiyya* #144 manuscript. *muqaddima* makes reference to "*al-Ġarība,*" which Bennūna argues refers to *Ġarībat al-Ḥusayn*, though this *nūba* is not found in the manuscript. Considering that pages have been lost from the document in more than one place, and that the manuscript. has been bound in a somewhat disordered fashion, it is not unreasonable to suppose that *Ġarībat al-Ḥusayn* was present one time. Bennūna also argues that the manuscript probably also contained *al-ʿUššāq*, even though it makes no reference to this *nūba*, because a selection from *al-ʿUššāq* appears in al-Būʿaṣāmī's *Īqād aš-šumūʿ...* (see Chapter 3 §1.4), which predates *Dāwūdiyya* #144 by about half a century. This argument is plausible, but it would be more convincing if the *Kunnāš* actually referred to al-Būʿaṣāmī's work, and given the other complexities already in the manuscript tradition, we should be chary about assuming that al-Būʿaṣāmī and al-Ḥāʾik were drawing from the same text stream.

3. They contain more than one *nūba* based upon a single *ṭab*ʿ (*Raysūnī*: *al-Iṣbahān* 1 and 2; *Dāwūdiyya*: *al-Istihlāl* 1 and 2[9]).

A possible explanation for these non-canonical *nawbāt* might lie in the fact that several of the modern *nawbāt* incorporate *ṣanāʾi*ʿ composed in *ṭubū*ʿ other than the primary one that the *nūba* is named for.[10] Interestingly, the *ṭubū*ʿ *al-ḥusayn*, *ʿirāq al-ʿarab* and *as-sīka/aṣ-ṣīka*[11] are all found in *al-Āla* today, so it would appear at first glance that the old *nawbāt* have been lost, but that some elements of them have simply been preserved and incorporated into modern *nawbāt*. However the picture not so simple as that.

The modern *Nawbat Ramal al-Māya* contains several *ṣanāʾi*ʿ in the *ṭab*ʿ *al-ḥusayn*, and a survey of *Dāwūdiyya* shows that thirteen *ṣanāʾi*ʿ found there in *Nawbat al-Ḥusayn* are indeed found in *Ramal al-Māya* today. Curiously, all but one of these holdovers are now performed in either *ṭab*ʿ *ramal al-māya* or *inqilāb ar-ramal*, not *al-ḥusayn*. The one exception, *Aḥmadu l-Hādī r-Rasūl*, a very famous and widely known *ṣanʿa* in *Nawbat Ramal al-Māya* (the first in Mīzān al-Basīṭ and the second in Mīzān al-Quddām), is performed in *ṭab*ʿ *al-ḥusayn*, which makes it a strong candidate for a melody that derives from the old *Nawbat al-Ḥusayn*. This and four others are found in the margins of the corresponding *mayāzīn* in *Wazzānī* and *Valderrama*, written with indication that they were performed in *ṭab*ʿ *al-ḥusayn*. Thus we have five *ṣanāʾi*ʿ (in *ṭab*ʿ *al-ḥusayn*, as indicated by *Nawbat al-Ḥusayn* in *Dāwūdiyya* and by the *Wazzānī/Valderrama* marginalia) that were "lost" after *Dāwūdiyya* but then recovered and inserted into *Wazzānī* and *Valderrama* before their full incorporation into the modern printed canon – four of them eventually being performed in different *ṭubū*ʿ and only one in *al-ḥusayn*.

Thus the evidence suggests that elements of an otherwise lost *Nawbat al-Ḥusayn* have been incorporated into the modern *Ramal al-Māya*, but it was not a direct or linear process. This may have happened in one of several ways, but the most likely is that *Dāwūdiyya* represents the oldest extant version of the *Kunnāš*, and that the text of *al-Ḥusayn* (at least some of it represented in *Dāwūdiyya*, but with the possibility of other, undiscovered manuscript versions of *al-Ḥusayn*) was a vector for incorporating the texts of these songs, the old melodies having been lost (with one probable exception) and new melodies being composed instead (after the source manuscript for *Wazzānī*

[9] Bennūna hypothesizes (1999 p. 15) that the author of *Dāwūdiyya* #144 "intended" *Nawbat ʿIrāq al-ʿAjam* with what Bennūna has labeled "*al-Istihlāl* 2." I do not find much textual connection between Bennūna's *al-Istihlāl* 2 and the modern *ʿIrāq al-ʿAjam*. Only two *ṣanāʾi*ʿ in the former are found in the latter, both in Mīzān al-Basīṭ.

[10] See Appendix 2: Summary of Ṭubūʿ.

[11] This *ṭab*ʿ (and its corresponding *nūba*) are spelled differently in different places, even within one work, such as Bennūna's: sometimes with س, sometimes with ص.

and *Valderrama* but before the modern canon). This underscores the complex relationship between oral and written processes in the tradition (in this case, the written version of an oral presentation nevertheless contributing to the re-incorporation of the text into the tradition in a new oral version), and it implies that musicians in the 19th century did continue to compose new melodies and incorporate them into *al-Āla*.[12]

Dāwūdiyya also contains *Nawbat ʿIrāq al-ʿArab* and *Nawbat as-Sīka / aṣ-Ṣīka*, and a similar situation obtains. *Ṭabʿ ʿirāq al-ʿarab* is found in the modern *Nawbat al-Istihlāl* and five *ṣanʿa* texts are shared between the old *Nawbat ʿIrāq al-ʿArab* as represented in *Dāwūdiyya* and the modern *Nawbat al-Istihlāl* (as represented in IJ / IM / MW). But one of these five, *Anta tazīd maʿnā*, appears in *Nawbat as-Sīka / aṣ-Ṣīka* in *Dāwūdiyya*, as well, and it is that version that appears to have survived from this old *nūba*, for it is performed today in *ṭabʿ as-sīka / aṣ-ṣīka* in *Nawbat al-Istihlāl*. This *ṭabʿ* also is performed today in *Nawbat Raṣd aḏ-Ḏīl*, but only two *ṣanāʾiʿ* (one of them being *Anta tazīd maʿnā*) have survived from the old *nūba*, neither of them in *Raṣd aḏ-Ḏīl*. Thus only one *ṣanʿa* text that is unique to *Nawbat as-Sīka / aṣ-Ṣīka* in *Dāwūdiyya* has survived. *Nawbat al-Istihlāl* as found in the modern canon therefore seems to have been the only receptacle for material from *Nawbat as-Sīka / aṣ-Ṣīka* (as presented in *Dāwūdiyya*), and that only in a very limited way.

The evidence of *Dāwūdiyya* (the only one of the eight manuscripts that contains this *nūba*) suggests that either the compositions in *ṭabʿ as-sīka / aṣ-ṣīka* found in the modern *Nawbat Raṣd aḏ-Ḏīl* are more recent compositions, and therefore probably dating from the 19th century or later, or else they derive from material that was circulating in "al-Ḥāʾik's time" but for some reason did not find its way into the written canon until after this particular manuscript. As with *Nawbat al-Ḥusayn*, the situation clearly was more complex than simply incorporating *ṣanāʾiʿ* from one lost *nūba* into a surviving *nūba*.

Relatively few of the *ṣanāʾiʿ* found in the modern canon are represented in *Dāwūdiyya*. The overlap between the two corpuses is significant, but far from complete, as is the correspondence between *Dāwūdiyya* and *Wazzānī / Valderrama*, as well. Of the 101 *ṣanāʾiʿ* in the modern canon belonging to the four *mayāzīn* of *Ramal al-Māya* that are found in the *Kunnāš*, 29 derive from *Dāwūdiyya*.[13] In contrast, the manuscript stream represented by *Wazzānī / Valderrama* actually has *more* material in these four *mayāzīn*

---

[12] This point shatters the notion put forward by Chottin and García Barriuso that "the door of composition" was somehow closed after the early 18th century.

[13] Obviously, the percentage of overlap drops even further if we include the 24 *ṣanāʾiʿ* in Mīzān ad-Darj, which is not found in the *Kunnāš*.

than *Dāwūdiyya*, only about a third of which derives from it (preserving a little less than half of the material found in *Dāwūdiyya*).[14]

There are only two possible reasons for this. Given the facts surrounding the incorporation of elements from *Nawbat al-Ḥusayn* into the modern *Ramal al-Māya*, and from *Nawbat as-Sīka / aṣ-Ṣīka* into *al-Istihlāl*, the more likely scenario is that *Dāwūdiyya* represents a very early stage in the development of the "original *Kunnāš al-Ḥā'ik*," so that quite a lot of material from "al-Ḥā'ik's time" has been lost and a great deal of other material (either *ṣanā'iʿ* that al-Ḥā'ik missed, or new compositions, or both) has found its way into the canon since that time. If, however, *Dāwūdiyya* does not represent the "original al-Ḥā'ik," we must find some other way to explain how a manuscript so far removed from the modern canon could appear in the middle of the anthologizing process and yet still bear the name, *Kunnāš al-Ḥā'ik*. In either case, simple incorporation of elements from lost *nawbāt* cannot fully explain the intertextual connections, which have been conditioned by a number of factors, the most important of them being the inferred existence of diverse, parallel traditions (both manuscript and oral) intersecting under the rubric *Kunnāš al-Ḥā'ik* – some of that material appearing in the main body of later manuscripts like *Valderrama* and some having been added into the margins (suggesting an origin in orally-preserved materials).

Marginalia play an important role in *Wazzānī* and *Valderrama*: many of the *ṣanā'iʿ* in *ṭabʿ al-ḥusayn* that these two manuscripts share with *Dāwūdiyya* are marginal additions from a parallel source outside them and alongside the (apparently earlier!) incorporation of *ṭabʿ al-ḥusayn* into *Ramal al-Māya*. Clearly *Wazzānī* and *Valderrama* represent a distinct text stream comprising some material found in *Dāwūdiyya* and other material from other sources, to which notations were added (some also deriving from *Dāwūdiyya*) that provided much of the material in *al-ḥusayn* now performed as part of *Nawbat Ramal al-Māya*. In addition, it shows that the now-canonical arrangement of *nawbāt* found in *Leiden*, *Raqīwaq*, *Wazzānī* and *Valderrama*, and attributed today to "al-Ḥā'ik", had already incorporated material from *ṭabʿ* (and *nawbat*?) *al-ḥusayn* before the impact of this second stream was felt on the written canon (or perhaps, before this second stream was annotated with other material). In sum, the formation of the written canon occurred gradually and included more stages and more material than the two stages recognized by the standard narrative: al-Ḥā'ik and then al-Jāmiʿī.

Dāwūdiyya is often spoken of by Moroccan scholars as the "original" *Kunnāš al-Ḥā'ik*, based primarily upon the following statement in the colophon:

---

[14] The material in Wazzānī / Valderrama represents a little over half of the modern repertoire.

نجز هذا الديوان المبارك السعيد ، الجامع المفيد ، على يد جامعه سامحه الله بمحض فضله ، آمين...

> This felicitous, blessed *dīwān*, comprehensive and beneficial, was completed at the hand of its collector, may Allāh lavish him with His pure grace, *amen*.[15]

This, and the date that follows (1202 [1788]) would seem to place this manuscript at the very birth of the modern *al-Āla*. At any rate it agrees substantially with the dates suggested by García Barriuso and Valderrama (and the date put forward by Chottin in 1939). If these indications in *Dāwūdiyya* are authentic, in one sense the picture becomes a little clearer, for at least it yields a date and a basic source text for the origins of the manuscript tradition. Although it complicates the simple notion of al-Ḥāʾik as founding father of the modern canon, it nevertheless suggests a smoother, more linear trajectory for the manuscript tradition than if we were to place any of the other manuscripts (or their sources) as predecessors to *Dāwūdiyya*: the saga of *Kunnāš al-Ḥāʾik* thus probably begins with *Dāwūdiyya* in 1788, passes through a period wherein the poetic contents and the arrangement of *nawbāt* are fluid and dependent upon local *nūba* traditions gradually being committed to writing, and ends with the cluster of (perhaps mutually-influencing) *Leiden*, *Raqīwaq*, *Wazzānī* and *Valderrama*. Figure 5.2 illustrates this possible trajectory.

If *Dāwūdiyya* is indeed older than *Wazzānī*, *Valderrama* and the other manuscripts bearing the modern canonical arrangement (perhaps even being the original *Kunnāš al-Ḥāʾik*, or a first-generation copy), it would mean that the canon recognized today as authentic does not derive entirely from al-Ḥāʾik himself (indeed, perhaps it only barely derives from al-Ḥāʾik at all!), and that the idea that this anthologist put the tradition on its modern footing is somewhat misleading. The data are very complicated, given the number of *ṣanāʾiʿ* involved in *Ramal al-Māya* (nearly 140 in *Dāwūdiyya*, 156 in the *familia al-Ḥāʾik* manuscripts – including marginalia – and 101 in the modern canon, with varying degrees of overlap and divergence among the three). Furthermore, as we have just seen, the very partial degree of overlap between the four manuscript stages represented here, along with the fact that the middle step represented an *increase* in the overall number of *ṣanāʾiʿ*, strongly suggests the presence of non-*Kunnāš* traditions that contributed material to what is now considered to be the *aṣīl* anthology, *Kunnāš al-Ḥāʾik*. Nevertheless, when we view these manuscripts at the level of structure, Ockham's Razor leads to the conclusion that the general scenario in Figure 5.2 is the most likely case. The anthologist al-Ḥāʾik thus remains a major figure,

---

[15] p. 519 in Bennūna, 1999.

who because of his fame became associated with later collections of *nūba* texts generally.

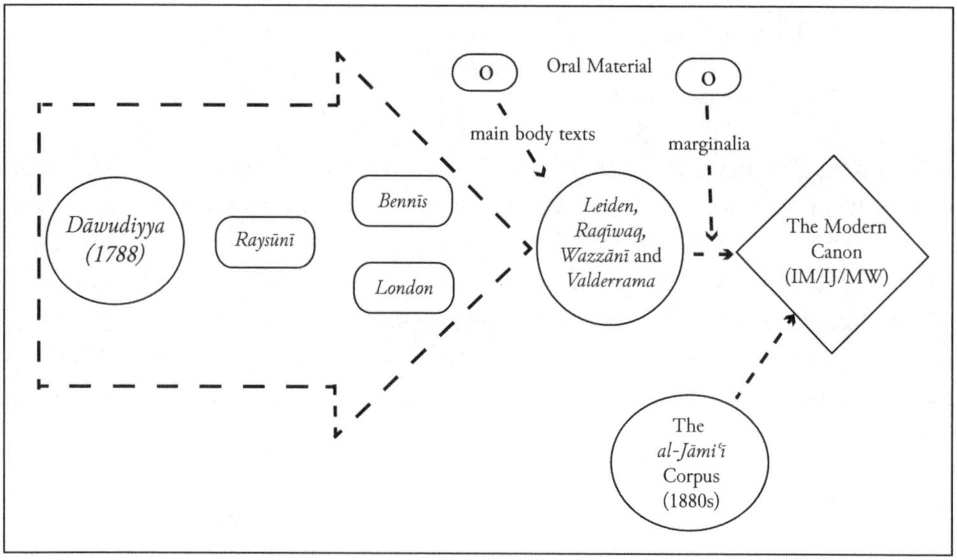

Figure 5.2: *Dāwūdiyya as beginning of the "al-Ḥāʾik process"*

Considering all this evidence together, we can state with confidence that the modern canon as represented by the printed anthologies is not simply a decayed version of *Kunnāš al-Ḥāʾik* that preserves the remains of a once-thriving tradition. Rather, the modern canon is the culmination of a process that included both the loss of some older documented material and the addition of previously undocumented material, as well. Figure 5.2 illustrates at least four distinct textual traditions flowing together within the larger process that has formed the modern canon. The first is represented by *Dāwūdiyya,* about half of which, passing through intermediate stages represented by *Raysūnī* and *Bennīs/London,* survived to be preserved in the "familia al-Ḥāʾik" manuscripts. A second stream contributed the material that comprises more than half of the "familia al-Ḥāʾik" manuscripts. This second stream included two distinct oral-textual traditions (represented as "O" in Fig. 5.2): "main body" texts and material added afterwards as marginalia in some (but not all) "familia" manuscripts (some of it common to *Dāwūdiyya,* as well). The fourth stream comprised even more material new to the modern tradition, approximately 45% of the total, much of which entered the canon via the al-Jāmiʿī corpus. One significant implication of this is that the oral component (the *ṣanāʾiʿ*-as-sung) was for much of the tradition's history rather larger than what has captured in writing in the *Kunnāš* stream. As late as al-Jāmiʿī's era anyway, a great deal of performed material was being preserved orally (or quasi-orally: perhaps local performers kept notebooks of their own) outside the *Kunnāš* stream.

In sum, the tale of *Kunnāš al-Ḥāʾik* is neither as simple nor as completely understood as has been widely assumed among scholars of the tradition. Comparison of the *nūba* arrangement among the various *Kunnāš* manuscripts raises fundamental questions about the origin and development of this foundational text in the *Āla* tradition. *Dāwūdiyya*, in particular, poses a problem for the traditional account of al-Ḥāʾik and his *Kunnāš*. Even if we assume that the manuscripts in the first column of Figure 5.1 (*Leiden*, *Raqīwaq*, *Wazzānī* and *Valderrama*) represent an original, authentic *Kunnāš al-Ḥāʾik* composed using the modern canonical order, the remaining manuscripts, and especially *Dāwūdiyya*, appear as aberrations, local variations of the anthologizing process. Somehow these other versions (at least one of which almost certainly predates this hypothetical "authentic *Kunnāš*") became overshadowed by a more robust (i.e.: popular and/or "authentic") manuscript tradition, which embodied the now-canonical arrangement.

Such a scenario certainly is possible. Textual traditions (and musical ones, as well) often are characterized by untidy processes that elude simple schematization. Yet we cannot avoid asking how the versions of the *Kunnāš* represented by these diverse manuscripts came into existence (whether before or after al-Ḥāʾik) and then were attributed to him. How did some of the material in the variant manuscripts come to be incorporated into the "al-Ḥāʾik" canon (often using different *ṭubūʿ*) if they did in fact come into existence as variations on (or corruptions of?) a quasi-standard model? These questions certainly do not vanish if we assume that *Dāwūdiyya* is the foundational manuscript of the *Kunnāš* process, but when we do, the logic of answering them becomes much simpler. If the anthologist al-Ḥāʾik is viewed as the author of *Dāwūdiyya*, we may see him as the eponymous initiator of a process of collection and revision that answered the needs of several generations of musicians and aficionados in more than one location around Morocco and culminated in the "familia" manuscripts. It would not be surprising at all if the name of the first figure recognized as attempting an all-embracing written anthology of the *nūba* tradition in Morocco were to become well known and then attributed to other similar efforts afterwards (much as contemporary Americans consult "Webster" when using a dictionary). If, however, al-Ḥāʾik arrived in the midst of this process, such an attribution appears somewhat less plausible, because it means that some other, earlier manuscript (a hypothetical source or sources for *Raysūnī*, for example) would have had to have been created, copied, and then had the name al-Ḥāʾik attributed to it after the fact.

Furthermore, we must also account for the loss of material present in manuscripts like *Dāwūdiyya,* and the simultaneous emergence of new *ṣanāʾiʿ*, circumstances which seem to suggest dynamic processes of compilation of oral material, recension and copying. How do we reconcile this with other evidence, presented in Chapter 3, that the four decades following the turn of the 19th century were politically, climactically, environmentally and economically chaotic?

Whatever answers are found to these questions lead inexorably back to the social value attaching to *al-Āla* in various places and times over the past two centuries, and therefore answering them would cast a great deal of light on the development of the musical tradition in general. A tentative first step would be simply to suggest that the performed tradition at any given point in its history was rather larger than the material that has survived in manuscript form. Al-Ḥāʾik hailed from Tetuan and was living in Fez when he wrote his anthology, it is said, but *al-Āla* was performed as well in other cities in the north of Morocco, including Meknes, Chefchaouen, Tanger and Rabat. It is likely that many later arrivals in the manuscripts had been performed for generations in other regions beyond Fez and Tetuan. Exactly how they came to be included in the modern canon, under the name *Kunnāš al-Ḥāʾik,* remains a mystery.

3. *The al-Jāmiʿī corpus*

Based upon data from eight of the best-known manuscripts of *Kunnāš al-Ḥāʾik* we have reconstructed a plausible outline of the historical development of the *Kunnāš,* one that points strongly to the importance of oral processes that operated within the tradition and lay parallel to the manuscripts that provide the main source material for the modern textual canon. It thus raises significant questions about the role of Muḥammad b. al-Ḥusayn al-Ḥāʾik in assembling the anthology that bears his name today. As interesting as such questions are to the text-critical historian, however, they cannot efface the important ideological role al-Ḥāʾik has played and continues to play within the mythos surrounding the modern *al-Āla.* As with the question of the "Andalusian-ness" of *al-Āla,* what is most important is the prestige attaching to *Kunnāš al-Ḥāʾik* as an emblem of the tradition. This prestige can be seen in several aspects of the tradition, including the way that al-Ḥāʾik overshadows the other important anthologist, al-Jāmiʿī. As important as al-Jāmiʿī evidently was to the survival of *al-Āla,* like the "Moroccan-ness" of the tradition he remains largely unknown outside the circle of specialists.

Cortés García (1995) argues that most of what passes today for the al-Ḥāʾik repertoire in fact derives from the al-Jāmiʿī corpus. However, my study of concert programs dating from my sojourns in Morocco, as well as observations of rehearsals by orchestras from Fez and Tetuan, indicate that the performed repertoire today includes *ṣanā ʾiʿ* and performance units found neither in the al-Jāmiʿī manuscripts I have studied nor in the most authoritative printed version of the al-Jāmiʿī corpus available, MW. It seems clear from this that orchestras still draw from a repertoire that includes material deriving from outside the al-Jāmiʿī corpus. The modern performed canon differs from the repertoire found in many of the *Kunnāš* manuscripts, but the difference need not be attributed only to the intrusion of the al-Jāmiʿī corpus as a reservoir of *Āla* material "rescued" from oblivion. Rather than assume that the *Kunnāš* began its career as a fully-formed and pristine text that later sank into decay and was rescued by al-Jāmiʿī, it seems to me more plausible to allow for the wonderfully messy and multilinear processes that often accompany the evolution of art forms like *al-Āla*.

Al-Jāmiʿī's contributions to the textual tradition, while apparently less substantial, were nonetheless important for the consolidation and perpetuation of the tradition as a whole. Unlike al-Ḥāʾik, however, we encounter fewer problems when trying to determine precisely what al-Jāmiʿī's contributions actually were. We will examine what remains of the manuscript tradition associated with the name of al-Jāmiʿī in order to clarify as well as possible the ways in which oral processes helped to shape this corpus, as well.

3.1. *Manuscripts*

Unlike *Kunnāš al-Ḥāʾik*, the manuscripts relating to the al-Jāmiʿī corpus contain no information that might give us clues to the life of its author, the *faqīh* Sīdī Muḥammad b. al-Wazīr as-Sayyid al-ʿArabī b. al-Wazīr as-Sayyid al-Muḫtār al-Jāmiʿī. Modern secondary sources yield no solid clues to either the anthologist or his father, who appears to have been a government official. Our chief source of information on al-Jāmiʿī is oral tradition. His career, insofar as it is known in this way, has been detailed in Chapter 3 §3. The corpus that bears his name apparently was compiled in the reign of Sultan Mūlāy al-Ḥasan I, some time around 1303/1885-6, and we can reasonably infer that al-Jāmiʿī intended it as a teaching aid at the conservatory he founded in Fez.

The chief modern exemplar of the al-Jāmiʿī corpus is the printed volume *Min waḥy ar-rabāb* (1982), assembled by the great musician and *raʾīs*, ʿAbd al-Karīm ar-Rāyis. Its wide availability (it has been reprinted at least twice) makes it a convenient resource for students in the conservatory, as well as for musicians. For those interested in background information on the *ṭubūʿ*, MW offers a short narrative summary at the beginning of each *nūba*, drawn from both al-Ḥāʾik and contemporary performace practice, describing each mode associated with the *nūba*, its author, and its humoral or temporal associations. MW thus fulfills an important function within the modern context. Yet, it has one or two limitations. The text is vowelled inconsistently, and the vocalizations seem to be unreliable in several places, especially when compared with IJ, in which more care seems to have been taken in this regard. Moreover, the anthologist (or his editor) misspelled the names of two poetic meters (مجتثّ as "مجتتّ" or even "مجثتّ", and هزج as "هجز"), and always uses the latter when رجز is indicated.

The manuscript tradition behind the al-Jāmiʿī corpus is far less extensive and complex than that of the *Kunnāš*. I have been able to locate only three complete manuscripts, all of them relatively late:

1. *R1327* – manuscript #1327 (on microfilm) at the Bibliotheque Générale in Rabat; dated 1330 (1912).
2. *Piro* – al-Jāmiʿī manuscript owned by Aḥmad Piro in Rabat; dated 1329 (1911) but said to be a copy of a manuscript dated 1303/1885-6.
3. *Belmalīḥ* – al-Jāmiʿī manuscript donated to the *Matḥaf Dār al-Āla* in Casablanca in 2004 by the Belmalīḥ family of Fez; said to have been copied in 1902.

In addition, the *Matḥaf Dār al-Āla* holds two other, incomplete manuscripts, each about one *nūba* in length.

Of these, *R1327* and *Piro* may be closely related: they appear to have been executed on the same kind of paper (watermarks are visible on pages 110 and 114 of the *R1327* microfilm) within a year of each other. *Piro*, however, is more elaborate, having a brief *muqaddima* that contains the poem on the *ṭubūʿ* attributed to al-Wanšarīsī and a drawing of the *šajarat aṭ-ṭubūʿ*. Like *Belmalīḥ*, *R1327* has no introductory material. Of the three manuscripts, only *R1327* has marginalia, which include numbers for the *ṣanāʾiʿ* and Mīzān ad-Darj written in the margins of al-Bṭāyḥī. These marginal notes are executed in the same hand as the main text, an indication that the manuscript is not an original. (*Piro* does have very occasional corrections written with a blue ball point pen.)

These three manuscripts are more inconsistent orthographically than the *Kunnāš* manuscripts I have examined, *Belmalīḥ* being by far the most inconsistent. Not only does this manuscript take more liberties (employing *alif* for *tā' marbūṭa* at the end of a hemistich, for example), but the copyist also made a number of obvious errors in spelling that went uncorrected. All three manuscripts show occasional signs of simple oral/dialectal intrusions, such as use of *nā* for *ana*, or the occasional exchange of final *ī* for *i*. Again, *Belmalīḥ* shows more of these features than either *Piro* or *R1327*.

Of particular interest is the arrangement of *nawbāt* in these manuscripts:

Raṣd (without Mīzān al-Qāʾim wa-Niṣf)
al-Ḥijāz al-Kabīr
ʿIraq al-ʿAjam
Ġarībat al-Ḥusayn

al-Māya
al-ʿUššāq
Raṣd aḏ-Ḏīl
al-Istihlāl
Ramal al-Māya
al-Iṣbahān
al-Ḥijāz al-Mašriqī (without al-Qāʾim wa Niṣf)

(In addition, *R1327* has the "orphan" *mīzān* Bawākir al-Māya, which is not present in the others.)

This is the same order as that found in the *Bennīs* and *London Kunnāš* manuscripts (see Figure 5.1). This can hardly be entirely coincidental, and so it raises some interesting possibilities. It would seem that al-Jāmiʿī had access to one of these manuscripts (or to the branches of the tradition they represent), and evidently he regarded this arrangement as acceptable, if not authoritative. Does this mean that *Bennīs* (and *London*, which was copied from it) represents the authentic tradition as it was recognized in Fez just prior to the 1880s (al-Jāmiʿī's era)? Yet the content of *Bennīs* coincides with that of *Wazzānī*, *Valderrama* and *Raqīwaq*, not with that of the al-Jāmiʿī manuscripts, which indicates that the latter nevertheless represent a distinct repertoire, or perhaps part of the Fez repertoire, that was rendered in writing parallel with or after *Bennīs*.[16]

Whatever the logic behind it, the similarity of the al-Jāmiʿī arrangement to that of *Bennīs* lends credence to the idea that a century after al-Ḥāʾik there still was more than one legitimate way to arrange *nawbāt* circulating in Morocco: the modern arrangement that derives from the *Kunnāš* manuscript tradition seems not to have had much influence upon al-Jāmiʿī in the second half of the 19th century as he was collecting and organizing his anthology.[17] The structure of the al-Jāmiʿī manuscripts, and their connection to the *Bennīs/London Kunnāš* manuscripts, thus strongly suggest that the modern canonical order of *nawbāt* existed as one option for organizing an anthology of *al-Āla*, but was not yet authoritative for all participants in the tradition in al-Jāmiʿī's time, and probably was not so until the second half of the 20th century.

Thus the al-Jāmiʿī manuscripts definitively move the canonization of the tradition's organization out of the 19th century and therefore support the idea advanced above that *Kunnāš al-Ḥāʾik* as known today is the product of an extended period of

[16] Another possible explanation was suggested by Professor ʿAbd as-Salām aš-Šāmī: these manuscripts were assembled by "difficulty of ṣanāʾiʿ." The first-year curriculum at the Maʿhad al-Waṭanī does seem to bear this out by drawing from nawbāt in the "easier" lower half of the list.

[17] Nor did it make much difference, apparently, to copyists of the al-Jāmiʿī manuscripts working in the early 20th century, since they made no effort to "correct" the unique order of nawbāt we find in them.

development probably lasting more than a century. Whether we believe that al-Ḥāʾik alone was responsible for the *Kunnāš*, as some have argued, or that the anthologist merely started a process of collecting that went through several distinct, local permutations before becoming authoritative, as has been argued in this chapter, there is little doubt that what is today regarded as *Kunnāš al-Ḥāʾik* did not achieve its final, authoritative form until relatively recently.

Careful, *ṣanʿa*-by-*ṣanʿa* study of *Ramal al-Māya* in the al-Jāmiʿī manuscripts shows that their contents are distinct from those of the *Kunnāš*. Many *ṣanāʾiʿ* from the *Kunnāš* manuscripts are not found at all in the al-Jāmiʿī manuscripts, or are found only in truncated or altered form, with, for example, only the *qufl* surviving from a *ḫumāsiyya*.

3.2. *Mīzān ad-darj and the al-Jāmiʿī corpus*

Mīzān ad-darj presents an interesting illustration of the processes by which oral material has made its way into the modern canon of *al-Āla* texts. *Darj* is now an accepted part of the performed canon, but it is not mentioned at all in *Kunnāš al-Ḥāʾik*, and a total of just three *ṣanāʾiʿ* appear as marginalia to *Ramal al-Māya* in the al-Jāmiʿī manuscripts. Yet altogether, the printed anthologies offer 24 *ṣanāʾiʿ* in Darj Ramal al-Māya. Therefore, *mīzān ad-darj* must have entered the textual canon at some point after the turn of the 20th century.

One particularly surprising absence from the al-Jāmiʿī manuscripts is the best-known *ṣanʿa* in this *mīzān*, *Qad ṭāla šawqī li-n-nabī Muḥammadi*, which is heard nearly every time this *mīzān* is performed. The absence of this *ṣanʿa* and the very small number of *ṣanāʾiʿ* in *ad-darj* in the al-Jāmiʿī manuscripts, strongly suggest that the incorporation of *ad-darj* as a separate *mīzān* in the modern canon was not a simple process of adding a previously coherent collection of *ṣanāʾiʿ*. As with the incorporation of the old *Nawbat al-Ḥusayn* into the modern *Kunnāš*, the interpolation of *mīzān ad-darj* into the *nūba* probably was the product of several factors, including performance practice and oral transmission.

At least some of the material that has become consolidated as *mīzān ad-darj* certainly was performed in Chottin's time, since he (1939) regarded this *īqāʿ* as one of the classical Andalusi rhythmic modes and noted the existence of the *mīzān* in the performed corpus. This information probably came from oral informants, since he would not have found this *mīzān* in *Kunnāš al-Ḥāʾik*, his principal textual source. *Ad-darj* was performed in the Spanish Protectorate zone at this time, as well, since García Barriuso (1940) commented on it. Both García Barriuso and Muḥammad al-Fāsī[18]

[18] 1962, pp. 83-84.

indicated that this rhythm was originally performed within *mīzān al-bṭāyḥī* (al-Fāsī defines the name *ad-darj* as deriving from the verb *daraja*, in the sense of "to include or incorporate"). Clearly, it was performed long before its appearance in the 20th-century anthologies.

Al-Fāsī's comment cannot be the whole story, however, because not a single *ṣanʿa* in the *Kunnāš* manuscripts in *Ramal al-Māya* (or its associated *nūba, al-Ḥusayn*) is now performed in Darj Ramal al-Māya, and only one *ṣanʿa* from Bṭāyḥī Ramal al-Māya in the al-Jāmiʿī manuscripts is now performed in Mīzān ad-Darj. Moreover, the material in the modern Darj Ramal al-Māya is, with one exception, unique to this *mīzān*: there are no other indications in the manuscripts – whether *Kunnāš* or al-Jāmiʿī – that any of these *ṣanāʾiʿ* have been moved or copied, which would be expected if ad-Darj was once performed as part of al-Bṭāyḥī. In short, it does not appear that *īqāʿ ad-darj* as used in al-Bṭāyḥī was a vector for the incorporation of *ṣanāʾiʿ* into a recently-fashioned *mīzān ad-darj*.

This is surprising, since it means that, with respect to most of the *ṣanāʾiʿ* now performed in Darj Ramal al-Māya, (a) they did not enter the tradition via the al-Jāmiʿī corpus, (b) nor did they take the "shortest route" into the new *mīzān* (i.e.: as performance units directly from al-Bṭāyḥī), and so (c) they came from another source entirely. So al-Fāsī's theory does not completely explain the appearance of *mīzān ad-darj* in the modern canon.

It is possible that the *ṣanāʾiʿ* that originally were performed in *īqāʿ ad-darj* were only "informally" regarded and performed as part of Mīzān al-Bṭāyḥī. This would explain their almost total absence from the manuscript tradition: they were not considered "authentic" until *ad-darj* was formalized into a proper *mīzān*. This would suggest that Mīzān ad-Darj offers a strong indication of oral intrusions into the literary canon.

According to both Sī Ahmed Piro and ʿAbd al-Fattāḥ Benmūsā, *mīzān ad-darj* was performed for a very long time in the *zawāyā* before it was incorporated into the standard structure of the *nūba*.[19] In other words, we see in *ad-darj* an indication that the music of the religious brotherhoods exerted some influence on *al-Āla*. There is support for this idea in an undated manuscript that associates itself with the al-Jāmiʿī corpus.

Manuscript #D1031 2762 at the Bibliothèque Nationale in Rabat is idiosyncratic in several ways (arrangement of *nawbāt* and *mayāzīn*, and use of colloquial Moroccan dialect – even including Moroccan-style consonant clusters clearly marked with *sukūn*!), but its *muqaddima* claims it is based upon al-Jāmiʿī's collection (which it dates as 1303/1886) and paraphrases portions of al-Ḥāʾik's. Nine *nawbāt* appear in it,

---

[19] Interviews, 6/17/04 and 4/20/05, respectively.

and each contains only a small selection of *ṣanāʾiʿ*, yet it includes *mīzān ad-darj*, integrated into seven of the *nawbāt* between al-Bṭāyḥī and al-Quddām (i.e., consonant with the modern arrangement). However, *ad-darj combines* with al-Bṭāyḥī in *ar-Raṣd* (Bṭāyḥī ar-Raṣd itself containing only one *ṣanʿa*) and *al-Istihlāl* (there being no *ṣanāʾiʿ* in Bṭāyḥī al-Istihlāl); and in *al-Iṣbahān* and *Raṣd aḏ-Ḏīl* it *precedes* al-Bṭāyḥī. The relationship of *ad-darj* to the *nūba* in this manuscript appears to be fluid and thus distinct from the *Kunnāš* manuscripts (where ad-Darj is not found at all), the al-Jāmiʿī corpus (where it is a marginal addition), and the modern canon (where it is integral to and a standard part of the *nūba*). This unusual and problematic manuscript documents a transitional context between a time when *īqāʿ ad-darj* was part of *mīzān al-bṭāyḥī*, and the present, in which this rhythm has its own movement in the *nūba* falling between *al-bṭāyḥī* and *al-quddām*. The inconsistent treatment of *mīzān ad-darj* in this manuscript, combined with its non-standard linguistic features, suggest that it preserves in writing a portion of the repertoire that had circulated orally in the author's community.

Live recordings from the early 1980s of Jawq al-Brīhī, under the direction of ʿAbd al-Karīm ar-Rāyis, further document the complex relationship of *mīzān ad-darj* to the *nūba*. In one case, the *jawq* is heard performing Qāʾim wa-Niṣf Ramal al-Māya, breaking for a vocal interlude, then resuming with Darj Ramal al-Māya. In another, the *jawq* inserts more than 20 minutes of Darj in the midst of Bṭāyḥī Ramal al-Māya. Even as late as the 1980s, a *jawq* from the conservative stylistic school of Fez could use *mīzān ad-darj* in places other than between *al-bṭāyḥī* and *al-quddām*. This reinforces the idea that this *īqāʿ* and *mīzān* (or at least, the *ṣanāʾiʿ* associated with them) until very recently occupied a complex and varying place in the performance ethos of *al-Āla*.

Clearly the emergence of *ad-darj* as a distinct and authentic *mīzān* was not a uniform process across Morocco, and the manuscript versions played only a minor part, probably documenting material and performance practices that had been preserved orally for some time – importantly, after the al-Jāmiʿī corpus was created. The placement of *mīzān ad-darj* and the paucity of *ṣanāʾiʿ* documented as being performed in this *īqāʿ* in various sources suggests divergent notions of what was canonical, even as late as the 1980s. Thus, the consolidation of *mīzān ad-darj* and its placement within the *nūba* structure were very late developments in which oral processes played an important, perhaps decisive role.

4. *Oral processes and the canon of Āla texts*

The manuscript traditions that lie behind the modern *al-Āla* canon preserve in their contents and structure unmistakable signs that oral processes of perservation and transmission played important roles in the formation of the musical tradition as we find it today. The hypothesis for the development of *Kunnāš al-Ḥāʾik* presented here explains some aspects of the manuscript tradition and demonstrates that from its inception, this anthology did not include all that was performed in the *nūba* genre. A great deal of material – indeed, most of what is performed today and preserved in the modern printed anthologies – circulated in al-Ḥā᾽ik's time and after as orally-preserved *ṣanā᾽iʿ* and performance units (very likely in diverse locales across the country) that over time merged with the *Kunnāš* manuscript tradition. If this material existed in written form at all, such manuscripts have not come to light.[20] Similarly, the al-Jāmiʿī corpus in its printed form (MW) incorporates more material than the available manuscript exemplars, which suggests that informal notes and other quasi-oral sources perhaps formed a significant part of the al-Jāmiʿī corpus from the beginning.

The material that most clearly distinguishes the modern repertoire from that of al-Ḥā᾽ik, *mīzān ad-darj*, seems to have entered the written repertoire very late. No documentary evidence of this facet of *al-Āla* predates 1902 (in an obviously later addendum to *Belmalīḥ*). Like the rest of the repertoire, this *mīzān* existed first as orally-preserved material, but it emerged into the written tradition only with the advent of comprehensive printed anthologies in the second half of the 20th century.

By its nature, the history behind orally-preserved material is very difficult to pin down, for it relies upon inferences that must be drawn at best from very recent written versions, and at worst from orally-preserved and presented material that may itself be local and idiosyncratic in any number of ways. Yet oral aspects do still persist. More than one *ra᾽īs* has commented to me on the number of "unknown" *ṣanā᾽iʿ* he has preserved in his memory, unknown in the sense of no longer being commonly performed and/or taught at the conservatory. No doubt, many of these unknown *ṣanā᾽iʿ* comprise melodies that once accompanied texts that are already present in some version of the *Kunnāš*. In such cases a comparison between the *ṣanʿa*-as-sung and the archaic written version might reveal the effects of oral transmission and oral presentation. In addition, some of these "unknown" *ṣanā᾽iʿ* may contain texts from outside the generally accepted canon that is based upon al-Ḥā᾽ik and al-Jāmiʿī. Collection and analysis of these examples might cast some light on poorly understood

---

[20] Some examples might be found in the context of various *zawāyā*, which use similar texts and musical settings. Even more intriguing is the possibility that the material preserved in *Iqād aš-šumūʿ* represents a local-version of the tradition that actually found its way into written form *prior to* the *Kunnāš* stream. The manuscript does not include *Ramal al-Māya*, so a comparative study with the material presented here is not possible; much more work needs to be done. However a brief comparison of two *mayāzīn* proves interesting, but inconclusive. Of the ten *ṣanā᾽iʿ* in Quddām al-Māya, only three are found in D144 (in the same order, though separated by different *ṣanā᾽iʿ* in each case), and the same three in MW (from a total of 18, 17%), and those same three plus one other in IJ (from a total of 22, 18%). Similar figures obtain for Basīṭ al-ʿUššaq in *Iqād aš-šumūʿ*, MW and IJ. All this shows that the material al-Būʿaṣāmī collected had a small but significant commonality with the branch of the tradition collected by al-Ḥā᾽ik which has survived virtually intact through the *Kunnāš* process into the modern setting.

aspects of the tradition's history, such as the role played by the *Madīḥ/Ṣamāʿ* tradition in the formation of the modern canon.

5. *Oral and textual streams as historical evidence*

The discussion in this chapter has focused upon describing the manuscript traditions that lie behind the modern textual canon of *al-Āla*, and I have argued that it is the product of a much more complex set of processes than has hitherto been recognized. These processes, however, have implications that go beyond arcane textual considerations.

Manuscript anthologies exist to serve people, especially performers, who in turn present their art to others. Each manuscript therefore points to a textual community that made use of it. Consequently, the very complexities in these manuscript traditions that make building a clear timeline of their development so difficult in fact imply corresponding complexity within the social-cultural milieu that surrounded *al-Āla* itself. The same can be said especially of the oral processes whose traces these manuscripts preserve. These lines of evidence point to the existence of at least four different, somewhat overlapping textual streams that themselves almost certainly represent distinct communities participating in the *Āla* poetic-musical tradition in the century and a half between al-Ḥāʾik and the birth of the printed canon in the 1950s.

Although this study points clearly to their existence, it may well be impossible now to recover much about these communities of *Āla* aficionados. The geographic or temporal origins of these manuscripts have yet to be clearly determined to a degree that would link them to particular communities, and the manuscripts themselves preserve little evdence of their provenances. (It may be that detailed comparative study of these manscripts in tandem with oral traditional material about them might shed some light in that direction.) Yet we know now that the *Āla* tradition of the 18th, 19th and early 20th centuries comprised several communities, each of which maintained its own canon of poetic-musical materials, and that this regional diversity has been slowly effaced since the middle of the 20th century through a process of modernization that has brought about both printed anthologies and formal institutions that together have standardized the repertoire.

Having explored the historical roots of *al-Āla*, and the social and institutional frameworks that supported it in various periods, we have been able to demonstrate a significant fact: Oral processes of preservation and transmission have been central to the tradition throughout its history, alongside and despite the presence of a complex but nevertheless robust literary dimension. From this point, we must try to understand how and why these oral features of the tradition have persisted into the present day. How is it that this poetic-musical tradition retains both literary and oral elements as part of its general ethos? What social-cultural functions do these two dimensions serve that allow them to persist within the one tradition? In Part 2, the cultural and historical data laid out in Part 1 become the raw material for proposing a theory of tradition based upon a general theory of value that seeks to explain this dual oral-literary character.

Al-Āla: History, Society and Text

Part 2 — Orality and Literacy: A Social Rationale

Prologue to Part 2

Part 1 presented evidence from the history of *al-Āla* for the changing social contexts that surrounded the music and helped shape its development. These contexts evolved over the course of eleven and a half centuries from the elite courtly milieu of Ziryāb's time, through a middle period in North Africa when the audience expanded to include people from many walks of life in Andalusian communities, to the modern era wherein the tradition has become part of the national culture of Morocco. This latter phase has seen dramatic changes in the social and economic frames which support and now preserve the music. Where once relations between patron or audience and musician were personal, even intimate, the music's audience has become much larger, but also much more distant. In the place of informal social institutions and arrangements that once embraced the music, formal institutions have emerged in the 20th century that control to a great extent the flow of resources into the tradition and its maintenance as a part of Morocco's cultural life.

It would be tempting to argue, based on this overarching trend, that the economics of modern life – especially, economies of scale – have overwhelmed the social aspect of the tradition. However, Part 2 puts forward an argument to the contrary, that the social and economic dimensions of the tradition are two facets of a larger issue: the importance assigned to action in a social context. The first two chapters that follow construct a theory of how tradition, seen through the lens of value, functions in society. This theory is then deployed in Chapter 8 to analyze the material on the Andalusian music tradition in Morocco developed in Part 1, seeking to explain the persistence of *mixed orality*, that is, the survival of oral processes within this otherwise literate tradition.

Taken together, the three chapters that follow aim to show that attention to the meaningful actions embodied in *al-Āla,* which give form to the social relationships within it, can provide insight into the historical and social dimensions of the tradition. Moreover, viewing *al-Āla* through this lens allows us to reach for an explanation of the tradition's problematic status in Morocco today. Within the web of valued actions informing *al-Āla* lie the keys to the tradition's survival.

The present work deals with the complex interplay between oral and written processes as they operate within a modern literary-musical tradition. To the extent that it engages with the oral dimensions of the Arabic poetic tradition, it is not without forebears in the study of oral narrative and poetic-musical traditions in the Arabic-speaking world. Four works, in particular, recommend themselves as potential models for the present study because of the emphasis they place upon oral performance as a constitutive element of oral-traditional discourses among Arabic-speakers: Steven C. Caton's *"Peaks of Yemen I Summon": Poetry as Cultural Practice in a North Yemeni Tribe* (1990), Saad A. Sowayan's *The Arabian Oral Historical Narrative: An Ethnographic and Linguistic Analysis* (1992), P. Marcel Kurpershoek's *The Poetry of ad-Dinān: a Bedouin Bard in Southern Najd* (1994) and Dwight Reynolds' *Heroic Poets, Poetic Heroes: The Ethnography of Performance in an Arabic Oral Epic Tradition* (1995). Beyond their evident focus on "oral literature," these works share with the present study a degree of engagement with the social-situatedness of oral discourses.

While none of them fully develops an explicit theoretical stance, implicit in each of these works is the understanding that its subject has been shaped and in some sense characterized by the demands of oral presentation. In this way, they offer comparable insights into the significance of orality as a cultural process. Among them, *"Peaks of Yemen…"* and *Heroic Poets* share the closest affinity to the present study, as they deal most directly with the social significance of poetic performance as such. The former explicitly presents itself as an "ethnography of poetry" in illustrating the role of poetry as a medium of social discourse, group identification and conflict resolution among certain Arabic-speaking tribes in Yemen. *Heroic Poets* treats three related genres of narrative poetry as they are performed today in Egypt. In addition to dealing with the social status of the poets, Reynolds explores the social meanings of the poetic performance itself and the ways that the social context helps to shape the performance and its contents. In slightly different ways, both authors make clear the profound social implications of oral composition and presentation.

This work distinguishes itself from these predecessors in that its subject is not an oral tradition, but a *mixed*-oral one. Reynolds especially confronts the social and cultural implications of composition, since the process of composing the Egyptian epics he studies typically coincides with the act of performance and is therefore socially conditioned to one degree or another. (Kurpershoek faces the additional issue of the transition of ad-Dindān's poetry from oral performance to print, which the author does not treat theoretically). The present study does not deal with the composition process at all. Indeed, it cannot, since the *Āla* tradition today is effectively fixed within boundaries defined by a written corpus, with no new compositions forthcoming or even conceived as possible. In the case of *al-Āla,* the issue becomes rather the methods by which existing material is preserved and transmitted orally parallel to (and in some ways implicated within) an important literary dimension.

In contrast to its predecessors, a major concern of this study – and especially, Part 2 – is to explain the social bases of both orality and literacy, and the reasons for orality's continued presence in the face of the evident cultural/discursive power of literacy. In this way, the discussion that follows offers a new and hopefully productive approach to orality and oral tradition.

Chapter 6
Toward a Theory of Tradition and Transmission

In Part 1, Chapters 1, 2 and 3 developed a picture of *al-Āla* that brought to the fore the social contexts that have surrounded the music, and in particular, emphasized the importance of formal and informal institutions that provided the framework for enacting the social relationships and economic arrangements that supported the music at various stages in its history. The focus on institutional circumstances continued in a different vein in Chapter 4, which addressed specifically the combined oral and literate methods by which one generation of musicians passes *al-Āla* on to the next. Al-Maʿhad al-Waṭanī, the National Conservatory, plays a prominent role in this process, being virtually the only formal institution that provides access for both amateurs and future professionals to organized instruction at the hands of master *Āla* musicians.

However, Chapter 4 also pointed to a degree of friction that emerges in the higher levels of instruction at the National Conservatory: The Conservatory's standardized system (a characteristic of formal institutions in general) exists in a dynamic tension with the individualized and personal mode of teaching that takes place at the higher levels of training, and indeed which has typified the musical heritage of al-Andalus since the era of Ziryāb. While not completely inimical to the demands of the institution, the personalized relationship between master and student must eventually supercede the institutional relationship if the student is to participate fully in *al-Āla* on its traditional terms. Dissonance arises when the social relationships implied in the economic framework embodied by the Conservatory system rub up against other significant relationships in the context of Andalusian music training. Master and student at the National Conservatory typically resolve this dissonance by adhering to the traditional mode of master-student relationships, while accommodating the institution chiefly when it demands some formalized interaction with it – including, not least, the monetary aspect. This example illustrates how formal institutions serve society as an extension or embodiment of a certain variety of economic order, one which organizes the world in terms of goods and services that have specific monetary values assigned to them, rather than according to more personalized and individualistic criteria by which, not coincidentally, monetary value as such becomes more malleable and somewhat less stable. It is, of course, no accident that the institution and the social rationale associated with it are very recent developments in the history of *al-Āla*, arising in the 20th century as a direct result of colonial contact.

The corollary to this may be found in the other contexts in which the tradition is learned and taught: informally outside the Conservatory for many *Āla* musicians, and mastery-level training that takes place at the hands of a *muʿallim* in a *jawq*. In both cases, the teaching takes place in an intimate setting suffused with interactions based upon personalized relationships and instruction. Even more, the relationships that characterize these cases are based upon fundamentally different assumptions from those emphasized by the Conservatory. For example, the economic dimensions of these relationships (more precisely, the terms of exchange and reciprocity) do not presuppose an intermediary guarantor of the curriculum or the results. Even the individual musician who devotes considerable time to learning from recordings and broadcast media cannot escape the necessity of close contact with other musicians who know the tradition well. Without such input, the budding musician will always lack the nuances, the unwritten rules of style and performance practice that distinguish an expert performance from that of a dilettante. Thus the economic order which surrounds *al-Āla* in the Conservatory is merely one aspect of the tradition that interacts with social dynamics that may or may not fit well with it.

A parallel and equally important theme emerging from Part 1 was the complicated relationship between written and oral modes of communication within the tradition itself. The story of Ziryāb's two "song holders" (Ġizlān and Hunayda) shows the master performing for the two servants a song he has heard in a dream, and then writing down the poetry.[1] Ibn Khaldun's story of Ibn Bājja "walking home on gold"[2] offers a similar example by using the verb ألقى على ("to deliver, present or hand over to someone"), which suggests that he physically handed his song (موشّحته) to the female singer. Of course, this scene as presented by Ibn Khaldun may be little more than a dramatization on the historian's part, the exact details not being so important to his purpose as the larger point of the story. Nevertheless, since a performance like this would not have taken place without rehearsal, this passage implies that, although the composer taught the song to the singer beforehand, she relied on a written text to perform the text correctly. This web of literate and oral processes has persisted down to the present day, as Chapter 4 made clear.

These two large themes, which may seem at first glance to have little in common with one another, in fact are connected. *Al-Āla*, and indeed any musical art form, provides a space for social interaction in several forms, including both the acts of performance, as well as the processes by which the art is preserved and handed on. Interactions between and among musicians, audiences and participants in the various institutions that support the music (all members of what we might describe as an

[1] See Chapter 2 §1.2a.

[2] See Chapter 2 §2.

Andalusian music community) focus on and around the musical tradition, so that one might view *al-Āla* in one sense as existing chiefly as the raison d'être for these social activities. The proposition that *al-Āla* is a function of its social context contradicts what is perhaps the more common view, that a musical form's social frame is somehow an outgrowth of its creation. This latter notion, that music has a life of its own as a creative act apart from and prior to the social interactions that surround its performance and transmission, enables the kind of cultural-historical perspective embodied in the standard narrative. As long as *al-Āla* is studied apart from its social frame, a complete understanding of its historical development and modern characteristics remain out of reach. Continuity in the art over time (the existence of aesthetic principles and performance practices that distinguish *al-Āla* from other genres) is an a priori feature of music that is fundamentally social: the rules and principles have been created by people, they exist to render the music recognizable to people, and they represent a connection between those who have created or performed in the past and those who do so now. Thus it makes no sense to speak of music that precedes the social context that actually makes it possible. This need not deny the validity of musical innovation: stylistic change always incorporates existing elements, building upon what has come before (as was argued in the Prologue to Part 1). Indeed, an artistic revolution depends to a degree upon a social climate that creates the conditions for innovation. Examples from the twentieth century abound: the birth of jazz in 1920s New Orleans, of rock 'n' roll in the American Southeast of the 1950s, of reggae in the shanty towns of Jamaica, of *rai* in post-independence Algeria, and so on. Obviously, what has just been said of music applies equally to poetry, and especially to poetry set within a musical frame.

Thus social context is indispensable to understanding *al-Āla,* whether through the historical processes of development and transmission discussed in Part 1 Chapters 1 through 4, or via the literary aspects of the tradition explored in Chapter 5. Little sense can be made of certain features of the tradition without taking account of how they serve to situate and integrate the music within a set of meaningful social relationships. In effect, this and the two following chapters propose a framework for an historical ethnography of the Andalusian music tradition in Morocco, which attempts to highlight those meaningful aspects of the tradition that lie at the intersection of the social, economic and historical discourses surrounding the Andalusian music today. To do this requires first a clear understanding of the nature and function of tradition.

1. *Tradition, whether oral or written*

Throughout the history as renarrated here, I have chosen to use the word *tradition* to refer to *al-Āla,* but what exactly is meant by the word? *Al-Āla,* is a musical form, including both text and music. Yet we are speaking also of a set of performance practices and aesthetic rules or principles that inform the music and text. Together these elements comprise a more-or-less coherent cultural form that is regarded as a cohesive whole by performers and audiences. Such a form, combining content, principles and practice, which is considered and transmitted as a whole over time, might be called a tradition. However, this is not quite sufficient, for tradition has other qualities, as well. In order to understand the significance of tradition in cultural terms, we must ask how these disparate elements actually came to be transmitted together, to be conceived of as a unity within a given cultural-historical frame. So let us look first at what previous scholars have said about tradition and its role in society.

The scholarly literature on tradition is large, but much of it reflects a certain preoccupation with the relationship between tradition and modernity (commonly understood in terms of economic development or cultural Westernization). In many cases, it is modernity that is really at issue, while the idea of tradition as such is not well framed and is assumed to be more transparent than it really is. Often, one finds an implied definition of tradition that is not consistent, suggesting sometimes symbolic aspects of culture, sometimes organizational aspects of social life – even within one work. Thus, much of the scholarly discussion on tradition has little relevance for the present study.

Samuel Eisenstadt lays out this problem clearly in *Tradition, Change, and Modernity* (1973).[3] His discussion of the foundations of tradition seeks to bridge the symbolic and the organizational. He follows Max Weber by emphasizing tradition's role in legitimizing certain kinds of social organization, but goes on to say that tradition provides the stock of ideas which help define reality, and organizational answers to the basic problems of human existence. This is "tradition" in the sense of "Great Tradition," and while it appears difficult to transpose such a conception onto an individual poetic-musical art form, this definition does at least indicate a particular kind of relationship between the practical and the ideological: tradition serves as a repository of concepts and repertoires that help define the parameters of behavior.

In *The Past in Ruins: Tradition and the Critique of Modernity* (1992), David Gross approaches the question of tradition from a different direction. In his argument for the importance of developing new ways of appreciating tradition within the context of modernity, he engages tradition in a less grand sense, defining it as:

> a set of practices, a constellation of beliefs, or a mode of thinking that exists in the present, but was inherited from the past … It is not the assumption that an act was previously performed that makes it traditional; rather, it becomes traditional when it is

[3] See especially pp. 119-121.

> replicated precisely *because* it was performed before. In every bona fide tradition, there is always an element of the prescriptive.[4]

Alongside this, Gross sets out three criteria for an "authentic" tradition. 1) It must link together at least three generations; 2) It must carry a certain amount of spiritual or moral prestige; and 3) It must "convey a sense of continuity between the past and the present" (10), that is, one must have the feeling that adhering to the tradition links one with the distant past.

Note that for Gross, tradition always contains an ideological element, whether or not there is a behavioral one. This is significant because this line of reasoning suggests an explanation for the blending of elements noted above that comprise the Moroccan Andalusian music tradition. Neither the textual/musical content of the Andalusian music, nor the aesthetic principles, nor the performance practice, individually is sufficient to constitute the tradition. For example, to perform *Ramal al-Māya* with electronic instruments (altering both performance practice and aesthetic principles) would be an innovation with a result that might be described *in terms of* the original, but would not be recognized as authentic (*aṣīl*) by participants in the tradition. Similarly, to perform different text and music using the contextual frame of the *Āla* tradition (instruments, costume, even stylistic elements, i.e.: performance practice and aesthetics without content), would achieve the same result: a sense of confusion in the listener, the feeling that something fundamental to the tradition has been violated. We might say that to make use of any of these elements without the others subverts the result, robs it of its authenticity. It is the belief (Gross would say *prescription*) that these facets necessarily belong together that allows them to form a tradition as such.

It is important to note that, though Gross has *social* traditions in mind in his discussion, the same parameters apply to *artistic* traditions as well. It is true that an element of aesthetic appreciation comes into play in the arts: A musical form may be perpetuated because of the beauty of its content, quite apart from any connection it may have to the past. However, we should distinguish here between *genres* and *traditions*. Certainly, aesthetic appeal plays a role in the survival of any genre of music, but what makes it traditional, as Gross notes, is its prestige as a marker or emblem of the distant past. This prestige lies at the intersection of content, principles and practice. Even though any or all of these elements may change over time, it is the perception that their combination is significant because it links performer and listener to a shared past that raises genre to the level of tradition.

---

[4] p. 8

The Moroccan Andalusian music thus meets Gross' complex test of a tradition:

1. That it links at least three generations is obvious: it can be shown to have existed in Morocco for two centuries at the very least (since al-Ḥāʾik), and probably derives from music performed in Morocco and al-Andalus much earlier than that.
2. That it carries prestige is evident from its historical associations with the monarchy, religious contexts and educated, literate society. Indeed, we have already noted that the very association of the music with al-Andalus conveys its prestige. Moreover, its deployment as a kind of national classical music in television and radio broadcasts places it in the domain of what Anthony Smith has called "civic religion," the privileged symbols that serve to evoke identification with the nation state.[5]
3. It is indeed repeated for its own sake, for its aesthetic qualities, but also because it represents for many people a link to a common heritage, in theory reaching back all the way to al-Andalus.

Finally, it carries a set of prescriptive elements, as Gross suggests a tradition should. For *al-Āla*, these determine what should be performed, how and in what contexts, prescriptions that, when violated, undermine the result.

Alongside Gross' three main criteria, I would add a set of processes that emerge as natural consequences: resonance, repetition and evolution are central features of performative traditions, like those in the arts especially. *Resonance* is a function of the tradition's prestige and derives from meaningful elements in the cultural context, such as a shared sense of history or a link to an idealized past. Resonance gives each reenactment of a musical tradition part of its affective force. *Repetition* of the tradition is governed by various rules or norms understood as part of performance practice, so that the very act of repeating the tradition within certain accepted (even *prescribed*) contexts adds to its emotional resonance, apart from the actual content of the performance, and reinscribes it as a meaningful practice. Repetition lends stability to resonance: every reenactment of the tradition within the norms that govern when and in what context it should be performed, tends to reinforce attachment to it. However, the process of reiterating the tradition's actual content over time also opens the door to elaboration and so to *evolution* of the tradition. Gross' observations on how traditions change help to clarify this point.

---

[5] 1991, p. 46.

Gross emphasizes that traditions change and develop over time, and that those traditions that do not change eventually die out. This is affected partly by the channels through which the tradition is handed on. Traditions that depend upon oral transmission tend to command greater emotional loyalty than those that have a strong written component, but they also change more easily, which makes them more malleable. Gross points out the mutability of tradition by linking its survival and maintenance to the "totality of social relations."[6] As social and cultural developments take place, a tradition comes to be viewed differently as well, and particular traditions are either adapted to fit the new situation (as long as some aspect continues to resonate) or abandoned. Repetition thus interacts dynamically with shifting social conditions to lead to evolution of the tradition (including both content and ideological/prescriptive elements like performance practice).

Such changes have operated throughout the history of *al-Āla*, particularly in the 20th century. Even as its custodians have sought to preserve the tradition as it stands, economic forces have been reshaping social mores and relationships in Morocco, which in turn have put new pressures on *al-Āla* as an expressive form: its associations with the past do not always resonate with younger generations confronted with the choices and symbols of the modern world. Thus Gross' view of mutability and the mechanisms by which the power of tradition erodes corresponds well with what we find in the Moroccan Andalusian music tradition.

However, Gross' model does not adequately answer a question that till now has lain in the background of the present study of *al-Āla*: why is any particular *literary* or *musical* tradition preserved and passed on? Both Gross and Eisenstadt recognize that social relations are important in a general way, but neither actually explains the appeal of any given tradition. How does social context shape the trajectory that a tradition like *al-Āla* follows? To answer this, another term is needed: *value.*

2. *The value of tradition*

Value has had a convoluted career within the social sciences. Broadly speaking, the term has been used in three ways: *linguistic value* (following Ferdinand de Saussure, and synonymous with *meaning*), *economic value* (Karl Marx being a central figure in this domain) and *social value* or *values* (a concept that Clyde Kluckhone and his associates sought without success to bring within the bounds of a coherent theory). Each has its application within its particular domain, but one might wonder whether the use of this one word in these three senses is more than an artifact of language.

---

[6] p. 14

David Graeber (2001) argues that there is in fact a connection amongst them. No value can be derived, he maintains, purely from within any of the three domains in question without reference to a specific social context. In Graeber's estimation, value can be understood as a way of describing the importance or meaning attaching to actions that take place within society: the meaning of *value* in any of these domains depends upon how that domain is situated in real-life circumstances.

Linguistic value depends upon the people who use language. De Saussure put forward the notion that meaning can be defined in terms of all the things that an object is not. This was in line with his general project of analyzing the *structure* of language (*langue*) apart from its *use* (*parole*). But Graeber points out that this ultimately leads to an infinite regression of negative definitions. The number of things in the universe that are not *a chair* is vast, as is the number of (possibly mistaken) "not-this" definitions, as well. Does this ultimately tell us what a chair in fact is? Who can decide whether any of these anti-definitions is correct or not? To arrive at a positive meaning, some impetus from outside the regression is needed, and that can only come from those who actually use language to talk about chairs. Therefore, it is social context (e.g. the *use* of the utterance *chair* in particular human interactions) that ultimately provides the substance of linguistic meaning. In practice, a person may indeed develop an understanding of *chair* by observing what the word never refers to (though this seems rather counter-intuitive, to say the least). Nevertheless, it is precisely people's application of the word to real-world objects that makes this possible.

This pragmatic line of reasoning points to a limitation inherent in de Saussure's desire to divorce *langue* from *parole*. Understandably, he regarded the messiness of language use as an unreliable foundation for a theoretical approach to language. However, he did not recognize that without *parole, langue* drifts free in a theoretical space that allows the tacit assumption that a language can somehow exist without a speaker. This does not mean that de Saussure's efforts were wasted by any means, for his work provided the foundations for the often fruitful efforts of structuralist analysis, which had a lasting impact beyond the boundaries of linguistics.[7] But Saussurean analysis of linguistic value ultimately must lead from *langue* back to *parole*, from *meaning* in the abstract to *use*.

Even in economics, which seems to the modern mind to offer a fundamental and convincing explanation of reality, value is tied to social context. Economists usually hold that value derives from disembodied forces, such as supply and demand, the cost of labor and materials, and so on; and indeed in societies where exchange takes place

[7] In focusing on contrastive meaning Saussurean linguistics emphasized meaningful categories as structural components of language, an abstraction that has been mirrored in anthropological theory, including the work of Claude Lévi-Strauss and Kluckhone's values project.

through money, these factors contribute to *the number of units of currency attaching to an object*. But this *cost* is not very useful as an explanation of *value* in an anthropological sense, for as Graeber points out, it is a circular explanation that really only makes sense in societies where the idea of a market exists. In these specific circumstances, economic theories can predict within limits how markets will change and what people will buy, but they have difficulty explaining *why*: why people choose to eat fowl and not cattle, why people diet to be thin in one society but prefer to be voluptuous in another, and so on. Moreover, societies that practice gift exchange (Trobriand islanders, famously, but others as well) present a problem for economic theories of value, since such systems appear to refute the idea that a person (a so-called "maximizing individual") always seeks his or her own self-interest and does her or his best to optimize that. Rather, the idea of a gift in any society implies action *against* one's evident self-interest, and gift economies entirely confound the notion that people merely maximize self-interest.

The response of economists has been to emphasize that people are driven to satisfy desires (which ultimately means they seek "pleasure" in one form or another), and that some of these desires are for non-material things. Graeber responds, "In order to carry out such an economic analysis, one almost always ends up having to map out a series of 'values' of something like the traditional sociological sense – power, prestige, moral purity, etc. – and to define them as being on some level fundamentally similar to economic ones."[8] In other words, the social relationships implied in the social values necessary to explain "pleasure" become transformed into thing-like objects that can then have an economic value attached to them. The problem becomes explaining in what sense prestige is like a bar of gold, and that solution ultimately drags social context back into the equation, because:

> even if one does manage to reduce every social relation to a thing, so that one is left with the empiricist's dream, a world consisting of nothing but individuals and objects, one is still left to puzzle over why individuals feel some objects will afford them more pleasure than others.[9]

Graeber finds it more useful from an anthopological point of view to see economic exchange as a kind of social interaction that expresses the significance of the relationship between the actors. This concept of economic value can apply to non-market as well as market economies. Whether the medium of exchange is money, or credit from a bank, or circuits of symbolic gift exchanges extending over hundreds of

[8] p. 8

[9] p. 9

miles; and whether the actors are patrons and clients, or "pleasure maximizing" consumers, the exchange itself is a way of assigning value to the actions associated with it, and therefore to the social relationships which surround and inform it.

This insight is perhaps less than obvious in modern economic exchanges that appear on the surface not to involve a social interaction at all. An online credit card purchase is one example of an exchange that at first glance seems to deny a social dimension. Yet a closer examination reveals that this exchange is saturated with social interactions. First, the purchaser engaged in a host of socially-informed economic activities in order to obtain the credit card, from holding down a job, to maintaining a bank account, and so on. These socially-valued relations form the background of the purchase itself. Let us then suppose the purchaser is buying a shirt. Is it a gift? Then the purchase becomes in part an expression of the buyer's friendship. Is it for her or his personal use? In either case, he or she has taken into account styles of fashion, color, size, appropriateness for certain occasions, whether or not the shirt will be "flattering" when worn – again, all socially-informed considerations that contribute meaning to the purchase.

The difficult part of the transaction is really the actual exchange itself, which appears not to involve any people other than the purchaser. But this is an illusion, for that shirt was made by someone (probably a woman or child in a developing country like India, Thailand or Viet Nam) and marketed online by someone else, and it will be delivered by someone else again. This transaction thus is bound up with a host of other transactions that culminate in the shirt's delivery to the buyer's door. These aspects, and more besides, embody relationships that the purchaser is enacting by ordering the shirt. The value expressed in the transaction is not simply the price in dollars. For the woman in India who made the shirt, the dollar (or the 50 rupees) she earned that day may be much more valuable than the fifteen-dollar online price is to the buyer in Indiana. Just as the "weight" of a dollar is greater in India than in Indiana, so the value of economic exchanges like these, which "bring together" actors from far-flung corners of the world, lies in the importance each attaches to the transaction, importance expressed partly in terms of currency but experienced on a human level.

The fact that the medium of communication is technological and not personal should not blind us to the very human significance of transactions like these. That we in technologically-oriented societies participate in them shows that we value some quality they possess — possibly the illusion of anonymity that makes them at once so efficient and yet apparently private. However, insight into the socially-situated value of apparently anonymous economic transactions lies behind the idea of the consumer boycott as a form of political action. The boycotts of Shell during the Apartheid regime in South Africa, of Exxon after the *Exxon Valdez* disaster, of Nike and the Gap, as well as

"Buy American" campaigns, all testify to the very real social meaning attaching to transactions that today could easily be carried out by a single person interacting (apparently) only with a machine.[10]

In the face of overly simplistic readings of Marx, which tend to emphasize material factors as determining social conditions, Graeber points out that it is people who *evaluate* material conditions and assign meaning to them, even as they use exchange to obtain resources, prestige and so on. While it may be true that, as Marx argued, the form of the economic system is shaped to a greater or lesser extent by the means of production, material conditions hardly supply a final explanation, for the meaningful contents of every economic system are strongly shaped by the social realities in which it operates. Economic value thus is an idiom for describing social status and the relative importance assigned within the social system to owning or exchanging various material objects and services.

The idea of *social value,* or *values,* has had a checkered history in anthropology. Kluckhone's values project among Native Americans of the U.S. southwest attempted to reframe anthropology as the comparative study of social value across cultures. The problem, according to Graeber, was that the search for an overarching theory of social value led to lists of values pertaining to specific societies without arriving at a mechanism for comparing them across cases. Kluckhone and his associates sought a comparative method by proposing fundamental questions that values purportedly address, hoping to identify common themes across cultures. Graeber points out that questions like these lie far removed from everyday life. It is extremely difficult to use such questions to explain why, for example, paternal cousins might be preferred as marriage partners, or why one variety of music is considered prestigious and another not. Ultimately, the values project never quite bridged the gap between the refined level of value-themes and the mundane world where values provide guidance for living.

It is precisely here that Graeber's theory of value is most useful to this study of the *Āla* tradition. Graeber shows that, as with linguistic and economic value, social value ultimately refers to the importance assigned to socially informed actions. For linguistic value, socially-informed action involves using language to communicate; while for economic value, action means participating in exchange. For social value, socially-informed actions are those that operate within or touch upon their social frame, manifesting most clearly in the context of social relationships. Prestige is an

---

[10] The credit cards that make these transactions possible were themselves originally marketed as markers of high status. Early television commercials for credit cards showed card holders breezing through airports and hotels without resorting to messy, lowbrow cash transactions. Only recently has "plastic" come to be widely regarded (and marketed!) as a necessity for everyone, rather than a luxury for the elite few.

obvious example of a value based upon action within a social frame. The common denominator among value systems that feature prestige is that, whatever the criteria for it, to have prestige is to act within the bounds of certain culturally defined and significant relationships. Such relationships entail certain behaviors and beliefs (often including acquiring and displaying culturally-prescribed material objects, forms of dress and so on) that express or represent those relationships and are in some sense prescribed by or for them.

If the language of this discussion sounds familiar, it is because Gross uses similar terms to talk about tradition. Recall that Gross points out the prestigious and prescriptive qualities that make for an authentic tradition. These two qualities show that a tradition that is alive and active in the society must also be valued by its participants and provide guidance for meaningful behavior in an actual context present in the social milieu.

Gross postulates a deep-seated psychological need in humanity for tradition, arguing that the success of tradition results from the confluence of need and opportunity. People have always needed material ways of coping with survival – finding food, water and shelter. The handing down of successful strategies, in Gross' view, was the origin of tradition and the reason for its success. The functionality of tradition, however, tends to become mystified behind the screen of the tradition's prestige, so that large institutions (notably the state) have been able to appropriate traditional beliefs and modes of behavior for their own ends. The affective power of the tradition, based as it is upon its social meaning, is turned to serve the institution. A poetic musical tradition can benefit from the same ideological turn, which explains the government's support of al-Maʿhad al-Waṭanī and the *mahrajānāt*: in associating itself with *al-Āla*, the monarchy presents itself as guardian of the common heritage of the nation, which is also (not coincidentally) linked to the Golden Age of al-Andalus.

By arguing that tradition emerges from and reinforces survival strategies, Gross recognizes one aspect of what might be called the survival value of tradition. He overlooks, however, the powerful role that tradition may play in group identity, which also contributes to group survival. As a repository of shared values (that is, of commonly-accepted social roles and behavior) a tradition can come to be seen as one of the bonds that unite people in a common heritage. An artistic tradition can be very influential in this respect, serving as an emblem or expression of collective self-identification and stirring deep emotional responses. As a dimension of group identity, tradition can command even more affective allegiance. This was true for *al-Āla* in the North African middle period, between the fall of Granada and al-Ḥāʾik, when *performing* the music helped Andalusian communities in Morocco self-identify by linking them to their common Andalusi heritage.

The perceived need for tradition also has led to various attempts to preserve or revive dead or dying traditions. While Gross sees nothing inherently wrong with this, he points out that some aims are hardly worth the effort. One is the attempt to preserve tradition as an *objet d'art*. This sort of museum collecting is not to Gross' taste, because he sees no inherent value in particular traditions as such, devoid of the social value they once embodied. While remembering defunct traditions has some historical logic, Gross regards traditionalism, tradition for tradition's sake, as a meaningless exercise. Since the "totality of social relations" (Graeber would say, "meanings attaching to certain acts in social context") which prevailed when the tradition was alive has changed, the idea that one can re-establish a moribund tradition simply by repeating it is ridiculous:

> [T]he price paid for artificially sustaining all or parts of any particular tradition is the misrepresentation, if not wholesale falsification, of that tradition.[11]

Seeing social value as the importance assigned to actions which inform social relations within a given cultural milieu provides insight into both the appeal of artistic traditions, and how participants in such traditions may accommodate changes in social conditions over time. Since social value is central to understanding the survival of tradition, changing social conditions represent a substantial threat to it. To the extent that a tradition is an inherited repository of beliefs and behaviors, its persistence can be explained by the value attributed to the social relations associated with those beliefs and behaviors. So long as a poetic-musical tradition continues to represent and inspire meaningful behavior in social contexts, it will be valued and conserved, and will continue to mediate accepted behavior in those areas it touches.

As social conditions change, the values associated with the contents of a tradition also change. For an indefinite period, the fit between the two can adjust without seriously altering the tradition, as long as it continues to command respect from (as long as repetitions continue to resonate with) its participants: the meanings derived from text can be bent to new purposes, taken to metaphorical levels or understood as historically significant; the emotions evoked by the music can change; and behavioral elements can be modified or assigned new significances that are relevant to the new social conditions. To a certain extent, new behavioral elements can even be added (e.g. changes in performance practice such as expanding the size and composition of the *jawq*). As long as social change is slow, as it was during the long stretch of time between 1492 and 1800, the process of adjustment can proceed naturally

[11] p. 107

and remain virtually unnoticed. However, if the disparity between value and content becomes too great too quickly, central elements of the tradition itself must change, or it faces extinction.

One of the most devastating influences on tradition has been economic change. Marx, of course, pointed out the dependence of much of what we today call *culture* upon the form of the economic system. The intimate links between economic conditions and social organization make tradition vulnerable. This is why economic modernization in the West has been associated with profound changes in social mores and institutions, with a parallel erosion in much of what is called traditional. Historians of the United States have pointed to the Industrial Revolution of the late 18th and early 19th centuries and its impact on family structure as a critical juncture for social changes. The advent of the "information age" in the early 1960s was accompanied by further changes in social relations, especially with regard to women. Throughout all these changes, tradition was intimately bound up with both social value and economic conditions, and therefore economic value. Since tradition depends upon social conditions that are profoundly influenced by economic developments, it is not surprising that when economic conditions change, tradition comes under pressure to change, as well.

The *Āla* tradition has been subject to precisely this kind of pressure. Chapter 4 discussed the unprecedented effort in the 20th century to preserve and maintain *al-Āla* as an element of Moroccan public culture. This project took the form of institutionalization and emerged specifically as a result of the colonial experience, parallel to and institutionally connected with the economic modernization of the country. However, at the same time, the social meanings and intimate settings long associated with the music among Andalusian communities, and the personal relationships attaching to it, have been rapidly shunted aside as the Moroccan economy has begun to modernize and as Moroccans have begun to create new meanings from the changing world around them. Formal institutions have stepped in to manage the tradition's adaptation to the new situation, but in the process, the social relationships surrounding *al-Āla* have been redefined. In short, the decay of tradition so often remarked on in the West, which took place in the course of perhaps two centuries (and was conditioned by other developments in science, economy and society), has overtaken Morocco in a matter of decades. Although both the government and the doyens of the tradition have focused on ancient and traditional methods of teaching, in the hope that this will preserve something of the spirit of the music, changes in the teaching context and the general economic and social climates in Morocco have profoundly altered performance contexts and meanings and thus the social prospects of the tradition. As important as the teaching methods are to the spirit of the tradition, the (perhaps unavoidable) changes in values that have come with modernization signal far more profound changes in the tradition's status.

So it comes as no surprise that the rapid impact of foreign influences that have sent economic and cultural effects rippling through Moroccan society are having an effect on *al-Āla* as well. Many young people today respect the *Āla* tradition for its *aṣīl* qualities, but it does not speak to them: it seems not to summon the meaningful social relationships they find (or seek) in their environment. Social values are shifting westward, so to speak, as youth in cities like Fez and Tetuan adopt European fashions in clothing, music and outlook. In this situation, the relative weakness of the Moroccan economy has left much that was traditional in Moroccan society vulnerable, including *al-Āla*.

3. *Tradition, value, and al-Āla*

The survival of *al-Āla* and some aspects of its present form, now come more clearly into focus. Viewing the Moroccan Andalusian music as a tradition in the sense outlined here can explain why it has survived for so long: its appeal has been a function of the values the music represents, that is, the meaningful acts and social relationships which the tradition embodies. Moreover, this leads us toward a way to analyze historical changes in the tradition in terms of the social contexts in which it has been performed.

In its earliest history in al-Andalus, the ancestor of *al-Āla* belonged to the elite and those who served them. The way the sources treat the music of Ziryāb's era and after imply that his music was regarded as a distinct genre from the music of the common people. The sources make a clear conceptual link between the prestige of Ziryāb's music in Cordoba and the refined courtly music of contemporary Baghdad. Quite apart from its aesthetic qualities, the music was one expression of the patron's taste, access to leisure and ability to command his own entertainment and reward social inferiors who entertained him well.[12] As with all economic transactions, this one achieved more than simply redistributing resources. Looking at the same transaction in the light of value theory, we can say that the economic relations inherent in the patron-

[12] The question of the musicians' social status is a bit more complex than this suggests. There were aristocrat-musicians of course, like Isḥāq al-Mawṣili's rival Ibrāhīm b. al-Mahdī in ninth-century Baghdad (who was the son of one caliph, the brother of two others and briefly even a pretender to the throne himself) and even prince-patrons who were themselves musicians. However these were exceptions: the patron-client system, though it varied somewhat with circumstances, was by definition a relationship between unequals. If an aristocrat like Ibrāhīm could afford to pursue music as an avocation, still he was in no way an equal of his patron-brother Hārūn, nor did his aristocratic birth do anything to raise the status of the majority of musician-courtiers who were entirely dependent upon the good graces of their patrons.

client relationship expressed the specific social distance between patron and musician or poet. At the same time, the patron-client system also enmeshed them in a value-informed relationship, which revolved around the prestige attaching to fine music and refined musical performance, and which tied the patron and all his courtiers and performing artiste slaves together in a web of meaningful relations. The musical tradition (both content and performance practice) served as vehicle for prescribed norms of behavior and beliefs about social position that existed among patron, artist and slave.

This musical form persisted and developed over the centuries because it served this purpose well, even as political changes swept over al-Andalus. The Umayyad caliphate collapsed, but courtly musical culture survived, and even flourished at the courts of the successor Ṭāʾifa states. It would seem that, though the political and economic landscape had shifted, the tradition of courtly musical entertainment retained its value in the new context (indeed, even as it had after its transplantation to al-Andalus from the Middle East). In other words, the fundamental social relationships within the patronage system that held sway under Umayyad rule continued under the Ṭāʾifa emirs. Furthermore, relationships between these princes appear to have come to the fore, as can be seen in the competition for prestige-earning talent. The musical tradition thus was now part of a tradition-value nexus that helped to express relationships among the elites (emirs and other aristocrats) of the various petty kingdoms.

All these relationships consist of the actions prescribed for reenacting the tradition (even if they are not necessarily viewed as such). The entertainments of the *majlis*, the repartee of *nadāma*, paying of stipends and gifts to client-musicians, composing of songs of praise or love and performing them, taking on student musicians or artiste slaves and teaching them, conveying the musician's latest composition to the prince's *sitāra*, all these and more comprised the behavioral contents of the musical tradition that were evaluated as meaningful in the context.

With the florescence of Andalusi literary culture during the era of the Ṭāʾifa states, the increased musical and poetic production almost certainly led to an expansion and diversification of the tradition, as competition among the emirs created more opportunities, more niches for talented poets and musicians who could earn a share of patrons' largesse. The political decentralization of al-Andalus made room for economic decentralization, which facilitated the cultural expansion, as more than one scholar has noted.[13] This expansion probably contributed to the stylistic innovations attributed by

[13] The foundational study of Andalusian poetry that takes account of its social and economic aspects is Henri Perés' *La poésie andalouse en arabe classique au XIe siècle: ses aspects généraux, ses principaux thèmes et sa valeur documentaire* (1953). Benaboud (1987) provides a very thorough study of the economics of the

at-Tīfāšī and Ibn Khaldun to Ibn Bājja.[14] With more opportunity for poets came more competition and greater possibilities for innovation and creative genius, which Ibn Bājja undoubtedly was.

Just prior to Ibn Bājja's era came the political unification of al-Andalus with North Africa under the Almoravids beginning at the end of the 5th/11th century. As noted in Chapter 3, most of the early references to Andalusi settlers arriving in North Africa date to this period, and these early settlers certainly brought with them some aspects of their musical culture (though whether this was the music of the Ṭāʾifa courts is unknown). This was a watershed for the Andalusian musical heritage, for as more Andalusis arrived in Morocco in the wake of Christian advances in Iberia, the courtly music of al-Andalus found a home among these established migrant communities. These developments marked the beginning of a major shift in the social milieu surrounding the tradition that ensured its survival beyond the end of Islamic rule in Spain.

At first, the wealthier people among the migrants, the leaders and landowners, probably had some interest in the music, but the courtly music may have had little influence among the migrants as a whole, most of whom were common folk, laborers and agriculturalists. It is unlikely that the elite music resonated with them. As the decades and centuries passed, and as the Muslim presence in and access to al-Andalus steadily shrank, the music probably took on new social meanings, new ethno-historical resonances, for the migrant Andalusi families in North Africa. Perés (1953) has remarked upon the popularity of garden and nature scenes in Arab-Andalusian poetry and has attributed this to a longing among the Umayyads for their former dominion in the Middle East. One might make the same conjecture about the Moroccan Andalusian music tradition, also rich in the same imagery. Did the Andalusi émigrés find in their poetic heritage an expression of their own yearning for the lost gardens of al-Andalus? Does this explain why so many of these poems found their way into songs that were ultimately incorporated into the *nūba* tradition?

Nowadays the chief venues for *al-Āla* performances are the *ḥafla* and the *mahrajān*. These events are almost the only occasions that still bring the community of *Āla* aficionados together, and as we have seen in Chapter 3, they are organized by the modern *jamʿiyyāt*. But this has not always been so. Oral traditional accounts indicate that prior to the rise of the music-lovers' associations in the mid-20th century, community events were hosted by wealthy community members. Beyond private salons in the houses of the community's leaders, wedding parties and other community

---

Ṭāʾifa period, and Soulami and Benaboud (1994) apply this perspective specifically to the literary life of al-Andalus.

[14] See Chapter 2 §2.

occasions such as religious festivals like the Prophet's Birthday brought the larger community together, and the soundtrack for such events featured *al-Āla*. Relationships between musicians and audiences of various kinds, and a sense of common heritage and community, were forged through these performances, just as with the economic exchanges between patrons and musicians that became part of the value set attaching to the music in its social dimensions. In this way, what had been a centuries-old courtly music tradition, rich in value among the aristocracy in Andalusi cities like Cordoba, Seville and Granada, became established as a musical tradition in North Africa as well, but within a different social frame, and thus with a different system of values.

The survival of the Andalusian music tradition in North Africa was due at least in part to its ability to embody social value among the Andalusian immigrant families. Many of these families were well-educated and well-placed socially, so that even if their musical culture may have lost some of its courtly prestige, it certainly had not lost its erudition and sophistication. It is not difficult to imagine that this musical tradition, already centuries old, at least provided a receptacle for beliefs about ethnic identity and solidarity; and surely its sophistication would only have added to its value, perhaps as an emblem of the golden era of al-Andalus.

Contemporary scholarship presently has little to say about exactly when and how *al-Āla* was adopted by the ruling classes in Morocco. The most obvious evidence is the present Alawite dynasty's longstanding affection for the Andalusian music tradition discussed in Chapter 4. Several monarchs are held to have been fond of the music, including Mūlāy Muḥammad b. ʿAbd Allāh (r. 1757-1790) and his brother (who is believed to have supported al-Ḥāʾik); and Muḥammad V (r. 1927-1961) who encouraged the music as a national emblem and had his son, Ḥasan II (r. 1961-1999) trained in it. The Andalusian musical heritage may have become part of dynastic courtly culture in North Africa as early as the 12th century (as shown by the arrival of Ibn Bājja after serving the Almoravids in Seville) or even before. Given the music's history as a courtly phenomenon in al-Andalus, it is not hard to understand the appeal the music would have had to the ruling elite of the successive dynasties in Morocco, perhaps as a vehicle for maintaining the same kind of elite social values in the new context. In the absence of outside influences (such as Turkish music, which had a profound impact upon the Middle East), the Andalusian music was the elite musical form of the era, the *traditional* form of courtly music of the Arab-Islamic west. It survived and was adopted into Moroccan dynastic culture because it resonated with – or perhaps, was adaptable to – the social values that the ruling elite sought to preserve and express.

Over the centuries since the loss of the last Muslim foothold in Spain, the musical tradition has taken on an increasingly North African quality. The synthetic character of the tradition today is unquestionable, even if this is not always appreciated by musicians or aficionados. At the level of text, Cortés García points out that of the songs in the tradition for which authorship is known (perhaps 25% of the total), more than a few can be shown to come from Maġribī poets.[15] To the extent that we find *muwaššaḥāt* of Andalusian origins within the tradition, we observe that not one has a non-Arabic *ḫarja*, as Christian Poché notes. Poché argues that the non-Arabic *ḫarja* was detached from the song-form after its departure to North Africa because there was no longer any *political use* for a linguistically mixed poetic form.[16] Put more accurately, the change took place in the *social environment*: there simply was no longer an audience that found poetry incorporating Romance expressions entertaining. Monroe (2004, 31-32 and 39-41) suggests that the Romance phrases in some Andalusi *muwaššaḥāt* drew upon the social meanings attaching to non-formal and non-Arabic linguistic registers within Andalusi courtly society. The non-Arabic *ḫarja*, if it was understood in North Africa at all, could only remind the audience of the lost dominion across the Mediterranean. The values inherent in multi-ethnic, multilingual Andalusi society no longer obtained; neither the elites of Morocco nor the transplanted Andalusian families had any use for non-Arabic expressions inserted into Arabic songs.

Finally, as argued in §4 of the Introduction, although recent scholarship has turned up indications that the modal/rhythm *nūba* system may have roots in Andalusi performance practice (probably after the 13th century), the present form of the *nūba* is almost certainly a North African creation. Earlier descriptions of suite forms from al-Andalus do not clearly highlight musical mode as an important organizing principle. The first indication of this feature in the Moroccan context is the oral tradition referring to ʿAbd al-Raḥmān al-Fāsī's[17] renovation of the themes of *Ramal al-Māya* sometime before the middle of the 17th century. Some form of suite organization approximating the present *nūba*, with its emphasis on *ṭubūʿ*, may have existed within a century or so of the fall of Granada. When and where it actually emerged remains an open question, but it certainly owes its full development to North Africa, as shown in al-Būʿaṣāmī's *Iqād aš-šumūʿ* and *Kunnāš al-Ḥāʾik* (and in the diversity of *nūba* forms in the North African Andalusian music genres generally).

The contemporary Moroccan Andalusian music tradition thus bears the marks of more than seven centuries of residence in North Africa. This is to be expected, of course, but the element that has been lacking in previous retellings of this long tale has been a clear explanation of the appeal of this music, of its survival as a tradition for so long in an entirely different context from its origins. Analyzing *al-Āla* with the value

---

[15] 1996, p. 109.

[16] 1995, p. 57.

[17] Or Abū l-ʿAbbās Aḥmad's – see Chapter 1 n. 14.

theory of tradition leads to a clearer understanding of its survival: an important part of its strength lay in its ability to adapt to changes in social context. More precisely, the meanings attaching to reenacting the tradition were flexible enough that participants in it could continue to value it despite the changing circumstances. Indeed, the loss of contact with al-Andalus and the vicissitudes of life in the Maġrib probably contributed to the adoption of *al-Āla* as a marker of ethnic identity, opening the way to new possible meanings for the poetic and performance practice contents of the tradition. For a long time after the arrival of the earliest Andalusi settlers in Morocco, these changes were slow. Once the music became established outside the elite milieu, social and economic relations remained relatively stable for a very long time, as did the tradition's value. However in the 19th and 20th centuries, the pace of change increased. It remains to be seen whether *al-Āla*'s value is flexible enough to weather the storm.

4. *Tradition, change and channels of transmission*

Traditions change, as the value theory suggests, because social conditions change. As long as the content of a tradition is congruent with the values active in the social milieu, the tradition will continue to serve the people as a container for prescribed beliefs and behaviors that help people define who they are. The history of *al-Āla* illustrates how the contents of an existing tradition may be adapted to serve in a new context. The contents can open to reinterpretation, particularly if the tradition already carried a degree of prestige that would make it appealing in the new situation. *Al-Āla* has survived for so long in North Africa because of this adaptability. In that sense, it has been a relatively successful artistic tradition.

The meanings associated with performative aspects of a tradition are less malleable than those of its textual contents. Like text, they can be reinterpreted to some extent, but within narrower limits. For example, when certain ways of enacting social deference (bowing and curtseying, let's say) fall out of favor, to maintain them merely for the sake of tradition creates a cognitive dissonance that cannot be sustained indefinitely. They become comical, even ironic and satirical. Eventually, behavioral norms have to change to fit the new situation, and they generally do so naturally, through common practice. If change is not possible (if the performative facet of the tradition is too deeply bound up with its social meaning, or if the behaviors come to carry negative associations), the tradition will wane and eventually die out. Again, artistic traditions are more flexible in this respect, but not without limits. Certain kinds of costuming are considered traditional at formal concerts of *al-Āla*, but are not necessary at informal gatherings where the music is played. Electric amplification of the instruments in the *jawq* at a formal concert is considered acceptable, even desirable;

electric or electronic instruments are out of the question; it is simply understood as part of the unspoken ethos of the tradition.

Moreover, traditions may exist within traditions, that is, some traditions comprise elements that are valued within the context of the tradition as a whole. The practice of oral teaching of *al-Āla* is an example of such a tradition within a tradition. A central feature of *al-Āla,* oral transmission itself embodies certain resonant behaviors that comprise the relations between teacher and student (or *muʿallim* and *jawq* member). These activities are valued for the ways in which they preserve a connection to the aesthetic and performative norms of the larger poetic-musical tradition. The survival of the Andalusian music tradition as a whole ultimately may be understood in the context of the values associated with it, and so too the tradition of oral transmission of the music and text can be understood in the same way. Changes in the method of transmission (the incorporation of written texts into the teaching method, for example) can be analyzed for the way they reflect changes in social values within the community of Andalusian musicians, and perhaps even within the larger society as well.

This points to another, very important aspect of the mutability of traditions: the channel or mode by which the tradition passes from generation to generation. The medium of transmission is an important element in Gross' analysis. He puts forward three modes, oral, written and institutional, and argues that of the three, the oral mode fosters the deepest emotional allegiance. Written and institutional modes of transmission, he maintains, are inherently more fragile. Gross treats these three modes as distinct phases of a tradition's history, however *al-Āla* provides ample evidence that they may in fact coexist and complement one another. The next chapter examines the oral and written channels, in search of a way to connect them to the value theory of tradition. Doing so will provide a way to explain the changes that have overtaken the Moroccan Andalusian music tradition and how they have been reflected in performance practice and text.

Chapter 7
Tradition, Both Oral and Written

Part 1 showed the extent to which the spoken and written word have worked together within the confines of the Moroccan *Āla* tradition throughout its history. In the background of the historical narrative put forward there lay the simple fact that Arab musicians did not have a practical means of preserving music on paper. Although a system of tabulature based on *ʿūd* fingerings was invented by al-Kindī in the 3rd/9th century, it was a descriptive tool that could serve at best as a mnemonic aid by preserving instructions for how to finger the notes of a melody. The articulations – note lengths, tempo, dynamics – had to be worked out meticulously from a verbal description, so that it was far simpler to learn the piece orally and memorize it that way. Even when the text of the poem was available as a written document, composers usually used oral methods in passing on their songs. The services provided by artiste slaves like Ziryāb's Ġizlān, Hunayda and Šanīf were done through the methods of oral transmission. Thus the poetic-cum-musical art among the aristocracy during the Umayyad and Ṭāʾifa periods in al-Andalus relied heavily upon oral recitation and oral transmission among composers and musicians in competition for favors from the patron, techniques that existed side-by-side with, and complementary to, written materials.

There is no indication that the music's spread to North Africa and the loss of cultural contact with Iberia changed this state of affairs in any significant way. Indeed, the evidence of the manuscript traditions that lie behind the modern printed anthologies of *al-Āla* texts shows that this state of affairs continued through the 19th century at least. Prior to the appearance of the modern printed canon, corpuses of oral texts were found in various places in Morocco. Committing the tradition to writing was a multilinear process involving these local versions of the tradition that appear to have shared some material, but which only emerged into the written record by stages (beginning in fact with al-Būʿaṣāmī's book, but only coming into its own after al-Ḥā'ik) that have culminated in the modern canon described in Chapter 5.

The interweaving of oral and written transmission persists to the present day, as the study of al-Maʿhad al-Waṭanī in Chapter 4 made clear. The oral component is still a highly valued aspect of the tradition both in the training of musicians and in the final product, the performance, as performing from printed text remains very unusual. Omar and the other musicians in Jawq Benmūsā are expected to have committed both the music and texts of the *ṣanāʾiʿ* to memory before performances. Most musicians performing *al-Āla* today have committed a significant portion of it to memory in the traditional way before joining a *jawq*. Such a level of familiarity with the tradition is one thing that separates musicians in a true Andalusian *jawq* from those in less specialized groups that perform the Andalusian music in addition to other styles.

Intimate knowledge of the tradition is acquired in one of two ways: either through formal training in the Conservatory (as was the case with Sī Benmūsā, Sī Briouel, Sī Chaachou, Omar, Khalid, Otmane and others); or via repeated exposure to the music informally (Bilāl of Jawq al-Hayik and ʿAzīz ʿAlamī of Jawq Briouel, for example). In either case, experience with a *muʿallim* in a *jawq* serves as the highest level of training, in which refinements in style and performance practice are taught and honed, and in which rare *ṣanāʾiʿ* and performance units may be taught, as well. In all these cases, transmission between generations of performers relies heavily upon the spoken word, with only minimal reference to printed text.

The spoken word historically has been privileged among Andalusian musicians for teaching, and it remains central to the authentic teaching process to this day. While printed anthologies have been integrated into this teaching model, they serve only as an initial reference when first learning a new *ṣanʿa* and never as central teaching tools. Indeed, they cannot serve as "teaching manuals" because their format does not preserve the *ṣanāʾiʿ*-as-sung. The absence of songbooks that capture the performed version of the *ṣanʿa* underscores the importance attaching to oral transmission of *al-Āla*, despite the sophisticated nature of its texts and the often complex relationship that exists between the text and the melody. Musicians – students, amateurs and professionals alike – maintain that rote memorization by oral repetition is an essential dimension of the tradition, which in their view endows it with an ineffable quality that cannot be taught in any other way. At the same time, participants in the tradition place strong emphasis upon *Kunnāš al-Ḥāʾik* as embodying the tradition in an iconic way. The modern anthologies that derive from al-Ḥāʾik and al-Jāmiʿī retain the format of the original and partake of its prestige. The Moroccan Andalusian music, as it is taught and performed today, thus may be regarded as the legacy of more than a millennium of interplay between two channels of transmission, the spoken and the written.

This chapter, and Chapter 8 which follows, explain the persistence of this system in terms of the value theory of tradition developed in Chapter 6. Of particular significance is the social power of the spoken word, which binds speaker and listener in a personal relationship founded upon meaningful action within a social frame, and is therefore value-laden. At the same time, we shall see that literacy and the written word each bear a value load that reflects a distinct kind of social relationship. A focus in this chapter on the meaningful social relations (that is, the values) that attach to the spoken and the written will open the way for the next chapter to explore the values that inform the oral and literate dimensions of the Andalusian music tradition in Morocco today, in order to explain why a mixture of the spoken and the written has proven to be so stable over time.

1. *Channels of transmission: orality and literacy*

The relationship between the spoken word and the written word within any discursive, artistic tradition is quite complex. In the terms of the value theory of tradition, these two channels of communication engage different value sets, which means they embody different kinds of meaningful action in the social frame, a fact which allows them to coexist within a single artistic tradition. But how exactly does this work? By analyzing the way they function within their social context, we can begin to explain the phenomenon of their coexistence. The scholarly discussion on oral and written text provides background for an analytical scheme that can harmonize with the value theory of tradition.

In the second half of the 20th century, literary critics and historians began to study in detail the literary qualities of text produced through these two channels, and to speculate on the cultural characteristics of societies that produce what some have called *oral literature*. Two authors in particular, Jack Goody and Walter Ong, arrived at similar conclusions about what happens to human society under the influence of the written word. In different ways each argued that the emergence of literacy in ancient Greece made possible a new kind of analytical perspective on the world. Both authors maintained that this paved the way for a host of intellectual and cognitive developments that have become associated with the Western intellectual heritage. Though much is problematic about their work, Goody's and Ong's ideas have been very influential.

In 1968, Jack Goody published an essay with Ian Watt entitled "The Consequences of Literacy," in which they argued that much of what is characteristic about Western intellectual thought can be traced back to the spread of literacy in the 6th century BCE, and the subsequent writing down of previously oral material. This activity allowed the Greeks to think critically about their own tradition by revealing inconsistencies and contradictions in the material they received from their forebears. Literacy thus promoted a more skeptical attitude toward the world and laid the foundation for formal logic, and thus for philosophy and science. In later works (1977, 1987), Goody expanded on this idea to suggest that writing introduced humanity to a visual-spatial way of thinking that allows people to explore more complex relationships between ideas, to create elaborate lists and tables of concepts, and in general to think more analytically than had been possible when knowledge was retained in memory only and transmitted only by word of mouth. According to Goody, literacy alters irrevocably the mental world, producing "differences in modes of thought, or reflective capacities, or even cognitive growth."[1]

In his book, *Orality and Literacy: The Technologizing of the Word* (1982), Walter Ong put forward a similar idea: that the appearance of alphabetic literacy represented a fundamental cognitive and cultural shift in human society. He described literacy as a technology that transformed society and culture. Building upon studies of ancient Greek literature by Eric Alfred Havelock (1963) and Milman Parry (1971), Ong insisted upon a radical separation between what are in effect two sociolinguistic matrices, the oral and the written. The textual products of societies untouched by written language (a state he referred to as *orality* or *primary orality*) are qualitatively different from those of literate societies because, he argued, they see the world differently. The introduction of the phonetic alphabet in Greece, he said, represented a fundamental shift from an acoustic mode that is essentially diachronic and frozen in the present moment of meaning to a visual-spatial orientation. This new way of thinking has the potential to be synchronic and therefore is able to objectify language, treating words as things and opening the way for syllogistic logic and the other intellectual developments that characterized the flowering of ancient Greek civilization. Ong maintained that literacy is necessary "for the development not only of science but also history, philosophy, explicative understanding of literature and any art, and indeed for the explanation of language (including oral speech) itself."[2]

According to Ong, because orality is limited to the present moment without importing any outside meaning, discourse in orality relies upon repetition and formulaic phrases to keep the listener focused on the point at hand. These become easily-recognizable building blocks for the narrative. Thus, he wrote,

> Oral folk prefer, especially in formal discourse, not the soldier, but the brave soldier; not the princess, but the beautiful princess; not the oak, but the mighty oak.[3]

Moreover, written text allows "backlooping," or rereading of earlier passages. In contrast, oral style is full of redundancies because the listener must depend upon repetitions to keep fresh the train of thought or argument being put forward.

Despite his protests to the contrary, Ong's argument (and Goody's, as well) seems to lead, directly or indirectly, to certain awkward inferences that were taken up

---

[1] 1977, p. 111.

[2] p. 15

[3] p. 38

by later authors. To some, Ong's book suggests a developmental (perhaps even teleological) model of "civilization" in which the invention of alphabetic literacy as a medium of didactic, narrative and artistic expression leads unavoidably to a more advanced kind of consciousness, that is, the Western mind. He seems to have anticipated the troubling implications of this, for he addressed the question of cultural relativism, stating clearly that neither orality nor literacy is superior, but that "both orality, and the growth of literacy out of orality, are necessary for evolution of consciousness."[4] Nevertheless, this disclaimer does not negate the theory's teleological implications.

Ong's work has become a touchstone in a debate about what differences, if any, exist between discourses produced by people from oral and literate societies, and what these differences might mean.[5] A number of challenges to his ideas have been raised. Here I want to focus on one facet of this discussion, which touches upon our analysis of the Andalusian music tradition: Ong's claims about the distinctive features of orality and literacy and the cultural-psychological gap dividing the two.

2. *Literacy and (partial) orality*

Of course, Ong recognized that speech-oriented culture did not simply vanish with the advent of writing, any more than people stopped talking to each other. Rather his argument concerns the influence of literacy on society as a whole. Hence he suggested a term for the residue of orally-oriented culture surviving within a literate setting: *secondary orality*. Yet with this term he seemed more interested in a new kind of orality that he says is emerging under the influence of electronic media[6] and did not use the concept to analyze in any depth the transition from orality to literacy. Yet if we are to believe his and Goody's assertion that literacy represents a fundamental shift in consciousness and culture, the boundary between the two modes would seem to be of crucial importance; and we might expect some reasonably easy way to determine when literacy has taken over as the dominant mode of discourse. However, both historical and contemporary evidence indicates that this has not in fact been the case.

---

[4] p. 175

[5] In addition to the works mentioned in this chapter, the anthologies by Olson and Torrence (*Literacy and Orality*, 1991), Günther and Ludwig (*Schrift und Schriftlichkeit*, 1994-1996), Brockmeier (*Literales Bewusstsein. Schriftlichkeit und das Verhältnis von Sprache und Kultur*, 1997), and Brockmeier, Wang and Olson (*Literacy, Narrative and Culture*, 2002) present various perspectives on the issues raised by Goody and Ong. Fox-Genovese (1999) revisits the debate with an eye to the question of modernity and literacy. There is also a growing body of literature on orality, literacy and electronic media, much of which looks to Ong (and before him, to Marshall McLuhan) for its initial inspiration.

[6] 1986, Chapter 5.

Various authors have shown in different ways that the emergence of literacy from oral culture is far from a clean break with the past. The chief underlying issue in their responses to Ong is the observation that both literacy and orality are social practices deriving from particular conditions and the needs of particular groups of people. In the words of Peter Roberts, “Literacy has no absolute or final essence.”[7]

Jesse Gellrich (1995) has looked at the oral-literate transition in medieval Europe. In Chapter 1 of his book on the uses of oral and written language, he points out that oral modes of intellectual discourse persisted well into the Middle Ages, long after literacy had taken hold among the educated classes. Moreover, the written word itself became a principal channel of expression for oral discourses.[8] The walls of academe, he says, did not keep out influences from the pre-existing orally-informed culture.

> Rather, the community of the text, or “textual community” as it has been conveniently called, was the result of social and oral habits interacting strongly with the special skills of reading and interpreting manuscripts. Such considerations clearly indicate that literacy no longer signifies a complete and final separation from the “oral tradition” of the past or present.[9]

Indeed, one of the difficulties Gellrich encounters is how and where to draw the line separating the dominance of orality from that of literacy. He says that scholarship on French and English literature of the later Middle Ages reveals that writing was not devoid of oral characteristics. Poets and rhetoricians employed the language of oral presentation, even in their written works. Reading itself was a vocal process, in part because the orthographic conventions of the day were phonetic (and words were not always clearly separated on the page), and in part because the *letter* was regarded as a representation of the *voice*.[10] Thus, what Huot called “the performative quality of the medieval book” was preserved in the themes and layout of documents from the era.[11] Gellrich continues: “Literacy, therefore is a cultural form tied specifically to social experience: it is ‘context-dependent,’ since it is responsible for the development of social patterns.”[12] Moreover, he points out that

---

[7] 1997, 46.

[8] p. 3

[9] p. 4

[10] This idea has had a very long history in Western thought, extending back at least as far as Augustine.

[11] p. 4

[12] p. 6

> medieval materials present us with a *structure* in which writing exists in specific relation to spoken language. It is this structure which prevails, not one valence or the other, speech or script, voice or letter; and it prevails not only in language but in society as well.[13]

For Gellrich, the key factor is not the survival of orality in a "secondary" form, but the ability of language in any form to obscure its own uses as a means to exercise power. Hence he argues that literacy was not consciously pursued as a cultural program, but rather "it was simply the way things were, which is another way of saying that literacy was context-dependent or 'ideological.'"[14] Gellrich thus argues against the notion of "secondary orality" as it has been commonly put forward:

> As a category for explaining the "residue" of oral properties in written language, "secondary orality" presumes that speech gradually loses the high ground to the advent of writing, whereas in medieval sources we have abundant evidence that the struggle is far from over. The practice of oral reading illustrates dramatically the controlling structure of the oral and aural word. Although reading marks the passing into history of a "primary" oralism, it still preserves the vestige of a social context in which communication by word of mouth took precedence. In this sense, a new and relatively autonomous "technology" existed from the beginning within the subordinating context of oral practice. Writing arrives already dependent upon context.[15]

Gellrich summarizes his argument, challenging the idea that literacy arrived and began exercising some kind of hegemonic power:

> My argument is that the power of change arises from the *displacement* inherent in the medieval assimilation of written and oral language. Either channel of communication can be the "voice" of dominion, but it proceeds from neither per se. The power of language consists in its capacity to deny opposition to its own utterance in either channel. Language "has" dominion when it becomes a kind of "domain" or "property" in its own right, held by a special few and protected by the class divisions of society. It has no context other than its own self-assertion. And in

[13] p. 7, emphasis in original.

[14] p. 16

[15] p. 10

> this sense its "property" is its "propriety." Thus the decontextualizing possibility of language in the written channel is a potential threat or antibody in the system of controlling meaning and asserting power. At all costs writing *must* be construed as voice, if the status quo is to continue.[16]

Thus the transition from oral to literate in Europe of the Middle Ages, according to Gellrich, was neither sudden nor effortless. Literacy was tied to social experience and beliefs about language, knowledge, rhetoric, and power. Because it was socially situated, we cannot separate it from the milieu in which it functioned. "Secondary orality" therefore is far more than traces of an old oral order ensconced within literate society, and there is no unproblematic opposition to be found in European history between "oral tradition" and "literate tradition," for the distinction between the two was obscured and displaced for a very long time for social and ideological reasons.

Ruth Finnegan offers a similar critique of the Goody-Ong proposition in *Literacy and Orality: Studies in the Technology of Communication* (1988), by drawing upon more contemporary data. As her title suggests, Finnegan extends the analysis of communication technologies beyond print and electronic media to encompass oral and written "technologies," as well. She argues that careful study of these first information technologies can tell us much about the impact of electronic media in our own day. With respect to orality and literacy, her central aim is to deny the existence of a "Great Divide"[17] between the two. Rather, she says, the history of human social and cultural development is complex and cannot be reduced to transitions between simple binary oppositions.

> The whole concept of opposed pure types of society is in any case now generally subject to criticism in the light of the many detailed studies of 'non-industrial' cultures. Binary typologies may be handy as a starting-off point for theorizing and are still influential, not least because of the continuing reverence within western higher education for the classic nineteenth-century sociological theorists. But the accumulating empirical evidence … demonstrates that the postulated characteristics of each type simply do not always predictably follow … Indeed contrasts among non-industrial cultures themselves are as striking as those between industrial and non-industrial.[18]

---

[16] p. 35, emphasis in original.

[17] pp. 12-14

[18] p. 142

She argues from empirical evidence that literacy is not a necessary condition of certain developments (analytic thinking, scientific skepticism, modernization, democratization), but rather merely is sufficient to allow societies to realize certain kinds of practices. Whether or not these are deployed depends on the culture's history and conditions. For Finnegan, as for Gellrich, the power of literacy depends upon context.

She points to several empirical examples to argue against the Great Divide. The Limba of Sierra Leone are shown in Chapter 3 to have a sense of detachment, inter-referentiality and objectification regarding their own language – precisely the kinds of conceptual skills and perspectives on language which the Great Divide theory claims are not possible in an oral society. Thus

> [T]he distinction commonly made between literate and non-literate societies may not be as clear-cut as is often assumed; and ... some of the specific characteristics of at least one non-literate society may not be as wholly attributable to the fact of their non-literacy as it might seem at first sight.[19]

In Chapter 4 she cites several cases of African oral literature genres that have tropes, allusions, metonymy and so on, which she maintains are just as complex as written literature. Also, she says Fijian poets do not follow the method of spontaneous formulaic oral composition, which Milman Parry argued was characteristic of oral discourses. Rather, they often use prior memorization and rehearsal with the goal of accuracy and fidelity in reproducing earlier versions of the text, an aim which Parry claims is not characteristic of orality. The Fijian example of an oral poetic tradition that is pre-composed undermines Parry's assumption that oral poetry naturally corresponds to spontaneous oral composition. Moreover, evidence from other oral and mixed-oral traditions in the South Pacific (the Maori, Australian aborigines and others) suggests that contact with literacy does not automatically efface oral tradition. Rather, Finnegan notes a complex interplay between the two, in which the writing down of oral literature feeds back into the oral tradition itself. "In the South Pacific, it seems, [oral and literate text] were not (as sometimes supposed) two separate and opposed modes but, both now and in the past, form part of one dynamic in which both written and oral forms interact."[20]

Ultimately, Finnegan argues, the effects of literacy on society depend on the uses to which writing is put and on who has control over the *means* of literate expression (education, writing materials, printing resources, and so on). Literacy can

[19] p. 58

[20] p. 122

indeed produce cognitive and cultural changes, she argues, but not merely as a medium in and of itself. The kinds of schooling and formal training which surround literacy are just as important. In this way, Finnegan emphasizes literacy as a social process that is shaped by the particular history and cultural specifics of the society in question. Literacy is therefore far more than merely a disembodied technology that transforms consciousness and society in predictable ways, as Goody and Ong seem to suggest.

John Miles Foley presents a third critique of the Goody-Ong model from yet another direction. In his introduction to *Oral Tradition in Literature: Interpretation in Context* (1986) Foley argues that, unlike the historical and literary contexts which surround a written text, the context within which we find oral text is necessarily dynamic and shaped by factors that cannot readily be captured on the page (speaker-audience relationships, performance practice, composite authorship of traditional texts, and so on). Hence "the usual notion of context as a set of verifiable authorial facts enabling effective criticism proves largely impertinent to oral and oral-derived works of literature."[21]

In his 1995 article, "The Implications of Oral Tradition," Foley discusses the structures that constitute oral tradition, maintaining that oral tradition depends upon the unexpectedly broad range of domains in which its language produces meaning, a phenomenon Foley calls *traditional referentiality*:

> Traditional referentiality, then, entails the invoking of a context that is enormously larger and more echoic than the text or work itself, that brings the lifeblood of generations of poems and performances to the individual performance or text. Each element in the phraseology or narrative thematics stands not simply for that singular instance but for the plurality and multiformity that are beyond the reach of textualization. From the perspective of traditional context, these elements are foci for signification, still points in the exchange of meaning between an always impinging tradition and the momentary fossilization of a text or version.[22]

He calls this type of signification *metonymic*, suggesting that individual elements of the traditional text stand in some sense for the whole, or for a larger cultural-literary framework or corpus that is "present even in its silence."[23] Foley remarks that what is

[21] p. 8
[22] p. 34
[23] p. 37

immanent in it, what "impinges, as distinguished from what is denoted explicitly",[24] is much greater than the scholar expects. Traditional texts abound in what appear to be stylized or formulaic phrases, and even seemingly innocuous imagery, that bear this metonymic load. These elements are structures that

> far from being mere phraseological and narrative counters that allow the poet to compose easily and without interruption – are *the very cognitive categories that underlie the artistic act*. These forms, in other words, provide nothing less than the foundation on which the aesthetic experience takes shape and the perceptual grid through which it is transmitted. It is not exaggeration to say that the traditional structures enable the aesthetic experience.[25]

While Ong regards such structures as merely mnemonic devices, Foley says these structures derive meaning from the social situation: unless both artist and audience know how to interpret these simple structures for the complex and immanent reality that stands behind them, "the illusion will collapse and the song will be silenced." (44) This does not mean that the referential meaning of the text is irrelevant, that there is no literary logic in using structures of this kind. "But the special magic of traditional metonymy works because there is an agreed-upon relation between structure and meaning, a relation that is, as we have seen, more than literary."[26]

Foley also emphasizes that the referential field of these structures, whether deployed in oral performance or in oral-derived text, is not limited to one line or even one text, but encompasses the entire tradition as a whole. For example, a poem from oral tradition might invoke a figure like "mighty-armed Achilles," but this expression summons Achilles not just in the given context, but also as a stereotyped Achilles in all his "mighty-armed" manifestations. And even more, the figure of Achilles itself becomes a metonym that calls to mind the whole narrative tradition of which it is a part, along with all the cultural associations that attach to the tradition and its performance. This semantic system is similar to fractal geometry: meaningful micro-structural elements reflect and evoke meaning on larger scales. In this situation one cannot speak of a phrase or usage being "first" or "subsequent," since every usage is coexistent with every other. Beyond the "conferred meaning" intended by the author there lies an "inherent meaning," which is both always already present, and yet unique by virtue of its current presence.

---

[24] p. 38

[25] p. 44, emphasis in original.

[26] p. 44

> The linear aspect of the text has only limited importance here, since whatever has a beginning, middle, and end in itself also has a larger identity vis-à-vis the poetic tradition. Traditional elements can no more "repeat themselves" than a much-told traditional tale can be frozen into a uniquely authoritative form … the primary relationship of these occurrences will be to the metonymic meaning each summons, and not to each other. Instead of "repetition," the oral traditional text implies *re-creation*, and it is this mode of signification its audience is asked to share.[27]

This has profound implications for the Goody-Ong model. Both Goody and Ong argue that orality, being acoustic and therefore evanescent, only feebly supports meaning outside the present moment. They maintain that the repetitious and seemingly redundant material characteristic of so many orally-derived texts is due to the need to constantly refresh the audience's memory and help them keep track of the flow of the narrative. Foley would say that this use of formulas, collocations and set phrases also evokes material (and therefore meaning) that exists outside the present moment of performance. Foley's analysis therefore gives far more credit to the memory of the audience and to its power in co-creating the performance. Traditional narrative, according to Foley, may in fact draw upon the contents of the whole tradition (already well known and familiar to the audience) to make present many potential meanings in a variety of domains. It is precisely this impinging of meanings beyond the obvious and present moment that Ong argues is characteristic of *written* text.[28]

Evidence for Foley's traditional metonymy might be inferred from one of the practices of the Egyptian oral epic poets described by Dwight Reynolds in *Heroic Poets, Poetic Heroes*. Reynolds describes how the *sīra* poets of the Nile delta use public performances of the Banī Halāl cycle at times to comment on current events in the community, poke fun at certain individuals, take revenge for wrongs done to them, and so on. Such digressions are inserted into the flow of the performance and are typically composed using language and characterizations drawn from the *sīra* itself. It is thus not difficult to see that part of the power of these asides lies in the way they draw upon the conventions of the *sīra* and thereby invoke the weight of the tradition for the immediate purpose.[29]

Similarly, the organization and linguistic content of *al-Āla* gives the *ṣanāʾiʿ* in the tradition metonymic potential. The language used in many *ṣanāʾiʿ* employs stock phrases, repetitions, redundancy and collocations that closely resemble the formulaic

---

[27] pp. 45-46

[28] 1982, pp. 33-36.

[29] See pp. 190-206.

structures found in oral-derived literature. These are most clearly seen in the context of thematically structured *nawbāt*. Among the eleven *nawbāt* of *al-Āla* are some that embody a single theme reflected in the poetic material comprising the *nūba* (that may also draw from the musicotherapeutic associations of the primary *ṭabʿ*). The two most striking examples are *Nawbat al-Māya* and *Nawbat Ramal al-Māya*. The theme of the former's poetry, sunset, derives from the association of *ṭabʿ al-māya* with that time of day.[30] *Ramal al-Māya* is devoted religious themes, especially to praise of the Prophet Muḥammad (though no specific link is held to exist between this theme and *tabʿ ramal al-Māya*). These (and other *nawbāt* that are less emphatically associated with a single theme) contain numerous elements characteristic of traditional metonymic text as Foley describes it. A few examples from one part of the tradition will illustrate this point.

For those familiar with the tradition from years of hearing and singing the *ṣanāʾiʿ*, singing one *ṣanʿa* or a series of *ṣanāʾiʿ* from *al-Māya*, for example, can evoke the contents of the entire *nūba*, because the imagery and linguistic formulas in this *nūba* all focus on sunset reveries, and there is a great deal of overlap and repetition of phrases in various contexts among the *ṣanāʾiʿ*. For example, the phrase شمسُ العشيّة ("the evening sun") is very common in the *nūba*, as is the semantically equivalent شمسُ الغروب ("the westering sun"). A quick glance through *al-Māya* as it is found in *Min waḥy al-rabāb* reveals that, of the 13 *ṣanāʾiʿ* in Mīzān Basīṭ al-Māya, three of them contain the formula شمسُ العشيّة and a fourth contains the formula شمسُ الغروب. Two other *ṣanāʾiʿ* have the word عشيّة ("evening") placed prominently at the beginning of the *ṣanʿa*. Thus nearly half of the *ṣanāʾiʿ* in this *mīzān* not only evoke the image of sunset, but do it in very specific language. Similar numbers obtain for these formulas in the other *mayāzīn* in *al-Māya*. No performance of this *nūba* can avoid deploying these formulas. Audience members hearing a performance of Basīṭ al-Māya will instantly recognize the *nūba* and its thematic content, and so a given *ṣanʿa* can bear a metonymic load, that is, it will have the potential to call to mind the whole of the *nūba* as a thematic-aesthetic unity.

These critiques of the Goody-Ong hypothesis converge on two useful observations. One is that orality and literacy are far from being bounded and mutually exclusive states. Rather, emergent literacy tends to partake of the existing social forms of orality. There would seem to be no other possibility, since the social forms of literacy must be created from some raw material; there must be some familiar context through which people can assimilate the new technology. The path of least resistance is simply to incorporate literacy as an improvement upon existing discourses on language, rather than as a revolutionary departure from what is known and accepted as the norm. Thus literacy, in cultural terms, does not appear to be a clear break from the past, though it

---

30 See Appendix 1.

may appear so millennia later when the literate versions of oral materials are examined out of context.

For this reason, the term *secondary orality* does not satisfactorily describe the interpenetration of the oral with the literate in the Andalusian music tradition. In its original formulation, the expression suggests a state where the oral persists merely as a residue within literate discourses, interesting perhaps, but subordinate in the end to the literate dimension. To avoid this implication, the expression *mixed orality* will be used here, because it allows that the oral component of the tradition may coexist on a more or less equal footing with the literate dimension.

A more important lesson to be drawn from the debate over the Goody-Ong hypothesis is that both orality and literacy are culturally constituted. We cannot understand either one isolated from the social relations in which it functions. Because we live within a discursive world saturated with books, newspapers and periodicals, government handbooks, instruction manuals, web pages and tweets, and because one particular mode of literate praxis has come to predominate in the developed world, we tend to assume that the cultural form of literacy we are accustomed to is universal and value-neutral. Rarely do we reflect upon the cultural-historical specifics of our brand of literacy, nor do we consider that other models of literacy are possible, being socially constructed according to locally valued action in context.

3. *Value in writing and speaking*

> When the receptor of tradition is the eye rather than the ear, a greater emotional distance from the tradition seems to be the rule.[31]

Here Gross has put his finger on the salient difference between the oral and written channels. The key feature of the spoken word is that it is performed: "real time" speech takes place in a more or less direct encounter between speaker and audience. As a result, the spoken word has the potential to unite both participants in a dynamic interaction that is mutually created and invokes the tacit social rules that govern such interactions. Of course, all forms of communication of course place the participants in some relationship to one another. Spoken interaction involves a two-way, ongoing negotiation governed by norms associated in that society with the particular context. Such norms may prescribe appropriate demeanor (to smile or not to smile, to maintain eye contact or not, etc.), appropriate posture and dress, appropriate forms of response (applause, verbal encouragement, minimal verbal response, respectful silence), and so on. In general, the relationship that obtains in direct oral communication is personal in

[31] Gross 1992, pp. 15-16.

a way that written communication cannot be. Traditions that rely to one degree or another upon the oral channel – including musical and literary traditions – thus benefit from the deeply rooted appeal of direct human interaction. In short, the spoken word by its very nature draws upon different values from the written word because it involves very different kinds of social behavior and interaction.[32]

Several authors, including Ong,[33] have noted that the written channel tends to distance the participants from each other and from the language that moves between them. Since the reader is removed from direct contact with the author, he or she can engage with the text as if it were detached from the author. At the same time, writing makes possible a discourse "which cannot be directly questioned or contested as oral speech can be because written discourse is detached from the writer."[34] Furthermore the reader receives the text in a moment removed from that of its creation, while the author receives feedback from the reader in a moment separated from the act of writing. Generally speaking, literacy tends to de-emphasize immediacy in favor of reflection, and systems of value associated with the written channel tend to emphasize the *ideal* rather than the *personal*.

The distance between author and reader also allows for the existence of two imaginary, idealized relationships mediated only by the words on the page and the ideas they contain, without reference to any other shared experience. Curiously, the reader may develop a "relationship" via the written channel with the author's literate and mental faculties alone, as they are represented on the page, and yet may know absolutely nothing else about her or him. For the same reason, the author writes but may have no idea at all that any given reader even exists. They are reciprocal yet unconnected relationships. At the same time, this distance lends authority or weight to the author's words through a sense of permanence deriving from the stability and objectifying power of the printed page: the reader may return repeatedly to the author's "pristine" words; they are reliable, substantial, dependable, in ways that speech is not. Finally, each reader's relationship to the author is typically formed from the individual's own meeting with the text that stands between them, without a larger social context framing that relationship, and so the relationships formed through the written channel alone, without a parallel oral component, tend to remain individualistic.

Of course, this is an oversimplification. In reality, the distance described here is

---

[32] We are dealing here with conversation, lecture and similar kinds of oral interaction. Other forms of spoken-word communication, such as recorded music or radio broadcasts, share most characteristics with written text – Ong's secondary orality.

[33] 1982, Chapter 4.

[34] p. 78

mitigated by the fact that both the reader and the text are suffused with social contexts, whether the reader be a fan of popular fiction drawn to the latest best seller because "everyone is reading it," or a student digesting (and later discussing) an assigned reading for a course. A newspaper article implies a readership that shares a direct interest in the subject; a billboard in Times Square presents information every day to the thousands of people who pass by. Yet the reader shares the experience not with the author (which would be analogous to a real-time conversation or lecture) but with others who have read the same text. So the social relations within this "community of the text," are of a particularly distant quality insofar as they do not partake of the spoken word. When speech enters the community of the text (when readers talk about what they have read), it engenders its own relations parallel to those emerging from the encounter with the text alone.

The oral channel emphasizes a complementary system of values. The spoken word tends to de-emphasize the *ideal* in favor of the *personal*, offering an immediate, common experience that embraces the speaker(s) and all the listeners present. The status of the speaker results from an ongoing negotiation between speaker and audience, a negotiation which the written word tends to replace with a gesture that is completely invisible to the author and beyond his or her reach: either the reader reads or not. (In the modern context, this tends to drift towards commodification: the status of the author depends upon her or his access to a readership, whose value is often expressed in economic terms.[35]) The listener's attention and response are required to sustain an oral interaction, and the context in which the interaction takes place represents part of the tacit agreement between speaker and listener. Moreover, since speaker and listener are connected by a shared experience, their relationship incorporates an array of information beyond the discourse itself. Some of it is personal, because speaker and listener encounter one another as people. Some information is highly mutable, unlike ideas fixed on a page, for speech varies and adapts itself according to social conditions in ways that written text cannot. This situates speech within entirely different kinds of social relations from those of written text. The speaker's authority therefore draws upon valued acts associated with the speaker personally and the context of the communication, and lacks the special authorizing power of written text.

Conversely, the relationship of author to reader is more stable and less dynamically negotiated. Both channels are mediated by culturally-informed beliefs, but literacy is mediated especially by beliefs about the nature of the written word and

[35] Reams have been written from Marxian perspectives about the commodification of society. The idea appeared briefly in Chapter 3 §4.4, in the discussion of the economics surrounding al-Āla today. Economic value was of course related to other forms of value in Chapter 6.

authorship. For literate folk, the written word can have tremendous, even magical power. Not only the content, but even the form in which it is presented can be tied to deeply-resonant beliefs, hence the preoccupation of some very religious folk with the holy book as sacred object.[36] We shall see in Chapter 8 that for many literate Arabs, the format of poetry carries substantial social value.

Viewed from the perspective of the value theory of tradition, the two channels of discourse invoke *separate but complementary kinds of social value.* Spoken-word interactions have a distinctive power to bind speaker and listener, engaging those aspects of comportment and attitude that are valued and meaningful in the cultural context. For example certain actions and manners are considered important for a music teacher, and manifesting them facilitates the teaching process by establishing an appropriate relationship between teacher and student. The necessity of manifesting these behaviors, and not others, is part of the value system informing the student-teacher relationship. These valued elements are combined with the values embodied in the behaviors assigned to the student, as well as in the norms governing the interaction; and all these dimensions of meaningful interaction are elements of the larger system of values. The personal, face-to-face character of oral interaction allows the specific conditions surrounding it to be constantly renegotiated (or acquiesced to) by the participants. These dynamic qualities make orality appealing and powerful. And they allow mixed orality to persist despite the simultaneous operation of literate processes (the use of reference books like *Min waḥy ar-rabāb*, the taking of notes on the text and its *tarāṭīn*, and so on), which involve other, less personal kinds of values to be enacted.

Applying the value theory of tradition to mixed orality thus addresses Jack Goody's puzzlement at the persistence of orality and memorization within a highly literate community and tradition. Speaking of the oral law in Judaism (the Mishna), he finds it

> strange … that at the very period in time when literacy made it possible to minimize memory storage, human society adopted the opposite track, at least in some contexts. As the editor of one published edition of the Mishna writes, "It is a point of curious interest to the modern mind that the great mass of knowledge and opinion … was retained in the schools for the most part, perhaps entirely, without the aid of writing. It was transmitted by

[36] This is institutionalized among Sikhs, who exalt the *Guru Granth*, but many Jews, Christians and Muslims practice ritualized devotion to their holy books, as well.

> memory alone, through the process of oral repetition, whence indeed came the title 'Oral Tradition.'"[37]

What seems so strange to Goody is easily explained by the value theory of tradition: oral teaching and oral argumentation have represented meaningful action within the community of Jewish legal scholars for many centuries. The presence of an oral mode of legal tradition, parallel with the Mikra (the written law), preserves certain kinds of social relations that arise from the performative aspect of orality and not from written discourse, and that have long been highly valued among legal scholars in the Judaic tradition. When we recognize that both the oral and the written are socially situated and serve complementary value sets, the paradox inherent in Goody's decontextualized analysis disappears.[38]

Ironically, part of the durability of oral tradition derives also from the malleability of its contents within the social context. Since the only resources for any rendition of a fully oral tradition are the memories of those who practice it, there is room for the tradition to expand or contract or change from within in any number of ways in different historical moments. Changes of this kind are comparatively easy to accommodate, as long as the tradition as a whole continues to resonate within the social context that surrounds it, because not all the details of the tradition are essential for its authenticity. What matters in the long run is that any given rendition is *locally* recognizable as traditional. Thus, a certain amount of variation from region to region is acceptable and to be expected within the confines of the tradition. The diversity of the Andalusian music communities uncovered by our study of the *al-Āla* manuscripts in Chapter 5 is therefore not surprising at all, since they existed wholly or largely as orally-preserved material that only emerged into the anthologies relatively late.

Written tradition, however, has other qualities. When tradition is committed to writing, transmission can be more precise, thorough and stable over time, but at the expense of immediacy and the emotional commitment that arises from it. Because writing tends to objectify text, tradition becomes more available to close, critical scrutiny in an abstract form. Its strength is its stability and *in*flexibility: the authenticity of each rendition can be tested by comparison with a known model. Change and adaptability within a literate tradition must derive from reinterpretation or direct augmentation of the contents from *outside* the text itself, as it were.[39]

---

[37] Goody (2000, p. 33) is quoting here W.A.L. Edwards (1911) *The Mishna on Idolatry 'Aboda Zara*. Cambridge: Cambridge University Press, p. xvi.

[38] Schoeler (1989a) treats the mixed-oral qualities of both the Torah and *ḥadīṯ* literature. See also Chapter 8.

[39] Moreover, the canonical text may acquire a certain prestige, sometimes even for those who cannot

The foregoing discussion leads to the idea that the two channels, oral and written, are fundamentally different and yet complementary when understood as cultural processes. Any tradition that exploits the middle ground, mixed orality, must navigate between the disparate demands of the two channels. Those who partake of the tradition naturally subscribe to the values embodied in each channel, and so as long as the contents of the tradition continue to resonate with (i.e., can be interpreted as speaking to) valued relationships in the society, both channels will reinforce the tradition's place in the cultural context. This is an organic process, shaped by and immersed in historical conditions, that evolves over time, not a fixed program consciously conceived and elaborated.

The performative characteristic of the spoken word is crucial to its power as a channel of transmission: its dynamism and affective impact point to a systematic explanation of its importance to and persistence within the tradition. The stability and authoritativeness of the written word engages other values within the cultural context. Within the different and complementary character of the two channels lies an explanation for how the two have coexisted historically in the Moroccan Andalusian music tradition.

---

read it themselves. The *Kunnāš al-Ḥāʾik* has this kind of prestige. Literacy sufficient for classical Arabic and Andalusi vernacular Arabic found in this anthology is not available to everyone in Morocco, yet this does not prevent the canonical texts from exercising considerable influence within the bounds of the tradition. There is no more definite way of asserting the authenticity of a given *ṣanʿa* than to say, "It's in al-Ḥāʾik." No further comment is needed. This point will be taken up in Chapter 8.

At the same time, in the situation of mixed orality, where oral processes coexist and complement written ones, it may still be possible for oral-style change to creep into the text. These may even be preserved in canonical versions of the text, if a particular written "capture" of the text takes place in an historical moment close enough to the point at which the written text takes on foundational or canonical status. This was the case with the *Āla* tradition, especially with the *barwala*, a subject dealt with at length in Pen, Voice, Text.

Chapter 8
The Moroccan Andalusian Music as Tradition, Talk and Text

1. *The dependence of al-Āla on oral processes*

From the earliest phase of its history, the musical tradition of al-Andalus, including its descendant, *al-Āla*, has lain at the intersection of two modes of communication: the oral and the written. Writing has served mainly to capture song texts in the form of poetry. Since the earliest glimpses we have of it (Ibn al-Quṭiyya's *Taʾrīḫ iftitāḥ al-Andalus* and Ibn ʿAbd Rabbih's *al-ʿIqd al-farīd*), the textual contents of this musical heritage have appeared on the page as lines of verse, many of them traceable today to well-known poets. The oral dimension, however, has played a different and perhaps more significant role. Quite apart from the fact of oral presentation inherent in any song form, the music was composed and taught using oral methods and has continued in this fashion throughout its long history.

Beyond the historical evidence, however, lies the fundamental fact that these musicians and composers made no effective use of musical notation, a situation that held true in North Africa until the colonial period, and by and large remains true to this day in Morocco with respect to *al-Āla*. Examples of notation systems did appear in the Abbasid period. The Middle Eastern polymaths Yaʿqūb b. Isḥāq al-Kindī (d. after 256/870) and Abū Naṣr Muḥammad al-Fārābī (d. 339/950) each developed a system for describing melodic modes; and in the *Kitāb al-Aġānī*, Abū l-Faraj al-Iṣfahānī included verbal descriptions of the musical meter and a kind of tablature that expressed notes in terms of *ʿūd* fingerings for the songs he presented. More than eight centuries later, some manuscripts of *Kunnāš al-Ḥāʾik* offer similar instructions for *īqāʿāt* and *ṭubūʿ* in that anthology. Although none of these methods served to represent melodies conveniently, such was, by and large, the state of music writing in the Arabic-speaking world until the adoption of Western-style notation during the colonial era. Even though the verbal contents of the music had been written down, and some composers may have kept notes that described the music of their compositions, for practical purposes music teaching and performance remained dependent upon rote memorization via oral methods.

Only in the 20th century, and chiefly in the last twenty-five years, have sustained attempts been made to transcribe the melodic content of *al-Āla*. However ʿAbd al-Fattāḥ Benmūsā pointed out the serious limitations of such efforts to date. One problem, he maintains, is that each type of instrument in the *jawq* plays the melody slightly differently. The available transcriptions provide only an outline of the melody, and individual instrumentalists then must interpret the musical script according to the conventions of their instruments. So even though rhythms and articulations appear on the page, a musician not already versed in the tradition cannot simply pick up a score and play the music of *al-Āla* without someone at hand to explain how the notations should be interpreted on the instrument. More important in Benmūsā's view is the fact that none of the transcriptions available today adequately represents the changing nuances of the melody at different points in a *ṣanʿa*. Each musical phrase of a *ṣanʿa* is repeated, often several times, sometimes with accompanying text and sometimes by instruments alone. As the text changes, the melody changes slightly, as well, but none of these subtle variations is captured by existing transcriptions. At best, the available musical transcriptions of *al-Āla* can serve only as supplementary material. They cannot replace oral transmission entirely, because the musician learning the tradition requires a knowledgeable instructor to explain how the melody should be played in order to match the text at each stage of the *ṣanʿa*. Given the often complex repetitions and sometimes counterintuitive division of words and phrases in the melodies of many *ṣanāʾiʿ*, this is no small limitation.[1]

The discussion in Chapter 4 of the teaching methods at the National Conservatory showed that written versions of the song texts present analogous problems. From the earliest known collection of *al-Āla* material, al-Būʿaṣāmī's (d. 1151/1738?) scholarly anthology, *Iqād aš-šumūʿ li-laḏḏat al-masmūʿ bi-naġamāt aṭ-ṭubūʿ*, through *Kunnāš al-Ḥāʾik* to the al-Jāmiʿī corpus and the modern anthologies, the textual contents of *al-Āla* have always been represented using the conventions of poetry. Existing anthologies provide only the basic text of each *ṣanʿa*, leaving out repetitions, line and word breaks, phrasing and *tarāṭīn*. They function, not as songbooks in the Western sense, but as collections of poetry that present *al-Āla* as a literary tradition. As a result, the written word has contributed to *al-Āla*'s preservation in part through its stabilizing effect on the text, but also because the particular conventions of representing poetry on the page situate *al-Āla* in the prestigious domain of literature. The survival of *al-Āla* in written form is therefore not difficult to understand, but the pen has conserved only an incomplete image of it that serves the musician but poorly.

Perhaps more difficult to explain is why the oral mode of transmission has continued to thrive despite the potential for written intervention. Unlike some other literate contexts such as western Europe, where written music and written texts have become standard tools for teaching and performance, writing has not completely

[1] Interview, 1/26/2005. Benmūsā is now working on a transcription of part of *Nawbat al-Iṣbahān* that painstakingly represents melodies exactly as they are played by the *kamān*, with the corresponding variations matched to the text, just as would be the case in a Western score. Of course, the project faces the fundamental diffuculty that Arabic and Western musical notation are written in opposite directions.

displaced orality as the principal mode of preservation and transmission of *al-Āla*. At first glance two plausible answers suggest themselves, but both prove to be incomplete on closer examination.

One would be that the lack of musical transcription methods contributed to the survival of orality, since it forced musicians and composers to rely on rote memorization. However the absence of an effective means for transcribing music really only begs the larger question: Why did neither the Andalusis nor the North Africans ever create a practical method of preserving music precisely in writing? In the Middle East, al-Kindī's system used letters of the Arabic alphabet to represent the notes of musical modes.[2] Sawa (1989) points out that al-Fārābī created a relatively accurate system of musical notation, based upon concepts and terms borrowed from grammar, prosody, arithmetic and geometry.[3] Surprisingly, al-Iṣfahānī refers to what appears to be a precise method of musical notation: on two occasions the singer-composer Isḥāq al-Mawṣilī *wrote* (meaning, apparently, *sent*) a song to his rival, Ibrāhīm b. al-Mahdī, who the *Aġānī* says performed the song just as Isḥāq created it.[4] Yet, few if any musicians ever adopted these notation methods for practical use, whether in the Middle East, al-Andalus or North Africa.

Sawa argues that this was because they were regarded as theoretical tools and therefore beyond the ken of most musicians and composers. A view in hindsight from the 21st century suggests two other reasons they never achieved wide acceptance. These systems were *verbal* descriptions (not *graphic* representations, as is the case with Western-style notation, for example). As such, they were rather complicated, demanding both the ability to read and careful study, in order to bring forth each musical phrase note-by-note. Thus they were not well suited for efficiently matching song text to melody, nor for rendering a song quickly without rehearsal. For these purposes, oral rendition and recourse to memory were more efficient. Moreover, for reasons that will be discussed below, the intrusion of written music into the master-student system would have represented a rupture of the social and economic relations that underlay the production of music in Morocco until well into the 20th century.

Another reason for the survival of orality in *al-Āla* could be that Moroccan musicians agree that the "best" method of learning *al-Āla* is through oral-rote memorization. Yet why should the preference for oral teaching by itself preclude

---

[2] It appears in his *Risāla fī l-luḥūn…*, Baghdad: 1965, p. 31.

[3] p. 255.

[4] كتب إلى إبراهيم بن المهدي بجنس صوت صنعه ومجراه وإجراء لحنه ، فغناه إبراهيم من غير أن يسمعه

"He wrote to Ibrāhīm b. al-Mahdī a type of song which he composed, and its fingering, its (rhythmic) movement and the progression of its melody. Ibrāhīm sang it without ever having heard it..." *Kitāb al-Aġānī*, Cairo: 1927, v. 10 p. 105. The other instance occurs in the same volume, p. 110.

precise written preservation of the music and texts as they are actually performed? The analogy typically drawn between oral-rote memorization of *al-Āla* and rote memorization of the Qurʾān by the same method illustrates well the problem with this explanation. True, both traditions attribute a certain emotional effect to the process of oral-rote memorization, and this has become part of the cultural ethos surrounding each. Yet both traditions also exist as written texts. Memorizing the Qurʾān in no way interferes with recourse to its written form during recitation, and indeed, this recourse is expected in the learning process. Why would the same not be true for *al-Āla*?

The difference lies in the differing values associated with the oral and written renditions in each tradition. In the case of Qurʾānic recitation, the written version is regarded as authoritative and sacrosanct, the pattern from which the oral rendition derives and against which it is always compared. Value therefore attaches to beautiful performance that adheres strictly to the text in the minutest detail. With *al-Āla*, on the other hand, the written version is not sacrosanct, and the text-as-sung *is* the model. Instead, value attaches to the performance alone, with little or no regard for minute attention to the written version, because different values animate its production and use.

A satisfying explanation for the persistence of mixed orality in the Moroccan Andalusian music must take into account the culturally constructed nature of the two channels and therefore the social context of the musical tradition itself. The solution lies in the differing and complementary ways that orality and literacy are valued. The present chapter aims to shed some light on the values that inform orality and literacy in the *Āla* tradition and to describe their social implications. It begins with the role played historically by mixed orality in Arabic literary life, which has contributed to the social value attaching to mixed orality in *al-Āla,* for the mixed-oral character of medieval Arabic letters provides the cultural model and social ethos which helps to validate the persistence of mixed orality in the modern Moroccan Andalusian music tradition.

2. *The oral and the written in Arabic literary history*

In the two centuries prior to Muḥammad, the Arabs created a substantial body of oral compositions, both prose and poetry, that were performed orally and constituted a significant part of the matrix from which the language of both the Qurʾān and the classical Arabic literary tradition of the Middle Ages evolved. None of these works survives in its original form, for the literate society that evolved after the advent of Islam transformed them. Yet from these roots the Islamic era also inherited a significant oral dimension that continued to influence literate processes.

By Muḥammad's time the urban areas of Western Arabia (Mecca and Medina) had been touched by the written word, as writing was in use for many practical purposes. The movement from primary to mixed orality was already well underway. Eventually Muslim literary scholars and historians collected and preserved the pre-Islamic oral heritage, though the collections of pre-Islamic poetry and tribal narratives that have survived bear the marks of written recension and editing by later Arab Muslim writers. Of interest here, however, is the extent to which oral processes continued to influence literature, especially poetry. The issues inherent in the imbrication of oral and written processes can be seen in the Arabic lexicon itself, in the later Islamic community's accounts of the first efforts to codify the Qur'ān, and in the role of orality in the preservation and transmission of poetry and scholarly literature.

2.1. *Lexical indications: "reading" and "reciting"*

From the earliest lexicographical indications, it is evident that *reading* and *reciting* were not clearly distinct activities in formal Arabic discourses. Two Classical Arabic verbs commonly are rendered in English as *to read*. One, تلا , carries the basic meaning of *to follow*, both in the sense of *to come after* and *to imitate*. This suggests *reading* as an act of following directions on a page, but dictionary examples for this verb do not indicate whether this is a private or a public act, that is, whether *recitation* as such is meant.[5] The more typical verb for the act of reading is قرأ , which certainly carried both meanings, as can be seen from various dictionary examples.

The entry for قرأ in *Lisān al-ʿArab* of Abū Faḍl b. Manṣūr (630/1232-711/1311) cites both "Abū Isḥāq an-Naḥawī"[6] and Majd ad-Dīn Ibn al-Athīr (543/1149-605/1209), defining قرأ as *to collect, gather* (جَمَعَ), and the verbal noun القرآن as meaning الجمْع (that is, *collection*) by which Abū Isḥāq meant that the holy book of Islam is the collection or anthology of the chapters (*suwar*, s. *sūra*) of the Revelation (to which Ibn al-Athīr adds: stories – *qiṣaṣ*, s. *qiṣṣa*; command – *amr*; prohibition – *nahy*; promise – *waʿd*; warning – *waʿīd*; and verses or signs – *āyāt*; s. *āya*). Abū Isḥāq goes on to give a second meaning in this context:

ومعنى قرأتُ القرآن : لفظت به جموعاً أي ألقيته

> The meaning of *qara'tu l-Qur'ān* is: *I spoke it altogether* (*without interruption*), that is, *I recited it*.

[5] See, for example, Lane's entry for تلا in his Arabic-English Lexicon, in which he summarizes the Arabic lexicographers Abū Manṣūr al-Azharī (282/896-371/982), Ibn Ḥammād al-Jawharī (d. 393/1007-8), and Abū aṭ-Ṭāhir al-Fīrūzābādī (d. 817/1415).

[6] This is Abū Isḥāq az-Zajjāj, the Baghdadi grammarian (*naḥawī*), who died in either 311/923 or 316/928.

Thus, according to Ibn Manṣūr's sources قرأ meant both to *collect* and to *recite* something aloud.[7]

Similarly, William Lane in his *Lexicon* cites *aṣ-Ṣiḥāḥ* of Ismāʿīl b. Ḥammād al-Jawharī (d. 393/1007-8), *al-ʿUbāb az-zāḫir wa al-lubāb al-fāḫir* of Raḍī ad-Dīn al-Ḥasan b. Muḥammad al-Qurašī aṣ-Ṣaġānī (d. 650/1252), *al-Qāmūs al-muḥīṭ* of Abū ṭ-Ṭāhir al-Fīrūzābādī (d. 817/1415) and the *Tāj al-ʿarūs* of Murtaḍā az-Zabīdī (1145/1732 or 3 - 1205/1791) defining the word first as meaning *to collect*. He then goes on to give the word in this context:

قرأ الكتابَ

According to Lane *al-Qāmūs* renders this sentence: *He read* [*the book,* or *Scripture*] or *recited* [*it*]. Then he cites *al-ʿUbāb*, which attributes the following gloss to Quṭrub[8]:

> *he read* or *recited* the Scripture *chanting* ... then, *he read*, or *recited*, anything *in any manner*, without, or from, or in, a book.

For the second definition, Lane's earlier source dates only to the first half of the 7th/13th century, a little bit later than Ibn al-Athīr. Nevertheless Lane shows that by that time, if not before, a gloss was attributed to Quṭrub (d. early 3rd/9th century) wherein the meaning of the verb قرأ did not necessarily reflect a separation between *reading* and *recitation*.

So these two concepts, which today we assume refer to distinct activities, were not clearly distinguished in medieval Arabic usage. If the absence of this boundary seems strange today, perhaps it becomes more understandable if we take into account the complicated relationship between the Arabic writing system and the spoken language.

A form of script recognizable as Arabic existed as early as the first half of the 4th century CE (derived from a cursive Nabataean form of Aramaic[9]), but it was scarcely a complete system. Though the present system of paired consonants distinguished by diacritical marks is quite old, probably only the *rasm*, or unmarked consonantal form,

---

[7] These various meanings are found in the Qurʾān. For تلا as to read/recite, see: 2.129, 151, 252; 3.58; 13.108; et al. For قرأ as to collect, see 17.14, 93; et al. For قرأ as to read/recite see: 16.98; 17.45; 75.18; 96.1, 3; et al.

[8] Quṭrub ("werewolf") was the nickname of Abū ʿAlī Muḥammad b. al-Mustanīr (d. 206/821) allegedly given him by his master, the great grammarian Sībawayh (d. 177/794). He was from Basra and was famous as a grammarian and lexicographer. See the article "Ḳuṭrub" by G. Troupeau (1986) in the *Encyclopaedia of Islam, New Edition*, v. V p. 567.

[9] See: Gruendler (1993).

was commonly used in the pre-Islamic era, even when important works such as contracts or famous poems were written down. If similar consonants were distinguished from one another, it was chiefly to avoid ambiguity. An early system of short vowel markers is attributed to Abū l-Aswad ad-Duʾalī (d. 69/688?), and at least one example of a fully-marked Qurʾān has survived from this time. But it is unclear how widely used this system was, and a fully developed form of the written language (including vowel signs, *tanwīn* and *tašdīd*) came later, commonly ascribed to al-Ḫalīl b. Aḥmad (d. 194/791) in early-Abbasid times. This suggests that for nearly two centuries after Muḥammad the written text was most readily understood when read aloud, and that writing was chiefly intended as a way to capture the spoken and/or memorized word on the page.

Certainly over time the written word in Arabic came to have a life of its own. Yet its roots lay in a system of signs that preserved traces of its original function as representing speech, and the lexical items relating to its use did not definitively separate it from the spoken word. This is consistent with what we understand from Gellrich of the emergence and incorporation of literacy as a cultural form in medieval Europe, since it implies that literacy emerged in the Arabic-speaking world, not as a unique and original technology, but implicated within existing oral processes.

2.2. *Orality and the Qurʾān*

The divine revelation came to Muḥammad as an oral-spoken phenomenon, a recited message, and he delivered it to a quasi-literate, mixed-oral society which recognized writing primarily as a practical tool. The early Islamic community placed great emphasis on rote memorization and oral presentation of the Qurʾān, quite apart from preserving the text in written form. However, the limitations inherent in having an orally-preserved scripture had to be confronted at some point if a revealed religion, explicitly dependent upon the Word, were to stand. The canonical collections of *ḥadīṯ*, compiled in the first half of the 3rd century of the Hijra, reflect the community coming to terms with this problem.

As long as the Prophet was alive, the young community had a reference for the text of the revelation, so that memorization could be valorized at the expense of the written word. With the passing of the Prophet in 10/632, the community lost its authoritative source for the revelation. If the traditional accounts are to be believed, what remained was a handful of partial written examples of revealed text (perhaps amounting to a single codex of the Qurʾān) and the (albeit skilled) collective memory of the community. The nature of these written exemplars and their practical use have been the subject of some conjecture by modern scholars, but the received body of traditions on the subject (and indeed, the compilation effort itself) reflects a awareness within the

Islamic community that the spoken word alone was insufficient. The oral-performative ethos that characterized the first decades of Islam eventually collided with the perceived need for a uniform scripture that could bind Muslims together in the far-flung corners of a rapidly expanding empire.

The standard *ḥadīṯ* collections present a two-part story concerning the original effort to compile the complete revelation into a standard written form. In the earlier phase the first caliph, Abū Bakr (d. 12/634), is informed that a number of leading *qurrā'* (s. *qāri'*: "reader, reciter") have been killed in the battle of Yamāma, and so ʿUmar b. al-Ḫaṭṭāb (d. 22/644) urges him to compile the written portions of the Qurʾān into a codex. The caliph worries about doing "what the Prophet of Allāh himself did not do." But he is persuaded to ask Zayd b. Ṯābit (d. ca. 37/660), whom the Prophet had called upon to write down some parts of the revelation, to find all the various pieces that had been committed to writing and collect them. The resulting compilation was used only by Abū Bakr, apparently, and was passed on to ʿUmar and then to ʿUmar's daughter, Ḥafṣa (one of the Prophet's widows, d. 45/665).[10] This story concerns itself with the possibility that some portion of the revelation would be lost, and the remedy is considered to be a written text for the caliph's use. This *ḥadīṯ* thus appears to be about the fragile nature of memory in an orally-based tradition.

Later, according to the *aḥādīṯ*, the third caliph, ʿUthmān, is told that soldiers from Syria and Iraq are arguing over differences in Qurʾānic recitation. Ibn Ṯābit is called upon once again, this time to head a commission that transforms the pages of Ḥafṣa's codex into an official version of the book. The commissioners are told that, where they find problems with the text they cannot resolve, they are to use the "tongue of the Qurayš" because the Qurʾān was held (by the transmitter – or inventor – of this *ḥadīṯ*, at least) to have been revealed in that dialect. A codex is prepared, copies are made and distributed to distant centers of the empire, and other written versions of the Qurʾān are destroyed.[11] This story concerns divergent versions of the text, another potential problem with oral transmission from memory.

The orthodox Islamic view is that these stories represent clear statements of historical fact. However they are problematic in several respects, and modern scholarship by W. Montgomery Watt (1977), John Burton (1977), John Wansbrough (1977) and others suggests that they belong to a later period in Islamic history. Burton and Wansbrough have argued, for different reasons, that Muḥammad already had some sort of codex of the Qurʾān before the project to prepare an "official" version was undertaken, and that he was excluded from the collection process as related in the

[10] *Ṣaḥīḥ al-Buḫārī*, Book 61 nos. 509 and 511.

[11] *Ṣaḥīḥ al-Buḫārī*, Book 61 no. 510.

aḥādīṯ in response to issues that emerged much later.[12] Regardless of when these accounts originated, they do reveal the early Islamic community wrestling with the value and authoritativeness assigned to oral rendition of the Qur᾿ān, on one hand, and a recognition of the fundamental problems involved with reliance on orality in a rapidly expanding and diversifying religious culture on the other.

Probably, the process of establishing and disseminating an authoritative text was not nearly so smooth and convenient as the *ḥadīṯ* accounts suggest. One indication of this is that the accounts themselves appear today as constructed using literary devices and tropes. For example, in both *aḥādīṯ*, the caliph repeats his reservations about doing "what the Prophet himself did not do" three times before finally being persuaded to take action. Likewise, Ibn Ṯābit also expresses qualms in triplicate. This ritualized triple-assertion appears in many contexts in *ḥadīṯ* and other literature. It may represent standard discursive practice of the time, or it may be evidence of the storyteller's art. Moreover, Albrecht Noth (1994) has identified the topos of "central command" as a theme that runs through much Arabic historiography of the 2nd/8th and 3rd/9th centuries, precisely the era in which the authoritative *ḥadīṯ* collections emerged. It is evident that the problem of central authority was at issue in historical and religious discourses of the day, so we should reserve judgment as to the caliph's ability to enforce his will on an issue as contentious as standardizing the holy book of Islam.

Most tellingly, the difficulties inherent in producing a univocal Qur᾿ān using the Arabic script of the period by themselves would seem to argue against the idea of an early authoritative codex. Not a few variations are to be found among codices of the Qur᾿ān dating through the early 4th/10th century, quite some time after the question of divergent readings of these texts had arisen. There was considerable resistance in centers like Kūfa, which had developed a rich tradition of Qur᾿ānic recitation/reading of its own, to imposition of a single written version that could call into question the authenticity of local practice. The wider adoption of more accurate writing conventions contributed to solving such problems, as did the recognition of a handful of local

---

12 Burton argues that the emergence of the legal science of *fiqh* led to a debate over abrogation (*nasḫ*), which forced jurists of the 3rd Islamic century to invent traditions that placed the collection project in the era of the Rāšidūn Caliphs (see esp. Chapter 8). Wansbrough maintains that the text of the Qur᾿ān remained quite fluid through at least the 3rd/9th century, with multiple interpretations of the consonantal text and even divergent versions operating in different parts of the empire, and that the traditions were designed to hide the relatively late compilation of the official text (see pp. 44-46 and 202-207). In either case, the argument goes, it would have been awkward had the Prophet himself assembled an imperfect or incomplete edition of the revelation, hence the need to remove him from the process, according to Wansbrough.

variant readings of the otherwise stable text as canonical, largely through the efforts of Abū Bakr Aḥmad b. Mujāhid (244/859-324/936).[13]

Eventually, the Qur᾿ān was indeed compiled into a written version that acquired the stamp of authority and was widely disseminated. The process that ultimately produced this authoritative version was extremely important, both for the religion and for the Arabic literary heritage as a whole. For the religion, it was a significant step away from reliance upon collective memory as a guide for the community. As such, it tended to interfere with the personalized style of discourse that orality fosters, and it raised the question of central authority within a system of religious discourses built largely upon such interactions. It was not a complete revolution by any means, since the oral methods of memorization and scholarly transmission, as well as oral practices like recitation, continued to operate within Arab-Islamic society.[14] Rather, the compilation of the Qur᾿ān amounted to an acknowledgement, however tentative, of the limitations inherent in reliance upon the voice and memory, and it affirmed the pen's power to standardize and homogenize. Moreover, the existence of a more-or-less official codex of the Qur᾿ān could only have encouraged reliance on writing: if the pen was worthy to capture the divine revelation, it must surely be fit to express human creative genius as well. The compilation of the Qur᾿ān did not spell the end of orality entirely, far from it. It was, rather, part of a realignment of the balance between orality and literacy within Islamic religious culture.

2.3 *Orality and the literary tradition*

Gregor Schoeler's concise study of the role of writing in early Islamic society, *Ecrire et transmettre dans les débuts de l'islam* (2002), notes that up to the time of the Prophet Muḥammad, the written word was instrumental, being used for contracts and other agreements, for letters to important persons, and in private notes used by *ruwāh* (s. *rāwī*, a formal reciter or transmitter of poetry and/or tribal legends). In early Islamic times, the oral nature of the Qur᾿ānic revelation, and the recitation and memorization required of Muslims in their daily religious observances, probably militated to some degree against the authoritativeness of written language, at least as far as non-instrumental uses were concerned. Practical considerations played a part as well, since

---

[13] On the compilation of the Qur᾿ān, see also T. Nöldeke (1919) ii pp. 11-27; A.J. Wensinck (1927) p. 131; R. Blachère (1959) pp. 27-34; W.M. Watt (1977) pp. 40-56; and the article "Ḳur᾿ān" in the *Encyclopaedia of Islam, New Edition*, v. V A.T. Welch (1986).

[14] Indeed, recitation of the Qur᾿ān still plays an important role in Islamic practice. The ritual prayer required of Muslims five times a day, *ṣalah*, itself involves repetition of portions of the Qur᾿ān; and beautiful, stylized recitation (*tajwīd*) has evolved into an important facet of religious culture. Most formal occasions today commence with a recitation of some part of the Qur᾿ān in this style.

the writing system was not completely phonetically precise, as we have already noted. Schoeler further points to the oral poetic tradition of the pre-Islamic era and the oral nature of the Qur᾽ānic revelation as formative factors in the evolution of an ethos of orality within all the scientific and literary endeavors in the medieval Arabic-speaking world.

Muḥammad was the product of a quasi-literate society characterized by mixed orality. Mecca in his era was both a pilgrimage center and a market for goods passing from Yemen, on the Indian Ocean, to the Mediterranean and Red Seas. Sellheim and Sourdel (1990) argue that this is just the sort of milieu where we might expect the earliest phases of literacy to appear.[15] The ability to read and write would have been a valuable skill for agreements and record keeping, though it may not have been necessary for everyone. Muḥammad, for example, is reported by Islamic tradition to have remained illiterate his whole life, even though he was employed by his first wife, Ḫadīja, in her caravan business.

Instead, we find the scribe (*kātib*), who was charged with fixing in writing the important documents of the day. Important agreements were "published" by being posted in the local temple or ritual center (in Mecca, the Kaaba), a practice that seems to have originated in classical Greece.[16] We are told by the *aḥādīṯ* that later in his career, the Prophet of Islam employed scribes for these purposes, the most famous being Zayd b. Ṯābit. Al-Buḫārī informs us that Ibn Ṯābit was employed by the Prophet on at least two occasions to write down portions of the revelation as they came to him.[17] Then again at al-Ḥudaybiyya, the Prophet "called for the *kātib*" to write down the terms of peace between the Muslims and the Meccans.[18] Finally, after the Prophet's death, the caliphs Abū Bakr and ʿUthmān both called upon Ibn Ṯābit the *kātib* in the process of fixing a canonical text of the Qur᾽ān.[19]

This functional use of writing did not necessarily translate into preserving the oral poetic heritage. The written collection and propagation of pre- and early Islamic poetry came rather later, and some discussion has focused on the degree of authenticity of this corpus as it has survived in the written collections of the 2nd/8th and 3rd/9th centuries. James T. Monroe (1972) offers a cogent summary of the various positions on this issue, and then turns to the Parry-Lord model of oral composition to argue that signs of oral composition could be seen as evidence that at least some elements of these poems did indeed originate in the pre-Islamic period, even if the versions we have

[15] p. 754-755.

[16] Schoeler (2002) p. 17.

[17] Book 61, Kitāb faḍā'il al-Qur᾽ān, Bāb kātib an-Nabī, nos. 509 and 511.

[18] *al-Buḫārī*, Book 50, Kitāb aš-šurūṭ, Bāb aš-šurūṭ fī l-jihād…, #891.

[19] *al-Buḫārī*, Book 61, nos. 507 and 510.

today contain later additions and alterations.[20] Using data from six major pre-Islamic poets, Monroe constructs an interesting statistical argument that these poets composed their works using a stock of collocations, phrasing patterns and rhythmic-structural elements that closely resemble oral-compositional building blocks found in other non-literate poetic traditions. These basic elements probably evolved through many generations of oral performances, the surviving exemplars having been composed and recomposed, only becoming fixed and attributed to particular poets at a relatively late stage. (It should be pointed out, however, that the scholarly community is not in complete agreement about this. It may well have been the case that the pre-Islamic poets composed and perfected their works prior to oral performance using a method perhaps analogous to that of the Fijian poets described by Finnegan – see Chapter 7 §2. This does not, of course, deny the essentially oral character of the resulting poems, only that they were created in the moment of performace.)

Orally-composed poems like these provided the aesthetic and linguistic background from which the elevated register of the Arabic language evolved, the *koiné* which was used for formal discourses and which was deployed with such remarkable effect in the Qurʾān. Furthermore, oral performance/presentation remained an important feature of the poetic enterprise in Arab society for many generations. However poetry soon lost its oral-compositional character, as literacy acquired increased importance after the advent of Islam. Until the middle of the 2nd/8th century, poetry was transmitted almost entirely orally, according to Schoeler. Up to that time, the *rāwī* (pl. *ruwāh*: the poet's "reciter") was responsible for preserving the poet's work and "broadcasting" it publicly. After the poet's death, it fell to the *rāwī* to keep the poet's memory and works alive. Schoeler suggests that later, some of these transmitters probably had written notes they used for reference purposes, but which were not made public, as the essence of the poetic culture still was considered to be the oral performance. (On occasion, however, a fair copy might be made for a patron's private use.)[21]

Over the centuries, Arabic poetry came increasingly under the influence of literacy. More-or-less authoritative collections (*dawāwīn*, s. *dīwān*) were assembled, often long after the poet's death, and these became the standard by which a poet's work was judged and remembered. Michael Zwettler (1978) argues that these works were conditioned by the demands of oral presentation. The *ruwāh*, often poets themselves, frequently amended the poems they were charged with preserving through "correcting" grammatical and lexical problems, and so on. In this way a given *dīwān* might be handed down via multiple manuscript traditions, producing today more than one

---

[20] On Milman Parry concerning orality, see Chapter 7 §1.

[21] 2002, pp. 18-20.

reading of the same text. It is perhaps an overstatement to argue, as Zwettler does, that the *rāwī*'s alterations entirely effaced the sense of an original text.[22] Nevertheless the ethos of orality certainly played a role in the production and presentation of Arabic poetry long after oral composition as such ceased to be the rule.

Thus even after written composition became the norm in the 3rd/9th century, the art of poetic rendition retained a significant oral component. Poetry was often a public activity, being used to praise the patron or shame him, to lament the deceased or woo the beloved, and from perhaps the 7th/13th century on, to celebrate or evoke mystical experience among members of the Sufi fraternities (in the form of either poetic recitation or song). The *Kitāb al-Aġānī*, too, testifies to the other public use for poetry in late Umayyad and early Abbasid times: courtly song, which as we have seen took root in al-Andalus in the early 3rd/9th century and certainly did not vanish with the succession of dynasties in the medieval Arab-Islamic world. Even non-standard, strophic forms of poetry, such as the *muṣammaṭ*, *muwaššaḥ* and *zajal*, partook of the oral-performed domain, at least from the 12th century on and probably earlier.[23] All these public, orally-oriented functions existed side-by-side with poetry's written aspects.

The shift from the more-or-less pure orality of the pre-Islamic era towards a poetic ethos more deeply touched by the written word can also be seen in the grand Arabic ode, the *qaṣīda*, at the level of literary style. Muhammad Badawi (1980) divides production of the *qaṣīda* into two eras, Primary and Secondary, the former coming to an end with the shift in religious values initiated by the triumph of Islam in the first half of the 7th century. The difference between the two can be seen in the language used, which Badawi maintains is partly a result of the different roles served by poets.

> In the first place the Primary *Qaṣīda* was not just a poem in the familiar, modern sense of the word; it had more than a *literary* function. It was a ritual, more akin to ancient Greek tragedy, a reenactment in recital of the common values of the tribe ....[24]

In contrast, Badawi argues, the Secondary *Qaṣīda* was predominantly a literary work, an elaboration in style and adaptation in theme of conventions and conventional structures already long established. Its function was not to promote group solidarity by extolling tribal virtues and attacking the tribe's enemies, but to earn the poet his daily bread through praising and entertaining the patron.

---

[22] pp. 24-26.

[23] Whatever one believes about whether or not the Andalusian strophic genres were originally intended to be sung, Ibn Sanā' al-Mulk (d. 1211) makes clear reference in his *Dār at-tirāz* to the musical use of *muwaššaḥāt*.

[24] p. 8

While Badawi does not mention the significance of orality and literacy in these developments, his analysis hints at it: the distinction he makes between the ritual and the literary qualities of the two types of *qaṣīda* strongly suggests an increased emphasis upon writing and written processes in the production and dissemination of the Secondary *Qaṣīda*. The author of the Secondary *Qaṣīda* was indeed an entertainer, as Badawi points out, but one who depended upon familiarity with both poetic convention and the body of existing *qaṣā'id*. While referentiality and a reflexive stance toward language do not by themselves require literacy (as Ruth Finnegan has pointed out), the preservation of the ancient poetic tradition in written form and later, the availability of authoritative *dawāwīn* of more recent poets, certainly promoted intertextuality of the kind described by Badawi. And most important, Badawi's analysis points clearly to the social factors shaping the poetic enterprise at the level of content and style, in both oral and written contexts.

Even when the written version of a poem was treated as in some sense authoritative, still its oral presentation might be regarded as prestigious and therefore bearing value. Witness the performance of Ibn Bājja's *muwaššaḥ* before Ibn Tīfalwīṭ. Leo Africanus' account of poetic competitions in the Kingdom of Fez at the turn of the 16th century[25] strongly suggests that the oral ethos in poetry and poetic presentation continued to play a prominent role in North Africa, even in an historical moment when courtly patronage was waning. Leo does not indicate whether or not the competing poets read their works from a page, but his account shows clearly that it was the oral presentation, not the written version, that earned the poet accolades and reward from the king. (Contrast this with modern literary awards such as the Pulitzer prize, in which the award goes to the best *book* of poetry, not the best poem or poems based upon a public oral presentation.)

The interweaving of oral processes with written text continued for centuries after Muḥammad and was not confined to poetry. Schoeler, in *Ecrir et transmettre* and in a series of articles (1987, 1989a, 1989b, 1997), explored the role of oral processes in the transmission of literate knowledge in medieval Islam, and their implications for our understanding of the genesis of the written texts. Schoeler's careful analysis of the surviving sources shows that in the two centuries after Muḥammad, in many areas of medieval Arabic letters, literate knowledge and its transmission were mediated by oral processes, so that the idea of a fixed text being passed on as a coherent whole is not accurate for much of the early period of Islam. Recitation of the master's text, whether from his own or a student's written copy, supplemented by the master's oral explication, was a common teaching method. Moreover, the master rarely taught from a

[25] See Chapter 3 §1.3.

fully-formed book as such. Instead, the actual compilation and recension of his work often fell to one or more of his students or his student's students, frequently working from notes taken during teaching sessions. The consolidation of the great written works that exemplified the early heights of the classical Arab-Islamic civilization took place in an environment where the uses of the work extended beyond the writing on the page, and where oral rendition helped to shape the text.

From the 4th/10th century on, literacy and the written word came to exert a greater influence on intellectual discourses. Orally-delivered commentaries on the great works of science, history, religion, law, grammar and poetics were themselves written down and studied, and these, in turn, became part of the larger intellectual discourse. Yet even when the books of important authors became authoritative in themselves and the subject of study and teaching by generations removed from direct contact with the author, oral rendition and personal communication between master and student retained their valued status in the teaching context. For example, authors like the Hanbali traditionist and scholar ʿAbd ar-Raḥmān b. al-Jawzī (1116-1201), and the geographer Yāqūt b. ʿAbd Allāh al-Hamawī (1179?-1229), continued to note chains of transmitters as their sources and emphasized personal testimony. As another example, Emile Michaux-Bellaire (1924) describes the use of oral techniques (*samāʿ*) in the production and dissemination of commentaries within the Maliki legal school in al-Andalus, which were subsequently written down and became part of the school's curriculum and were themselves taught by the same technique.

Indeed, Seyyed Hossein Nasr (1995) goes so far as to argue that the classical Arabic intellectual heritage cannot be understood properly without taking into account the presence of oral traditions that existed side-by-side with the written text and supplied important interpretive and exegetic dimensions to what was found on the page. Orality thus fulfilled an important function in the transmission of knowledge:

> Such books became more than simply the written text. Rather, they came to accompany and in a sense became immersed in the spoken word, through an oral teaching transmitted from master to student and stored in the memory of those destined to be the recipients of the knowledge in question.[26]

Moreover, this oral component served an overtly social purpose, as well:

> Oral transmission helped to establish the authority of teachers who were to follow, and it served as the criterion with the aid of which one could distinguish one student from another as far as

[26] p. 57

> his closeness to the master and understanding of the latter's message were concerned…[27]

Scholar-authors whose ideas might arouse the ire of religious orthodoxy would commit to writing chiefly the most inoffensive dimensions of their work, leaving the more problematic aspects of their thought to be transmitted orally. This allowed them some measure of control over how their work was received, allowed them to clarify ambiguities which might arise, and helped insulate them from the wrath of the orthodox. So important has this oral dimension been in the intellectual, cultural and spiritual life of the Arab-Islamic world, that Nasr argues that

> [its] importance must be asserted in the face of all the historicism and positivism which have sought to reduce the reality of the Islamic intellectual tradition to written texts and historically established influences. Historical studies and careful attention paid to the written text … cannot become exclusive and totalitarian without destroying the integrity of the Islamic intellectual tradition.[28]

3. *Mixed orality, past and present*

The foregoing discussion illustrates the extent to which oral processes interpenetrated with the written word within the confines of the medieval Arabic literary tradition generally, a phenomenon referred to here as the *ethos of orality*. The language itself did not distinguish definitively between the private act of reading and the public act of recitation, so that a specific context was required in order to determine which activity was meant. Furthermore, in many areas of literary activity oral presentation played a significant role either in the transmission of knowledge (in the case of scholarly activities) or as an aim in itself (the production of poetry, and study and use of the Qurʾān). Nowhere is this mixed-oral character more evident than in the traditions surrounding the compilation of the Qurʾān and its dissemination as an authorized text. Both the *aḥādīṯ* and the historical evidence surrounding the issue reveal the Islamic community wrestling with the problem of balancing the voice and the pen.

Mixed orality in *al-Āla* today reflects the same issue within a modern context, a connection at the level of cultural praxis extending centuries into the past. Like the ancient teaching methods of medieval Arabic scholarly circles and oral teaching and rendition of the Qurʾān, the oral dimensions of *al-Āla* engage the types of social value

---

[27] p. 58

[28] p. 66

enacted by oral interactions: the intimate, personal relationships that arise when individuals interact face-to-face.

Where the values inherent in each of these examples differ, it is due to the socially meaningful specifics of each case. Chapter 4 spelled out some of the parallels and contrasts between the teaching of *al-Āla* and memorization of the Qurʾān, but others could be emphasized here. The methods are similar and produce similarly valued results: a deep and intimate familiarity with the contents of the tradition. Yet the social contexts of the two traditions are quite distinct, and as a result, they are valued differently in many respects. Memorizing the Qurʾān usually begins in childhood, and this fact places Qurʾānic memorization and recitation very deep in the personal history of the individual. One literally "grows up with" the Qurʾān. In addition, the sacred character of the text and its recitation infuses the activity of memorizing by oral repetition with values deriving directly from the religious culture surrounding Islam. Recitation of the Qurʾān commands respect and alters the social atmosphere unlike any other activity: conversation dies away and silence falls as attention turns to the recitation. In contrast, *Āla* students vary considerably in age, with the most advanced being in their 20s and 30s, and neither the text nor its performance is considered sacred. Audience conversation may continue throughout an entire *Āla* performance, interrupted only by applause between sections of the music. Though one may "grow up with" *al-Āla* as a significant presence in the home and community, the values involved are very different. Consequently, though *al-Āla* bears considerable prestige among participants in the tradition, its value operates in a very different way from Qurʾānic recitation, the gap between the sacred and the profane being the chief distinction between the values ascribed to the two traditions.

The ethos of orality that permeated medieval Arabic intellectual culture reverberates through orality in the modern *Āla* tradition as a kind of cultural background to the social and economic relations operating within it. The common denominator between the historical and the modern contexts is the evoking of personal connections. These personal connections have been important historically for how they interlock with the economic relations surrounding the transfer and uses of knowledge, whether it be intellectual knowledge or the knowledge and skills necessary to perform music.

Through the personal connections promoted by orality, the medieval scholar was able to exert some control over how his knowledge was used, and by whom. He could protect himself from some of the repercussions of controversial ideas and above all, he could help guarantee his own position by keeping his students (and potential successors) in a close partnership. In this social and economic milieu, the ethos of orality served a very useful purpose for the scholar. Much the same could be said of the master musician, who also depended upon his ability to control his proprietary knowledge, as we saw in Chapter 4. For the master musician, orality served the important function of binding his student to him, building bonds of intimacy, dependence and affection that reduced the potential for competition between them and provided a kind of retirement insurance though the student's support once he had become a master in his own right. Written versions of text and music represent a threat to this system, since they offer the potential for learning without the intimate bonds fostered by orality. In an environment where survival depended upon one's ability to build personal relationships with both patrons and students, oral processes served the master far better than writing could. Thus there was substantial endemic resistance to perfecting written music, and likewise, the incomplete rendering of *ṣanʿa* texts as poetry represented at best a minimal danger to the value-content of the master-student relationship.

The corollary to this is the problematic situation facing masters of *al-Āla* today within the present conservatory system. The institution denies the master complete authority to decide whom he will work with, what he will teach and how. The personalized values promoted by orality no longer dominate this musical craft, but instead have been relegated to only the most advanced levels of instruction. Orality is being reduced to merely a technique, stripped of much of its value. Only resistance from the doyens of the tradition has stood in the way of reducing the tradition completely to writing, and the standardization of relationships and erosion of the role of orality in the teaching process that naturally would follow.

4. *Poetry, prestige and the pen in al-Āla*

The pen also serves the tradition, though valued in a complementary way. As the discussion of literacy in Chapter 7 revealed, the pen has a greater potential than the voice to promote a reflective stance toward its subject. The values evoked by literate processes emphasize the detached and the impersonal: along with the power to analyze and reflect upon written text comes a greater ability to distinguish between text and context, and to value the former according to criteria that are less dependent upon direct and personal relationships. This can be seen in the way that the literate dimension of *al-Āla* evokes the prestige attaching to poetry in the Arabic literary tradition. Since its earliest phases, the ability to read and use written language in the Arabic-speaking world was imbricated with the socially informed techniques of oral presentation and pedagogy. Oral rendition was regarded as the dominant mode of discourse into which writing entered and by degrees gained the upper hand, just as Jesse Gellrich (1995) shows was the case with the emergence of literacy as a cultural form in pre-enlightenment Europe. This indicates once again that the value of emergent literacy cannot be fully appreciated without reference to the oral processes that interpenetrate with it.

Yet all that has been said about the ethos of orality within Arabic literary activities should not obscure the fact that for centuries poetry in Arabic has been valued as a literary activity as well, an embodiment of mastery and expressive skill in the language. The history of Arabic letters since the pre-Islamic era provides ample evidence of the prestige attaching to poetry. In the orally-oriented era prior to Islam, poets were the spokesmen of their tribes, the propagandists and rhetoricians in whose hands lay the power to exalt or ruin reputations. Their influence even in the time of the Prophet Muḥammad was inescapable. Although the Qur'ān severly condemns those poets of the Qurayš who mocked the Prophet, he himself employed poets as propagandists on behalf of Islam.[29] Simply put, poetry was the medium of political discourse in his era. Moreover, poetic diction contributed significantly to the language of the revelation, so much so that the Prophet himself was at times accused of being merely a poet.[30] Although the poetry of the pre-Islamic and early Islamic eras shows evidence of orality, it has survived only in written recensions assembled much later, versions that probably underwent considerable editing and revision at the hands of (literate) compilers. Nevertheless, the effort undertaken to compile the poems itself indicates the importance attaching to poetry in the medieval Arabic-speaking world. In addition to its place as the medium of elevated expression, poetry was considered to be a resource for explicating the Arabic language, and in particular, for clarifying obscure expressions found in the Qur'ān, to the point that linguists of the classical period often went to live with expert Bedouin informants who came from tribes that still practiced oral poetic rendition, and even brought some of them to teach at their schools in Basra and Kūfa.[31]

In nearly every area of Arabic letters we find poetic insertions – authors deploying portions of the rich Arabic poetic tradition as proofs, illustrations, illuminations, elucidations and even mnemonic aids. Linguists and grammarians made ample use of verse as evidentiary examples and as summary encapsulations to aid in memorization. Historians and biographers also routinely supplied verses written by or

[29] The most famous of these poets was Ḥassān b. Ṯābit (d. ca. 40/660). Two verses from this poet may be found in the modern *Nawbat Ramal al-Māya*: the twelvth ṣanʿa in Mīzān al-Quddām (*Lammā naẓartu ilā anwārihi saṭaʿat...*).

[30] The accusation is found in Qur'ān 37:36, and the rebuttal in Qur'ān 69:40-41. Cantarino (1975) provides a clear and succinct discussion of the role of poets and poetry in ancient Arabia. Zwettler (1978, Chapter 4) discusses the *rāwī*'s role in the mixed oral mode of poetic production, and Versteegh (1997, Chapter 4) gives an excellent summary and bibliography of scholarly opinion on the poetic koiné and its role in the development of the formal Arabic of Muḥammad's time.

[31] See Régis Blachère (1950) and Joshua Blau (1963) on the evolving status of these Bedouin informants.

about their subjects, and the literature of refined conduct (*adab*) is saturated with poetry. Even in the secular and religious sciences and philosophy, authors used verse for similar didactic purposes.[32] *Kunnāš al-Ḥāʾik* contains in its introduction a poem that summarizes the *ṭubūʿ*, their relationships among themselves, and their connections to humoral and temporal phenomena. Throughout the history of the language, poetry has been regarded as a prestigious form of expression, so authors naturally sought to elevate their prose works through ample use of it.

Given the intimate connection between verse and song, it is scarcely surprising that anthologies of *ṣanāʾiʿ* from the Andalusian music should be presented as collections of poetry. The conventions of poetic presentation (notation of the poetic genre and meter of the verses, and especially, arrangement in separate lines on the page with a caesura between hemistiches) obviously recommend themselves, since many texts in *al-Āla* are borrowed from well-known poets of al-Andalus, North Africa and the Middle East. At the same time, not only did verse appear to be the natural format for song collections, but the act of representing the *ṣanāʾiʿ* using the poetic conventions cast them as belonging above all to the Arabic poetic heritage. Song, conversely, had no cultural standing among Arabic speakers that could compare with poetry or modify its conventions. The conventions of poetic presentation simply do not allow for representing the complicated repetitions and other details that distinguish the sung tradition from the literate one; to render a *ṣanʿa* on the written page precisely as it is sung would be to fracture and scatter the aesthetic and discursive power of the poetic representation, an unthinkable act of aesthetic violence.

Knowingly or not, the anthologists of *al-Āla* imported the prestige and aesthetic influence of poetry into the musical tradition by following the existing models for representing it on the page. The value attaching to poetry in Arabic-speaking societies (that is, the importance assigned to being able to read, recite and understand poetry and poetic expression) became a significant part of the value system permeating the musical tradition. Especially in the modern context, *al-Āla* owes much of its prestige and aesthetic power to its *aṣīl* (both "authentic" and "noble or pure") associations with high literature, even when portions of the tradition are in fact composed in colloquial language. *Muwaššaḥāt* and *azjāl*, respected nowadays as emblems of the Andalusi golden age and bona fide components of the grand Arabic poetic heritage, offer evidence to the audience of the prestige of the Andalusian music. The many deviations from classical poetic diction one finds in the *tawāšīḥ* and *azjāl* do not detract at all from the tradition's prestige. On the contrary, they are in fact regarded as relics of the

[32] A common genre was the *muzdawij* ("doubled, paired"): a poem in which verses were rhymed in pairs (or, rarely, triplets). Typically, some comparison or contrast was made within the frame of the rhyming verses.

Andalusi dialect and therefore evidence of the authenticity of the text, proof of the connection with al-Andalus, even if a substantial number of the actual verses belong not to medieval Iberia but to North Africa.[33] The prestige of the Arabic poetic heritage is an essential element in the prestige of the *Āla* tradition.

This holds true in the 20th century even for the *barwala*, Moroccan colloquial poetry within the tradition. This song form did not appear within the written canon until after al-Jāmiʿī, at the end of the 19th century.[34] Since at least the mid-20th century, the *barwala* has been regarded as an authentic element of the tradition, even to the point of being represented on the page using the conventions of *tawšīḥ*, despite the many problems encountered in rendering the spoken dialect in writing. Still, the *barwala*'s integration into the tradition has not been smooth, as data from *Ramal al-Māya* reveal. *Barāwil* in Darj and Quddām Ramal al-Māya show a great deal of variation among the three modern printed anthologies of *al-Āla*: not only are phrasing and lexical items apparently more fluid than for other song forms, but even the conventions for rendering the words in writing vary among the three anthologies, so that it can be difficult to decipher the intended text without the aid of an expert familiar with the tradition. Perhaps some of this variation may be attributed to regional differences within the canon, but in any case, the decisive criterion seems to be what is sung, rather than what appears on the page.[35]

The production of an anthology, the act of collecting and presenting a literary-musical tradition in written form, is a powerful intervention into the history of that tradition. We will never know to what extent either al-Ḥāʾik or al-Jāmiʿī was aware of the power of the written word, the sense of permanence it lends, the aura of authenticity and canonicity it weaves about its subject. Nevertheless, in committing the tradition to writing and casting it in the format of poetry, the anthologists situated *al-Āla* in a highly valued domain whose prestige is recognized even among people who

---

[33] At least 8 of the 24 poets identified with verses in *Ramal al-Māya* spent all or part of their careers in North Africa, and the names of three others about whom little is known suggest they were connected with North Africa in some way.

[34] This does not necessarily mean that it only developed in the century between al-Ḥāʾik and al-Jāmiʿī, as Cortés García infers: As indicated in Chapter 5, both Ahmed Piro and Benmūsā maintain that *mīzān ad-darj*, a major repository for *barāwil*, existed at the time of al-Ḥāʾik. Moreover, the communities that supplied the oral text streams identified in Chapter 5 certainly predated al-Ḥāʾik and may very well have made use of the *barwala* in performance.

[35] Nevertheless, preservation in written form has not fully integrated the *barwala* into the domain of high poetry to the extent that has happened with the *muwaššaḥ* and *zajal*. Sī Benmūsā admitted to me that he has at times altered *barāwil* texts when preparing concert programs, having no compunctions about bowdlerizing racy passages he considers inappropriate for women and children to hear. He would hesitate to do so for the more *aṣīl* song forms, *tawšīḥ* and *zajal*. The structure and status of the *barwala* within the tradition is discussed more fully in Pen, Voice, Text.

cannot themselves effectively read and understand the verses. Not only did the anthologies facilitate the modernization of the tradition's teaching and economic relations, as has been shown in Chapter 4, they promoted the very idea of *al-Āla* as a definable literary-musical form, traditional and authentic in and of itself.

Furthermore, a written anthology encourages a reflective, intellectual stance in the reader toward its contents, a stance which for *al-Āla* facilitated the unique value attaching to the corpus. In principle, at least, the written anthology allows its owner to read and appreciate the poetry for its own sake apart from its performed context. As with any "community of the text," the social value of the *al-Āla* anthology unites its owner with others who have read and appreciated the same anthologized poems. Cortés García observes that it was not unusual even in the early 20th century for families of Andalusian origin and lovers of the music to have a copy of the *Kunnāš* made by a fine copyist, written in three or more colors in beautiful script. This accounts for many of the manuscripts pertaining to the music scattered in various public and private libraries around Morocco.[36] The impetus behind some of these copies surely must have involved both the prestige of the musical tradition itself and an appreciation of its contents as poetry. For a literate audience of ethnic Andalusians and *al-Āla* aficionados, the written anthology embodied an implied link between the value set represented by poetry, and that embodied in the Andalusian music. All of these facets coincide with what has already been noted about the social conditions surrounding literacy and the written word.

5. *Mixed orality and al-Āla*

The Moroccan Andalusian music is a mixed-oral tradition: the voice and the pen function together, each evoking a different set of values that together represent the importance attaching to participation in the tradition, whether as musician, concert organizer or audience member. Whereas the value of the written facet of the tradition corresponds to the importance attaching to literacy, erudition and so on, the value attaching to orality within the tradition involves the personal nature of the relationships formed in the face-to-face contact inherent in oral communication. The written aspect of *al-Āla* comprises primarily the anthologies of *ṣanʿa* texts, but what exactly is meant here by the oral component of the tradition?

Of course, as performed music, the structure and textual contents of *al-Āla* have been conditioned to some degree by the demands of oral presentation. Certainly the arrangement of *ṣanāʾiʿ* in *nawbāt* and *mayāzīn* reflects performance practice within the tradition, and likewise the structure and thematic arrangement of all the *ṣanāʾiʿ*

[36] 1996, Chapter 8.

have been shaped by the techniques of musical composition and presentation. Moreover, the communal experience of the *ḥafla*, the site wherein the two main participants in the tradition — performers and audience — meet to enact the tradition, is a significant source of value. That the performers engage in a meaningful social act is self-evident, but the same can be said of the audience, as well. Those who attend an *Āla* performance, whether a small private party or a large *mahrajān*, are far from being mere passive consumers of the music. First, they have made the effort to come to the *ḥafla* (which at least involved an investment of time), and perhaps spent some money in the process (an act whose value is expressed in monetary terms). Even more important, their presence, responses to the performance, and communal behavior before, during and after the performance, are all meaningful acts within the social context of the *ḥafla* and animate it as a socially meaningful phenomenon. The *ḥafla*, the oral-performative presentation of *al-Āla*, is the quintessential meaningful social act within the tradition, its very *raison d'être*.

But orality in *al-Āla* differs from that in a purely oral tradition. The particular mixed-oral character of *al-Āla* involves an orality that does not really permeate the performance context in the same way as oral poetic traditions: Because the textual contents of *al-Āla* are already fixed and bounded, *Āla* performers do not generate the performed version from a stock of compositional elements; and they are not free to improvise, rearrange and recast the material in response to the audience.[37] In short, the mixed orality of *Āla* performance de-emphasizes intimacy and spontaneity to some degree, for the socially meaningful act does not involve dynamic, in-the-moment composition, but rather adherence to the (fairly restrictive) conventions of performance and respect for the boundaries of the tradition as a whole. As the "classical music" of Morocco, *al-Āla* stands at a certain distance from its audience, valorized in part for its aesthetic of formality and the elite aura that the conventions of performance weave around the music.

A more salient domain in which orality functions in *al-Āla* is the teaching process, the transmission of the tradition across generations via oral methods, where the emphasis is on relationships among musicians. The value of oral transmission lies in the affective qualities it engages, whether they be among musicians whom oral interactions bring into contact with one another, or at the level of individual familiarity with the tradition that rote memorization by oral repetition cultivates. The two are related in value terms, since the intimacy that comes with participation in the tradition partakes of the shared experience of immersion in it and the sense of community that

---

[37] This is as true in private *ḥafalāt* as in the grand soirees staged by the *jamʿiyyāt*, though the intimacy of the informal gathering does allow for more liberties in the structure of the performance. See the description of one such private *ḥafla* in Chapter 3 n. 53.

grows from performing it together. At the apex of these oral-communal experiences sits the *muʿallim*, the *raʾīs al-jawq* who serves as guide and exemplar in the evolution of the ensemble toward an appropriately authentic rendition of the music. The emphasis on intimacy and communality is one reason why the project of recording *al-Āla* has not met with approval from all participants in the tradition. Audio recordings are problematic in part because they tend to encourage stylistic homogenization by obscuring regional variety, but also because like written music, they introduce the possibility of musicians learning the tradition without a master. Audio recordings thus imply a potential violation of the personal relationship between master and student inherent in oral transmission, even as they make the tradition available to a wider audience.

Philip Schuyler's article (1979) and the discussion of al-Maʿhad al-Waṭanī in Chapter 4 underscored the problems that the conservatory system has created for the master-student relationship. The value theory of tradition brings these issues into even sharper focus by aligning the economic dimensions with the social ones along the axis of value. They are really two facets of the same question, which has to do with the meaning attaching to acts in a social context: the master's livelihood depends upon his command of a valued repertoire; and both the value of the repertoire, and that of the system by which it is maintained and passed on, are interwoven with the social context of orality. The one-on-one, oral, rote-memorization method provides the essential conditions for preserving both affective, immersive familiarity with the tradition, and the valued social relationships that interlock with it. The conservatory pulls apart these economic relationships that once were central to the tradition, substituting itself as the arbiter of economic value and standardizing the terms under which master and student work. Furthermore, the conservatory demystifies the tradition by making it more widely available in a standardized form. New kinds of meaningful action intrude, and thus a new kind of value is introduced that incorporates discourses of national memory and belonging, and attempts to import notions of modernity as well. We might view the modern history of *al-Āla* as the working out of ancient mixed-oral values within an environment increasingly shaped by both the power of the pen and the impersonalizing forces so characteristic of modernity.

Ironically, this shift was in fact made possible by the existing imbrication of literacy with orality (a cultural ethos extending back, ideally if not always in practice, all the way to the time of the Prophet Muḥammad), which provided canonical texts in a reasonably useful form that could be deployed to define and (in theory, at least) standardize the repertoire. The very anthologies that served to define the tradition and establish it as a distinct musical art form for previous generations became, in the middle of the 20th century, one medium though which the foundations of the value system behind the tradition have gradually shifted. The extension of literacy into the teaching context was for *al-Āla* as important a shift in value terms as the compilation of the Qurʾān was for religious practice in Islam or the gradual evolution of Arabic poetry away from its oral roots.

In practice, however, the force behind such a significant shift depends upon maintaining the authenticity of the tradition, and for *al-Āla* that still belongs to the masters: they alone hold the tradition in its *aṣīl* form, and so they alone are capable of passing on an authentic version of it. Because the tradition still depends upon orality for its transmission (for the reasons discussed at the beginning of this chapter) the conservatory system must continue to rely upon rote memorization by oral repetition, a method whose social value is negligible at the lowest levels of instruction, where classes are large and populated with many relatively casual students. The social effects of oral-rote memorization become magnified as class sizes shrink at higher levels, and therefore its value expands accordingly. The value of orality in *al-Āla* is greatest in precisely the most significant context for the tradition, since only at the highest, most rarified levels of teaching are the most *aṣīl* dimensions of the tradition taught and thus preserved.

The importance of mixed orality to *al-Āla* has not hitherto been fully appreciated by participants in the tradition. The tension that once existed between proponents of literate/technological preservation and those who saw in non-oral preservation a threat to the authenticity of the tradition has been rendered irrelevant and swept away by the tide of sound recordings that has emerged in the last thirty years or so. The perceived advantages, inherent in recordings, of extending the music's audience and preserving its contents appear to have trumped concerns about the corresponding losses in diversity and subtlety. Resistance to change, typically expressed as a reluctance to accept intrusions into and innovations within the canonical corpus of *ṣanāʾiʿ* and its time-honored performance practices, has forced a relatively stable truce: the contents of the tradition are now bounded by the written canon, which alone is considered authentic and worthy of performing and recording. The concern has become that nothing should disturb these tangible and time-honored aspects of the tradition.

However, the more subtle significance of the oral component in the tradition, the values that it engages, have yet to be generally recognized as constituent elements of the tradition. Rote memorization by oral repetition is valorized for its *affective* power, but scarcely for its *social* significance. Instructors like Professor Šīkī lament the scarcity of committed students without yet fully recognizing that it is a natural consequence of the value-content of the tradition as it stands. The oral teaching method requires a level of familiarity and social intimacy that limits the number of committed students of the kind hoped for by the doyens of the tradition. In other words, expanding access to the tradition has not coincided with an expansion in the valued contexts available to it. Professor Šīkī (and indeed the conservatory system itself) very nearly have fallen into the gap between the two. At the same time, the process of institutionalization tends to inculcate the impersonal, the professional, the modern, and so on – all qualities that can only clash with the *aṣīl* social values inherent in the old oral methods.

Finally, the laudable desire to expand access to the tradition and extend its reach as the country's national classical music cannot actually ensure its survival in an authentic form, as that is presently defined. The economic interventions inherent in the conservatory system tend to undermine the valued social relations inherent in the oral-traditional method. Furthermore, institutionalization requires standardization, and that implies a non-valued rapprochement between the tradition-as-practice and the tradition as (preserved) corpus. The two cannot be allowed to come too close together, lest the result either disperse the tradition's *aṣīl* integrity, or vitiate its underlying matrix of socially-valued relationships, or both. This same tension between authenticity and standardization emerged in the case of the Tunisian *Mālūf*, and was resolved by the government's complete standardization of the tradition and committing it to writing for ideological purposes.[38] In the case of *al-Āla* this tension has remained within the value system of the tradition, and has led to the institutionalizing of mixed-oral teaching methods in a way that may not fully answer the needs of the tradition.

Throughout its historical evolution, from its origins within the Andalusi system of elite patronage permeated with personalized relationships, to the modern era of relatively impersonal formal institutions, the elite music of al-Andalus and its descendant in Morocco have retained a mixed-oral character. The affective nature of oral presentation, as well as the social and economic rationales that informed its transmission across generations, have together ensured a role for orality in the face of an always-immanent literacy. The two channels answer to different purposes and embody distinct values that complement one another in the social praxis that comprises *al-Āla* today.

At the same time, the two modes of transmission interact with one another, as well. Rote memorization by oral repetition draws to a limited extent upon written versions of the canon, used chiefly as template or reference in support of the oral method, clarifying lexical items, pronunciation and so on. In this way, the written canon provides a boundary on variation in the sung text, although incompleteness necessarily limits its utility in this regard. On the other side of the ledger, the various processes of oral rendition and transmission have left their mark on the printed corpus, as well. Texts of *ṣanā'iʿ* sometimes vary among the three principal printed editions,

[38] See Ruth A. Davis, 1997a and 1997b.

between different instances of the same *ṣan ͑a* text in different parts of the tradition, and between the *Āla* anthologies and the poets' anthologies from which some texts derive. (A full discussion of the effects of orality on the written tradition will be found in my forthcoming book, *Pen, Voice, Text: Nūbat Ramal al-Māya in Cultural Context.*)

Although it has been convenient to isolate orality and literacy as cultural processes, in order to outline their distinctive characteristics and the value-laden contexts that they bring into being, such a separation is somewhat artificial. In the embodiment of text and music within this socially-enacted tradition, the voice and the pen are not entirely separate but function together as mutually implicating dimensions of the tradition. Participants in the tradition value both aspects, but do not necessarily distinguish between them. Rather they tend to regard the tradition as a unified whole in both its oral and written dimensions. Experts in the tradition may recognize certain obvious differences between what is found on the printed page and what is sung, but that does not mean that either is considered more *aṣīl* or that either can or should stand alone. Audience members may use concert programs to help them sing along with the performance (and perhaps even prize them as mementos of their interest in *al-Āla*), but the deviations of sung text from printed text they find in the program do not give cause for confusion or doubt as to the authenticity of either the text or the performance. On the contrary, the printed text is *expected* to depart from the *ṣan ͑a*-as-sung: that is just the nature of the tradition as they find it.

As constituted today, at the beginning of the 21st century, *al-Āla* represents a socially valued artistic link to a musical and poetic heritage stretching, in principle, across nearly twelve centuries from the courtly music of Ziryāb in Umayyad Cordoba to modern Morocco. The values that the music embodies have changed dramatically over the centuries, which is a testimony to the durability of the tradition and the flexibility that mixed orality can provide.

Appendix 1
A Glossary of Arabic Technical Terms Used in the Moroccan Andalusian Music Tradition

Names of instruments, and musical and poetic and structural terms are given here according to their current usage in Fez. This glossary is intended to be used as a quick reference. For most nouns, the singular is given, followed by the plural in parentheses. In many cases detailed explanations may be found in the text. Most of these terms come from formal Arabic; expressions from Moroccan colloquial Arabic are marked MA, and the formal Arabic equivalents are given.

al-Āla : one of the names for the Andalusian music in Morocco; signifies that the music is played on instruments (*āla*), as distinct from the a cappella *Samāʿ* (q.v.).

al-ʿamal : a passage of vocal and instrumental music in the 13th-century *nawba* of al-Andalus, according to at-Tīfāšī; performed alone in *aṣ-ṣawt* (q.v.), and with a prelude, *al-istihlāl* (q.v.), in *an-našīd* (q.v.).

barwala (*barāwil*) : a North African poetic form composed in Moroccan colloquial Arabic, and found chiefly (but not exclusively) in *mīzān ad-darj* (q.v. *mīzān*).

al-basīṭ : an *īqāʿ* (q.v.) in duple meter characteristic of the first *mīzān* (q.v.) of the *nūba* (q.v.).

baytayn : a vocal interlude, without tempo, in which the singer improvises freely on two lines of verse; may appear at any point in a performance, though it is not obligatory.

al-bṭāyḥī (MA, > *ibṭāʾiḥī*) : an *īqāʿ* (q.v.) in triple meter characteristic of the third *mīzān* (q.v.) of the *nūba* (q.v.).

buġya (*buġayāt*) : an introductory instrumental passage with a fixed melody that is played without tempo and outlines the primary *ṭabʿ* (q.v.) of a *nūba* (q.v.); each *nūba* thus has its own *buġya*.

darbūka : a vase-shaped hand drum from the Middle East.

darbush : a cylindrical red "Fez" style hat with a black tassel, part of the traditional musician's costume in Morocco.

ad-darj : an *īqāʿ* (q.v.) in duple meter characteristic of the fourth *mīzān* (q.v.) of the *nūba* (q.v.).

dawr (*adwār*) : a "turn" or repetition of the principal melodic phrase of a *ṣanʿa* (q.v.).

farqa (MA, > *firqa*; pl. *firaq, farqāt*) : a small ensemble of between three and seven musicians.

al-Ġarnāṭī : a style of music, said to have originated in Muslim-ruled Granada and similar to *al-Āla,* found primarily in the region straddling the Moroccan-Algerian border between Oujda and Tlemsen.

ġuṣn (*aġṣān*) : the main body of a *muwaššaḥ / tawšīḥ* (q.v.) or *zajal* (q.v.) strophe whose rhyme scheme varies from strophe to strophe.

ḥamdān : one of the three "secondary" *ṭubūʿ* (q.v. *ṭabʿ*) that appear in *Nawbat Ramal al-Māya* (q.v.).

kharja : in Arab-Andalusi poetry, the closing two lines of the final strophe of a *muwaššaḥ* (q.v.); may be composed using expressions from colloquial Arabic, Romance or Hebrew. None of the *muwaššaḥāt* performed in the Moroccan Andalusian music has a non-Arabic *kharja.*

al-ḥusayn : one of the three "secondary" *ṭubūʿ* (q.v. *ṭabʿ*) that appear in *Nawbat Ramal al-Māya* (q.v.).

inqilāb al-ramal : one of the three "secondary" *ṭubūʿ* (q.v. *ṭabʿ*) that appear in *Nawbat Ramal al-Māya;* said to be derived from the *ṭabʿ al-māya.*

inšād : a vocal interlude, without tempo, in which the singer elaborates on a fixed melody and text; may appear at any point in a performance, but often used to separate two *marḥalat al-mīzān* (q.v. *marāḥil al-mīzān*).

al-inṣirāf : the third and fastest of the three *marāḥil al-mīzān* (q.v.); traditionally the climax of a *mīzān* (q.v.), but may be performed on its own.

īqāʿ (*īqāʿāt*) : a fundamental rhythmic pattern associated with a specific *mīzān* (q.v.); the five *īqāʿāt* used today in Morocco are *al-basīṭ, al-qāʾim wa-niṣf, al-bṭāyḥī, ad-darj* and *al-quddām;* may be in either duple (4 or 8) or triple (3 or 6) meter.

al-istihlāl : 1. (cap.) the fifth *nūba* (q.v.) in *al-Āla,* according to the modern order; the *ṭabʿ* (q.v.) associated with this *nūba;* 2. a vocal or instrumental prelude in the 13th-century *nawba* of al-Andalus, according to at-Tīfāšī: *an-našīd* (q.v.) comprises *al-itstihlāl* followed by *al-ʿamal* (q.v.).

jallaba : a hooded, long-sleeved robe, usually white or cream-colored, which is part of the traditional musician's costume in a *jawq.*

jawq (*ajwāq*) : an orchestra, especially an Andalusian music orchestra, numbering from seven to 20 musicians.

kamān : (from the Turkish *kamanja*) a violin played resting vertically on the left knee; since the 19th century one of the standard instruments in Andalusian music ensembles.

al-madīḥ : 1. praise poetry generally, and specifically of the Prophet Muḥammad, concentrated in but not exclusive to *Nawbat Ramal al-Māya* (q.v.); 2. (cap.) an a cappella style of music found among certain Sufi brotherhoods, related modally, rhythmically and textually to *al-Āla* (q.v.); sometimes used synonymously or in conjunction with *as-Samā'* (q.v.).

maṭla' : 1. the opening line of a poem, used to identify it; 2. more particularly, the first one or two lines of a "complete" *muwaššaḥ* (q.v.) or *zajal* (q.v.) that bears the repeating rhyme.

melḥūn : (MA, > *malḥūn*, "colloquial speech") "folk" music in colloquial Moroccan Arabic, modally, rhythmically and instrumentally distinct from *al-Āla* (q.v.).

marāḥil al-mīzān (s. *marḥalat al-mīzān*) : the three "stages" of a *mīzān* (q.v.) performance arranged according to increasing tempo – *al-muwassa'*, *al-qanṭara* and *al-inṣirāf*.

mīzān (*mayāzīn*, MA > *mawāzīn*) : a "movement" within a *nūba* (q.v.), distinguished by and named for one of the *īqā'āt* (q.v. *īqā'*); the five *mayāzīn*, in order, are: al-Basīṭ, al-Qā'im wa-Niṣf, al-Bṭāyḥī, ad-Darj, al-Quddām.

mu'allim (pl. *mu'allimūn*) : the highest and most respected level of mastery in the Moroccan Andalusian music: an orchestra leader who teaches the fine points of the tradition, having arrived at a deep knowledge of it under the tutelage of a master from the previous generation.

munšid : a singer, especially a soloist who performs *baytayn* (q.v.) or *inšād* (q.v.).

muwassa' al-mīzān : the first and slowest of the *marāḥil al-mīzān* (q.v.). See also: *taṣdīrat al-mīzān*

muwaššaḥ(a) (*muwaššaḥāt*) : a form of Arab-Andalusi strophic poetry characterized by a varying rhyme scheme and sometimes a varying metrical pattern; composed in Classical Arabic, but may have a non-Arabic *kharja* (q.v.). Sometimes used synonymously with *tawšīḥ* (q.v.).

an-našīd : a movement in the 13th-century *nawba* of al-Andalus, according to at-Tīfāšī, comprising an instrumental prelude, *al-istihlāl* (q.v.), followed by vocal and instrumental music, *al-'amal* (q.v.).

nāy (*nayāt*) : a reed or bamboo flute of Persian origin, played vertically; occasionally used in Moroccan Andalusian ensembles.

nūba, (MA, > *nawba*) (*nawbāt*) : the chief structural form of the Moroccan Andalusian music: a suite of songs and instrumental interludes theoretically defined by modal unity; typically composed of five *mayāzīn* (q.v. *mīzān*), each having a specific rhythmic pattern. There are at present 11 *nawbāt* in the Moroccan Andalusian music tradition: *Ramal al-Māya* (q.v.), *al-Iṣbahān*, *al-Māya*, *Raṣd adh-Dhīl*, *al-Istihlāl*, *ar-Raṣd*, *Ġarībat al-Ḥusayn*, *al-Ḥijāz al-Kabīr*, *al-Ḥijāz al-Mašriqī*, *'Irāq al-'Ajam* and *al-'Uššāq*.

al-qā'im wa-niṣf : an *īqā'* (q.v.) in duple meter characteristic of the second *mīzān* (q,v,) of a *nūba* (q.v.)

qalīd (*qalā'id*) : a form of Classical Arabic poetry, monorhymed and monometric like the *qaṣīda* (qv.).

al-qanṭara : the "bridge," the second of the three *marāḥil al-mīzān* (q.v.), performed in a moderate tempo.

qānūn : a lap zither of Turkish origin (and usually of Turkish or Egyptian manufacture) having 36 strings; it has become a common instrument in the larger Andalusian ensembles.

qaṣīda, qaṣīd (*qaṣā'id*) : the most highly developed form of Arabic poem, monorhymed and monometric, non-strophic but with a polythematic structure.

al-quddām : an *īqā'* (q.v.) in duple meter characteristic of the fifth *mīzān* (q.v.) of a *nūba* (q.v.)

Quddām Bawākir al-Māya : one of two *mayāzīn* (q.v. *mīzān*) that do not belong to a *nūba* (q.v.), recently assembled from "orphan" *ṣanā'i'* (q.v. *ṣan'a*) whose original *nawbāt* have been lost.

al-Quddām al-Jadīd : see Quddām Bawākir al-Māya.

qufl (*aqfāl*) : the line or lines of a *muwaššaḥ*/*tawšīḥ* (q.v.) or *zajal* (q.v.) following the *ġuṣn* (q.v.) that bear the repeating rhyme.

rabāb : a two-stringed, boat-shaped rebec characteristic, even emblematic, of the Moroccan Andalusian music.

ra'īs (also MA *rāyiṣ*) (*ru'asā'*) : the "chief," or leader, of a *jawq* (q.v.).

Ramal al-Māya : (cap.) the first *nūba* (q.v.) in the modern canonical arrangement, devoted thematically to praise of the Prophet Muḥammad and comprising the *ṭubū'* (q.v. *ṭab'*) *ramal al-māya, inqilāb ar-ramal, al-ḥusayn* and *ḥamdān*.

as-Samā' : Sufi music related modally, rhythmically and textually to the Andalusian music, but typically performed a cappella; often used synonymously or in conjunction with *al-Madīḥ* (q.v.).

ṣan'a (*ṣanā'i'* or sometimes *ṣana'āt*) : in general 1. a song with both a specific rhythm and melody, distinct from *tūšiya* and *buġya* (which are instrumental), *baytayn* (which is vocal, improvised and untimed) and *inšād* (which is untimed but with fixed melody and text); or in the special sense here of 2. any song that is not *šuġl, tawšīḥ, zajal* or *barwala*.
- (*ṣan'a*) *rubā'iyya,* (*ṣan'a*) *khumāsiyya,* (*ṣan'a*) *sudāsiyya* : four-, five- and six-line songs with varying rhyme schemes, typical of *al-Āla*.

ṣawt : a song; a movement in the 13th-century *nawba* of al-Andalus, according to at-Tīfāšī, comprising vocal and instrumental music (*al-'amal,* q.v.) without an instrumental prelude (*al-istihlāl*, q.v.).

sitāra (*sitārāt*) : an orchestra composed of women, named for the curtain behind which it performed when men were present; originally a feature of Andalusi courtly society, by the Ṭāʾifa period the word referred also to "domestic" ensembles that performed for aristocratic parties.

šuġl (*ašġāl*) : 1. in *Kunnāš al-Ḥāʾik* manuscripts, any non-strophic *ṣanʿa*; 2. in the modern tradition, any *ṣanʿa* which contains *taraṭīn* (q.v.).

ṭabʿ (*ṭubūʿ*) : a musical mode, analogous to a *maqām* in the Middle East; characterizes a specific *nūba* (q.v.); Moroccan musicians recognize 25 primary and secondary *ṭubūʿ*: *ramal al-māya, inqilāb ar-ramal, ḥamdān, al-ḥusayn, al-iṣbahān, az-zawarkind, al-māya, raṣd adh-dhīl, as-sīka* [also *aṣ-ṣīka*], *al-istihlāl, ʿirāq al-ʿarab, ar-raṣd* [also known as *ra's al-māya* or *raṣd al-māya*] *al-ḥuṣār, al-mazmūm, az-zaydān, ġarībat al-ḥusayn, al-muḥarrara, al-ḥijāz al-kabīr, al-mašriqī aṣ-ṣaġīr, mujannab adh-dhīl, al-ḥijāz al-mašriqī, al-ʿirāq al-ʿajam, al-ʿuššāq, adh-dhīl* and *ramal adh-dhīl*

ṭār : a small frame drum with cymbals embedded in the frame; one of the oldest percussion instruments used in the Andalusian music tradition.

ṭarab : ecstasy, a pleasurable feeling induced by musical performance; *aṭ-ṭarab al-andalusī* : a name for *al-Āla* that emphasizes the physical-emotional effects performances produce in the listener.

taṣdīrat al-mīzān : the first *ṣanʿa* (q.v.) of the *muwassaʿ al-mīzān* (q.v.), following a *tūšiya* (q.v.) and generally establishing the tempo for the *muwassaʿ*.

aṭ-ṭarab al-andalusī : one of the names for the Andalusian music in Morocco; emphasizes the music's emotional and therapeutic effects.

tarāṭīn : (> *raṭana* = to speak gibberish, to speak unintelligibly) nonsense syllables, such as *ha-na-nā* and *ṭāy-ṭiri-rāy*, which are part of the textual and melodic structure of a *šuġl* (q.v.); synonymous with the Middle Eastern term, *tarannum*.

tawšīḥ (*tawāšīḥ*) : 1. a *ṣanʿa* (q.v.) whose structure resembles a *muwaššaḥ* (q.v.), usually poly-rhymed and often poly-metric, and composed in Classical Arabic but without *kharja* (q.v.), or 2. a *ṣanʿa* whose text has been assembled from more than one source, typically poly-rhymed and often poly-metric and therefore similar to a *muwaššaḥ*.

tūšiya (*tawāšī*) : an instrumental interlude within the context of a *mīzān* (q.v.); a *tūšiya* always follows *buġya* (q.v.) at the beginning of a *mīzān* performance; other *tawāšī* may be found within the *mīzān*, occasionally even interpolated into the middle of a *ṣanʿa* (q.v.).

ʿūd : the Arabic lute; today, the Middle Eastern version with 9 or 10 paired strings is a standard instrument in any Andalusian Music ensemble.

zajal (*azjāl*) : 1. a type of Arab-Andalusi poem, similar to the *muwaššaḥ* (q.v.), but composed in Andalusi colloquial Arabic and lacking a non-Arabic *kharja* (q.v.), 2. a *ṣanʿa* (q.v.) whose text is composed in Andalusi colloquial Arabic and possibly derived from an Andalusi *zajal*.

Appendix 2
A Summary of Ṭubū ʿ Associated With Each nūba

(following ar-Rāyis, 1982, and Guettat, 2000)

Nūba	*Ṭubū ʿ*	*Associations*
Ramal al-Māya	*ramal al-māya* *inqilāb ar-ramal* *ḥamdān* *al-ḥusayn*	midnight
al-Iṣbahān	*al-iṣbahān* *al-zawarkind*	nighttime
al-Māya	*al-māya*	sunset, blood
Raṣd adh-Dhīl	*raṣd adh-dhīl* *as-sīka / aṣ-ṣīka*	midnight
al-Istihlāl	*al-istihlāl* *ʿirāq al-ʿarab*	morning
ar-Raṣd	*ar-raṣd*[1] *al-ḥuṣār* *al-mazmūm* *az-zaydān*	morning
Ġarībat al-Ḥusayn	*ġarībat al-ḥusayn* *al-muḥarrara* *as-sīka / aṣ-ṣīka*	midday
al-Ḥijāz al-Kabīr	*al-ḥijāz al-kabīr* *al-mašriqī aṣ-ṣaġīr* *mujannab adh-dhīl* *al-zawarkind*	evening
al-Ḥijāz al-Mašriqī	*al-ḥijāz al-mašriqī*	morning
al-ʿIrāq al-ʿAjam	*al-ʿirāq al-ʿajam*	morning
al-ʿUššāq	*al-ʿuššāq* *adh-dhīl* *ramal adh-dhīl*	pre-dawn

[1] aka *ra's al-māya* or *raṣd al-māya*

Bibliography

ʿAbd al-Wahhāb, Ḥasan Ḥusnī (1965-1972) *Waraqāt ʿan al-ḥaḍāra al-ʿarabiyya bi-Ifrīqiya*. 3 vols. Tunis: Maktabat al-Manār.

Abu-Haidar, J.A. (1991) "The *Muwaššahāt* in the Light of the Literary Life that Produced Them" in *Studies on the Muwaššah and the Kharja [Proceedings of the Exeter International Colloquium],* Alan Jones and Richard Hitchcock, ed. Reading, UK: Ithaca Press Reading for the Board of the Faculty of Oriental Studies, Oxford University. 115-122.

al-ʿAlamī, Muḥammad Abū ṭ-Ṭayyib b. aš-Šarīf (1888 (1315)) *al-Anīs al-muṭrib fī man laqīhi muʾallifuhu min udabāʾ al-Maġrib*. Fez: Ḥajriya.

Aḫlīfa, Muṣṭafā (2003/1423) *al-Ajwāq al-nisawiyya bi-madīnat Tiṭwān*. Tetuan: Maṭbaʿa al-Khalīj al-ʿArabī.

Aḥmad, Muṣṭafā Abū Ḍayf (1983) *al-Qabāʾil al-ʿarabiyya fī l-Andalus ḥattā suqūṭ al-ḫilāfa al-umawiyya (91-422H/710-1031M).* Casablanca: Dār an-Našr al-Maġribiyya.

Ahmed, Munir-ud-Din (1968) *Muslim Education and the Scholars' Social Status Up to the 5th Century Muslim Era <11th Century Christian Era>*. Zürich: Verlag "Der Islam".

ʿArībī, Ḥasan (1995) "Taqālīd al-mūsīqā l-andalusiyya fī Lībyā" in *Taqālīd al-mūsīqā l-andalusiyya fī duwal ḥawḍ al-baḥr al-abyaḍ al-mutawassiṭ: bi-munāsibat adh-dhikrā al-thamānimi'a li-tajdīd bināʾ madīnat Ribāṭ, 27 Māy 1995,* ʿAbd al-Karīm Bennānī, ed. Rabat: Jamʿiyya Rabat al-Fatḥ. 42-48.

Attia, Meir, David Golan and Jacques Azran (1997) "Note sur le compositions musicales préservées dans la musique juive andalouse au Maroc" in *Relations Judéo-Musulmanes au Maroc: Perceptions et Réalités,* Robert Assaraf and Michel Abitbol, ed. Paris: Stavit. 303-306.

Al-Azmeh, Aziz (1979) "The Muqaddama and Kitab al-ʿIbar: Perspectives from a Common Formula." *The Maghreb Review*. 4.1. 17-20.

——— (1981) *Ibn Khaldūn in Modern Scholarship: A Study in Orientalism*. London: Third World Centre for Research and Publishing.

Badawi, Muhammad M. (1980) "From Primary to Secondary *Qaṣīdas*: Thoughts on the Development of Classical Arabic Poetry." *Journal of Arabic Literature*. 11. 1-31.

Bauman, Richard and Charles L. Briggs (1990) "Poetics and Performance as Critical Perspectives on Language and Social Life." *Annual Review of Anthropology*. 19. 59-88.

Benaboud, M'hammad (1987) "Economic Trends in al-Andalus in the Period of the Ṭā'ifa States (11th Century A.D./5th Century A.H.)." *Islamic Studies*. 26.1. 1-30.

——— (2003). "The Problem of Ethnic Groups in Al-Andalus," in *Islam in the Middle Eastern Studies: Muslims and Minorities*. Akira Usuki and Hiroshi Sato, ed. Osaka, The Japan Centre for Area Studies, National Museum of Ethnology. 75-95.

Benchekroun, Mohamed B. A. (1974) *La vie intellectuelle marocaine sous les Mérinides et les Waṭṭāsides*. Rabat: Imprimerie Mohamed V.

Benmūsā, ʿAbd al-Fattāḥ (1998) "Nawbat al-Āla bayna at-tadwīn wa-at-tanẓīr," in *Ḫulāṣa aʿmāl al-nadwa al-manẓūma ʿalā hāmiš al-Mahrajān al-Waṭanī al-Sābiʿ lil-Mūsīqā l-Andalusiyya.* October 8-10, 1998. 19-26.

——— (2001a) "Ādāʾ nawbat al-Āla ʿinda al-madrāsa al-muḥāfiẓa." *al-Jawāhir.* March 30, 2001. 22-29.

——— (2001b) "Nawbat al-Ġarnāṭī wa nawbat al-Āla bayna al-muṣṭalaḥ wa al-ādāʾ," in *al-Baḥth fī t-turāth al-Ġarnāṭī : ḥaṣīla wa āfāq,* v. 2 Muṣṭafā al-Ġadīrī, ed. Oujda: Maṭbaʿ Šams/Jāmiʿa Muḥammad al-Awwal - Kulliyat al-ādāb wa al-ʿUlūm al-Insāniyya. 99-108.

——— (2003) *al-Mūsīqā l-andalusiyya "al-Āla" : al-maṣādir wa al-madāris.* Fez: Maṭbaʿat al-Afaq.

Bennāni, ʿAzz al-Din (1995) *Boghyat et Tawashi: de la musique andalouse marocaine.* Rabat-Souissi: Académie du Royaume du Maroc.

Bennūna, Malik [Bennouna] (1994) "Huellas y raíces de poetas orientales in la música andalusí," *in La Sociedad andalusí y sus tradiciones literarias / Foro Hispanico 7.* Otto Zwartjes, ed. Amsterdam: Rodolpi. 25-38.

——— (1999) "Muqaddamat al-muḥaqqiq." *Kunnāš al-Ḥāʾik.* Malik Bennūna, ed. Rabat: Matbaʿat Akadīmiyya al-Mamlakiyya al-Maġribiyya. 7-24.

Ben Srhir, Khalid (1992) *Morocco in the British Archives: the Correspondance of John Drummond Hay 1846-1886 (Al-maġrib fi l-aršīf al-brīṭānī murāsilāt John Drummond Hay maʿa-l mahzan).* Rabat: Wallāda.

Blachère, Régis (1950) "Les Savants iraqiens et leurs informateurs bédouins aux IIe - IVe siècles de l'Hégire," in *Mélanges Offerts à William Marçais par l'Institue d'Études Islamiques de l'Université de Paris.* Paris: Éditions G. - P. Maisonneuve et Cie. 37-48.

——— (1959) *Introduction au Coran* Paris: Besson and Chantemerle.

Bois, P. (1995) "L'Anthologie al-Āla du Maroc: une opération de sauvegarde discographique," in *La Musique et le Monde (Internationale de l'Imaginaire, nouvelle série, 4),* J. Duvignaud and C. Khaznadar, ed. Arles: Babel Maison des cultures du monde. 75-90.

Bosch-Vilá, J. (1971) "Ibn al-Ḳūṭiyya." *The Encyclopaedia of Islam, New Edition.* v. III. V.L. Ménage, B. Lewis, Ch. Pellat and J. Schacht, eds. Leiden: E.J.Brill. 847-848.

Brockelmann, Carl (1971) "Ibn ʿAbd Rabbih." *The Encyclopaedia of Islam, New Edition.* v. III. V.L. Ménage B. Lewis, Ch. Pellat and J. Schacht, ed. Leiden: E.J. Brill. 676-677.

Brockmeier, Jens (2002) "The Literacy Episteme: The Rise and Fall of a Cultural Discourse," in *Literacy, Narrative and Culture,* Jens Brockmeier, Min Wang and David R. Olson ed. Richmond, UK: Curzon. 17-34.

Brockmeier, Jens and David R. Olson (2002) "Introduction: What Is a Culture of Literacy?" in *Literacy, Narrative and Culture,* Jens Brockmeier, Min Wang and David R. Olson ed. Richmond, UK: Curzon. 1-13.

Bilʿarabī, al-Ṣadīq (1998) *Nuṣūṣ fī tārīkh al-mūsīqā l-andalusiyya.* Marrakesh: Dār Walīlī li-ṭ-Ṭabāʿa.

Blau, Joshua (1963) "The Role of the Bedouins as Arbiters in Linguistic Questions and the *Mas'ala az-Zunburiyya*." *Journal of Semitic Studies*. 8.1. 42-51.

al-Būʿaṣāmī, Muḥammad (1995) *Iqād aš-šumūʿ li-ladhdhat al-masmūʿ bi-naġamāt aṭ-ṭubūʿ*. ʿAbd al-ʿAzīz b. ʿAbd al-Jalīl, ed. Rabat: Akādīmiyyat al-Mamlaka al-Maġribiyya.

Burton, John (1977) *The Collection of the Qur'ān*. Cambridge: Cambridge University Press.

Cantarino, Vincente (1975) *Arabic Poetics in the Golden Age*. Leiden: E.J. Brill.

Chapoutot-Ramadi, Mounira (1997) "Thirty Years of Research on the History of the Medieval Maghrib," in *The Maghrib in Question: Essays in History and Historiography*. Michel Le Gall and Kenneth Perkins, ed. Austin: University of Texas Press. 35-61.

Caton, Steven C. (1990) *"Peaks of Yemen I Summon" Poetry as Cultural Practice in a North Yemeni Tribe*. Berkeley: University of California Press.

Chottin, Alexis (1929) *La Musique marocaine*. Paris.

——— (1931) *Corpus de musique marocaine, fascicle 1, Nouba de Ochchak*. Paris: Huegel.

——— (1939) *Tableau de la musique marocaine*. Paris: Guenther.

Ciantar, Philip (2006) "Nostalgia, History and Sheikhs in the Libyan *Ma'lūf*: Contemporary Meanings in the Shadows of the Past," in *Muwashshah: Proceedings of the Conference on Arabic and Hebrew Strophic Poetry and its Romance Parallels, School of Oriental and African Studies [SOAS], London, 8-10 October 2004*, Ed Emery, ed.. London: School of Oriental and African Studies, pp. 55-70.

Cohen, Judith R. (2002) "Ca no soe joglaresa: Women and Music in Medieval Spain's Three Cultures," in *Medieval Women's Song: Cross Cultural Approaches*. Anne L. Klinck and Ann Marie Rasmussen, ed. Philadelphia: University of Pennsylvania Press. 66-80.

Combs-Schilling, M. Elaine (1999) "Performing Monarchy, Staging Nation," in *In the Shadow of the Sultan: Culture, Power and Politics in Morocco*, Rahma Bourqia and Susan Gilson Miller, ed. Cambridge: Harvard University Press. 176-214.

Corriente, Federico. (1977) *A Grammatical Sketch of the Spanish Arabic Dialect Bundle*. Madrid: Instituto Hispano-Arabe de Cultura.

——— (1980) *Gramática, métrica y texto del cancionero hispanoárabe de Aban Quzmán (Reflejo de la situación lingüistica de al-Andalus tras concluir el periodo de las Taifas)*. Madrid: Instituto Hispano-Arabe de Cultura.

——— (1988) *Poesía estrófica (cejeles y/o muwaššahāt) atribuida al místico granadino aš-Šuštarī* Madrid: Instituto de Filologia Departamento de Estudios Arabes.

——— (1989) *Ibn Quzmān: Cancionero andalusí*. Madrid: Ediciónes Hiperión.

——— (1994) "Textos andalusíes de cejeles no quzmanianos en Alhillī, Ibn Saʿīd Almagribī, Ibn Xaldūn y en la *Geniza*," in *La Sociedad andalusí y sus tradiciones literarias / Foro Hispanico 7*, Otto Zwartjes, ed. Amsterdam: Rodolpi. 61-104.

——— (1997) *Poesía dialectal árabe y romance en Alandalus (cejeles y xarajāt de muwaššahāt)* .Madrid: Gredos.

——— (2002) *A Dictionary of Andalusi Arabic*. Leiden: E.J. Brill.

Cortés, Manuela (1990) "Organología oriental en al-Andalus." *Boletín de la Asociación Española de Orientalistas*. 26. 303-332.

——— (1993) "Vigencia de la transmisión oral en el *Kunnāš al-Ḥā'ik*." *Rvta: Sociedad Española de Musicología, Actas del XV Congreso de la Sociedad Internacional de*

Musicología, separata II. Música Islámica y Judía y su relación con lo hispánico. 16. 1942-1952.

——— (1995) "Nuevos datos para el estudio de la música en al-Andalus de dos autores granadinos: As-Sustārī e Ibn Al-Jatib." *Musica Oral del Sur.* 1. 177-194.

——— (1996) *Pasado y presente de la música andalusí.* Seville: Fundación El Monte.

——— (1997) "Perfil de la nawba durante el período omeya," in *El Saber en al-Andalus.* Seville: Univesidad de Sevilla. 51-64.

Crone, Patricia (1991) "Mawlā." *The Encyclopaedia of Islam, New Edition.* v. VI. E. van Donzel C.E. Bosworth, W.P. Heinrichs and Ch. Pellat, ed. Leiden: E.J. Brill. 874-882.

Una Crónica anónima de ʻAbd al-Raḥmān III al-Nāṣir (1950) E. Lévi-Provençal and Emilo García Gómez, ed. Madrid and Granada: Consejo Superior de Investigaciónes Científicas Instituto Miguel Asín.

aḍ-Ḍabbī, Abū Jaʿfar Aḥmad b. Yaḥyā b. ʿAmīra (2005) *Buġyat al-multamis fī taʾrīḫ rijāl ahl al-Andalus.* Ṣalāḥ ad-Dīn al-Hawwārī ed. Beirut: al-Maktaba al-ʿAṣriyya.

Davila, Carl (2006) "Andalusian Strophic Poetry Between the Spoken and the Written: The Case of the Moroccan Andalusian Music," in *Muwashshah: Proceedings of the Conference on Arabic and Hebrew Strophic Poetry and its Romance Parallels, School of Oriental and African Studies [SOAS], London, 8-10 October 2004,* Ed Emery, ed. London: School of Oriental and African Studies, pp. 99-113.

——— (2009) "Fixing a Misbegotten Biography: Ziryāb in the Mediterranean World." *al-Masāq* 21 (ii). 121-136.

——— (forthcoming) *Pen, Voice, Text: Nūbat Ramal al-Māya in Cultural Context.*

Davis, Ruth F. (1986) "Modern Trends in the Arab-Andalusian Music of Tunisia." *The Maghreb Review.* 11.2-4. 58-63.

——— (1989) "Melodic and Rhythmic Genre in the Tunisian *nūba*: a Performance Analysis." *Ethnomusicologia II, Atti del VI European Seminar in Ethnomusicology (Quaderni dell' Accademia Chigiana, 45).* Siena: Accademia Musicale Chigiana. 71-109.

——— (1996) "Arab-Andalusian Music in Tunisia." *Early Music.* 14.3. 423-437.

——— (1997a) "Cultural Policy and the Tunisian *Maʾlūf*: Redefining a Tradition." *Ethnomusicology.* 41.1. 1-21.

——— (1997b) "Traditional Arab Music Ensembles in Tunis: Modernizing *al-Turāth* in the Shadow of Egypt." *Asian Music.* 28.2. 73-108.

de Larrea Palacin, Arcadio (1956) *Nawbat al-Iṣbahān.* Instituto Gen. Franco.

Dozy, Reinhart (1881) *Supplément aux dictionnaires arabes.* Leiden.

ad-Dūrī, ʿAbd al-ʿAzīz (1983) *The Rise of Historical Writing Among the Arabs (Bahth fī našʾat ʿilm at-taʾrīḫ ʿinda l-ʿArab).* Lawence I. Conrad, trans. Princeton: Princeton University Press.

Eisenstadt, Samuel Noah (1973) *Tradition, Change, and Modernity.* New York: John Wiley and Sons.

Elam-Amzallag, Avraham (1997) "La *ala* andalouse chez les Juifs et les Arabes du Maroc," in *Relations Judéo-Musulmanes au Maroc: Perceptions et Réalités,* Robert Assaraf and Michel Abitbol, ed. Paris: Stavit. 295-302.

El-Hibri, Tayeb (1999) *Reinterpreting Islamic Historiography: Hārūn al-Rashīd and the Narrative of the ʿAbbāsid Caliphate* Cambridge: Cambridge University Press.

El Mansour, Mohamed (1990) *Morocco in the Reign of Mawlay Sulayman.* Wisbech: Middle East and North African Studies Press Limited.

El Moudden, Abderrahmane (1997) "The Eighteenth Century: A Poor Relation in the Historiography of Morocco," in *The Maghrib in Question: Essays in History and Historiography,* Michel Le Gall and Kenneth Perkins, eds. Austin: University of Texas Press. 201-211.

Farmer, Henry G. (1928/1973) *A History of Arabian Music to the XIIIth Century.* London: Luzac.

——— (1933) *An Old Moorish Lute Tutor.* Glasgow: The Civic Press.

——— (1965) "Ghināʾ." *The Encyclopaedia of Islam, New Edition.* v. II. Ch. Pellat and J. Schacht B. Lewis, ed. Leiden: E.J. Brill. 681-688.

Faruqi, Lois Ibsen (1981) *An Annotated Glossary of Arabic Musical Terms.* Westport, CT: Greenwood Press.

al-Fāsī, Muhammed (1962) "La musique marocaine dite 'Musique Andalouse'." *Hésperis Tamuda* 3. 79-106.

Fierro, María Isabel (1989) "La obra histórica de Ibn al-Qūṭiyya." *Al-Qanṭara.* 10.2. 485-512.

Finnegan, Ruth (1988) *Literacy and Orality: Studies in the Technology of Communication.* Oxford: Blackwell.

Foley, John Miles (1986) "Introduction." *Oral Tradition in Literature: Interpretation in Context,* John Miles Foley, ed. Columbia: University of Missouri Press. 1-18.

——— (1995) "The Implications of Oral Tradition," in *Oral Tradition in the Middle Ages,* W. F. Nicolaisen. Binghamton: Medieval and Renaissance Texts and Studies. 31-57.

Fox-Genovese, Elizabeth (1999) "'What Oft Was Thought, but Ne'er So Well Expressed': From Oral Culture to the Written Text, Again." *Review of National Literatures and World Report: Literature as a Unifying Cultural Force.* 22-32.

García Barriuso, Patrocinio (1940) *La música hispano-musulmana de Marruecos.* Larache: Artes Graficas Bosca.

García Gómez, E. (1943) *Poemas arábigo-andaluces* (4th edition). Madrid: Espasa-Calpe.

Gellrich, Jesse M. (1995) *Discourse and Dominion in the Fourteenth Century: Oral Contexts of Writing in Philosophy, Politics and Poetry*. Princeton: Princeton University Press.

Goody, Jack (1977) *The Domestication of the Savage Mind.* Cambridge: Cambridge University Press.

——— (1987) *The Interface Between the Written and the Oral.* Cambridge: Cambridge University Press.

——— (2000) *The Power of the Written Tradition.* Washington DC: Smithsonian Institution Press.

Goody, Jack and Ian Watt (1968) "The Consequences of Literacy," in *Literacy in Traditional Societies.* Jack Goody, ed. London: Cambridge University Press. 27-68.

Gozalbes Busto, Guillermo (1989) *Estudios sobre Marruecos en la Edad Media.* Granada: T.G. ARTE, Juberíes & CIA, S.A.

Graeber, David (2001) *Toward an Anthropological Theory of Value : The False Coin of Our Own Dreams.* New York: Palgrave.

Granja, F. de la (1970) "Un cuento oriental en la historia de al-Andalus." *Al-Andalus*. XXXV. 211-222.

——— (1986) "Ibn Māʾ al-Samāʾ." *Encyclopaedia of Islam, New Edition*. v. III. V.L. Ménage Ch. Pellat and J. Schacht B. Lewis. Leiden: E.J. Brill. 855.

Gross, David (1992) *The Past in Ruins: Tradition and the Critique of Modernity*. Amherst: The University of Massachusetts Press.

Gruendler, Beatrice (1993 *The Development of the Arabic Scripts: From the Nabatean Era to the First Islamic Century According to Dated Texts*, Harvard Semitic Studies. Boston: Scholars Press.

——— (2003) *Medieval Arabic Praise Poetry: Ibn al-Rūmī and the Patron's Redemption*. Routledge Curzon Studies in Arabic and Middle-Eastern Literatures. London: Routledge Curzon.

Guettat, Mahmoud (1980) *La musique classique du Maghreb*. Paris: Sindbad.

——— (2000) *La musique arabo-andalouse: l'empreinte du Maghreb*. Paris: Éditions el-Ouns.

Guichard, Pierre (1977) *Structures sociales "orientales" et "occidentales" dans l'Espagne musulmane*. Paris: Mouton.

al-Ḥāʾik, Ibn ʿAbd Allāh Muḥammad b. al-Ḥusayn al-Tiṭwānī al-Andalusī (1353/1935) *Majmūʿat al-afānī al-mūsīqiyya al-andalusiyya maʿrūfa bi-l-Ḥāʾik*. Ambīrkū al-Makkī, ed. Rabat: al-Maṭbaʿ al-Iqtiṣādiyya.

——— (1972) *Majmīʿat al-Ḥāʾik li-ṭ-ṭarab al-andalusī*. Aḥmad b. al-Ḥasan Zuwītin, ed.

——— (2003) *Kunnāš al-Ḥāʾik (facsimile edition)*. Ed. and preface by Manuela Cortés García. Granada: Consejería de Cultura, Centro de Documentacion Musical de Andalucia.

Hājji, ʿAbd al-Raḥman ʿAli (1969) *Taʾrīḫ al-mūsīqā l-andalusiyya*. Beirut.

Ḫāliṣ, ʿAbd al-Laṭīf Aḥmad (1982) "Taqdīm." *Min waḥy al-rabāb*. Rabat: Matbaʿat al-Najāh al-Jadīda. 7-22.

Ḫāliṣ, Ṣalāḥ (1961) *Išbīliyya fī l-qarn al-khāmis al-hijrī : dirāsa adabiyya taʾrīkhiyya li-nušūʾ dawla Banī ʿAbād fī Išbīliyya wa-taṭawwur al-hayāt al-adabiyya fī-hā 414-461*. Beirut: Dār al-Thaqāfa.

——— [Salah Khalis] (1966) *La vie littéraire à Séville au XIe siècle*. Algiers.

Hartmann, Martin (1897) *Das arabische Strophengedicht. I. Das Muwaššah*. Weimar: Emil Feber.

Havelock, Eric Alfred (1963) *Preface to Plato*. Cambridge: Belknap/Harvard U. Press.

al-Ḥumaydī, Abū ʿAbd Allāh Muḥammad b. Abī Naṣr (1997). *Jadhwat al-muqtabis fī dhikr walāt al-Andalus*. Ibrāhīm al-Ibyārī ed. Beirut: Dār al-Kutub al-ʿIlmiyya.

Ibn al-Abbār, Abū ʿAbd Allāh Muḥammad (1955-56). *Al-Takmīla li-Kitāb aṣ-ṣila*. ʿIzzat al-ʿAṭṭār al-Ḥusaynī ed. Cairo: Maktabat al-Ḫānjī.

Ibn ʿAbd al-Jalīl, ʿAbd al-ʿAzīz (1988) *al-Mūsīqā l-andalusiyya al-maġribiyya*. Kuwayt: Maṭābiʿ al-Risāla.

——— (1992) *Muʿjam muṣṭlaḥāt al-mūsīqā l-andalusiyya al-maġribiyya*. Rabat: Maʿhad al-dirāsāt wa al-abhāth lil-taʿrīb.

——— (2000) *Madḫal ilā tārīḫ al-mūsīqā al-maġribiyya*. Casablanca: Maṭbaʿa al-Najāh al-Jadīd.

Ibn ʿAbd Rabbih, Aḥmad b. Muḥammad (1997/1417). *al-ʿIqd al-farīd*. Mufīd Muḥammad Qumayhah. Beirut: Dār al-Kutub al-ʿIlmiyya.

Ibn Ḫāqān, al-Fatḥ b. Muḥammad (1966) *al-Qalā'id al-ʿiqyān fī maḥāsin al-iʿyān*. Muḥammad al-ʿInānī ed. Tunis: Al-Maktaba al-ʿAtīqa.

Ibn Ḥayyān al-Qurṭubī (2003) *Al-Sifr al-thānī min Kitāb al-Muqtabis*. Maḥmūd ʿAlī al-Makkī, ed. Riyāḍ: Markaz al-Malik Faysal.

Ibn Ḥazm, Abū Muḥammad ʿAlī (2001) *Ṭawq al-ḥamāma fī ilfa wa-l-ālāf*. Iḥsān ʿAbbās ed. Tunis: Dār al-Maʿrif li-ṭ-Ṭabāʿa wa-n-Našr.

Ibn Jallūn Tuwaymī, Ḥājj Idriss (1979) *At-turāth al-ʿarabī al-maġribī fī l-mūsīqā : mustaʿmalāt nawbāt al-ṭarab al-andalusī al-maġribī : šiʿr, tawšīḥ, azjāl, barāwil — dirāsa wa-tansīq wa-taṣḥīḥ Kunnāš al-Ḥā'ik*. Tunis.

Ibn Khaldūn, Abū Zayd ʿAbd ar-Raḥmān b. Muḥammad (1992) *Tāriḫ Ibn Khaldūn (Kitāb al ʿibar wa diwān al-mubtada'i wal-khabar)*. Beirut: Dār al-Kutub al-ʿIlmiyya.

——— (2004) *Muqaddima*. Muḥammad al-Iskandrānī ed. Beirut: Dār al-Kitāb al-ʿArabī.

Ibn Khurradādhbih, ʿUbayd Allāh b. ʿAbd Allāh (1969) *Muḫtār min Kitāb al-Lahw wa l-malāhī*, ed. Ighnātyūs ʿAbduh Ḫalīfa al-Yaūʿī, Beirut: Maṭbaʿa al-Kāthūlīkiyya.

Ibn Manṣūr, ʿAbd al-Laṭīf Muḥammad (1977) *Majmūʿ azjāl wa tawšīḥ wa ašʿār al-Mūsīqā l-andalusiyya al-maġribiyya al-ma'rūf bil-Ḥā'ik*. Rabat.

Ibn al-Quṭiyya, Abū Bakr Muhammad b. ʿAmr (1982) *Ta'rīḫ iftitāh al-Andalus*. Ed. Ibrāhīm al-Abyār. Beirut / Cairo: Dār al-Kutub al-Islāmiyya.

Ibn Saʿīd, ʿAlī b. Mūsā b. Muḥammad b. ʿAbd al-Malik (1964) *al-Muġrib fī ḥulā al-Maġrib*. Šawqī Ḍayf ed. 2 v. Cairo: Dār al-Maʿārif.

Ibn Salamah, Mufaḍḍal (1938) *Ancient Arabian Musical Instruments* (*Kitāb al-malāhī wa-asmā'ihā min qibal al-mūsīqā*). James Robson and Henry George Farmer, ed and trans. Glasgow: The Civic Press.

Ibn Zaydān, Mūlāy ʿAbd ar-Raḥmān (1347/1929) *Itḥāf iʿlām an-nās bi-jamāl aḫbār ḥāḍirat Miknās*. Rabat: Maktabat al-Waṭanī.

al-Isfahānī, Abū l-Faraj ʿAlī b. al-Ḥusayn *Kitāb al-Aġānī*. (1989) 13 v. Beirut: Dār Ihyā' at-Turāth al-ʿArabī.

James, David (2009) *Early Islamic Spain: The History of Ibn al-Qūṭīya*. London: Routledge.

Jayyusi, Salma Khadra (1992) "Andalusī Poetry: The Golden Period," in *The Legacy of Muslim Spain*, Salma Khadra Jayyusi, ed.. Leiden: E. J. Brill. 317-366.

Jones, Alan (1980) "Romance Scansion and the *Muwaššahāt*: An Emperor's New Clothes?" *Journal of Arabic Literature*. 11. 36-55.

——— (1988) *Romance kharjas in Andalusian Arabic Muwaššah Poetry*. London: Ithaca Press.

——— (1991) "'Omnia vincit amor'," in *Studies on the Muwaššah and the Kharja [Proceedings of the Exeter International Colloquium]*, Alan Jones and Richard Hitchcock, ed. Reading, UK: Ithaca Press Reading for the Board of the Faculty of Oriental Studies, Oxford University. 88-103.

Jones, Alan and Richard Hitchcock, (1991) "Some Ramarks on the Present-Day Tradition of Andalusian *Muwaššahāt* in North Africa," in *Studies on the Muwaššah and the Kharja [Proceedings of the Exeter International Colloquium]*, Alan Jones and Richard Hitchcock, ed. Reading, UK: Ithaca Press Reading for the Board of the Faculty of Oriental Studies, Oxford University. 160-197.

Kazimirski, A. de Biberstein (1860/1944) *Dictionnaire arabe-français*. Beirut: Librarie du Liban.

al-Kindī, Abū Yūsuf Yaʿqub b. Ishāq. (1965) *Risāla fī l-luḥūn wa-an-naġam*. Ed. Zakariyyā Yūsuf. Baghdad: Maṭbaʿa Šafīq.

Kurpershoek, P. Marcel (1994) *The Poetry of ad-Dinān: a Bedouin Bard in Southern Najd*. Leiden: E.J. Brill.

Lachiri, Nadia (1993) "La vida cotidiana de las mujeres en al-Andalus y su reflejo en las fuentes literarias," in *Árabes, judías y critianas: Mujeres en la Europa medieval,* Celia del Moral, ed. Granada: Universidad de Granada. 103-121.

Lakhdar, Mohammed (1971) *La vie littéraire au Maroc sous la dynastie ʿalawide.* Rabat: Éditions Techniques Nord-Africaines.

Lane, Edward. W. (1863) *An Arabic-English Lexicon*. 1984 reprint edition in 2 vols. Cambridge: Islamic Texts Society.

Laroui, Abdallah (1977) *The History of the Maghrib, An Interpretive Essay*. Ralph Manheim trans. Princeton: Princeton University Press.

Latham, John Derek (1965) "The Reconstruction and Expansion of Tetuan: The Period of Andalusian Immigration," in *Arabic and Islamic Studies in Honor of Hamilton A.R. Gibb,* George Makdisi, ed. Leiden: J.R. Brill. 387-408.

Leder, Stefan (1989) "The Literary Use of the *Khabar*: A Basic Form of Historical Writing," in *The Byzantine and Early Islamic Near East, 1. Problems in the Literary Source Material. Studies in Late Antiquity and Early Islam,* Averil Cameron and Lawrence I. Conrad ed. Princeton: Darwin Press. 277-315.

——— (1990) "Features of the Novel in Early Historiography – The Downfall of Xālid al-Qasrī." *Oriens*. 32. 72-96.

Leo Africanus (1600) *A Geographical Historie of Africa (Written in Arabicke and Italian by John Leo a More, borne in Granada, and brought up in Barbarie).* John Pory, trans. London: Imprensis George Bishop.

Levi-Provençal, E. (1987/1913-1937) "al-Rāzī." *The Encyclopaedia of Islam, Volume 3.* M.Th Houtsma, A.J. Wensinck and T.W. Arnold eds. 1137-1138.

——— (1991/1922) *Les historiens des chorfas.* Casablanca: Afrique Orient.

——— (1932) *L'Espagne musulmane au Xème siècle: Institutions et vie sociale.* Paris: Larose.

——— (1951) *Conférences sur l'Espagne musulmane.* Cairo: Imprimerie Nationale.

Literacy and Orality. (1991) David R. Olson and Nancy Torrance, ed. Cambridge: Cambridge University Press.

Literales Bewusstsein. Schriftlichkeit und das Verhältnis von Sprache und Kultur. (1997) Jens Brockmeier, ed. W. Fink: Munich.

Liu, Benjamin M. and James T. Monroe (1989) *Ten Hispano-Arabic Strophic Songs in the Modern Oral Tradition: Music and Texts.* Berkeley: University of California Press.

Loopuyt, M. (1988) "L'enseignement de la musique arabo-andalouse à Fès." *Cahiers de Musiques Traditionelles.* 1. 39-45.

Lowney, Chris (2005) *A Vanished World: Medieval Spain's Golden Age of Enlightenment.* New York: Free Press.

Makdisi, George (1981) *The Rise of Colleges: Institutions of Learning in Islam and the West.* Edinburgh: Edinburgh University Press.

al-Manūnī, Muḥammad (1989) *Les sources arabes de l'histoire du Maroc à l'époque contemporaine 1790-1930.* Rabat: La Faculté des Lettres de Rabat.

al-Maqqarī, Abū l-ʿAbbās Aḥmad b. Muḥammad (1968) *Nafh aṭ-ṭīb min ġuṣn al-Andalus ar-raṭīb*. Ihsān ʿAbbās, ed. 8 v. Beirut: Dār Ṣadr.

Marín, Manuela (1988) "Nomina de sabios de al-Andalus (93-350/711-961)." in *Estudios Onomástico-Biográficos de al-Andalus, Volume I*, Manuela Marín, ed. Madrid: Consejo Superior de Investigaciones Cientificas. 23-182.

Maroufi, Nadir (1995) "Structure du répertoire andalou: quelques problèmes de méthod," in *Le Chant arabo-andalou: essai sur le Rurbain ou la topique de la Norme et de la Marge dans le patrimoine musical arabe*. Nadir Maroufi, ed. Paris: Éditions l'Harmattan. 11-24.

Mediano, Fernando R. (1996) "L'Élite savante andalouse à Fès (XVème et XVIème siècles)," in *Orientations: Poetry, Politics and Polemics: Cultural Transfer Between the Iberian Peninsula and North Africa*, Geert Jan van Gelder, Ed de Moor and Otto Zwartjes, ed. Atlanta: Rodopi. 83-94.

Michaux-Bellaire, E. (1921) "Essai sur l'histoire des confrèries marocaines." *Hésperis*. 1, 1st Trimester. 141-159.

Michel, Nicolas (1997) *Une économie de subsistences: le Maroc précolonial*. 2 vols. Cairo: Institut Français d'Archéologie Orientale.

Mitjana, Rafael (1906) "L'Orientalisme musical et la Musique arabe." *Le Monde Oreintal*. 1. 200-224.

Monroe, James T. (1972) "Oral Composition in Pre-Islamic Poetry." *Journal of Arabic Literature*. 3. 1-53.

——— (2004 [1974]) *Hispano-Arabic Poetry*. Piscataway: Gorgias Press.

——— (1986) "Poetic Quotation in the *Muwaššaha* and Its Implications: Andalusian Strophic Poetry as Song." *La Corónica*. 14.2.

——— (1987) "The Tune or the Words? (Singing Hispano-Arabic Strophic Poetry)." *Al-Qanṭara*. 8.

——— (1989) "Which Came First, the *Zajal* or the *Muwaššaha*? Some Evidence for the Oral Origins of Hispano-Arabic Strophic Poetry." *Oral Tradition*. 4.1-2 January-May, 1989. 38-74.

Nasr, Seyyed Hossein (1995) "Oral Transmission and the Book in Islamic Education: The Spoken and the Written Word," in *The Book in the Islamic World: the Written Word and Communication in the Middle East*, George Atiyeh, ed. Albany: State University of New York Press. 57-70.

Nöldeke, Theodor (1909-1938) *Geschichte des Qorāns*. 3v. Leipzig: T.Weicher.

Noth, Albrecht (1994) *The Early Arabic Historical Tradition, a Source-Critical Study*. Princeton: The Darwin Press.

Olson, David R. and Deepthi Kamawar (2002) "Writing as a Form of Quotation," in *Literacy, Narrative and Culture*, Jens Brockmeier, Min Wang and David R. Olson ed. Richmond, UK: Curzon. 187-198.

Ong, Walter J. (1982) *Orality and Literacy: the Technologizing of the Word*. New York: Methuen.

Oman, Giovanni (1991) "Maṭbaʿa." *The Encyclopaedia of Islam (New Edition)*. v. VI. E. van Donzel C.E. Bosworth, W.P. Heinrichs and Ch. Pellat ed. Leiden: E.J. Brill. 794.

Parry, Milman (1971) *The Making of Homeric Verse: The Collected Papers of Milman Parry*. Adam Parry. Ed. & trans. Oxford: Clarendon Press.

Pellat, Charles. (1990) "Ḳayna." *The Encyclopaedia of Islam, New Edition.* v. IV. E. van Donzel C.E. Bosworth, B. Lewis and Ch. Pellat, ed. Leiden: E.J. Brill. 820-824.

Perés, Henri (1953) *La poésie andalouse en arabe classique au XIe siècle: ses aspects généraux, ses principaux thèmes et sa valeur documentaire.* Paris: Adrien-Maisonneuve.

Poché, Christian (1995) *La Musique arabo-andalouse.* Arles: Cité de la Musique / Actes Sud.

al-Qādirī, Muḥammad b. aṭ-Ṭayyib (1977-1986) *Našr al-mathānī li-ahl al-qarn al-ḥādī ʿašr wa-th-thānī.* Rabat: Maktabat aṭ-Ṭālīb.

Racy, ʿAli Jihad (1991) "Creativity and Ambience: An Ecstatic Feedback Model from Arab Music." *The World of Music.* 33.3. 7-28.

ar-Rāyis, ʿAbd al-Karīm (n.d.) *al-Durūs al-awwaliyya fī l-mūsīqā l-andalusiyya.*

——— (1982) *Min waḥy al-rabāb.* Rabat: Matbaʿat al-Najāḥ al-Jadīda.

ar-Rāyis, ʿAbd al-Karīm and Mohamed Briouel (1985) *Al-Mūsīqā l-andalusiyya al-maġribiyya: Nawbat Ġarībat al-Ḥusayn.* Casablanca: al-Ḥājj ʿAbd al-ʿAzīz Hilmī.

Razzūq, Muḥammad (1996) "al-Ḥijra al-andalusiyya ilā l-Maġrib." *Revue d'Études Andalouses.* 17-30. June, 1996.

——— (1998) *al-Andalusiyūn wa-hijrātuhum ilā l-Maġrib ẓall al-qarnayn 16-17.* Casablanca: Afriqiyya al-Šarq.

Renaud, H.P.J. (1921) "La peste de 1799 d'après des documents inédits." *Hésperis* 1, 2nd Trimester. 161-182.

Reynolds, Dwight F. (1995) *Heroic Poets, Poetic Heroes : The Ethnography of Performance in an Arabic Oral Epic Tradition.* Ithaca: Cornell University Press.

——— (2000a) "Music." *The Literature of Al-Andalus. Cambridge History of Arabic Literature* Raymond P. Schiendlin María Rosa Menocal and Michael Sells, ed. Cambridge: Cambridge University Press. 60-82.

——— (2000b) "Musical 'Membrances of Medieval Muslim Spain." *Charting Memory: Recalling Medieval Spain.* Stacy N. Beckwith. New York: Garland. 229-262.

——— (2013) "Lost Virgins Found: The Arabic Songbook Genre and an Early North African Exemplar." *Quaderni di studi arabi* (special issue on music and literature, forthcoming).

Ribera, Julián (1922) *La Música de las Cantigas: Estudio sobre su origen y naturaleza con reproducciones fotograficas del texto y transcripcion moderna.* Madrid: Tipografia de la Revista de Archivos.

Ricard, Prosper (1932) *Le conservatoire de musique marocaine de Rabat.* Rabat.

Roberts, Peter (1997) "The Consequences and Value of Literacy: A Critical Reappraisal." *Journal of Educational Thought.* 31. April. 45-67.

Rosenthal, Franz (1968) *A History of Muslim Historiography.* Second revised edition. Leiden: E. J. Brill.

Sadan, J. (1993) "Nadīm." *The Encyclopaedia of Islam, New Edition.* v. VII. E. van Donzel C.E. Bosworth, W.P. Heinrichs and Ch. Pellat, ed. Leiden: E.J. Brill. 849-852.

al-Šāmī, ʿAbd al-Malik (1997) "Bayna al-fikr al-mūsīqī al-mašriqī wa al-andalusī: ʿanāṣir min al-ittifāq wa al-iḫtilāf," in *Athar al-Mūsīqā l-andalusiyya fī l-anmāṭ al-īqāʿiyya al-maḥalliyya.* Jamʿiyya Ribāṭ al-Fatḥ, ed. Rabat: Dār al-Manāhil. 43-50.

——— (1998) "Naḥwa taqwīm tajriba tasjīl anṭūlūjiyyat al-Āla al-andalusiyya." *Ḫulāṣa a'māl al-nadwa al-manẓūma 'alā hāmiš al-Mahrajān al-Waṭanī al-Sābi' lil-Mūsīqā l-andalusiyya* October 8-10, 1998. 39-46.

——— (2001) "Turāth al-mūsīqī al-andalusī: dirāsa fī muṣṭalaḥ al-nawba." *unpublished ms.*

Sawa, George Dimitri (1985) "The Status and Roles of the Secular Musicians in the Kitāb al-Aghānī (Book of Songs) of Abu al-Faraj al-Iṣbahānī (D. 356 A. H. / 967 A. D.)." *Asian Music.* 17.1. 69-82.

——— (1989a) *Music Performance Practice in the Early 'Abbāsid Era, 132-320 AH / 750-932 AD.* Toronto: Pontifical Institute of Mediaeval Studies.

——— (1989b) "Oral Transmission in Arabic Music, Past and Present." *Oral Tradition.* 4.1-2. 254-265. January-May, 1989.

Schoeler, Gregor (1985) "Die Frage der schriftlichen oder mündlicen Überlieferung der Wissenschaftlichen im frühen Islam." *Der Islam: Zeitschrift für Geschichte und Kultur des islamischen Orients* 62. 201-230.

——— (1989) "Weiteres zur Frage der schriftlichen oder mündlicen Überlieferung der Wissenschaftlichen im frühen Islam." *Der Islam: Zeitschrift für Geschichte und Kultur des islamischen Orients* 66. 38-67.

——— (1989) "Mündliche Thora und Ḥadīth: Überlieferung, Schreibverbot, Redaktion." *Der Islam: Zeitschrift für Geschichte und Kultur des islamischen Orients* 66. 213-251.

——— (1997) "Writing and Publishing: On the Use and Function of Writing in the First Centuries of Islam." *Arabica.* 44. 423-435.

——— (2002) *Ecrire et transmettre dans les débuts de l'islam.* Paris: Presses Universitaires de France.

Schrift und Schriftlichkeit. Writing and its Use. (1994-1996) H. Günther and O. Ludwig, ed. Berlin and New York.

Schroeter, Daniel J. (1988) *Merchants of Essaouira: Urban Society and Imperialism in Southwestern Morocco, 1844-1886.* Cambridge: Cambridge University Press.

Schuyler, Philip D. (1979) "Music Education in Morocco: Three Models." *The World of Music.* 21.3. 19-31.

Sellheim, R. and D. Sourdel (1990) "Kātib." *The Encyclopaedia of Islam, New Edition.* v. IV. Leiden: E.J. Brill. 754-757.

Seroussi, Edwin (1990) "La música arábigo-andaluza en las baqqashot judeo-marroquíes: Estudio histórico y musical." *Anuario Musical.* 45. 297-315.

——— (1997) "La musique andalouse-marocaine dans le manuscrits hébraiques," in *Relations Judéo-Musulmanes au Maroc: Perceptions et Réalités,* Robert Assaraf and Michel Abitbol, ed. Paris: Stavit. 283-294.

Shannon, Jonathan H. (2003) "Emotion, Performance and Temporality in Arab Music: Reflections on Tarab." *Cultural Anthropology.* 18.1. 72-98.

Soulami, Jaafar Benelhaj and M'hammad Benaboud (1994) "La Sociedad y la literatura andalusíes durante el período de los Taifas," in *La Sociedad andalusí y sus tradiciones literarias / Foro Hispanico 7,* Otto Zwartjes, ed. Amsterdam: Rodolpi. 151-162.

Sowayan, Saad A. (1992) *The Arabian Oral Historical Narrative: An Ethnographic and Linguistic Analysis*. Wiesbaden: Otto Harrassowitz.

Smith, Anthony D. (1991) *National Identity*. Reno: Unversity of Nevada Press.

Sperl, Stefan (1996) "Qasida Form and Mystic Path in Thirteenth-Century Egypt: A Poem by Ibn al-Fāriḍ," in *Qasida Poetry in Islamic Asia and Africa*. v 1, Stefan Sperl and Christopher Shackle, ed. Leiden: E.J. Brill. 65-81.

as-Srāyrī, Idrīs (1998) "Taḥdīth manẓūr al-muḥāfiẓa ʿalā at-turāth al-mūsīqī al-andalusī." *Ḫulāṣa aʿmāl al-nadwa al-manẓūma ʿalā hāmiš al-Mahrajān al-Waṭanī al-Sābiʿ lil-Mūsīqā l-Andalusiyya*. 9-15. October 8-10, 1998. 9-15.

Stern, Samuel Miklos (1955) "Two Anthologies of Muwaššah Poetry: Ibn al-Ḫaṭīb's *Gayš al-tawšīh* and al-Šafadī's *Tawšīʿ al-tawšīh*." 2. 150-192.

——— (1974) *Hispano-Arabic Strophic Poetry*. Oxford: Clarendon Press.

Ṭayfūr, Abū Faḍl Aḥmad b. Abī Ṭāhir (1994) *Kitāb Baġdād*. Muḥammad Zāhid b. al-Ḥasan al-Kawtharī ed. Cairo: Maktabat al-Ḫānjī.

at-Tifāšī, Aḥmad b. Yūsuf (1968) "aṭ-Ṭarāʾiq wal-alḥān al-musīqiyya fī Ifrīqiya wa-l-Andalus" (Chapters 10 and 11 of *al-Mutʿat al-asmāʿ fī ʿilm as-samāʿ*), Muḥammad b. Tāwīt aṭ-Ṭanjī, ed. *Abhāth* 21: 1, 2, 3. 93-116.

Touma, Habib Hassan (1998) *Die Nubah Mayah: zur Phänomenologie des Melos in der arabisch-andalusi Musik Marokkos: Eine Strukturanalyse der nūbah Māyah*. New York: Georg Olms Verlag.

Valderrama Martínez, Fernando (1953) *"Kunnāš al-Ḥāʾik" aw Majmūʿat aġānī maġribiyya min al-qarn al-thānī ʿašar al-hijrī*. Tetuan: Dār al-Ṭabāʿa al-Maġribiyya.

——— (1954) *El Cancionero de al-Hāʾik*. Tetuan: Editoria Marroquí.

Versteegh, Kees (1997) *The Arabic Language*. Edinburgh: Edinburgh University Press.

Wansbrough, John (1977) *Quranic Studies: Sources and Methods of Scriptural Interpretation*. Oxford: Oxford University Press.

Watt, W. Montgomery (1977) *Bell's Introduction to the Qur'ān*. Edinburgh: Edinburgh University Press.

Wehr, Hans (1994/1960) *A Dictionary of Modern Written Arabic*. Ithaca: Spoken Languages Services.

Welch, A.T. (1986) "Ḳurʾān." *Encyclopaedia of Islām, New Edition*. v. V. Leiden: E.J. Brill. 400-429.

Wensinck, Arent Jan (1927) *A Handbook of Early Muhammedan Tradition*. Leiden: E.J. Brill.

Wright, Owen (1992) "Music in Muslim Spain," in *The Legacy of Muslim Spain*. Salma Khadra Jayyusi, ed. Leiden: E. J. Brill. 555-579.

——— (1993) "Nawba." *The Encyclopaedia of Islam, New Edition*. v. VII. E. van Donzel C.E. Bosworth, W.P. Heinrichs and Ch. Pellat, ed. Leiden: E.J. Brill. 1042-1043.

——— (1998) "al-Mūsīqā fī l-Andalus," in *Al-haḍāra al-ʿarabiyya al-islāmiyya fī l-Andalus (Arab-Islamic Culture in Andalusia)* v1. Salma Khadra Jayyusi, ed. 803-835.

Wright, William (1859/1997) *A Grammar of the Arabic Language*. Cambridge: Cambridge University Press.

Yafil, Edmond Nathan (1904) *Majmūʿ al-aġānī wal-alḥān min kalām al-Andalus*. Algiers: Yafil and Seror.

Yahya, Dahiru (1981) *Morocco in the Sixteenth Century: Problems and Patterns in African Foreign Policy.* Harlow, UK: Longman.

Zwartjes, Otto (1997) *Love Songs from Al-Andalus: History, Structure and Meaning of the Kharja.* Leiden: E.J. Brill.

Zwettler, Michael (1978) *The Oral Tradition of Classical Arabic Poetry, Its Character and Implications*. Columbus: Ohio State University Press.

Index

ʿAbd al-Malik (al-ʿAlawī) 140

ʿAbd ar-Raḥmān I 100

ʿAbd ar-Raḥmān II 48, 53, 73, 76-81, 83-87, 93-100, 103, 108, 112-3, 116-7, 119-20, 128, 130,

ʿAbd ar-Raḥmān b. ʿAlī b. Nāfiʿ (son of Ziryāb) 76

Abū Qaṭīfa 78 n8

Abū l-ʿAtāhiya 110 and n80

Abū Ṣalt Umayya ad-Dānī 50, 54

Aḫbār Ziryāb 29 n15, 80-1, 84-9, 91-95 and n51, 105, 108, 112-13, 114, 185

Aḥmad al-Manṣūr (al-ʿAlawī) 140

al-ahzāj (song type in Ziryāb's "primitive *nūba*") 29

al-Āla (as name for the tradition) 7-8, 44-46, 184

ʿAlāl al-Baṭla 59, 134

ʿAlamī, ʿAzīz 20, 26, 209-10, 212, 272

al-Aʿraj, Muḥammad b. Maṭrūḥ 103-4

Al-Azmeh, Aziz 85-6

ʿAllūn and Zirqūn 48, 53, 93, 95, 109

ʿAllūyah 106-7, 109-10, 111, 114-15

al-Aʿmā 125 and n108

ʿamal 30-32; Ibn Bājja's improvements upon 55-56, 124

Ambīrkū al-Makkī 150, 220

al-Amīn 67, 113-15, 119

al-Andalus: attribution to 7-8, 16-7, 28-34, 39-40, 43-7, 134, 152-3, 184, 186, 187-90, 254, 260, 265-6, 310-11; Andalusi migrations and migrants to North Africa 56-8, 138-9, 141, 143-4, 147-9, 160, 217, 260

ʿAntara 103 and n68

Aslam b. Aḥmad 80, 94 n51, 97, 105-6, 111, 112, 114

Attar, Anas 20, 172

al-Bāhilī, Abū l-Ḥakam 55

al-Balāḏurī 64

Barrada, Driss 206, 209, 212

barwala 14, 15, 18, 34 135, 147, 156, 313 and nn34, 35

al-basīṭ (song type in Ziryāb's "primitive *nūba*") 29; (see also: *īqāʿ* and *mīzān*)

baytayn 12, 13, 31, 167-8 n58, 186-7

Benmūsā, ʿAbd al-Fattāḥ 13, 154, 155, 156, 169, 208, 213-217, 237, 273, 291-2, 311 n35; on genealogy of Dār ʿAdīl 158-9

Bennūna, Malik 49 n15, 113, 114, 150, 222, 225 n8, 226 n9,

Bišr b. al-Muʿtamir 102 n65

Bouamar, Awatif 199

Brīhī, Muḥammad 158-60, 163, 212, 213

Briouel, Mohamed 12, 26, 193, 206-10, 213-14, 216, 272

al-Būʿaṣāmī, Muḥammad, and *Iqād aš-šumūʿ* 33, 149-50, 153, 158-9, 221, 225 n8, 239 n20, 267, 271, 292

buġya/mšāliya 11-13, 25; *zawāyā* not involved in preserving 142

Caton, Steven C. 246

Chaachou, Mehdi 167 n58, 186, 203, 215-16, 272

Chottin, Alexis 28, 40, 44-47, 50, 52, 53, 59, 68, 134, 143, 144, 148, 149 n35, 161 n53, 163-4, 189, 190, 227 n12, 229, 236

Cortés García, Manuela 29-31, 33-4, 50, 150 n37, 152, 154, 155 and n45, 156, 160, 222, 232-3, 267, 311 n34, 312

costuming 24, 253

aḍ-Ḍabbī 105 n74

Dār ʿAdīl 156-9, 177, 192, 193, 198, 199

darbūka 6, 20, 23, 176, 194, 203, 211

Dār at-tirāz 303 n23

Davis, Ruth F. 25 n1, 175 n68